Lavinia Warner graduated in history and psychology from the University of Wales before embarking on a career in television. In order to film the highly-acclaimed documentary 'Women in Captivity' and research this book, she contacted more than fifty survivors of Japanese prison camps and visited the scenes of this story in Malaysia and Indonesia. She subsequently created TENKO, the hugely successful fictional BBC-TV drama series about women prisoners of the Japanese. Lavinia Warner currently works as a producer/director for both the BBC and ITV, specializing in documentary.

John Sandilands is a freelance writer. Having begun his career as a newspaper reporter, he now contributes widely as a feature writer to major magazines in both Britain and America. He has also worked for television in current affairs and light entertainment and has written documentaries for both the BBC and ITV. In 1978 he wrote the script for a 'This Is Your Life' programme on Dame Margot Turner, who had survived $3\frac{1}{2}$ years in a Japanese prison camp. The researcher for the programme was Lavinia Warner, and their determination to know more about other women prisoners of the Japanese led to their book.

WOMEN BEYOND THE WIRE

Lavinia Warner
& John Sandilands

Hamlyn Paperbacks

A Hamlyn Paperback

Published by Arrow Books Limited
17-21 Conway Street, London W1P 6JD

A division of the Hutchinson Publishing Group

London Melbourne Sydney Auckland
Johannesburg and agencies throughout
the world

First published in Great Britain
by Michael Joseph 1982
Hamlyn Paperbacks edition 1983
Reprinted 1983 and 1984

Printed and bound in Great Britain by
Anchor Brendon Limited, Tiptree, Essex

ISBN 0 600 20802 8

This book is dedicated to
those women who did not
return and have no memorial.

Contents

Malaysia: Indonesia West

Acknowledgments

The writing of this book depended on the co-operation of those female survivors mentioned in the text, and many more, and we wish to acknowledge with gratitude the generosity of all those women who placed their valuable time, knowledge and artefacts at our disposal. Special mention must be made of Shelagh Lea for her constant help and the loan of her precious diary; of Phyllis Thom, Norah Chambers and Phyllis Liddelow for the loan of their own fascinating accounts, and of Molly Smith for her assistance throughout and for reading the manuscript. In Singapore, our thanks go to Harry Dyne, Zaida Short, Cynthia Koek and 'Buck' Buckeridge for help and hospitality; in Sumatra, equally, to Sister Catherinia, the nuns of Charitas Hospital, and A. Zawawe Said of the Indonesian Government; and in Australia, to Betty Jeffrey, for her warmth and wisdom.

The authors would also like to thank: Harold Payne OBE, President of the Federation of the Far Eastern Prisoners of War; The Imperial War Museum; Tristram Powell, Leslie Megahey and Carol Akillian of the BBC; the 'This Is Your Life' programme at Thames TV; and the author, Michael Hardwick, whose early encouragement was invaluable.

Integrated illustrations courtesy Shelagh Lea, Norah Chambers and Ena Murray.

ALONE

A meditation on community life.

I never can be quite alone,
My soul I scarce can call my own,
Five hundred voices fill the air,
Five hundred figures cross the square.
I eat, my neighbour jostles me,
I try to sleep, for lullaby
A hum of voices fills my ear,
I wake! Pounders and choppers hear,
I dress before a hundred eyes,
A public bath the camp supplies
I read, embroidered is my tale
By stories of how others ail,
I write, the cook says 'Time to eat.'
'Remove your paper!' I retreat,
I sew, and scatter all my pins
To make way for some household tins,
A story I wou'd faint relate
Is interrupted, 'Bring a plate'
'For onions!' 'Ration baskets please!'
'Wood.' 'Sugar.' Such cries never cease.
To quiet corner I repair
For meditation: lo! the air
Is rent by children's piercing yells,
Shrill blast of whistles, clang of bells.
Alone! Alone! When shall I be
All by myself in privacy?
When that day comes, mayhap I'll own
I rather fear to be alone.

by Margaret Dryburgh 1943

Introduction

It is probably quite rare that the moment when a book is conceived can be pin-pointed almost to the minute. This book had its origin at 7.25 p.m. on the evening of Wednesday, 25 January 1978. It is possible to be as precise because it was then that a 'This Is Your Life' programme drew to its close and did so in such a moving and dramatic fashion that it was a beginning as well as an end.

The central figure of the programme that evening was a woman: Brigadier Dame Margot Turner, former Matron-in-Chief of Queen Alexandra's Royal Army Nursing Corps. It was an impressive enough achievement to have risen from the rank of nursing sister to become a Dame of the British Empire and to command a body of military nurses with a history extending back to Florence Nightingale. In Dame Margot's story, however, there was a great deal more to tell.

From the fall of Singapore in 1942 to the ending of the Far Eastern war three and a half years later, she had been a prisoner of the Japanese, one of hundreds of women held in the remote jungle camps of Sumatra after the evacuation fleet from Singapore had been destroyed by the enemy. She had reached captivity via shipwreck and days spent alone on a flimsy raft under the burning sun of the South China Sea. Even by the standards of courage and resourcefulness within the appalling camps she was an authentic heroine.

A group of her companions in that ordeal had been assembled from far and near to recall her story, many of them, in the well-known tradition of 'This Is Your Life', meeting Dame Margot, and indeed each other, for the first time since the war. It was my job, as researcher on the programme, to locate these fellow survivors and bring them together, and from the start they were a source of fascination.

They were not young, nearly forty years having passed since the events they were being asked to describe, but there was an alertness and a firmness in their manner that did not make age the first aspect of them that a stranger would notice. They tended to be conventionally dressed: muted colours, discreet fabrics, neat coiffures. You would not single them out except for that air of self-possession. Nor could you imagine that they would regard drawing particular attention to themselves with anything but the most profound reservations.

At every stage of the programme's preparation they tested politely but warily for any hint of extravagant attitudes or indifferent taste. They were there to pay a tribute to Margot Turner, whom they all regarded highly, and even an audience of some twenty million viewers was not going to tamper with their natural restraint.

In the event, as the programme unfolded, they were admirable. They told their stories with brevity and humour then withdrew gracefully to take their places with the rest of the guests. There was no suggestion of the extraordinary revelation that was in the offing as the programme came to its end. At the denouement the women had agreed to sing a hymn composed in the camps by a missionary who had died there. It was known to them as 'The Captives' Hymn' and it had been sung at all the religious services which had continued, against bitter odds, every Sunday until freedom came.

Now this little group of survivors from those days gathered around Margot Turner and, unaccompanied as they had been then, and a little hesitantly at first in these strange surroundings, they began to sing. But as the words flooded back and their confidence grew there was a truly remarkable transformation. The years visibly fell away from them and the cloak of their reserve disappeared so that they were young women again, vulnerable, beleaguered, a little afraid but taking strength from each other, as they must have done then.

Sensing the uniqueness of the moment the camera lingered on their faces and through its insistence all were quite discernibly immeasureably distant in time and place from a television studio in central London and under the gaze of millions of strangers. It was suddenly apparent that an extraordinary sisterhood had existed between these women in those days when they had faced a common peril and had last sung 'The Captives' Hymn' together.

It was that glimpse of such a powerful bond between women who had gone on to lead the rest of their lives so much like everybody else that made it imperative to know more about them and the experience they had shared all those years ago.

It was plainly not only Dame Margot's story that was remarkable but an infinity of others, each with a singular perception of that long captivity.

In the histories of the war in the Far East I found that there was very little reference to the plight of this particular group of prisoners, the refugees from Malaya who, by accident of war, were cast up on the shores of Sumatra in what was then the Dutch East Indies and is today a part of the republic of Indonesia. They were principally civilians and so had no bearing on the conduct of the military campaigns, nor any political significance except to the authorities in Britain who were embarrassed by their inability to rescue them or even to offer any aid.

There were two personal accounts written shortly after the war by Australian military nurses who had been caught up in the evacuation of Singapore and imprisoned with the rest.* There was a biography of Margot Turner, who had gone on to be a woman of importance in the wider world and which of course included her wartime exploits. Thereafter I could find no official tracing of the progress of the many hundreds of civilian women who fled before the Japanese advance down Malaya in 1942, then took, too late, to the sea.

Great numbers of them died but, although a memorial exists in Australia to the military nurses from that country, there is nothing similar recalling the civilian women here. The wives of Service officers who died came under the jurisdiction of the Commonwealth War Graves Commission and were taken from their resting places in the jungle to be buried again in the war cemeteries of Java. The rest were left in the shallow graves, over which the jungle soon grew again. 'Sumatra' occupies but seven pages of the seven volumes of the Roll of Honour of Civilian War Dead, 1939–45, which rests in Westminster Abbey. The names of women mentioned in this story can be found there, classified without elaboration in Volume VII under 'Deaths at Sea and Abroad'.

The most significant memorial to many, and to the whole experience, clearly lay in the recollections of those who had survived and, beginning with that small group who had sung 'The Captives' Hymn' with such passion, I extended my research to talk eventually to more than fifty women in several parts of the world. As a kind of way-station on what was to prove a long quest, I was the reporter on a documentary for BBC Television in 1979. An ingredient of this was a return to Sumatra by Margot Turner and an Australian former nursing sister called Betty Jeffrey to revisit the sites of the camps and the locations of their misadventures on the route to imprisonment.

In this way I was able to travel down the Malayan peninsular where the headlong military retreat of 1942 took place, uprooting the lives of all in its path. I was able to walk on the beaches of Banka Island, off the main shore of Sumatra, where those who had lived through bombard-

* Betty Jeffrey and Elizabeth Simons – see Bibliography.

3

ment from sea and air first struggled to land. I visited Muntok, the little town on the island which gave its name to the camp which existed there. Muntok was a name stamped in the memories of all in this story because that is where so many of the women died.

There was a striking similarity in the personalities of those who survived: a confidence and a strength and a predisposition to the same kind of humour, understated and wry. At the same time they were vividly defined as individuals, each with characteristics that made them separately memorable. They were all persons of consequence and I came to have a high respect for them on many levels.

Oddly, few of them had used their capabilities to build formal careers in their lives after the camps. Of course there was not, in their time, the same pressure to believe that a career was central to a woman's wordly standing, but then they had come through an experience which had already broken many of the rules which then applied to womankind. When that extraordinary episode came to an end, however, they resumed a conventional existence, much as if it had never been. Many, indeed, had not spoken of it in any detail since, certainly not to a stranger, and it often required a great deal of coaxing to retrieve their recollections.

Once the reluctance passed they talked freely and with evident relief at the opportunity to unburden. Diaries were produced together with letters and photographs and objects which had survived. It seemed that, frequently for the first time, it had become possible to see in detachment this most curious passage in their lives.

Gradually the phenomenon of the emotions that were visible in that rendering of 'The Captives' Hymn' became more comprehensible. For all the privations of those years, which are detailed here, there was something of immense value too. These are some of the conclusions of these women in regard to an experience from which, at the last, they barely escaped with their lives:

'Looking back I still feel the warmth of those women I had the privilege to live with for nearly four years. In that sense I left the camps with regret. We hated saying goodbye to each other. It was a terrible break. We had all been together in the struggle to survive and we knew each other so well.'

'I grew up in those camps. I came out of myself and realized my strengths. I shall always be grateful for those years. It was the best school there could have been.'

4

'One learnt to live with and understand people better. The old order of politeness broke down and one got to the bare bones of living.'

'Before camp I had led a sheltered, privileged life. In camp there was no privacy. You couldn't go into a room and shut the door. I mixed with all sorts of people and it made me understand them and feel that in future I could mix with everybody. I was so much more trusting of human nature than when I went in.'

'Funnily enough, camp life was an extremely rich period. Yesterday had happened, tomorrow might never come, so you lived for the day and the people who were there. There were no other encumbrances whatsoever.'

'You could be eccentric if you wanted to be and nobody commented. A lot of us did what I suppose would now be called off-beat things. You were free to indulge in whatever it was that you wanted to pursue that in some way expressed yourself. Not before or since have I lived a life as rich. You could be exactly who you were – find yourself, I would say. Once we came out we were less free.'

'Because we had no men to help us it was only our strength and nobody else's. I learnt that women can be very brave, very tenacious. If it had not been for that we would not be here now.'

'Before the war I hadn't been too keen on women's company. I came away from the camps liking women and respecting their resource.'

It was impossible not to persevere in trying to discover the whole circumstances of this unique imprisonment, and there was another product of that memorable Wednesday evening. The script for Dame Margot Turner's 'This Is Your Life' was prepared by John Sandilands, a journalist not entirely free from the sometimes chilly professional detachment considered proper to that trade. He was just as deeply moved when 'The Captives' Hymn' was sung that night and he was equally determined to know more of what lay behind the sudden transformation of those ladies. The result was the continuing collaboration from which this book has emerged.

It must be said that it expresses our personal distillation of the women's varied perspectives on the events it describes. We have purposely restricted ourselves to this one body of women who were processed through certain camps in southern Sumatra after the fall of Singapore, though we are of course aware of other women who, elsewhere in the Orient, suffered as bravely and who also died in profusion. We have presented the Japanese as they were perceived by these women at that time because this pursues the same logic.

We now believe that the women's captors followed instincts and practices as ingrained as those of the women themselves. Bushido, the martial code of Japan, could not conceive of a preference for capture rather than death: 'Better to die with honour than live in shame.' That credo would certainly account for their attitude to male prisoners taken in war but here, in addition, is an exposition of the traditional Japanese view of women which appears in a revered volume, *Onna Daigaku, The Whole Duty of Woman*: 'The five faults that beset the female mind are: indocility, discontent, slander, jealousy, and silliness. Without doubt these faults exist in seven or eight out of every ten women, and it is from these that arises the inferiority of women to men.' The Japanese allegiance to that last conclusion was apparent in their treatment of the females who fell into their hands. It must be assumed that they knew no better.

Their own lives were unrelentingly harsh and the Japanese peasants, certainly, were no strangers to hunger and hard work. We describe, for example, the hardship of the women when they were put to the labour of cultivation. They were given only sickles and heavy primitive hoes to clear and turn the ground and they were obliged to use them even for the preparation of graves. But these, we discovered, together with mattocks, were the standard agricultural implements of Japan, even at that time, and were employed there for the same tasks. Nothing could be found which even began to account for the horrendous cruelty of the *Kempei Tai*, the Japanese secret police, but secret police, wherever they exist, seem to defy rational analysis.

Several of the women have since made trips to Japan. Almost without exception they showed no trace of an enduring hatred or a desire for revenge:

'I'm not sorry or bitter. I can't say I love the Japanese but I wouldn't go out of my way to hurt them.'

'At first I felt I hated the Japs but you can't go through life hating and now I am full of respect for what they have achieved since the war finished.'

Our endeavour began with a revelatory moment and continued to be surprising and enlightening to the very end.

Lavinia Warner
October 1981

Chapter 1

The road to Muntok, even these many years later, is not among the great highways of the world. A reluctant road hacked out of jungle on a little island, still of no great importance in the South China Sea, it winds past small, brooding villages, the houses standing like storks on thin, stilt legs, and through dark, green, spiky vegetation which laps its edges or lies in shattered geometric patterns, brought down by the monsoon, among the damp potholes. There is the sense of heading bumpily into nowhere in particular; of one species of discomfort leading only to another. The kind of journey that is made unwillingly, without appetite or positive hope of a welcoming end.

It was a long drive to Muntok, once the landrover had left the small airport at Pangkalpinang, the principal town of Banka Island. It took four hours to cover seventy miles, and darkness fell abruptly, as it does in Sumatra. When the vehicle slowed to negotiate gullies and rickety bridges, and the streams of monsoon water which suddenly flowed across the road, it was possible to hear the night sounds of the jungle, raucous and mysterious, a sort of muted hysteria in the sullen, humid blackness that gathered close around.

In the front seat Sister Catherinia sat very straight as if defying the lurching progress of the car. The headdress of her nun's habit, outlined by the headlights, gave her an impenetrable detachment as she made this journey through a place of so many memories. In the camp at Muntok where so many of the women had died of hunger and exhaustion, compounded by disease or the simple departure of the will to live, the night hours had invariably been lethal. There was a vicious strain of malaria which had become known to the women as Banka Fever, a sickness that came, in their minds, to hang like an evil miasma over the squalor of the prison compound. While the fever was rampant a night-bird would sing beautifully in the jungle in the dangerous small hours and was called by the natives the Death Bird. Could Sister Catherinia, survivor of that terrible time, help but listen for its singing now?

The landrover, driven by an ancient, impassive Indonesian, loaned, like the vehicle, by the Church community at Pangkalpinang, gave a terminal lurch as it struck some hidden pothole and the sister turned to me for a moment – the quick instinctive gesture of someone who has devoted a lifetime to looking after others. Sister Catherinia was one of the heroines of the women's odyssey of imprisonment, a specialist in giving succour amid awfulness, but remembered particularly for a singular skill at mending hutment roofs, her shabby habit tucked indecorously up around her thighs. She was seventy-two now, her bony Dutch face made grave by endless responsibility; but when she laughed, as she did at this moment, across her shoulder in sympathy, her eyes crinkled behind her glasses. She became ageless, a spirited young girl prepared for any kind of hardship. That quality, too, must have helped to keep her alive in this selfsame jungle those many years ago.

She had volunteered, without hesitation, to take a stranger of another generation back to a place which she must dearly have wished never to see again. Indeed, in the thirty-five years since Sister Catherinia had last left Banka Island, battened down with hundreds of other women in the stinking hold of a Japanese steamer, she had never been back, although at the war's end she had continued to live in the East, much as she had done before the Japanese came.

Her missionary post was now in Java, but she had flown up to Sumatra to meet me and re-visit the camp at Muntok as if it were a duty like any other, an automatic response to someone else's need. The result was this uncomfortable journey through the damp jungle darkness with the strong likelihood of an unpalatable conclusion. Muntok, like many of the camps where thousands of women were held prisoner, cut off from the world as thoroughly as if they had been despatched to another planet, has no reputation as a place of pilgrimage, so comprehensively has time swallowed up the extraordinary experience of the women prisoners of the Japanese in the Second World War.

Other places of imprisonment or persecution have acquired a certain cachet down the years, at least the significance of a metaphor if not a memorial: the Nazi concentration camps, the stalags, Colditz Castle, and in the Far East, the camps at Changi and on the Railway of Death in Thailand have their place in the history of that time. The camps of the women in Sumatra, Borneo, Java and the Philippines were never to achieve a lasting fame or even notoriety, although in terms of mortalities they produced the death-toll of a major battle.

Muntok's name was seared only in the minds of those who had known it in those astonishing days and we were not at all sure of what we would find there now. Thirty-five years could not dramatically alter the geography of the locality. Sister Catherinia would remember the landmarks, the loom of the mountain there, and the distant smell of the sea. But the jungle which edged so hungrily up to the road might have encroached again and swallowed the site in the universal green. In a developing country like Indonesia, striving for a place in the industrialized world, even Banka Island could have succumbed, like the mainland, to the growing demands for off-shore oil and mineral resources. The camp might now be buried beneath machinery and concrete slabs and prefabricated buildings.

We spent the night in one of these, the rest-house of a tin-mining complex which had sprung up on the outskirts of the little town of Muntok. The hospitality had been organised by Sister Catherinia through the same far-reaching network of contacts that had conjured up the landrover and its driver. The next day a local official was going to make himself available to us as a guide, impressed perhaps by Sister Catherinia's belief that some of the women's graves must still exist near the site of the camp. The notion of the dead left untended always seems to create more of an impact on the official mind than the living in the same condition.

I had no idea what to expect when the daylight came, beyond Muntok's associations with misery and illness and hopelessness. From talking with the women who had survived it I had understood only the dread that the place instilled. The camp had made two appearances in the women's story. Banka Island itself had a powerful significance to many who had passed into imprisonment via the fall of Malaya because it lay on what was then the escape route for ships attempting to steal away from the stricken city of Singapore, making for what was thought to be the safety of the Dutch East Indies. It was in the narrow waters of the Banka Strait that they were pounced on by the ubiquitous Japanese bombers and warships which ruthlessly sank one ship after another leaving their packed cargoes of women and children to be washed up like flotsam on the shores of Banka.

Rounded up by the Japanese troops who were making themselves masters of the Dutch Far Eastern Empire, the captives were taken first to Muntok to begin their internment. It was there that they were obliged to take stock of the unique circumstances that had transformed them in a matter of weeks from a privileged elite in the sybaritic surroundings of pre-war Malaya into ragged paupers at the mercy of an enemy whose barbarity was already a byword.

If the whole experience had been set down as a series of tragic etchings, as it might have been by some chronicler of torment like Gustav Doré, Muntok could have stood as the gateway to hell. Through the inexplicable machinations of the Japanese, the women of this particular story were moved from there to other camps on the mainland, of varying dreadfulness, but were then brought back to Muntok at a point when their fortunes were reaching their lowest ebb. In this way, Muntok came to stand, too, for the climax to their misery. Weakened by hardship and hunger, they were ripe for dying when they arrived there for the second time, and so many of them did.

In the event, this morning thirty-five years later gave not a single indication of what had gone before. It was a Sumatran morning of washed clarity after the sticky warmth of the night, the light translucent and the air clear although the sun was already hot. From the verandah of the guest-house there was a glimpse of royal blue sea and, closer to hand, the little town was beginning to come to life. Market stalls blossomed on either side of its principal street, vivid with multi-coloured produce which picked up the brilliance of the flowering tropical trees that were scattered about like drifts of confetti.

The local official arrived, small and bustling as if he were about to conduct a guided tour of some new municipal amenity and we set off to drive the few miles to the camp. It was still hard to imagine that there would not be some landmark to denote the significance of the place – a crumbling archway perhaps, a sagging notice-board, or a few flowers in a jam jar at the wayside. Instead the vehicle pulled up with a final jerk beside an open space the size of a football pitch and, indeed, there was some iron piping rigged at one end as a makeshift goal.

The official, who had been talking animatedly to Sister Catherinia in his native tongue, fell silent as if uncomfortably aware of an anti-climax at the end of the journey which had brought his visitors from so far away, and in the quiet there came, incongruously, a waft of the exceptionally joyful, high-pitched chatter which envelops the children of Indonesia wherever they gather. At one end of the ground, in front of the trees which bounded the open space, there was a long, low building which was clearly a schoolhouse. The camp at Muntok was now, if it were anything other than a wasteland, the playground of the school.

Sister Catherinia stepped down slowly and intently as if searching for some bearings. She set off finally, at a determined pace, and I walked with her, the official dutifully bringing up the rear. As she paced about she began to talk, though far more, I felt, to herself than to me. 'Here, I think, was the hospital. No. There, perhaps, was the hospital and here the place of cooking.' For all but her, there was only one patch of scrubby grass or baking mud to set against another, but as she spoke in her soft, low, broken English, that unlikely place took on a hallowed quality and the sister's quiet dignity made one think of how it must have been. Suddenly her eyes fixed upon something at the far end of the ground and she quickened her stride. We caught up with her at the edge of the trees and were able to see what she had discovered – one of the former wells was still intact. All three of us gathered about it, peering into its depths as if they had something more important to offer than a faint reflection of cloudy water. It was an insignificant well, a mere hole in the ground delineated by a low wall of ancient stones, although the fact that it still existed served as some kind of denouement to what was otherwise a painfully low-key return. It seemed, anyway, to fulfil that need for Sister Catherinia because she felt sufficiently strengthened to continue with the real purpose of this small pilgrimage. She spoke at length with the Indonesian, pointing a little uncertainly here and there, until his gestures synchronised with hers and it was clear that a consensus had been reached. She walked towards the trees on the other side of the ground, where a faint path led into the jungle. We followed it for a considerable distance because this was where the dead had been carried to prevent them spreading their contagion among the living. They were taken down this path to graves painfully dug with makeshift tools by women already threatened by death themselves: an authentic Via Dolorosa in this anonymous jungle so far removed from anything that the women had held dear.

We stopped at last in a small clearing. Sister Catherinia bowed her head; there was nothing that anybody could say because there was nothing to see but the matted undergrowth of the jungle floor. Except for those who could remember, with difficulty, where the dead of Muntok had been taken, there was no sign for the rest of the world, and, in all the strange absence of a true memorial to the civilian women prisoners of the Japanese in Sumatra, this was the moment which most conveyed the lack.

Half the women and children who were imprisoned with Sister Catherinia, some seven hundred when all were finally assembled, died, but that number alone conveys only one dimension of the three and a half years of an imprisonment that can justifiably be called unique. It was a singular set of circumstances which brought together in close confinement and conditions of appalling hardship a prison population which, in the first place, was not quite like any other.

The uniqueness began with the whirlwind Japanese assault of December 1941 which swept down the Malayan Peninsular and thundered into the 'impregnable' fortress of Singapore. It was an unthinkably swift victory, one of the most comprehensive of modern warfare and, in military terms, an exercise of textbook neatness. A small, compact, highly mobile force took on an army of vastly greater size and turned its strength into a weakness so that the giant blundered about, hampered by its own weight and entangled by its own limbs.

Within weeks of their landings on the north-eastern coast of Malaya the Japanese were masters of the whole peninsula and the surrender of Singapore was in their hands. Soon afterwards there followed the easy conquest of another Imperial colony, the Dutch East Indies. As the Japanese engulfed these territories they acquired all the customary spoils of war. There were the rich resources of Malaya, the rubber plantations and the tin mines which were among the most rewarding in the world. There were the vast maritime facilities of Singapore with its packed warehouses and its oil refineries, and the machinery, mostly intact, of the large army that they had so briskly torn apart. In addition, incomparable as trophies, the conquerors fell heir to the remarkable bric-a-brac of the British Imperial life-style: that unique artefact, the colonial bungalow of the period, its decor alone an abiding wonder in the Oriental world, and still weirder manifestations like carefully nurtured cricket pitches and golf courses, manicured tennis courts, swimming-pools, and clubhouses where the ritual whisky-sodas had been downed – the whole intricate paraphernalia of the complex tribe who had been masters of Malaya for more than a hundred years.

Surveying all this, so easily won, the bringers of a New Order to the subject races of Asia must have felt especially exultant, like boys unleashed at last in a previously unattainable orchard. The soldiers of the Empire, moreover, beaten and disarmed, marched tidily into imprisonment in the normal way of the vanquished in war. Indeed, there was only one entailment to the Japanese victory that could cause them less than unadulterated joy. A further by-product of acquiring, practically intact, a celebrated segment of the British Empire was infinitely less assimilable. Together with the prizes and trinkets of victory came what must have seemed to the Japanese literally a monstrous regiment of women.

It was extremely unfortunate in a way, for an army of such straightforward efficiency, a military machine trained and programmed merely to crush its enemies, to encounter women as a factor to be taken into consideration. The only previous land conquest of the forces of Nippon in the modern era was a tract of China, and in China the treatment of prisoners of war, as understood by Europeans, did not apply. Japan never ratified the Geneva Convention, the international agreement governing the treatment of prisoners, not least because to acknowledge the Convention was to contradict the Bushido Code. The Code, which raised martial conduct to the level of a culture and even a religion to millions of Japanese males, treated defeat in war as a terminal condition, a humiliation so powerful that death was actually preferable. Surrendering was considered to be such an unpalatable equivalent to death that those who surrendered were deemed to have waived their right to any existence at all.

By this token, if men in defeat were creatures without dignity, fourth-rate beings at best, then women were effectively off the scale altogether. And these were colonial women, by definition individualistic and dangerously far removed from the Japanese conception of the feminine role.

It was not least of the errors and mishaps of the fall of Malaya, that the confrontation ever came about. If the campaign had not been so extraordinarily swift and the authorities less purblind, the majority of the women would have been evacuated long before the end. As it was, they remained, and in a number and variety that only a community of that kind could maintain.

Pre-war Malaya was one of those softer places of Empire to which women went willingly in countless roles, attracted by the climate, the social opportunities, and a native population which was quiescent, tractable, and anxious to serve. At one level there were the wives, consorts rather, of the *tuans*, the white masters of the peninsula – planters, mine managers, the major entrepreneurial figures of a prosperous country. Then there were the wives of a vast range of colonial administrators: civil engineers and surveyors, policemen and fire-chiefs, customs men – the whole apparatus of running an imperial possession.

Thereafter there was another infra-structure: schoolteachers, governesses and missionaries, secretaries, ladies' companions, nurses. The nursing population of Malaya had increased dramatically shortly before the invasion, because rumours of war had brought the military in strength, and with them the field hospitals and female military nurses in profusion. Finally, there were the women of the native populations, amahs and cooks, laundresses and maids, close attendants who were made indivisible from the Europeans by the colonial order of things, and who added inevitably to the total when the holocaust came.

The immutable nature of this colonial order was in part responsible for the disaster. An unshakeable edifice to all outward appearances, calm and unchanging with its hierarchies settled and its racial boundaries finally drawn, it was not equipped for the sudden arrival of interlopers who not only disregarded its principles but were bent on casting them out altogether. The Greater Eastern Co-Prosperity Sphere, the Japanese euphemism for their seizure of most of the Orient, took as the major tenet of its propaganda the concept of Asia for the Asians, with the white races banished to whence they came.

In the early stages of the invasion of Malaya, this was a matter so unthinkable that the whites reacted slowly rather than racing away helter-skelter when the yellow tide, always a threatening undercurrent, rose and became an engulfing wave. As the Japanese pushed down the peninsula, surrounding the defensive positions of the Empire forces and then eroding them in the way that the incoming sea destroys sand-castles, the non-combatants withdrew reluctantly. There was an almost universal assumption that the little yellow men would be halted and then ejected, and that normality would return.

For this reason Singapore, long-acknowledged as impregnable, was regarded as the place to which one would go if the worst came to the worst. When the Japanese pressure proved unremitting, the women and children of white Malaya – the 'useless mouths' as they became known even to the authorities when the worst actually came – had to start moving southwards immediately. Beginning at a dignified pace, hold-ing their children by the hand and casting only an occasional glance over the shoulder, they were forced to break into a jog-trot and then a headlong run, clasping the children in their arms. Singapore filled with women, then overflowed, but the evacuation was too late. Nobody could quite concede that the last days of this part of the Empire had actually come.

It was this which stamped the imprisonment of the women and made it unlike any other. Those who fell into Japanese hands fresh from Malaya did so not only physically but mentally unprepared for such an event. It was not simply the speed of events but their unlikelihood that left them largely intact in their personalities and their social attitudes. For women accustomed to a status which turned even a humble British governess walking through the crowded streets of Singapore into a kind of miniature Imperial progress among the Malays, Chinese, Indians, and all the other races of that polyglot place, there could scarcely have been a greater trauma.

Nothing in their previous lives, except perhaps that spark of adven-turousness which had taken them East in the first place, could have readied them for a world in which two feet of bed-space represented their only personal domain and the distinctions of race were so diametrically reversed that whiteness became the stigma, and bowing to the strutting representatives of Asia a necessity of every day. Even the seemingly immutable rules of caste and class, immovable pillars of colonial society, were stripped of their comforting solidity as the whole framework of their existence was tested brutally by the enforced egalitarianism of total poverty.

There was another factor which bore a specific relevance to this particular species of women: the sudden and bewildering severance from men. When the shooting stopped and the Japanese resolved their dilemma not by slaughtering the women or repatriating them but simply by herding them together and locking them up, there remained an enclosed female society, imprisoned in the exceptional isolation of Sumatra.

These many years afterwards it is possible to see these events not only as a conventional story of hardship and suffering and danger, but as a singular experiment: a 'laboratory' in which there was a great deal to be learned about women. Long before it became fashionable to examine women for their strengths rather than their weaknesses, to ask what they are able to accomplish rather than underlining what they cannot, here was a case-history with all its elements neatly laid out.

Women obliged to express themselves according to their true natures, not in conformity with some imposed pattern. Women forced to set up their own structures, devise and apply their own politics and social order and discipline. Women encouraged to adapt, to be resourceful and inventive. Women dependent upon their physical abilities. Women supporting and relying on each other, constantly testing the notion of sisterhood, and able to compare it with its male equivalent. Women deprived of traditional support systems such as make-up, perfume, proper clothing, and even the hygiene which society seems so often to regard as primarily a female responsibility.

All this under interminable stress: there was hunger, sickness and fatigue to contend with, and men beyond their worst imaginings, literally their masters in every aspect of their lives and backed up by rifles and bayonets. Ironically, it can now be seen that what was illuminated by the women's imprisonment, was its exact reverse – Women's Liberation.

Chapter 2

Raffles Hotel expressed to perfection the mood and manners of Malaya in 1941, the year which preceded the fall of Singapore – 'The Fall', as it came to be known, lending an appropriately biblical overtone to such a cataclysm. In the memories of nearly all the women of Malaya who were to pass into imprisonment, 'Raffles' crops up somewhere to express a high-point of pleasure or emotion, or drama of meeting or parting in the prelude to the storm.

If the loss of Singapore effectively marked the end of the British Empire, the dance-floor of Raffles was elegantly exact as the setting for the last waltz. Somerset Maugham had already written the hotel's high-colonial ambience into legend: its potted palms and its sun-blinds; the huge fans revolving lazily on its high ceilings; its cool colonnades in shadow but with a hint of the heat and ferment of the Orient wafting across its faultless lawns.

In his stories of the East, Raffles figured as a kind of crossroads at which a variety of *dramatis personae* encountered one another: planters from up-country, broken-hearted or merely broke; *femmes fatales*; remittance-men in dingy white ducks and with their Panama hats at an untrustworthy angle; District Commissioners pondering the destiny of their small plots of Empire, assisted or befuddled by gin-slings fetched by white-coated waiters, moving deftly among the rattan.

Raffles was the stereotype from which various copies were made to give the Western world its conception of the life-style of the more romantic type of white person who had gone 'Out East' in the '20s and '30s. In 1941, while so much of the West starved or burned or cowered, this image was by no means far-fetched where Raffles was concerned.

It was still possible to eat a five-course dinner there and dance the night away, threatened by nothing more immediate than the exceptional press of couples on the dance-floor. The overcrowding gave birth to a syncopated, close embrace to music which was known locally as crush-dancing and was much in favour. It was part of an atmosphere that was distinctly hectic for the normally decorous social life of the colony and which was almost certainly attributable to the proliferation of uniforms among the evening gowns.

There had been a marked build-up of military forces in Malaya throughout the year, but this did not initially strike the colonists as alarming and presaging turmoil and war. The presence of the military merely represented an interesting new ingredient in an existence which otherwise seemed likely to continue, quite unruffled, for ever. In their turn the soldiers, sailors and airmen posted to Malaya, rather than remaining penned in the beleaguered fortress of the UK or despatched to the bitterly demanding deserts of North Africa, could be excused for arriving in something of a holiday mood. Forgivably ignorant of local rules, they could behave quite scandalously but cause no more than pretended shock concealing amusement.

The Australian contingent, stationed there because Singapore was the great bastion on which even Australia's security was deemed to rest, were especially capable of blundering through almost any carefully constructed skein of colonial conventions. With their own tradition of breezy egalitarianism and the irresistible appeal of their dashing slouch hats they coped quite effortlessly with whatever social strictures they encountered.

In Johore Bahru, just across the narrow strait which divided Singapore island from the mainland, a beautiful and extremely well brought up young woman called Molly Ismail, the daughter of a barrister, accepted an invitation to an evening out in the city, in November 1941, with an equally young Australian officer. He was an ADC on the staff of General Gordon Bennett, Commander of the Australian 8th Division, which is how they came to meet at one of the 'At Home's' of the Sultan of Johore, an Eastern potentate with such a taste for Englishness that his resplendent oriental palace in Johore Bahru was furnished in the style of Windsor Castle.

The Sultan's soirées were slightly taxing occasions. They were in the mould of similar rituals conducted by the upper echelons of English society but with certain interesting Eastern variants. Those attending an 'At Home' at the palace, for example, were not supposed to leave the company before the Sultan himself withdrew. If he was feeling particularly sociable his guests would watch the prospect of dinner recede steadily as the evening wore on.

Molly had a recollection of one 'At Home' which she attended with her parents when she was bidden, accompanied by her mother, to take a drink with the Sultan and it turned out to be his wish, firmly expressed, that his son should take her riding the following morning. Neither Molly nor the Sultan's son wanted to puruse this plan but her father's whispered counsel was to smile sweetly and agree since the Sultan, an expansive potentate, had imbibed extremely well already and would have forgotten all about it by the following day.

Molly was a classical product of Malayan society. She could remember, from her early childhood, tigers roaming in the lush jungle beyond the lawns of her family's home and putting out saucers of milky coffee for the panther cubs which sometimes found their way to its porch. Her adolescence was much more formal. It was spent in that migratory pattern established by the British which sent them back and forth to England with a regularity that made the Peninsular and Oriental Steamship Company – 'the P & O' – one of the most prosperous on the oceans.

There were long periods of leave in the homeland and it was understood that the education of children could properly be conducted only in the United Kingdom. For Molly, memories of panther cubs grew remote as she attended a girls' school in the discreet London suburb of Putney. She was eighteen years old when she returned to Johore Bahru to take her place in what seems, now it is no more, the vast and absorbing game of social life in its colonial form.

The ritual attached to invitations was completely inflexible: new arrivals left their visiting cards with you, and you returned the compliment, following up, if credentials were in order, with an invitation to cocktails or dinner. If you accepted you were then obliged to invite the inviters and so on, ad infinitum, in the long and cautious exploratory process by which relationships were formed. The matter of marriages between young people was a crucial side-show, usually the province of mothers who contrived suitable pairings with the dedication of racehorse breeders. Exchanges between the young were monitored most carefully for signs of impending permanence so that an evening out with such an obvious transient as a young Australian in Malaya solely on military business was a charmingly carefree departure from the pressures of match-making.

For the occasion Molly wore a long evening gown of green tulle, made by one of the innumerable, diligent Indian tailors of the colony who, by their nimble fingers and knack for creating almost instant confections, removed from the women of Malaya even the slight but perennial strain of having to think about what to wear. The Australian was in his uniform and, of course, they went to dine and dance at Raffles.

Raffles, too, was the introduction to Malaya for a contingent of British army nurses who were part of the build-up of military forces there in 1941. They were nursing sisters of what was then known as Queen Alexandra's Imperial Military Nursing Service – 'QAs', less imposingly, to all in the Services – and held officer rank in the military hierarchy, but as soon as their ship docked at Singapore they were whisked away, like so many débutantes in their long, white, tricoline dresses and red capes, to join the throng at Raffles.

Sister Margot Turner was among the party and, much as she enjoyed the evening, she was not entirely pleased with such determined levity. She was a tall, handsome young woman, possessed even then of the dedication and energy that would raise her to the heights of Brigadier and Matron-in-Chief of Queen Alexandra's Royal Army Nursing Corps, as QAIMNS later became, and more imposing still, a Dame of the British Empire. Her professional instinct was to move towards the conflict, not further away from it.

Margot had been serving in India, her first overseas posting, since November 1938, and she heard the declaration of war in Europe, in September 1939, on the radio in her quarters in an Indian hill-station. She remembered fretting throughout 1940 as the great events of that year unfolded half the world away – Dunkirk, the invasion threat to Britain, the blitz on her cities. She persistently requested a return home and eventually a posting came. In March 1941 she went down to Bombay for embarkation and boarded a ship which, in the wartime manner, was sailing under sealed orders. Even the Captain was unaware of his destination until the vessel had put to sea. Margot assumed that it would sail west to the war but as the sun set on the first day at sea it went down, blood-red into the ocean, in the wrong direction. The ship, in fact, was bound for Singapore.

To strollers in the warm night air of that brightly lit city, the blackout in Britain was a misery that remained in the back of the mind, just as the abundance of food there occasionally evoked thoughts of the privations of rationing in the Old Country, but it was a natural human reaction to fail to dwell constantly on others' misfortunes. The turmoil in that other hemisphere rumbled away over an impossibly distant horizon, a fretful thunder but one which never moved closer.

In the middle months of 1941 the battle in North Africa took one of its livid turns and the radio bulletins followed the action, but for listeners in the colony the vast curve of the earth between the deserts and the green and beautiful Malayan peninsula muffled the deadly nature of the struggle. It wasn't chic to discuss the war during the course of an evening at Raffles – either over the early evening drinks or at table, and certainly not while crush-dancing to the strict-tempo orchestra which reeled off foxtrots and quicksteps and tangos and waltzes, one following smoothly on from another in the dance-music manner of the period.

When Margot's hospital unit moved up-country to a remote

community called Tanjong Malim, seventy miles to the north of Kuala Lumpur, life was scarcely more exacting. Responding to this novel infusion of healthy young women, the local planters reactivated their club which had fallen into disuse, and invited the nurses to dances there. With subtle amendments appropriate to their gender, the QAs were largely accorded the privileges of the young male officers of the fighting services, the dashing bachelors whom the Empire traditionally cosseted to make up for the loneliness of their duties in far-flung lands. Since they were birds of passage it was possible to issue invitations to QAs, singly or *en bloc*, without setting in motion any of the alarming match-making machinery which enmeshed the resident spinsters. Dancing to gramophone music in the tropical night it required a particularly powerful effort to remember the existence of war. A posting to Malaya qualified as active service, but Margot wrote to her mother to confess that, although this was so, she had never been so inactive in her life.

Those who had been longer acquainted with the languor of Malaya were not as restive. Still further to the north, at Alor Star, the principal town of the state of Kedah, a civilian nurse called Phyllis Briggs was one of four nursing sisters at the hospital there. She would later look back at the last year of peace in the peninsula and find the kind of recollections that people now bring back from successful holidays abroad.

There was a military airfield at Alor Star and the increased complement of Army and RAF officers at this potentially strategic location added considerably to the frequency and fun of the standard range of social diversions. Off-duty life blossomed into a round of parties and dances, mixed foursomes at golf and mixed doubles at badminton with a kaleidoscope of charming new partners. With a full day to spare it was possible to drive to Port Butterworth, sixty miles away, and take the ferry to Penang Island, one of the jewels of the Far East. From the verandah of the swimming club Kedah Peak rose up across the tranquil water with a beauty that would stay in Phyllis's memory for a lifetime.

Yet further northwards, dangerously so as it was to prove, another young woman called Norah Chambers was equally content. Norah was the wife of a Government engineer, John Chambers, and part of a typical small, up-country white community in the north-eastern town of Kuala Trengannu: a classic colonial nucleus of Police Commissioner and customs officials, forestry officers and a doctor – some twenty Europeans in all.

Norah had arrived in Malaya in 1927 with her mother and two sisters to join their father, who was an engineering consultant in Perak, and had luxuriated at first in the sudden cessation of household chores as a little squadron of soft-spoken and compliant Chinese servants spirited all drudgery away. But if there was a defect in the colonial life it was the slight ennui which crept into such an easeful existence. When marriage and the move up-country came, Norah was conscious of the need for more activity. A slim, vibrant woman, she had been a student at the Royal Academy of Music in London and she began teaching the violin to local children, a most delicate occupation for one who was to show such steel later on.

A specific remedy for all up-country tedium was a shopping trip to Singapore, much as a visit to London might beckon to ladies finding the Home Counties momentarily stifling and in 1941 such an outing was especially refreshing. The city, which filled the southern extremity of a 225-mile-square island at the foot of the Malayan peninsular, was a British invention in terms of its commercial and social importance. Founded by an Englishman, Stamford Raffles, who bought the island from the Sultan of Johore in 1819, it had never been invaded or even seriously threatened in all its history and, politically and economically stable, had grown to become fourth ranking among the ports of the world by the 1930s.

This effortless burgeoning appeared to be due entirely to the infallibility of the white masters of Malaya. Only about thirty thousand Europeans lived among two million Malays, as many Chinese, some seven hundred thousand Indians and the large population of Eurasians whose blood was a mixture of European and Asian strains. There were even a thousand Japanese resident at the time of the invasion.

Both the British and the polyglot peoples they governed came to believe that the order of things would never change in the colony. Whatever might arise, the Asians and the Indians and all the rest had grown used to thinking that the *tuans* would be equal to it, and in war, especially, they were assumed to be without peers.

The *tuans* themselves felt such confidence that it was even possible, in the prevailing atmosphere, to relax the rigid barriers between the whites and those of other hues. At one time the compulsion to differentiate between this one breed and all the rest was so deeply entrenched that it was 'not done' for European women to appear in the fascinating streets of the ethnic enclaves of the city, the teeming Chinese quarter or the area where the Indians had created intact the sights, sounds and smells of Calcutta or Bombay.

By 1941 it was possible even to shop in these areas, an exciting experience for newcomers like the nurses fresh from England but, in a way, more intriguing still for local ladies to whom Chinatown, say, had grown over the years to resemble some forbidden city, remote and mysterious like Lhasa. In the camps later on, wearing rags, women thought back wistfully to the wonders of stalls piled high with fabrics of every kind and with tailors nearby who could transform them into copies of European fashions in not much more time than it took to unfold a picture torn from some glossy magazine sent from the other side of the world. Reduced, in the future, to the doleful contemplation of their muddy bare toes, it was possible to recall the ease of acquiring a pair of hand-made shoes. The only effort necessary was to place the feet on a piece of paper while a pencil was run around their outline.

For those whose thoughts would come to dwell exclusively on food, there were memories of Technicolor heaps of exotic eatables in China-town. In the European section of the city there was a cake-shop and café in Battery Road, known as 'GH's' after its owner, an Australian called Mrs Howe. At marble-topped tables the clientele would recklessly ignore their waistlines in exchange for the joy of Mrs Howe's gâteaux and home-made icecreams.

At the pinnacle of pleasant indulgence was Robinson's emporium in one of the city's smartest thoroughfares, Raffles Place. The store was Singapore's direct equivalent of Harrods and occupied the same sort of niche in women's daytime lives that Raffles Hotel took over at night. 'I'll meet you for coffee at Robinson's' was a catch-phrase so well understood as a synonym for all that was attractive and well-ordered in Malayan living that it survived, spoken wryly, even into the camps.

Robinson's stood, unself-consciously, for all that the British had made of Malaya, their achievement at turning an untamed, jungle country not only into a beautiful playground but a place of profit. Theirs was a game, set and match success at imposing on the country everything they valued and enjoyed with hardly a concession to anybody else in the process. There were assistants of half a dozen races working in Robinson's, immaculately recreating the ambience of Knightsbridge or Piccadilly, but the departmental supervisors were, almost without exception, white. Over coffee in the air-conditioned restaurant, in 1941 a recent and impressive addition to the amenities, with the attentive representatives of lesser breeds hovering to catch each passing whim, it was extremely hard to imagine anyone overturning a way of life so elegantly serene.

None of the amendments to time-honoured routine in that last year of peace seemed to prove anything but benevolent. Both Molly and her mother, Peggy Ismail, devoted considerable time to the Servicemen's canteen in Johore Bahru which provided comforts for the Other Ranks since they were so far from home. Working in the canteen qualified precisely as the sort of useful voluntary endeavour which ladies throughout the Empire always took up dutifully if the need was there. Such tasks had the additional value of lending point and purpose to days sometimes lacking in significant direction and there was a further bonus here. The Other Ranks, for those unfamiliar with their *modus vivendi*, proved both interesting and educative.

Their dietary requirements were as strictly regulated as those of some Eastern monastic order: complex permutations on an invariable theme of sausages, beans, toast, eggs and chips with mugs of tea. Molly and her mother would have liked to introduce something a little more adventurous to the menu, but later on, when they faced starvation, they were to think back to this sturdy fare at least as wistfully as they conjured up the gâteaux at GH's in their imagination.

There were also faint Eastern resonances to the pastimes of the fascinating tribe that frequented the canteen: ping-pong and sing-song, although they went about both with a vigour that owed little to Oriental delicacy. But there were charming surprises. Amid the hearty choruses 'Bless 'em All', 'Roll out the Barrel', 'Run, Rabbit, Run' – fresh off the troopships the soldiers had imported the 1940 Hit Parade whole from Blighty – one young NCO turned out to have a superb tenor voice. Mrs Ismail found out that he was a pianist, too, and gave him the freedom of her house to practise whenever he was off duty. Molly remembered waking up from her nap one sultry Malayan afternoon to hear, in the distance, the piano being played beautifully by a Bombardier from Yorkshire.

Raffles, of course, was out of bounds to Other Ranks as indeed, in the main and by unspoken rule, were the well brought up young ladies of the colony. Molly had made a further engagement with her Australian officer and they were to dine and dance again at Raffles on the evening of Sunday 7 December 1941. In retrospect this was to prove very much like making a date for the eve of Armageddon. The appointment had to be cancelled because, late that day, the ADC was whisked abruptly up-country in company with his General, and to an unknown fate because Molly, in fact, was never to hear of him again.

All over the peninsula social arrangements for that evening went suddenly awry. One hundred and fifty miles to the north of Johore Margot Turner had accepted an invitation to dinner in Kuala Lumpur from one of the doctors at the hospital in Tanjong Malim and their commanding officer offered them a lift there in his car. In the town the CO went to the cinema and Margot and her escort to a hotel dinner dance, having arranged a rendezvous at midnight for the journey back to Tanjong Malim.

As Margot and the doctor danced that evening there was an interruption as military police moved among the crowd ordering all military personnel to report to their units immediately. With seventy miles to cover in order to comply, Margot and the medical officer went to the Kuala Lumpur Club – known to the locals as The Spotted Dog, to arouse a few echoes of home – to wait for the CO and his car. They had just got up to dance again when more Redcaps, brisk and serious-faced, stamped in and repeated the same instruction. In the small hours, on the way back to the hospital, a road-block loomed out of the darkness, manned by more unsmiling soldiers.

It was at 4am precisely, that same morning, that Molly Ismail stood on the verandah of her parents' bungalow in Johore Bahru and, looking across the Strait, saw the bombing of Singapore begin. She was not afraid. 'I had no feeling that either I or my family could be harmed,' she was to say of the swiftness and unreality with which the thunder moved overhead.

In fact, for some twenty-four hours before the first bombs fell on Singapore it was known that a Japanese fleet was at sea, twenty-seven troop-transports off Cambodia Point, the southern tip of what was then Indo-China, and steaming westwards. In the darkness of the early hours of 8 December 1941, and known only to the highest Command and the soldiers spread thinly along the beaches at Kota Bahru on the north-eastern coast of the peninsula, the transports came finally to anchor. There, starting at 1.15am, the Japanese Imperial Army began to pour ashore in their rubber assault-craft to begin the invasion of Malaya.

For an event that was to mark the beginning of the end of a way of life that had matured to such a remarkable texture across the span of 150 years, the first landings lacked a certain drama when the news of them was revealed. The soldiers on the beaches knew that something exceptionally ferocious and unmanageable was coming at them from the blackness, but the radio announcement which Margot Turner heard as daylight came on that Monday morning, and which explained the oddities of the previous evening, was terse and professionally calm.

Like so much that was to follow in the same vein, this sang-froid was misleading. As soon as they were ashore in numbers the Japanese began to exercise the techniques of stealthy encirclement and headlong advance that were to carry them down the peninsula with such vehemence. It was a warlike style so alarming and unfamiliar that almost at once a cloud of panicky rumour began to precede their movements, an enervating uncertainty about their presence, here or there, that was as effective as a poison gas spreading in front of their spearheads.

Of the women whose story we shall be following, Norah Chambers was the first to find her life transformed as radically as if an earthquake had struck.

The remote and inviting expanse of beaches which attracted the

Japanese warlords, as they bent over their maps deciding where best to strike at Malaya, were among the playgrounds of the inhabitants of Kuala Trengannu. As soon as the landings were announced the Chambers sent their five-year-old daughter Sally south to Kuala Lumpur by road, but as a routine precaution rather than in alarm. The radio from Singapore continued to speak coolly of the Japanese incursion, as if it would be dealt with promptly, and the little community of Europeans in the township were not of the calibre to turn tail in any conventional emergency.

The crises of the assault on Malaya, however, were never to be of the formal kind. A powerful blast of rumour now insisted that fresh landings were taking place to the south at Kuantan, threatening encirclement to a whole sector of the north-east. Within days of the first attack, the Resident Commissioner for the Kuala Trengannu area, unable to reassure anybody that they were not in a trap which was about to close, counselled immediate withdrawal to the civilian population. They were told to leave everything behind and concentrate on saving their freedom, if not their lives.

With peril existing beyond doubt to the north, a Japanese-infested sea to the east, and the new and unfathomable threat to the south, the only feasible escape route lay across wild country into the mountains to the west. So it was that the companions of innumerable beach-parties and picnics and civilized gatherings in lovingly tended gardens for tiffin or sundowners in the tropical dusk, found themselves involved in an extraordinary trek. They were organized into three small groups for the escape, taking no more personal possessions than the clothes they stood up in. The group that included Norah and her husband carried a few tins of food and, in addition, were equipped with a rifle and a torch. Norah remembered, as if it were the only remaining vestige of a previous order, that a Malay policeman led the way carrying the torch.

As a journey on foot into untamed territory the march that followed would have been daunting to professional explorers, let alone lady violin teachers and colonial civil servants. Ravines crossed only by rough-hewn tree-trunks led to virgin jungle pockmarked with buffalo-wallows filled to shoulder height with mud and excrement in which blood-thirsty leeches proliferated. Shelter at night was provided by a few palm-fronds laced together and food was a handful of bully-beef washed down with the water from streams. To add to this range of hardships there was the conviction that this was terrain ideal for an enemy already credited with a demon's ability to materialize at will. Norah was not a woman to shriek at shadows, as she was to prove beyond question, but she recalled that every thicket came to look ineffably sinister and that every clearing felt as if it were being swept by cruel, slit-eyes.

Filthy and exhausted the party eventually reached, after five days and six nights, the north-south railway line on the far side of the central mountain range, and gazed up the track with but slender expectation of a train. To their astonishment a train appeared and, underlining the bewilderment with which Malaya passed from peace to war, the dirty and disreputable-looking band of escapers were actually asked to pay their fares to Kuala Lumpur!

Very soon there would be a flood of refugees surging southwards and their plight would be much better understood, but in Singapore still, at that moment, the trek would have aroused nothing but astonishment among the morning-coffee drinkers at Robinson's or at the dinner tables of Raffles Hotel. It would take rather more than a few bombs and the flight of some up-country people by such an uncomfortable method to shake the profound sense of security which existed within the fortress.

On 2 December, just six days before the onslaught at Kota Bahru, two battleships of the Royal Navy, the *Prince of Wales* and the *Repulse*, arrived in Singapore to reinforce the Far Eastern fleet. Margot Turner heard the news of their presence on the same small radio which had brought her the tidings of the outbreak of the European war. So far from assisting in a security clamp-down on the movements of two capital ships in potentially hostile waters, the radio was proudly indicating to all who cared to listen that the British power in this quarter of the globe was now more invincible than ever.

In just over a week from that announcement the battleships had been sunk off the eastern coast, bombed to oblivion by Japanese aircraft – and that was but the beginning of the worst single reverse that the British Empire ever suffered in war. Singapore and all the lovely land of Malaya had much to discover, and the women of that country, especially, had an unparalleled upheaval to endure.

Chapter 3

That first Japanese air-raid on Singapore brought death and injury and the destruction of property, but it had a little of the air of a firework display. The lights of the city were full on and along the waterfront crowds of the native population stood gaping upwards as the anti-aircraft guns stuttered into action in the early hours of 8 December.

The Japanese venom struck mainly at Chinatown, but a stray bomb hit Robinson's air-conditioned restaurant and it seemed almost as if this projectile alone counted as the official opening of hostilities. An Englishwoman living in Raffles Place was hurled out of bed by the blast and, responding to the conditioning of such a long period of peace; she immediately phoned the police station. The police, responding in their turn, perhaps, to a deep-seated need to preserve the myths of invincibility, even with the enemy overhead, replied that the pyrotechnics were part of a practice alert. 'In that case,' the caller said, with justifiable indignation, 'they're overdoing it. Robinson's has just been hit!'

There could have been no clearer indication that the fight was not to be confined to Chinatown. When he was told by the commanding General that the Japanese had landed that same morning, four hundred miles to the North, the Governor of Malaya, Sir Shenton Thomas, is said to have remarked, 'I trust you'll chase the little men off', thus perfectly conveying the notion that this was simply a question of unruly Asiatics and that the proper equilibrium would rapidly be restored. In fact, the little men had a strong foothold within hours of their landing. At Kota Bahru the brave first resistance of the British troops was suddenly undermined by rumours that the Japanese had already broken through to the rear and a helter-skelter retreat began.

This was the beginning of the pattern of panic that was to reduce a force of powerful numerical superiority to a near rabble; and the Japanese air offensive was equally effective in inducing terror and a blind urge to be elsewhere. Two days after the invasion the view across

27

the water from Penang that had so entranced Phyllis Briggs on her outings from the hospital at Alor Star had a chilling new addition. From the waterfront at George Town, on the island's coast, it was possible to see the bombing of the RAF airfield at Port Butterworth over the strait, and once again the Malays and Chinese and Indians gathered, almost childishly trusting, to watch the show.

At 11 o'clock the following morning, Thursday 11 December, an immaculate formation of Japanese planes arrived over George Town itself and, leisurely and unopposed, as if at practice, rained death down on the city. More than a thousand were killed before the aircraft droned away, leaving a great curtain of dust in the still morning air. A pupil at the Anglo-Chinese Girls' School, a fifteen-year-old called Phyllis Liddelow, was actually sitting for her School Certificate in a hall in the town when the drum-rolls of the pattern bombing began and, with the rest of the candidates, she sat out the massacre beneath the flimsy protection of her desk.

Phyllis and her twelve-year-old sister, Doris, who was also at the school, were the daughters of a British civil engineer and a Thai mother. Both their parents were in Thailand, at Phuket, just across the Malayan border, and, in order to attend the school, the sisters were staying with their Scots-Irish godparents in Penang. They can still remember being rushed through streets in which vivid flames lingered, back to the house where they were told to take only what they could pack into a pillow-case apiece. Their godfather paused to shoot his five fox-terriers – 'I'll not have them eaten by the Chinese,' he said – then they were hurried down to the harbour past piles of dead on whom kerosene was being poured before they were set alight. 'I looked at this with detachment as if I were merely observing a part of history,' Phyllis says now. Besides their prettiness, a certain fatalism must have come with the sisters' heritage and the same curious detachment from the harsh and unpalatable was to help them through an adolescence spent in the camps.

They were rushed on to a boat which immediately sailed for Singapore, that symbol of safety, and were among the first to take part in an escape, the effects of which were to resound to the very end of the Malayan war. Soon afterwards, in spite of a firm undertaking by the government in Singapore that no discrimination would exist if an evacuation became necessary, the military commander of Penang ordered all European women and children away. Overnight, in the strict secrecy attending what was designated as a military operation, the Asiatics, who had worked diligently alongside the European women in the aftermath of the raid, were abandoned. This was to prove a deadly blow to the reputation of the *tuans* and was to affect the thinking on evacuation when Singapore was directly threatened. Nobody wanted a repetition of that precipitate flight from Penang.

But all over the Peninsula the bad times had begun for those who, such a short time before, had been luxuriating in the sun. At Alor Star Phyllis Briggs's treasured off-duty was cancelled on the very first day of the war as the Japanese bombers came over in waves and the hospital began to fill with wounded, arriving right round the clock. That far north the distinctive, continuing rumble of gunfire was added to the thunder of passing convoys of trucks, shaking the wooden bungalow where Phyllis lived, its doors barricaded during the night hours in a futile gesture of protection from the possibility of wandering Japanese.

Their reputation already as vindictive wraiths, capable of striking at will, must have affected the choice of a melodramatic password when arrangements were made for the evacuation of the hospital. The message 'Curtain Fallen' was to be passed over the telephone and the nurses, each of whom had been told to pack their belongings into two suitcases, were immediately to abandon everything else and go.

The servicemen's families had been evacuated almost straight away and Phyllis remembers an infinitely sad by-product of their departure. Sally Scarf was a nursing sister at the hospital but also the wife of an RAF officer serving at Alor, and when the inexorable machinery of military organization ground into action her status as a service wife took precedence over her nursing duties. She had gone by the time the hospital received its very first casualty, a mortally wounded RAF officer who was none other than her husband. 'Pongo' Scarf, typical of the hearty young men who had brought so much gaiety to the beach-parties and the badminton matches, died without seeing her again.

Phyllis, tiny, sweet-faced, and delicately feminine, now a retired resident of Bournemouth, clearly never lacked determination. 'I made up my mind that Pongo would be buried properly,' she said. She managed to procure a coffin from the local jail. She had a little Morris car and, with another sister, she followed the ambulance bearing Pongo to the cemetery. On the road they met a car carrying two Army padres in the opposite direction and persuaded them to go with them and say a prayer. 'I wanted to be able to tell Sally that we had done all we could.'

The little Morris took to the road again four days later when the hospital, cleared of its patients, was evacuated. In the last hours Phyllis had another painful responsibility: a motherless baby lay forlornly with no relative arriving to collect it and, relying on an instinct to trust the impassive, uncomplaining Asiatics who had served the whites so well, she finally handed the infant to an Indian *ayah*, who received the small bundle in the usual unquestioning way.

On the way south, an air of disintegration gathered rapidly, manifesting itself in incidents which remained clearly in Phyllis's memory. At Taiping the school had been converted into a military hospital staffed by QAs fresh from Singapore, still starched and brisk. Phyllis and the civilian sisters with her were relegated to only the simplest menial tasks as if they were of a breed impossibly less valuable than this nursing elite. Or so it seemed until the tide of casualties from the north turned into a flood and suddenly all became equal.

At Taiping, too, a young Army wife, travelling down with a nursing sister because she was pregnant, went into premature labour. As if to compound the growing disaster she brought forth a baby suffering from spina bifida. Even Phyllis's vivid memory tailed away in the matter of its fate, although she recalled that a massive dose of morphia was discussed in this setting where all the rules and training of a lifetime were abruptly beginning to be held up to a different light.

At Ipoh the streets were deserted and ghostly because a bad raid the day before had persuaded the population to heed a terse Government Order, '*pergi ulu*', which meant, 'Go into the jungle', and was some of the soundest advice the Government was to proffer to the native population.

An instinct for the familiar took Phyllis to the sort of place she would probably have made for if visiting Ipoh in the days when it was alive with its normal bustle. This was the Railway Hotel and miraculously it was still serving food. On the same day she addressed herself to a Redcap, a military policeman, with some small query, only to discover that he was a British General. The red band of the Staff, showing through the dust on his cap, had led her to the kind of ghastly gaffe that would have kept old Malaya laughing for a week.

There was a distinct sign of burgeoning collapse when she called at the home of a friend in Ipoh who told her that his wife had already left for Singapore and that he would give away anything that Phyllis and her companion wanted from that temple of privilege, the bungalow of a *tuan*. Phyllis no longer felt sufficiently confident in the future, as worn and dejected soldiers trailed past in continual retreat, to want to take anything that would add to the burdens of the small Morris.

When the journey began again, however, with Kuala Lumpur as the next objective, one nursing sister was determined to save her husband's car, even though she was a woman driver of comic-postcard inefficiency. She set off with a Chinese *amah* in the passenger seat. Phyllis followed her down a road crammed with rickshaws and ancient buses and natives pushing bicycles piled high with their belongings, baskets of live chickens set atop like squawking talismans, and watched horrified as the car ahead suddenly shot from sight over a steep drop. A young rubber tree saved the vehicle from extinction in the ravine below, but as its occupants scrambled back to the road it was possible to observe a Chinese *amah* proving anything but impassive for once.

At Seremban, the next stop in the odyssey, the hospital was filled to overflowing with wounded soldiers, and the war seemed to be gaining fast on the escapers as the Japanese planes caught up again. In the infernal racket of the raids the Matron's little dog was driven hysterical by fear and was put to sleep – one of the innumerable tiny tragedies that accompanied the great ones.

There were oddly normal oases amid the chaos. Phyllis slept on a camp bed in the room of a sister called Jennie MacAlister who was engaged to a planter and was methodically getting ready for her wedding, quite unaware that it would be postponed for four years, most of them spent bereft of anything like a trousseau in the Sumatran camps.

The Christmas of 1941 might have brought a brief respite, but it crept up and went by almost unnoticed in a hospital where the length of the working hours made sleep the only treat. It was a time that later cropped up frequently in the women's recollections since the Christmases that followed for such a long time were survived in conditions incomparably worse.

Up at Tanjong Malim, Christmas Eve was the day that Margot Turner began her journey south. The noises of battle were rumbling down towards No. 17 Combined General Hospital and an ambulance train arrived and left loaded with battle casualties who had more than fulfilled Margot's need to be fully engaged in active service. The train had its own medical staff and the people from Tanjong Malim were left behind to await another, but the station was obliterated by bombs and that point of departure went out of the reckoning.

It was a raid of such fury that the Chinese and Indian hospital servants quietly availed themselves of '*pergi ulu*' and were seen no more. That night the staff were told to take what they could carry and start walking down the line to meet a train that, with any luck, was making its way up. It was a walk which brought them all abruptly face to face with that dependency which flourishes when servants exist. Burdened like oxen they trudged through the steamy, breathless night thinking agonizingly about bearers and water-carriers and all the rest of the myriad invaluable auxiliaries to European life in the East.

Part of their load was possibly a unique curiosity to be found on the move in the midst of Malaya at such a time – a complete Christmas dinner: turkey, plum pudding, mince pies, all cooked but with no opportunity to be eaten. The train turned up and played hide-and-seek with the Japanese bombers all the way to Seremban, where the bombers won the game, obliging the whole group to spend part of their Christmas in a drain.

Another train took them aboard for the journey to Singapore, hampered at first by the fact that the engine driver had also shown a sensible preference for the jungle. Two British soldiers got it under way and on the stretch that followed they also managed to warm up the Christmas dinner. In spite of its age, it still proved, by mutual consent, to be the best of its kind ever, not least because it was accompanied by tots of neat whisky.

But that Christmas, as though to quench any notion that life had done anything other than take a dramatic turn for the worse, there came news that inarguably confirmed the Japanese as an enemy of appalling ferocity, authentic nightmare figures rather than the vaguely spooky automatons of the jungle battles. Technically a few hours later, but in fact simultaneously with Malaya, given the time differences of the vast Pacific, the British Crown Colony of Hong Kong had been attacked with equal efficiency. By Christmas morning the Colony had surrendered after a gallant, last ditch defence but, in a sudden excess of rage, the victorious Japanese bayoneted soldiers who had already laid down their arms, so beginning an episode that was to shock a world already becoming inured to the horror of war.

At St Stephen's College in the district of Stanley an emergency hospital had been set up and was packed with wounded. A Red Cross flag was prominent over the door but Japanese infantry burst in and, when two doctors went to meet them, pointing to the Red Cross, they were shot and then bayoneted repeatedly as they lay on the ground. The wounded were next, their bandages ripped from them before they were bayoneted too. Then it was the turn of the nurses to pay a traditional further penalty of women in war. An orgy of rape began and, when it ended a day later, seven of them were dead as well.

A Japanese explained to a sister in the midst of it all that this fury was to avenge the death of the younger brother of an officer engaged in the attack on the Stanley district, lending a logic to the seeming mindlessness but making it somehow even more appalling. There were other stories of rape, some with additional embellishments to the torment, like the presence of senior British officers as an audience held at bayonet point. And European women were used for a variety of bizarre roles: they were reported seen standing up in the bows of Japanese launches moving about the Harbour as a human screen against sniper fire. A Japanese sentry was seen standing on guard in an exquisite mink coat, as horrifying as a monkey guying human kind.

All of this reached Malaya only in fragments, muted by the rigid censorship exercised from Singapore, so that the full terror had a distant quality, like a scream half heard in the dark. Elizabeth Simons, an Australian Army nurse who was to write an account of her imprisonment with an extraordinary regard for the ridiculous, even *in extremis*, recalls her astonishment when an English Army officer recommended in full seriousness that the military nurses should be shot by their officers if in terminal risk of capture by the enemy, much as if they were the Matron's little dog at Seremban or the five poor fox-terriers in Penang. Only later did they realize, and slowly, that the situation was sufficiently dreadful to make the suggestion almost humane.

In any event, everything that was taking place, either in Malaya or the world beyond, made of Singapore a symbol of stability in an environment otherwise racing towards a turbulence in which nothing safe and dependable remained. Simply getting there became, in every mind, the object that gave some semblance of order to every disjointed day.

Phyllis Briggs resumed her progress on 10 January when the Army ordered a general withdrawal towards the city. The wounded were put into trains and Phyllis set her faithful Morris on the road again, taking a sister called Mary Gentles as her passenger. Driving through Johore the skies opened and the roof could not contend with the furious tropical rain. Mary Gentles responded by putting up her purple umbrella inside the car and fended off the water very efficiently although not much later she was to drown when yet another vessel was sent to the bottom of the South China Sea.

Before leaving Seremban, the girls were given two thousand cigarettes and some bottles of champagne to take with them, the idea of bequeathing the Japanese even these limited comforts being repugnant to everybody. Whenever they encountered soldiers on the road Mary threw packets of the cigarettes to them from her place in the passenger seat, a strange Lady Bountiful beneath her purple brolly.

At the Singapore General Hospital the travellers were offered the blissful haven of beds in one of the wards, but in the small hours of the morning an interminable raid led to their being rousted out and obliged to spend the rest of the night in a corridor downstairs. The next morning, sleepless and miserable, they drank the champagne.

By now most of the nurses in Malaya had found their way to Singapore and they were distributed wherever there was need. Phyllis was sent to a former maternity hospital which had now become a centre for air-raid victims. Malays, Chinese and Indians were brought in direct from the bombed streets, sometimes dying and sometimes already dead. The hopelessly injured among the ceaseless tide were given large doses of morphia, the routines of hospital practice being sketched by writing the amounts administered on strips of plaster which were then stuck on to their foreheads.

There was another example of the kind of tidy thinking which becomes second nature to trained nurses. Phyllis automatically noted a recurring motif among the pattern of the wounds which were presented and sought an explanation. This was that the six-foot monsoon drains beside the roads were frequently, and sensibly, used for shelter during the air bombardment. But the Chinese, particularly, had a habit of putting their heads down and their bottoms up, leading to a positive epidemic of cases of shrapnel in the buttocks.

But if it was possible to grin at that discovery, privately and for a brief moment amid the turmoil, there were so many horrors that even most of a lifetime would not erase. 'Some of the patients had infected wounds crawling with maggots,' Phyllis said. 'It was the one thing that made me feel quite sick. One Chinese woman had half her face blown away. I have never forgotten her pleading eyes. Large maggots were crawling out of what was left of her nose.'

The bombs rained down throughout the month of January as if high explosive had joined the seasonal rituals of nature in the tropics, where the heavens weep or the droughts come with equal indiscrimination. In the same implacable way the planes arrived over Singapore, always in immaculate formation and invariably made up, for those who cared to count in the middle of such a maelstrom, of twenty-seven, fifty-four or eighty-one aircraft. Their method was just as predictable. A marksman in the leading aircraft made the decision for all as to when the lethal downpour should commence, and they complied in unison so that the effect was literally that of a sudden storm.

It was possible to watch the bombing, as though at a theatrical performance, while eating lunch at the Swimming Club on the coast a little way outside the city, an example of a schizophrenia which allowed some in Singapore to eat and drink and dance and swim while others died or gazed appalled at crawling wounds. It was not a division caused by callousness or class, but by the nature of the place and the ordering of that society which could not change its habits briskly even under the duress of high explosives. Many did their duty valiantly in the worst of it and then, in some brief respite, took a taxi to the Swimming Club for tiffin, a simple translation of the ethos which allowed both the Swimming Club and a jungle to co-exist on a small island in the China Seas.

Not that the Swimming Club retained for long its pre-war chic. Then, beside the big, tiled pool there were tables under beach umbrellas, attended by impeccable Chinese waiters. There were showers, a post office, electric irons, a dining-room a dance floor. Quite by chance, all of this, with the possible exception of the dance floor – and even that when every space beneath a roof became a haven for the wounded and the dying – was tailor-made for refugees of the singular kind that came to Singapore. Women who arrived from the north, with not much more than a suitcase of possessions but a lifetime's heritage of hygiene and care in their personal appearance, made their way to the club, changed into bathing suits, washed their clothes in the ladies' changing-room and then swam or casually ordered a drink by the pool while their things were laid out to dry in the hot sun. It was a time when, of all its appurtenances, the club's electric irons came most prominently into their own.

All over Singapore familiar structures were subtly altering their usefulness in the same way. The restaurant at Robinson's, damaged in the opening raid, was borne, as if wounded, down to the basement where it served not only as a reassurance that something at least of the old life had remained intact, but as a meeting ground for displaced customers from all over the Peninsula. People who had got cut off from family or friends in the long, pell-mell progress southwards could order a coffee from waitresses as friendly and compliant as usual, knowing that if those they had mislaid were going to turn up anywhere, sooner or later, as ever, it would be at Robinson's.

St Andrew's Cathedral near the Padang in the centre of the city, that most resolutely British stretch of bright emerald turf where cricket was played, had always looked as though it had been transferred too, whole from somewhere in southern England. A cool, slightly austere place within, in the manner of Anglican churches, it was to become littered with the wounded, the lost and the helpless, a sanctuary in the medieval sense.

The Englishness of St Andrew's was profound. The Choirmaster of forty years standing was a Mr Brown, so energetic in encouraging the young of the city to discover the joys of music that he was widely known as 'the man who put the Sing in Singapore'. He was a colonial gentleman in the classic mould, having made an appearance earlier in the city's history as Major Brown and played a part in the only other martial event of any significance, a mutiny among the Indian garrison in 1916.

His wife, pursuing the distaff side of the same tradition, was a most imposing example of the British presence since she weighed some fifteen stones, although she was what was then known as 'delicate', a sufferer from persistent poor health. She was equally energetic, however, doing numerous good works, despatching exquisitely thoughtful parcels to air-raid victims in the United Kingdom until bombs began to rain down, with biblical impartiality, upon the givers in Singapore as well as the receivers in the UK.

Their daughter Shelagh, then twenty-six, was a secretary in the

Ministry of War Economy and she was to pass, with her mother, into captivity in Sumatra. Mr Brown, who stayed behind in Singapore, was sent to the notorious men's camp at Changi, where he continued to be a most valuable member of that somewhat different type of community. When he and Shelagh were reunited after the war he confirmed his Anglo-Saxon heritage completely by never once mentioning his experiences after the Fall or enquiring about hers.

Shelagh subsequently married a rector and was to live in Wiltshire when all these events had become history. She continued, life-long, the family tradition of benign involvement in other people's lives. Not least among her attributes, she proved to be one of those people who, when they part from you swearing to keep in touch, actually do. She had been very active after the war at maintaining the links between the women who had forged such a bond through their shared suffering, proceeding in that determined way of even the most ladylike females of the Empire.

Shelagh was a devotee of the viola and she insisted on taking the portly instrument with her when she and her mother were forced to flee. The viola was eventually sunk in the Banka Strait and, though it would have proved such an unmanageable liability, its loss remained an abiding sorrow throughout the imprisonment.

A number of women harboured similar regrets through a period in which all smaller disasters might easily have passed from the memory. Molly Ismail and her mother, among the very last British women to be evacuated from Johore Bahru because of their conviction, born of such long security, that the whole nightmare would somehow recede, had to pack what they could into four suitcases as the Japanese spearheads approached. In an agony of indecision – justified, since when Molly returned in 1945 the house had been looted, her father's books burned and their beautiful garden swallowed again by the jungle – they settled for clothes and a few objects of sentimental value. Looking around until the last moment, Mrs Ismail succumbed to some new cushions which she had just acquired and, struggling, packed them too. They were not to survive for long. A teacher at a school for Army offspring in the city, Mamie Colley, a woman of remarkable strength of mind, bewailed throughout her years in camp the abandonment of a whole chestful of beautiful Chinese linen, although it was left behind in a house which she only left when a Bofors anti-aircraft gun was set up in the garden.

Not all such stories ended badly. The indefatigable Morris belonging to Phyllis Briggs was stolen in the feverish days shortly before the end, but in that same period, Netta Smith, a civilian nurse originally from Aberdeen, still had a car and, a true Aberdonian, decided to sell it. A Chinese bought it for six hundred Straits dollars, the price Netta had originally paid for it, which was balm to her Scottish soul. Pursuing the ancient instincts of her race, she put it straight into a bank, as if banks at least would surely be spared the prevailing shot and shell. The instinct was infallible. On her release she went straight there and found her deposit intact, a miracle of such proportion that she threw caution to the winds and treated herself and her friends to a beano. In the same way, a girl who stuffed a bundle of family photographs behind the organ pipes in St Andrew's Cathedral at the last minute, loath to destroy them but even more unwilling that they should be taken by the Japanese, came back post-war, stuck her hand behind the pipes and retrieved them.

The final turmoil that brought all these things about was still a little way in the future in January 1942. Although the air-raids came like a tiger's claws rending at the city, the beast itself was still on the mainland, at the Strait of Johore, which continued to act like an invisible stockade, at least in the minds of those schooled to believe that Singapore Island could never fall.

The relentless palliative propaganda of the Government also clung to the notion that all, to a great extent, was still well in spite of the hordes of refugees and the swelling tide of retreating Servicemen, either wounded or already carrying the exhausted pallor of beaten men. The tone of official announcements was exhortatory: 'WORKERS, every hour counts in the battle of Singapore. Don't let the sirens stop your work. The enemy bombers may be miles away. They may never come near you. Carry on until the roof-spotters give the signal to take cover . . . Every hour's work makes Singapore stronger.'

The attitude was ostrich-like but there was considerable charm in continuing to believe that this was a passing storm and certainly, with hindsight, Singapore, so near its end, was absurdly normal for much of the time. The shops were still full of the goods required by a prosperous colony. There was a choice of a dozen different makes of refrigerator for those unaware that they would presently be ordered to leave with only what they could carry. The latest books from England were somehow still finding their way into the bookshops. On 16 January the *Straits Times*, Singapore's principal newspaper, carried among its myriad advertisements an announcement of the arrival from England of Morley's pure silk stockings ('for thrifty loveliness!') and a recent shipment of, most ironically, British safes.

The *Straits Times* printed also a string of messages in its Personal Column which, properly interpreted, had the sinister sound of the tiger's claws scratching at the very door – 'J. Baldwin is enquiring after the whereabouts of his wife, Mrs Alice Adeline Baldwin, and daughter, Miss Phyllis G. Baldwin' . . . 'Suitcases belonging to Mr W. J. C.

Blunn, Mr J. Whyte, Mr B. K. Mallison and Mr Watson are lying in the office of the Department of Supply, Fullerton Building' – but Robinson's store reported record over-the-counter sales. The remarkable store also featured a special display of women's and children's fashions, to the considerable chagrin of those who had come down-country with only what they stood up in and had omitted to bring cash among their portables.

There was dancing every night, and even at tea-time. There was the cinema, and the possibility to eat extremely well, although the rounding up of all Japanese nationals at the start of hostilities had stripped the surrounding waters of their most diligent fishermen. The local Malays, by custom, caught only enough for themselves. In this climate the matter of leaving Malaya altogether, given that in Britain the evacuation of women and children from areas of potential danger took place before a single bomb had fallen, was seriously side-tracked.

Years later, when the women were asked, in view of the more sinister aspects of life in the Peninsula at that time, the simplistic question, 'Why on earth did you stay?' the replies went to the heart of the tragedy. To leave then would have been to give up everything, and everything, in the context, included the particular circumstances of being a European woman in the colony in the first place. Besides the necessity of leaving husbands and fathers and brothers and lovers who would be obliged to remain, there was the powerful feeling that it was 'not done' to 'run away'. This deep-seated hangover from the days when the women of the Empire faced up to ceaseless tribulations was actually endorsed by the authorities who were obsessed with 'saving face' in the presence of the native populations. It was made plain, though unofficially, that the shameful abandoning of the Asiatic women and children after the bombing of Penang should not occur again. Mr Brown, from the cathedral, included among his duties the job of film censor and was specifically instructed to ban scenes in which Asiatics could be seen offering violence to Europeans. He was invited to visit a Malayan film set one day and took Shelagh along; she privately noted that the very scene they watched so politely in its making was one which would almost certainly fall to her father's scissors later on.

All this was quite in vain. In mid-January a big battle on the west coast which, among its toll, left only eight hundred Indian troops out of four thousand committed, pushed the front line back to within fifty miles of Singapore and brought the Japanese into Johore, the last state before the city. As soon as the news made its way down the mystical Chinese grapevine, which existed in both peace and in war, the Chinese traders in Singapore insisted on cash down from the *tuans*. This abrupt ending of a system of credit notes which gave the word 'chit' to the

English language and was one of the most fundamental obeisances to the white presence, was a kind of death-knell when sounded by a people so shrewd and intelligent.

In that same mid-January at least one liner sailed, half-empty, for Britain and could undoubtedly have saved many women and children from the prison camps, but each one of those who failed to fill it would have offered some convincing reason for remaining in Singapore.

The nurses felt they had to stay to cope not only with the wounded but with the normal flow of human calamities. Norah Chambers, who had begun the battle with that spectacular trek into the mountains, was kept in Singapore not only by the same attitude which held others but by the sickness of her father who was hospitalized with a serious liver complaint quite unconnected with the hostilities. Her problems were also increased through the illness of her husband, John, who developed typhus as a result of a rat-bite acquired on the trek. He was put in the same hospital as her father and, to the accompaniment of bombs, she spent her nights there, dividing her time between the two men. 'For what it was worth,' she recalled, 'I covered them with pillows when the planes came over. Most of the patients were put under their beds but my two were too ill to move.' John actually came very near to death but in spite of the extraordinary circumstances, the episode, for Norah, involved the conventional trials of nursing sick relatives. The whole family was now assembled in Singapore: her younger sister Ena, with her husband, Ken Murray, a businessman in the city, and her other sister Barbara, also married and with two young sons.

Because of the boys Barbara took the opportunity of a passage on a ship leaving for Australia and this faced Norah with the most awful choice of her life so far. Her daughter, Sally, had reached a state of anxiety that made her tremble every time she heard the noise of explosions, and it was clearly better that she should leave as well. Norah's feelings were those of all who remained. Should she let the little girl go while there was still hope that the situation might be saved? Was it wrong or sensible to split the family now before the most extreme circumstances prevailed? Would it not be worst of all to wait and discover that the decision had been made too late?

Sally sailed with her aunt, leaving her mother on the dockside: 'It was a terrible moment because I had to ask myself whether I would ever see her again.' At the end of January such dilemmas began to resolve themselves when a broadcast report of a speech by Winston Churchill to the House of Commons filtered through the smokescreen of censorship and jaunty propaganda. The speech was clearly intended to prepare the ground for resounding setbacks: 'We have had a great deal of bad news from the Far East and I think it highly probable . . . we shall have a great deal more.' Coming from such a source this sounded more ominous, in a curious way, than the bombs themselves. Within days the authorities made four troopships available and set up an apparatus for the evacuation of those 'useless mouths' who wished to go.

There now began a sequence of events much in keeping with the general muddle that had reigned ever since the invasion. The P & O steamship company was put in charge of this exercise and the continuing urge to decorum was implicit in the fact that 'bookings' had to be made at a time when it would have been more sensible simply to pack the ships with all the people they would hold.

The P & O office had been moved from the now deeply unhealthy centre of the city to a bungalow five miles out, which in better times had been the home of the company's chief in Singapore. A classic *tuan*'s place of residence, its immaculate lawns were rapidly ruined by the endless trek of potential passengers who, in truth, were by now fleeing refugees.

There were two tables in a large room inside, one for those who wished to go to Britain and one for those who preferred Colombo, but as apprehension grew as the notion of an escape took hold, the lines blended untidily and formed a monstrous queue which passed the doors and finally extended tragically into the distance beyond. Scenes took place which woefully amended the image of cool pride which had so long attended the European women.

In the road which led across the winding drive to the bungalow scores of cars were left, parked in fearful haste, some with their wheels half in the ditch. Police tried to unravel the line of women clutching or tugging at their tearful children and trying to edge into the shade of the trees to escape the pitiless sun without losing their place in the queue. There was a worse hazard. Periodically Japanese planes swept overhead, sending the mob scattering for the cover of the ditches before wearily emerging to wait again.

Despite the chaos, the long history of colonial bureaucracy exerted itself, giving rise to hysterical arguments about missing passports and papers, nationality and marital status, and, inevitably, money. In the authorities' absurd attempts to preserve the last shreds of white prestige, many people only discovered when it was too late that the Government had agreed to advance the fares of those who could not afford to pay their way home.

The painful dignity was preserved to the last. In an already burning dockland the women were obliged to queue again to pass through one small gate to the quayside where a lone P & O clerk sat at a tiny table with a pencil and a ledger, slowly inscribing in copper-plate every passenger's name. As the last of the ships finally sailed, the first of the retreating army began to cross the Johore Causeway on to Singapore Island and the city now became a place of even more contrasts and absurdities and countless human dramas.

Ruth Russell-Roberts, a beautiful former Hartnell mannequin, married to a Captain with the 5/11th Sikhs of the 22nd Indian Brigade, had steeled herself for the separation from her one-year-old daughter, Lynette, whom she left in the care of a friend on one of the ships. She now turned away to face another problem – whether or not her husband was dead. He had been involved in the heavy fighting the Brigade encountered in the battle for Johore, and at that moment with the 22nd cut to pieces, was hiding in the rubber across the Strait looking for his own escape route and wondering if Ruth had got away.

He crossed the water in a small boat and made his way to the Naval Base where his magnificent exertions, which had cost him even his boots and left him in his socks, were rewarded with a forty-eight-hour pass to visit the city. He was reunited with Ruth, and the pair at once restored a little of Singapore's former romantic Maughamesque chic. They proceeded precisely as if the Japanese had never come at all. First call, quite inevitably, was at Robinson's to cash a cheque and acquire some new clothes, not forgetting a few handkerchiefs, interspersed with hearty 'hellos' as chums passed by, just as they always had done at Robinson's. To a Chinese silk-merchant then, to buy sufficient material for two pairs of pyjamas since it was still possible to find an Indian tailor ready to make them up at the usual lightning speed. Lunch at the Cricket Club, to the Tanglin Club for a swim, and in the evening, of course, to Raffles where Dan Hopkins and his Band played dance music until midnight, just as if the Japanese Imperial Army were not already at the Causeway and poised for the final mortal thrust at the city.

It was to take the Japanese only two more weeks to accomplish the death-blow but, amid the death and destruction, it is possible to find fragments of gaiety and romance even at the last. Molly Ismail, re-encountering a dedicated suitor from Johore Bahru, an English planter who was now an officer in the Malay Volunteers and awaiting the Japanese onslaught in Singapore, assented to his proposal of marriage and they set off together in his car to buy the engagement ring. In Orchard Road an air-raid overtook this otherwise idyllic journey and they both ended up in a monsoon drain, the murmured endearments appropriate to such a time being totally drowned by an anti-aircraft gun barking furiously in an open space just behind them. That evening, with a hooped diamond safely on Molly's finger, they returned to Orchard Road and celebrated with smoked salmon and champagne at the Café Wein.

41

As a depressant to a healthy and happy conjoining of the sexes, the Japanese bombers seemed fairly ineffectual. Phyllis and Doris Liddelow, reunited with their father who had come down from Thailand because he was involved in Intelligence work for the Services, were supposed to be chaperoned by a gentleman they remember only vaguely as 'the Major' while Mr Liddelow was at work. Fresh from the constraints of a Catholic school and in a city rapidly falling to pieces, they took advantage of the Major's absences to pursue a friendship with two boys they had met and they jitter-bugged, not without difficulty, to records by the Andrews Sisters and Bing Crosby as the bombs were falling.

All over the city there were attempts of one kind or another to forget the encroaching disaster. Aimless and exhausted soldiers from shattered units wandered the streets, getting drunk whenever the opportunity presented itself. The cinemas did a roaring trade, drawing long queues until just before the Fall. But the Japanese were now lined up along the Johore shore and to the racket of the bombs on the island was added a new sound, the whine and crump of shells. Margot Turner had survived the peregrinations of the 17th Combined General Hospital which was now set up in the barracks at Changi in the north-east corner of the island overlooking the Straits. She had grown almost used to the bombing but coming under artillery fire was a new experience with even nastier overtones. The shells came in without even the mild preliminaries of an air-raid warning and the existence of the guns, lighting the night sky with their flashes, was a constant reminder of the close physical presence of the savage little Japanese soldiery.

The Japanese ignored the big Red Crosses on the hospital buildings and the patients screamed in dreadful cacophony at every near miss. On 6 February they were moved into Singapore but a small staff of sisters remained to clear up, including Margot and a New Zealand sister who was a friend of hers. That night the artillery zeroed-in, in a last burst of spite, and Margot and the New Zealander, freed of the necessity of seeming cool and imperturbable in front of patients, crawled under the billiards table in what had once been the Officers' Mess, taking with them a bottle of brandy from the medical stores. 'After a number of swigs,' Margot said, 'the barrage didn't seem nearly as terrifying.'

Two days later the Japanese hurdled the last barrier and landed on the north-west coast of the island. Singapore radio broadcast a short announcement of the event together with the assurance that they would be driven off, but Singapore was now showing its distress. For miles into the mainland jungle and across the shining waters of the South China Sea, vast palls of smoke were visible, the demolition of oil tanks and stores adding to the funeral plumes of the blazing warehouses down by the docks, which the bombers had hammered so unmercifully.

By 10 February the invaders had reached Bukit Timah, only five miles from the city, and now in its streets there were signs of a terminal rupture of the civilization which had made it for so long such a pleasant place to be. On 12 February Phyllis and Doris Liddelow added to their growing stock of experiences. Making their way towards the docks they sniffed a curious smell, not entirely unpleasant, which turned out to be the odour of large amounts of money burning. Despite a predictable run on the banks some five million Straits dollars were destroyed to prevent them falling into the hands of the Japanese. At some banks crates of notes were simply hauled into the gutter for cremation.

For a community which had always savoured its alcoholic intake – the very home of the famous, gin-laden, Singapore Sling – there was a reek which even more clearly presaged irreversible doom. Conscious of the Japanese orgy of rape and murder in Hong Kong, which had been fuelled not least by looted drink, the Governor himself ordered all large stocks of liquor in the city to be destroyed. The Customs officials set an example by denuding their bonded warehouses, and from the cellars of Robinson's there issued a tide of the juices that had comforted Maugham's lonely planters, turned District Commissioners morose and made the ladies of the colony sparkle even more than before. It took half a dozen men to destroy the thousands of bottles by the simple expedient of hurling them at a brick wall. The sheer volume of fumes was intoxicating and the delicate Mrs Brown, when she passed by the place with Shelagh, felt distinctly odd. Arriving home, now a room at Raffles Hotel, she was obliged to take a nap.

The Browns had taken refuge at Raffles because they had been driven from their home by a particularly fierce raid on the city. Shelagh remembered the arrival of the war at their private address with the kind of repugnance that an extremely houseproud lady might extend to the discovery of large, muddy footmarks on the Axminster carpet and over the chintz of the settee. On the morning after the raid she found shrapnel in her bed and, looking out of the window, was horrified to see huge craters in the garden.

A move was made to the bungalow of friends in, of all places, the Bukit Timah Road, which happened to be the enemy's principal line of advance so that she inadvertently found herself pretty much in the front-line. The rattle of small-arms fire over a rise made it plain that the interlopers intended to carry their impertinences even further, in fact were just up the road. 'I was much more infuriated than frightened,' said gentle Shelagh. 'I had the feeling for a moment of wanting to grab a gun and go charging off at them along the road.'

43

As the city shrank back towards the docks a number of women were left like lonely little islands amid the storm. 'Good God, a woman!' cried the officer in charge when Mamie Colley appeared just as he was setting the Bofors gun down on her lawn, promising, she remembered, to take care not to disturb her flower beds. Mamie's usefulness as a school-teacher had ended as early as 6 February for all practical purposes. She had kept her classes going right through the raids, reassuring the children to a degree where they were more frightened of the vicious soldier ants in the drains where they sheltered than of the bombs. One by one, though, they had left until only three remained, and on the 6th she felt she should write to Army HQ and ask if she should close down. Her husband was in the Army, and with that resignation which descends on Army wives regarding the inscrutable ways of the military, she wasn't as surprised or hurt as she might have been when HQ admitted they had forgotten all about her. With the school closed, Mamie felt she should stay on in Singapore in case she could be of value in some other way and she laid in stocks of food against a long siege. Very much a schoolmistress still, she was to question with wry amuse-ment, many years later at her home in the London suburb of Ham, the wisdom of her choice of emergency rations – pounds and pounds of a hastily chosen and extremely bitter cooking chocolate, intended as a secret source of energy if the going should get particularly tough. Against the possibility of a deliverance from the inferno, which would take her out of the hemisphere altogether, she packed a suitcase with woollies for chilly England. When the time eventually came for her to lift it, this proved almost impossible to get off the ground. Her other piece of luggage was a hat-box the contents of which she viewed even more ruefully when she opened it at what was to prove her real destination: Banka Island.

The nurses, inevitably, were in the gravest danger of being marooned as the throttling grip tightened on Singapore, being bound through that long tradition to remain with their patients. And this was nursing of an order rarely seen since Scutari. The 2/10th Australian General Hospi-tal had come all the way down from Malacca and was divided between a Chinese school, a guest-house and, as the wounded flood continued to pour in, one neighbouring house after another as their owners fled. The location was close to the Bukit Timah Road and at one point was almost entirely surrounded by Japanese infantry and the vicious little one-man tanks which looked like dustbins on wheels but were as dangerously persistent as hornets. An Australian nursing sister called Betty Jeffrey finished up in yet another part of the hospital, a series of six marquees set up on the lawn tennis courts of a big house. A vivid raconteur who was to produce an excellent book about her experiences when she finally reached home, even Betty was hard put to describe the overwhelming press of wounded. When beds ran out they lay everywhere: on stretchers on the floor of the house, on its verandahs, in its garage, eventually in grave-like trenches which the troops had dug.

The marquees suffered grievously from gunfire emanating, sometimes, from as little as two hundred yards away. Gaping holes appeared in the fabric and doctors and nurses, making their rounds with all the calm they could muster, reacted to the screeching passage of a shell by an instinctive bending of the knees as it passed overhead. When the rain came, in its tropical fervour, the tennis courts on which the marquees stood became a sea of mud and the beds sank by degrees until only their mattresses were above the surface. To compound this spectacle, such a caricature of the hygienic disciplines of hospital life that the nurses couldn't help but find it funny, there was a further addition to the conventional routines of nursing. During the fiercest storms of bombs and shot, tin hats were placed on the patients' heads and when these ran out, the rest were forced to sit beneath up-ended bed-pans.

Deliverance came for the Australian nurses via an order that was the ultimate blow to all they had learned of their profession. It was conveyed by the Matron, from higher authority, on 11 February: thirty specified sisters were to abandon their duties and leave in two groups for evacuation. It was a dreadful moment. Betty, who was in the first group, had been in the process of making a hot poultice for the hand of a man who was badly injured. There was only one tiny primus stove for heating water and she had finally got some to boiling point. 'I just said, "No, I can't go, I've gone to too much trouble doing this. I'll leave with the next lot."' The decision cost her three and half years of Japanese imprisonment. The first group made it all the way back to Australia.

The last days of Singapore were very near now. The oddities continued. In a city where the services – gas, water, electricity, drainage – were collapsing under the pounding, and the smoky air reeked of decaying bodies, burning buildings and high explosive, the *Straits Times* property column continued to advertise accommodation: 'To let with immediate entry, furnished bungalow, Chancery Lane' . . . 'Flat to Let, furniture for sale, incl. refrig. and crockery'. . . . This in a place where looting had inevitably broken out among a native population who had spent their lives pressing their noses to the window of white people's easeful lives.

But gaping wounds were appearing in the innermost fabric of this city which for so long had best expressed the supremacy of the *tuans*. The amazing Robinson's, temple of that primness in business matters which prevails in high-class stores, actually began to give their stock away. Mothers with children reduced to only what they stood up in were each given two complete outfits: one to wear, and one, immaculately wrapped, to take away.

Even Raffles Hotel had succumbed at last. Shelagh Brown, passing through the immortal ballroom at the end, saw its chic in tatters. It was full of drunken soldiers and the dance floor was a sea of empty beer bottles. 'A city dying', she said, still having to restrain disgust so many years later, 'is a revolting sight.'

Not even the lethally optimistic authorities of Singapore could any longer pretend that nothing much was changed. The last issue of the *Straits Times*, reduced now to a single sheet, still carried below its title an exhortation by the Governor: 'Singapore Must Stand; it SHALL Stand', and even in such a critical shortage of space it included a stern Governmental decree. 'A Warning', it was headed: 'People in the rural area refusing to accept currency notes issued by the Board of Commissioners of Currency, Malaya, are warned that action will be taken against them and that they are liable to severe penalties.'

There was in fact nobody in the rural areas, except the Japanese, capable of penalizing anyone, and the same applied to most of the city. Mercifully, but much, much too late the pretence was dropped and a general evacuation of women and children was ordered. The existence at last of a direct order freed a body of people, who had always prided themselves upon their discipline, from the many constraints which had held them for so long in a visibly doomed situation.

It was now a matter of duty to make for the docks and the last trek began. But for the nurses who had lived with such a torrent of wounds and death from the beginning, there was still an especial problem. Remaining in Singapore provided the *raison d'être* of their professional lives.

Phyllis Briggs, who had joined the battle so early with the arrival of poor Pongo Scarf at the Alor Star hospital on the first morning of the war, had barely rested since, except for the brief time it took a young Government engineer from Penang, now a soldier, to propose to her, and be accepted, when they met again in the wreckage of Singapore. The marriage, a trifle awkward to arrange in the circumstances, was to take place if both could ultimately make their way to Australia.

On 10 February, a Tuesday, Phyllis's Matron called the staff together to tell them that any sister who wished to leave could do so the following day because ships would be sailing on the Thursday. 'It would have been easier if we had been told that a number of volunteers were required to stay,' Phyllis later considered, in reviewing what was for so many a life or death decision. She 'wanted to do the right thing' and slept on the problem to announce the next day that she would leave later if there were more ships to go.

That day a shell passed right through the operating theatre, killing one of the doctors. Guns were set up in the hospital compound firing, with their ear-splitting roar, almost non-stop. The wounded continued to pour in so that a log-jam of suffering formed in the entrance and the stairs and hallway became sticky with blood. The following afternoon, tortured by doubts, Phyllis went to her rooms, collected two suitcases and got into the vehicle that was to take those sisters who were leaving to the docks.

Next came a crowded launch. There were three ships in the harbour, but at each of them the launch was turned away because they were already full. It began to return to the wharf. 'I was quite pleased,' Phyllis remembered. 'I felt so dreadful at having left the hospital.' But just as those in the launch were about to disembark the first ship signalled that she could take them all aboard. They came up the side of a vessel called the *Mata Hari*, a cargo boat with a scratch crew collected from sunken ships and accommodation for nine passengers. There were 320 souls aboard when she sailed, but just before she did so another launch appeared carrying Australian soldiers armed with tommy-guns with which they threatened the crew as they demanded a passage.

The officers produced revolvers and warned them off and the *Mata Hari* got under way across a known minefield, a journey of breath-holding fearfulness made even more unbearable by the fact that the buoy intended to mark the ending of the area of hazard could not be picked out, so that the skin-crawling continued without respite to the open sea. Phyllis stayed on deck, on top of a hatch, to avoid the hermetic press of bodies down below and she looked back at the city. It was dark now at sea, but the sky above Singapore was red with fire, the flames visibly leaping and stabbed repeatedly by bursts of shellfire. It was an inferno of the kind that Dante saw, and it was impossible not to feel a sense of escape. But it was not an auspicious day to begin a journey. It was now the early hours of Friday the Thirteenth.

Chapter 4

The evacuation fleet was given the dignity of an Admiral in charge, but it was the remnants of the presence of a great maritime nation in those seas, and Singapore Harbour, finally, was the ultimate focus of the whole, shattering defeat. To make for the harbour was to admit that all was lost in that beautiful colony and if it was a bitter place for the male population of Malaya, for the women it was a precipice.

The evacuation was intended primarily to save the women and children on the island, and to go, more often than not, meant a separation from the menfolk on whom the whole edifice had so long depended. Once aboard the ships the women were, often for the first time ever, truly alone and in charge of their own fate.

The rendings ran the whole gamut of relationships: wives separated from husbands, girlfriends from lovers, sisters from brothers, daughters from fathers, all possible permutations of a close-knit society driven wholesale to the edge of the sea. The same launch that carried Phyllis Briggs so unwillingly away from the life that she had known contained the young Liddelow sisters, and Phyllis Liddelow's recollections of the last of Singapore perfectly capture the panicky emptiness of letting go.

The girls' young brother, Colin, had joined them and their father and the night before their escape Mr Liddelow took them to stay at the Adelphi Hotel. 'In the lounge that evening the atmosphere was calm,' Phyllis remembered, 'as if everyone knew what was about to happen. I actually thought: "The calm before the storm". Couples sat with their heads together. Some of the women were weeping quietly with their husbands or their boyfriends stroking their hair. There were family groups like ourselves staying close. My father was wonderful. He told us that we were bound for Australia and that he gave the Japanese a year of occupation before we could return to beloved Mummy and home.'

The calm did not survive the following day when the family made their way on foot to the burning shambles of the quayside. The pavements were littered with wounded soldiers who had run out of the energy to struggle onwards to the sea and of any hands to help them on their way. Men, in the mass, did not invariably show the stoicism attributed to them in the chaos of those last hours before the Fall. At the quayside there was a tableau of fatigue and despair as 'the useless mouths' sat patient and dejected on their luggage as if portraying their dependency and helplessness.

At this moment of maximum requirement for reassurance and comfort a British soldier cracked into hysteria and, amid so many dreadful memories, Phyllis was always to hear his shrieking: 'It's too late! These women and children are doomed! The Japs aren't human – they're savages . . .' Two more soldiers dragged him away from the blank shock on the faces around him, but there were endless other auguries of total collapse for all to see. Further along the quay shiny new cars were pushed over the side with thunderous splashes, and employees of the Hong Kong and Shanghai Bank were still disposing doggedly of all the inviolate contents of those bastions of security, hefting them into the water in long, coffin-like crates.

The docks were within range of the Japanese artillery and salvoes fell from time to time among the wharves. During the afternoon twenty-seven bombers swept in from the west and the whole mass of humanity below them cowered, except for a long double line of Army nurses who remained standing, straight and calm in their tropical uniforms, disdaining even to look upwards as the shadow of death roared over them. A ghastly twilight had set in, the smoke-darkened sky riven with the unnatural red of fires and shell-bursts, before it became the turn of the Liddelows to move towards a boat.

The movement was galvanic when it came, and the classic cry went up, 'Women and children first', because not all the men stood aside as tradition suggested they should. The launch filled rapidly until only two places were left; the Liddelow girls wanted to wait for another boat but their father lifted them both aboard, promising to follow with Colin on the next. The launch moved off and an expanse of water opened between them. 'That was the darkest moment of our young lives,' Phyllis said. 'We knew somehow that we would never see Daddy and Colin again. We asked to be taken back and some men even begged on our behalf, but there was no turning back. When we went aboard the ship and looked back at Singapore it was impossible to grasp that such a short time before we had all been together. We sobbed ourselves to sleep.'

The partings in those last hours took many forms. Ruth Russell-Roberts and her husband Denis, that glamorous couple who had already demonstrated their chic amid disaster by so casually shopping and cocktail-sipping in the ruins of the city, went aboard the *Mata Hari* in reasonable comfort in the course of the afternoon of that same day. Ruth's passage had been arranged by Malaya Command and there was even a cabin for her on the little, thousand-ton P & O steamer now converted, rather half-heartedly, into a warship by the addition of a four-inch gun at her stern and a venerable machine-gun on her upper deck.

Denis helped to carry her luggage below as if she were leaving for an unimportant voyage rather than a journey into infinity, and before he caught the launch back to the quayside, to whatever fate awaited him there with the rest of the beaten army, they bade each other farewell with archetypal restraint. Denis Russell-Roberts has recorded their last exchange: 'The best I can hope for you is that you will become a prisoner of war,' Ruth said. 'And for you darling,' Denis replied. 'We must pray it will be Java and then Australia, eventually England.'

Elsewhere in the ship the anguish could not be subdued. As an army sergeant said goodbye to his wife and baby his wife became hysterical and threatened to jump overboard with the child if he went ashore. The sergeant was still locked in the horrible quandary when the ship's master, a memorable man called Captain Carston, found a sudden vacancy for a ship's clerk, pressed him into Naval service and rescued him from the choice of being either a deserter or the cause of suicide.

On all sides there were themes developing within the greater drama. Of the hundreds of passengers crammed into a vessel normally endowed with accommodation for only nine many would die, but others would emerge from the faceless throng of frightened refugees to reach a stature of the kind that only the crucible of the camps could bring about in ordinary lives. The dutiful Mamie Colley was aboard, having decided at last that there was nothing more she could do for the city of Singapore and having laid her monkey and her dog to rest in the last hours before her departure. There was a humble Presbyterian missionary lady called Margaret Dryburgh whom the camps were to turn into a kind of saint. There was a young Jewish woman called Zaida Short, travelling with her sister Hilda. Zaida was to become a considerable businesswoman after the war on foundations laid when her shrewdness and resource were put at the disposal of others during the imprisonment, as taxing an apprenticeship in the management of goods and cash as it is possible to imagine.

Nobody could see then how their lives would interweave in the future. Ruth Russell-Roberts, on the first day at sea, noticed a young Chinese girl not only for her lively face but for her immaculacy in her tight-fitting cheongsam after an appalling night on a deck smothered in the oily soot of burning Singapore. She was a nurse named Angela Kong Kum Kiew who was to become simply and affectionately 'Kong' to everybody in imprisonment and a friend of inestimable value to Ruth when friendship became beyond worth. Another nurse called Christine Bundy talked long during the voyage with Lieutenant Norman Cleveley of the Royal Signals, unaware that this was the first stage of courtship. They met again and married after the war.

In all the ships of the makeshift flotilla it was the same. There were forty-four vessels in the main evacuation fleet, of which only a handful were to survive either sinking or capture, but the women whose destinies were to be brought together in the Sumatran camps of this story were distributed mainly among four of them. These, besides the *Mata Hari*, were the *Vyner Brooke*, the *Giang Bee* and the *Kuala*. Later when individuals came to relate their experiences, the names of these ships took on a powerful significance because there was a particular type of misery attached to the ultimate fate of each.

The *Vyner Brooke* was a freighter made into a Naval vessel mostly by the addition of HMS to her name, since her armament was so scanty. She was invariably an interesting credential for several reasons, but not least because she took off the Australian Army nurses who were to be such a vivid element in the life of the camps. Betty Jeffrey, when she decided to leave the hospital on the Bukit Timah Road a day later than she should have done in order to be free, was driven through a savage air-raid into the city to stop at St Andrew's Cathedral. There all the Army sisters were assembled along the pews, some in their starched captals, some in tin hats, some in the round, boarding-school felts of the walking-out uniform.

Elizabeth Simons, that able observer, was among them and she wrote: 'We waited in the dim coolness, invaded here and there by the late afternoon sunshine which streamed through the windows. Within a few minutes an air-raid siren whined and the ack-ack gun mounted at the cathedral door stammered into action. . . . News of our going had spread and several men brought in letters for us to deliver when, or if, we reached Australia or some other peaceful point south. In our turn we sent messages to friends to whom we had been unable to say goodbye. These messages were probably never delivered and the letters certainly were not.'

The nurses were collected by ambulances which failed to penetrate the seething chaos round the docks so that the journey was completed on foot, amid the stench and heat, to a tug which, late in the day, threaded between the hulks and masts of sunken ships down the harbour to the *Vyner Brooke*. Two hundred and fifty souls were eventually packed into a ship equipped for twelve passengers. Mrs Brown and her daughter Shelagh were aboard, having cut themselves off from the vastly reassuring presence of Mr Brown to face the greatest challenge of their lives. So was Norah Chambers who had got her sick husband, John, away and was also accompanied by her sister Ena, their grievously ill father and their mother having decided to remain in Singapore. There was a cockney girl called Maudie James, the wife of a soldier still on the island, who was to make her own lively impact among so many uniformly rounded English vowel sounds.

The *Vyner Brooke* was treated to a final air-raid just before she sailed. As she did so the full mad palette of colours in which the city died was reflected in the harbour water with a Wagnerian addition of erupting sound. It was through all this turmoil that Norah Chambers heard quietly, in those first dejected moments when the ship got under way, the familiar and comforting lilt of the ebullient Aussie anthem, 'Waltzing Matilda'. It was the Australian nursing sisters refusing to be utterly vanquished.

'What a cheery bunch they were!' Norah was to exclaim, many years later. It is also true that of all the women who were so brusquely thrown on their own devices by the utter collapse of all they had previously known, only the nurses were completely sanctified in behaving at once with independence and practicality and showing all the other brave qualities normally thought to be found exclusively in men in times of great adversity.

The nurses, under the dynamic Matron Paschke who was their senior officer, took charge of what food there was on board, organizing matters so that everyone got at least something to eat, including the ship's officers and crew. This last was a supreme piece of thoughtfulness. The idea that the male species were generally impervious to such fallibilities as doubt and fear and inadequacy had been severely tested by the unmitigated disasters of the past three months, but it would still have been possible to believe that ships' officers, at least, remained steadfast and required no succour from anybody, even in the matter of a bite to eat.

In fact, the plight of those manning the ships was very much the same as that of the passengers. They were caught up in the rout every bit as much as the women, both genders being thrown in this extremis literally into the same boat. It is interesting that they clung to their time-honoured postures towards each other to the very end.

An officer on the *Vyner Brooke*, a seasoned and humorous mariner called A. J. Mann, who left an enthralling account of his view of the flight from Singapore, was a perfect masculine stereotype. When the Australian nurses came aboard he offered his cabin to two of them on the grounds that he wouldn't be spending much time in it during the taxing passage ahead. He left them there with their luggage, seemingly very content, but when he went back later both nurses and suitcases had gone. He assumed that Matron had 'rounded them up' and was prepared to concede that this was because she didn't want the officers to be inconvenienced. 'If it was the other reason,' he concludes primly, 'she need not have bothered as it was not an occasion to think of such things.' On the other hand, later on in the embarkation he was leaning on the guard-rail of the after well-deck, smoking his pipe and wondering how far the ship would actually get with the tide of humanity that was tumbling aboard when he was approached by 'a very lovely-looking Eurasian girl'. She confessed her plight over a sleeping place in such a packed vessel and, according to Lieutenant Mann, actually uttered the age-old cry of feminine helplessness: 'I don't know what I shall do!' The Lieutenant rose gallantly to the occasion: 'I said, "Well, I have a cabin which you can make use of. I shall be on the bridge most of this trip, I anticipate, and also at a time like this one must make the best of things." '

Over 'a glass or two of "Dimple" Scotch' in the cabin he learned a little of his guest's history. Her boyfriend had been an RNVR Lieutenant, killed when his ship hit a mine off the coast of Malaya. 'Her name was Marie, I think, and she was very attractive in an Eastern way. I estimated that she was half Portuguese and half Malay but whatever it was the result was very pleasing.'

Mann was at the beginning of a journey in which he would show astounding courage, endurance and skill in getting all the way to Batavia on various kinds of floating materials, a true mariner's saga, but the episode of Marie occupied much of his narrative. When the ship got under way there was a rare moment of calm in her dreadful last voyage and he did go back to his cabin: 'There on the top bunk was Marie, peacefully asleep. She had kept her frock on and it had worked up a little, showing an expanse of smooth skin the colour of old ivory. . . .'

It is a vulnerable image and in fact the women were sailing towards a crescendo of jeopardy. Having endured the fury of twentieth-century war until the very breath of the enemy infantry could almost have been felt on their faces they were now approaching the greatest hazard yet. In addition to the prowling bombers, hungrily devouring more of the sky, since Singapore had been ingested, a Japanese fleet lay squarely across the escape route to the south. In the narrow waters of the Banka Strait two heavy cruisers, an aircraft carrier and three destroyers, under Admiral Ozawa of the Imperial Japanese Navy, were disposed to support the next move in the construction of the Greater Eastern Co-Prosperity Sphere.

As if ticking off items on a shopping list, Tokyo had scheduled for 14 February 1942 the invasion of the very lands that seemed to offer safety to the refugees from Singapore – Sumatra and the other islands of the Dutch East Indies. As a by-product to this there was one last tragic blunder to add to the mountainous stupidities surrounding the loss of Malaya. Admiral Ozawa's ships had been located by the Dutch at almost precisely the moment the evacuation fleet was setting out and frantic coded messages were tapped to the last remaining radio receiving station in Singapore. They were met with total perplexity. As a kind of swan-song for the tidy-minded bureaucracy of a notably well-conducted colony, the official in charge of the code-books had made his exit, dutifully taking them with him. Even the escape fleet, it was to turn out, had sailed the wrong way.

The *Vyner Brooke* steamed on behind, the pathetic pop-gun mounted on her forecastle, but at about two o'clock on the afternoon of the 14th six Japanese bombers found her in the Strait and proceeded to bomb her with measured ferocity. Twenty-six bombs missed as she twisted and turned like a frantic animal, but the twenty-seventh smashed through the forward hatch, exploded inside and blew a hole in her keel. Lieutenant Mann's recollection of the hit is a sailor's swift and clinical reckoning of damage sustained, but in all the accounts of the loss of the ship there is a curious matter-of-factness. Perhaps the moment was so shocking and terrifying that it could only be retained in the memory if preserved in neat and undramatic sequence.

The ship began to list and settle almost at once. In a further pass by the bombers a series of near-misses blew the bottom out of the lifeboats on the port side, but in the jam-packed 'tween-decks there actually was no panic. At the order to abandon ship, Norah Chambers remembered, everybody just went quietly up on deck. A girl in front of Norah had a wound in her back. 'I could see the poor lass was very badly hit,' Norah said, 'and I mentioned this to her. She simply said, "Oh, am I?" ' It was much as if a fellow-passenger had been calling polite attention to a slipping petticoat. The girl reached the deck but a few minutes later died.

The planes came back for a final spiteful peppering of machine-gun fire, and in the end only three lifeboats reached the water in serviceable condition. The way to the sea was by rope ladders, or merely ropes, and Mrs Brown, who had been proscribed from vigorous activity for so long in Singapore, made this exacting descent without great difficulty in her life-jacket and floated gently away. Her daughter Shelagh, essaying a rope, did not manage half as well and, falling into the water, followed a blind instinct to get away from the sinking ship as fast as she could.

The paths of the pair might have separated for ever at that moment except that a sailor who had helped them with their life-jackets the previous evening told Shelagh, 'Your mother's over there and she's calling for you.' 'It was absolutely thanks to him that we got together again,' Shelagh said. She could have been speaking gratefully of some thoughtful host who had engineered a valuable reunion. 'I joined mother and it was just like meeting a friend in Piccadilly Circus. Quite extraordinary!'

The Australian nurses handled the event as if shipwreck procedure had always been a part of their training. They helped the old and the hurt into the water and when their own turn came to go they found Matron Paschke effortlessly in charge. She supervised their departure much in the manner of the leader of a hike that was becoming a bit untidy. 'We'll all meet on the shore girls,' Betty Jeffrey remembers her telling the sisters, 'and get teed up again!'

In fact, Matron Paschke couldn't swim a stroke and there was a very strong chance that none of them would see either the shore or each other ever again. Betty made the same mistake as a number of survivors in sliding down a rope too quickly and lost most of the skin off her hands in transit. But oddly, of those who escaped death or wounds in the initial attack, one of the most difficult experiences of the sinking overtook someone struggling to get back on to the ship.

This was an American called Eric Germann who had been helping to fight a fire in Singapore docks immediately before joining the *Vyner Brooke* and, as a result, came aboard wearing a pair of high leather boots and a fireman's helmet. In the continuing story of Eric Germann the fact that he was dressed as a fireman for a voyage in the South China Sea grows less odd with the discovery of what later befell him, but even at this early stage his history was fairly singular.

He had helped to lower a lifeboat and had scrambled into it to continue with its management when it filled instantly with water, having been holed in the air attack. He watched women lowering themselves into the water and bobbing immediately away in the current and decided to go back on board to help to get some life-rafts afloat. He was an excellent swimmer, having once been a lifeguard in America, but in the few strokes necessary to reach a rope-ladder his boots dragged him under; when he got there he hooked a leg over the lowest rung and began unlacing them beneath the water.

In this position, with his face under water as he struggled, he found that descending women, many still wearing high-heeled shoes, were using his head as a stepping stone to reach the sea. Worse was to follow. Free of his boots, Germann began to ascend the ladder and was instantly cursed by women coming down in language which, he later recounted with some admiration, was 'just as fluent as any man's'. The cause of their aggravation remained a source of wonderment to him that lasted into the hell of a Japanese camp. They were shrieking at him for apparently climbing the wrong way up the ladder in order to look up their skirts! It was a response that can be taken as clearly marking the dividing line between one way of life and another for the women because, once imprisoned, modesty was one of the very first casualties of their new existence.

Eric Germann reached the deck speechless with astonishment and indignation and was promptly endowed with a four-year-old boy by a passing passenger. This was Mischa Warmen, the son of a White Russian couple from Shanghai and victim of the only recorded case of panic aboard the ship. When the bombs started falling his father jumped overboard in terror and at once began to drown because he couldn't swim. His wife screamed for assistance and a British soldier jumped in after him, but when the soldier reached the frantic man he was locked in a strangling embrace. Both disappeared and Mischa's mother collapsed on the deck, abandoning the little boy to his fate until Germann's appearance.

Mischa behaved very well. Told that he was going for a swim he calmly put both arms round his rescuer's neck as they jumped from the ship's side, and when they surfaced together he chuckled delightedly. Germann found a lifeboat for him and put him inside before he went off to help others. The cool water of the Strait, in fact, was at first fairly welcome after the din and heat and tension of the bombing and sinking. Elizabeth Simons, who could be relied upon to record exactly how things looked, or felt or smelt, remembered that the nurses held a sort of mass meeting in the water, rather as if they were a group of high-spirited girls sneaking an afternoon swim at Bondi. 'At first it was really pleasant, quite a "lark" in fact to be swimming in the cool water. We had not bathed for some time and even a perfunctory wash had been impossible on the ship, so the clean coolness of the tropical sea on a beautiful afternoon was more of a delight than a hardship to most of us.'

The *Vyner Brooke* took about twenty minutes to sink, the approximate time of her disappearance traceable by the number of watches which stopped at around twenty minutes to three when they had their first encounter with seawater. Mavis Hannah, who was to remain a classic Aussie, sharp, wry, dry, practical and unquenchably determined, could still display her watch, hopelessly seized up at that hour, as it was throughout her life in the camps, together with a surprising number of other items that were immersed that day in the Banka Strait: a pair of scissors, some buttons, her pay-book, some safety-pins attached to a little bag and dramatically rusty to underline their provenance. An inventory of her possessions at the time included morphia, a syringe, two dollars, lipstick and a handkerchief and a powder compact. She still had the mirror from the compact, since it too accompanied her all through the internment, although she said she never looked in it once during her time in camp because she felt that imprisonment had made her look so ugly.

Mavis also possessed a piece of her uniform stained with oil, because the refreshing water of the Strait was quickly marred by the *Vyner Brooke*'s life-blood, welling from her tanks as she settled and to become a ghastly, stinking element which all the swimmers remembered. The sea – a ten-mile stretch of it lay between the survivors and the nearest land, and all of it riven by vicious currents – quickly lost its first charm. As the afternoon drew into evening and then into night and those who had not drowned floated on, the choppy waters caused life-jackets to chafe the chin and neck into intolerable discomfort. Norah Chambers and others found themselves, after a time, surrounded by long, octopus-like tentacles which proved to be their own skin unravelling in strips from hands damaged by the burning friction of the ship's escape-ropes.

The nurses continued to minister whenever they could as if no amount of hardship could quell the instinct. Elizabeth Simons and two other nursing sisters had joined a raft which also contained a British sailor, hideously burned. The sailor was practically naked and the hot sun was increasing his agony so Elizabeth took off her dress and wrapped it round him for protection, while another of the sisters miraculously produced a needle and some morphia from an emergency kit in her pocket and performed an injection as the raft lurched and bobbed. Towards dusk three civilian women drifted across to join the company. One, unconscious, drifted away but the other two proved to be a mother and daughter. In another strangely urbane encounter Mrs Brown and Shelagh had struck up an acquaintance with some new people while strolling with the current in the Banka Strait.

There was something of the same social air to another meeting which took place at around the same time in those busy waters. The *Mata Hari*, once clear of the terrifying minefield and into the open sea, hove to in the small hours of the morning of the 14th to pick up six survivors from the water, and one of them turned out to be a friend of Phyllis Briggs. He was a young RNVR man and, a painful reminder of far better days, had been one of her badminton partners in those carefree times in Penang. The newcomers had a chilling piece of information to offer: their vessel had been sunk by a Japanese destroyer. Alerted to the menace ahead of him for the first time, Captain Carston gave up his intention of making straight for Java and decided to dodge between the islands on the way south, hiding during the day and sailing by night.

On that first night at sea the Liddelow sisters also dwelt on what lay behind them before the world had turned dangerous and crazy. Thinking of the separation from their father and their brother they sank into an utter slough of misery which only endless weeping could express. 'Do you know,' Phyllis said, smiling as people sometimes do when they recall, much later on, some total surrender to despair, 'I think we shed all the tears we had that night. In the next three and a half years neither of us ever cried again.'

When daylight came Captain Carston anchored in the shelter of a small island, which gave his little ship some chance of blending with the landscape, but a flight of bombers spotted her and pulverized the sea around her so thoroughly that Phyllis, with her propensity for detached observation, was able to examine her feelings about imminent death. 'A lot of people began praying loudly,' she said, 'but I remember thinking fairly calmly, "Well, this is it." It's surprising that when you feel your last moment has arrived you fall to wondering how exactly it's going to happen. I didn't think of being blown to pieces, but in such a crowded ship I felt we might be trampled to death and drowning, of course, seemed a very likely end.'

The Japanese caused a sufficient turmoil around the ship evidently to satisfy themselves that she had sunk somewhere in the maelstrom and then flew off. In fact, she had only one casualty and Captain Carston had time during the rest of the daylight hours to deal with what must have seemed to him a delicate problem – the existence of only three European-style WCs aboard, normally for the use of the officers. He made the command decision that all the European closets and also a proportion of the Asiatic squatting models should be reserved exclusively for the women, which was to prove the last discriminatory gallantry of that kind that they were to encounter for years.

With this matter, at least, satisfactorily resolved, the *Mata Hari* steamed on, playing hide and seek among the islands, and the Liddelows, after their initial paroxysm of despair, were treated to just a little of the gaiety that teenagers are entitled to in any normal world. A sing-song developed, as a form of release after that miraculous escape from the bombs, with the songs, accompanied by several mouth-organs, taking on a defiantly patriotic air – 'Rule Britannia' and 'There'll Always Be An England', repeated over and over. In lighter vein there was the 'Beer Barrel Polka' and 'Ferry Boat Serenade'.

Once again the Liddelows, unescorted, discovered their ability to attract young males. Card games came after the sing-song, followed by a long session of Monopoly, on a board that someone must have considered vital when snatching up their possessions. It was the twenty-first birthday of one of the young men and he dressed up in a tail-coat that someone else had found himself unable to abandon, and provided some hilarious tomfoolery. Later there was a story that he had rounded off his day by consuming a bottle of Lea and Perrins sauce and passing out on the deck.

It all had the semblance of a party and was the last the Liddelows would see of their conventional adolescence. The following night, in a strange, dreamlike sequence in the darkness, the *Mata Hari* fell squarely among the Japanese fleet. It was appalling mischance. Shadowy warships pinioned her in their searchlights, but merely held her, broodingly, without opening fire.

Up on the bridge Captain Carston had a decision to make that rested squarely on the difference between the sexes and could perhaps only have arisen in circumstances as unique as the fall of Singapore. Carston was the captain of a naval vessel confronted by the enemy and his course of action in normal circumstances was clearly laid down. Here there was a fresh factor to consider. Denis Russell-Roberts, an officer steeped in the time-honoured attitudes of the Services, presented Carston's case when the surrender of his ship seemed imminent.

'Training and tradition,' he wrote, 'were calling upon him to uphold the honour of the service in which he served. They were demanding that, at the very least, he should deny the enemy a prize-of-war. Ambition was telling him that this was the only opportunity he would ever be given of realizing his aspirations, of proving himself worthy to command a King's ship. The testing time had come; but could anything vindicate the exposure of women and children to the horrors of a naval engagement? Did the lives of these innocent non-combatants count for less than tradition and honour? They had been committed to his care and he was conscious of the faith and trust which they had placed in him.'

What the Captain had no way of knowing at that time was that his apparently childlike charges, infinitely dependent and trusting towards his masculine omnipotence, were actually of a toughness and resilience that would in great part survive an ordeal by comparison with which a naval engagement might well have been more acceptable. In this moment, however, the most likely resolution to an impasse growing more eerie as the minutes passed seemed to be a sudden torrent of shells which would blow his ship from the water and Carston was desperately anxious to convey to the Japanese that she was filled with helpless souls.

Among the scratch crew it was Lieutenant Cleveley of the Royal Signals who was set to sending a message to that effect in Morse, but when no reply came from the threatening night the women on deck were asked to stand up in the searchlights' glare, a living frieze to indicate innocence of any warlike intent. Still nothing happened. The searchlights snapped off and in the sudden blackness the *Mata Hari* stole away.

For two hours more she sailed, daring to believe that she was safe, but then, out of nowhere, another beam stabbed her and a signal lamp curtly ordered her to stop or take the consequences. Captain Carston, having held his private battle with his fighting instincts, now surrendered his ship. It was Sunday, 15 February and on that day, too, Singapore finally fell.

A destroyer materialized alongside and a Japanese boarding party came over the *Mata Hari*'s bulwarks, the nagging, faceless menace of the savage enemy at last a tangible reality. Phyllis Briggs recalled: 'For a few moments there was complete silence but there was no panic. I remember feeling icy cold in spite of the heat on deck.' Captain Carston, his uniform jacket immaculate despite the rigours of the voyage, met the Japanese officer with a smart salute and the necessary exchanges were conducted in chivalrous fashion. The *Mata Hari* had become a prize-of-war. Her White Ensign was struck and the Rising Sun sent to her masthead. The first of the captives were in the bag.

For the survivors of the *Vyner Brooke*, still struggling in the Strait, such a fate was beginning to take on the aspect of a merciful deliverance. All notion of the immersion in the cool water as a 'lark' had long since left Elizabeth Simons as she clung, now numb with cold, to the raft which Mrs Brown and Shelagh had joined and which, in addition, was supporting an invaluable English sailor called Stan. Stan scanned the horizon regularly, an ingrained Naval habit, and before darkness fell he discerned some dark hulls in the distance. This decreased the loneliness at least, although it was of no immediate practical help.

The night brought great and small tragedies. The burned sailor lost his grip and drifted away to an unknown end. Elizabeth slipped her spectacles into the pocket of Stan's shorts for safekeeping and, in all that followed, they slipped out again, leaving her with an abiding hardship. But buried in the blackness there was a colossal new hazard. In their unwelcome intimacy with the water, those on the raft first felt the shuddering vibrations of a ship's propellers before a vast dark outline took shape in the gloom. In such a plight it was natural to hope that succour was at last on hand and Stan immediately shouted, 'Help! British women!', perhaps the last time that anyone could assume this to be an automatic passport to proper treatment and respect from whomsoever heard the call.

In fact, and significantly, there was no response. Smaller shapes began detaching themselves from the main one, as though the sinister mass were giving birth, and these proved, as they came close, to be landing craft crammed with armed men. Astoundingly, the raft and its cargo had got themselves mixed up in the Japanese seaborne invasion of Sumatra.

Elsewhere among what proved to be the invasion fleet, Betty Jeffrey had attached herself to another raft packed with civilian women and Australian nurses, among them the doughty Matron Paschke, jubilant at her success in staying afloat. At first two Malay sailors plied the makeshift oars, but they made a very poor job of it and the Aussies briskly reorganized matters so that four of their number took it in turns to row. Another sister spent the night hours cuddling two small children who were aboard, a Chinese boy of four and an English girl about three years old. They were sufficiently comforted to sleep, except that once the little girl awoke and said in a tiny voice, 'Auntie, I want to go upstairs.' This turned out to be a nursery euphemism for peeing, but so strong had been the discipline of some now-distant *amah* or *ayah* in peaceful Malaya that the child, even saturated in seawater, would not relieve herself until her pants had been removed.

This infinitely vulnerable parcel of humanity came so close to the invasion craft that those clinging to the sides of the raft had to push against the boats' sides with their feet. At one point, engines idling before the start, Japanese soldiers looked down at them and spoke a few words in their native tongue, but then the landing craft came together in a fan-shaped formation and sped away towards the beach.

The souls in the water were literally flotsam amid this greater enterprise, their proliferating miseries of interest only to themselves. Shelagh Brown, with the habit of caring for her mother long set, found that a big clump of seaweed would act as a kind of blanket against the chill. When Mrs Brown's shoulder-bag persistently added to her difficulties by wrapping itself round her neck, Shelagh removed it and tied it to the raft, as a result of which Mrs Brown, too, was subsequently deprived of her specs.

Mrs Brown, however, was already showing all of the qualities that underlay the reputation of the women of the Empire. Before the advent of the raft she had supported an injured woman in the water for hours, and now she was called upon to effect what, in the circumstances, was nothing less than a major physical feat. For hours more the landing craft plied to and fro between the transports lying off shore and the beach, ferrying men and supplies to the point of landing and resolutely ignoring the human detritus in their path. The danger of being run down and shredded by their propellers was acute.

Daylight came, emphasizing even further the eerie sensation of being, if not invisible, then without the slightest importance, but at last a barge responded to the weak pantomime of signals from the raft and even altered course to come alongside. One of the crew leaned over to drag the women aboard as roughly and unceremoniously as if they were fish. Utterly spent, even the nurses found this transition almost unmanageable, and when it came to the turn of Mrs Brown her unusual weight, compounded by a cumbersome lifebelt, made her journey from the lurching raft a mountainous task. Shelagh, acutely aware of what it would cost her mother to make such a prodigious effort, experienced a moment of terrible anxiety as it crossed her mind that the Japanese sailor, in a climate of such slender concern, might consider the job altogether too taxing and simply throw her back. But applying fresh reserves of determination, Mrs Brown insisted more or less by moral force on rejecting such an indignity and finally gained the well of the boat to crumple, like the others, in an exhausted, soaking heap. Even less sure of a welcome than the women, Stan and one of the Malay sailors remained with the raft and tied it to the stern of the barge.

On board, Shelagh, weakened still further by relief, found the unimaginable luxury of a hot pipe leading from the engine and was sufficiently frozen to be able to sit on it, but as the glorious warmth was restoring her yet another hazard manifested itself. One of the officers on board the barge was wearing a sword in the Japanese martial manner, somewhat ludicrously since a Japanese sword was always to seem much bigger than its wearer, although without losing any of its menace. After a moment of reflection the officer abruptly drew the weapon from its scabbard.

At that time and in that place there could scarcely have been a gesture which more comprehensively expressed the appalling danger into which the women had fallen. A naked sword belongs so wholly to a kind of race memory of ancient barbarity that, even in a museum or in ceremonial use, it retains its savage aura. In the hands of a being as incomprehensible and unpredictable as a Japanese warrior it perfectly conveyed to the women their captors' power over life and death.

It was a moment of such intense strangeness and loneliness, out there on the water, that Shelagh's thoughts were wistful rather than fearful. 'I had time to think,' she said, 'that if I was to die I would so much sooner do it warm and dry on the beach.' Then the long, razor-sharp blade rose and fell in the sun and the officer neatly removed the top of a coconut which he filled with water and offered to the group.

It was a fair introduction to the consistently indecipherable temperament of the Japanese, an endlessly volatile mixture of normality, even small kindness on occasion, and fury and illogicality. In the years to come the women were to become used to the existence of this polarity, without ever coming to understand it very much better, and as an unstated threat to add to the more obviously apparent sources of fear and insecurity it retained its effectiveness to the end.

Indeed the final confrontation with this mysterious enemy which lay at the completion of the various journeys from Singapore was almost as potent a source of alarm as the journeys themselves, each of which had its own unpalatable character. The *Giang Bee*, formerly a Chinese-owned coastal steamer, converted as indifferently as the others to naval use and just as hopelessly overcrowded with an eventual total of about 290 passengers, had a terrible passage. She had only four lifeboats, capable of holding thirty-two passengers each, and her captain initially declined to take any women and children at all with such slender provision against so many frightful possibilities.

He was ordered to embark them by the naval authorities, weighing one kind of danger against another, and the *Giang Bee* set off south into the narrow waters that had already earned the nickname Bomb Alley. She was caught, inevitably, by the planes on her first day at sea, and in a pathetic gesture towards safeguarding those aboard her from the rain of high-explosive, the passengers were ordered to lie face down on the deck. Molly Ismail and her mother, who were among them, had been talking to two young Dutch boys just before the attack developed and now Molly lay with her mother on one side of her and the boys on the other. The obscene din of the bombing followed, spiked by screams and prayers as hits were registered on the little ship. When it was over Molly turned to the boys at her side and found that the heads of both had been severed.

Molly herself was bleeding from a shrapnel fragment in her head, but all this was to be only the beginning of the *Giang Bee*'s torment. As she limped on three Japanese destroyers raced over the horizon towards her spitting a stream of messages in Morse code which were completely unintelligible to her hard-pressed captain. In his dilemma he stopped and struck his ensign, the recognized signal for the surrender of a warship, and to make it even plainer that the vessel in no way merited the angry attention of three destroyers snapping at her like wolves, he too put the women and children on view on his decks.

For a moment it seemed that the nightmare of incomprehension had ended because one of the destroyers stopped and put a launch in the water, but when the boat was within one hundred and fifty yards of the *Giang Bee* a Dutch aircraft appeared and, in the storm of fire that was aimed at this interloper, the launch turned back. The destroyers now lay silent with their guns visibly trained on their quarry and once again a long, eerie wait began. Darkness fell and the *Giang Bee* was picked out with searchlights, and when the strain of keeping women and children for so long beneath the threat of gunfire grew intolerable her captain ordered his four boats to be lowered.

The boats would clearly have to be packed far beyond their capacity, but now some further effects of the bombing came to light. The first boat reached the water and was carried away into the darkness astern on the strongly flowing tide, but almost at once there were screams and cries that she was foundering. Splinters had riven her planking so severely that she had no chance of surviving. More horrifying still, the glare of a searchlight caught the very moment when another boat, hanging outwards from the davits in the process of being lowered, suddenly plunged pell-mell into the water, spilling its occupants like chaff.

Molly and her mother were waiting their turn to enter that boat, and it was a moment so ghastly that Molly could not recall ever previously having spoken about the incident to anybody else. The pair found places in one of the two boats that survived and continued their journey towards imprisonment, but the misery of the *Giang Bee* was not yet over. About a hundred passengers were still on board and in a final, desperate effort to communicate with the silent, implacable enemy, the ship's tiny harbour dinghy was dangerously committed to a turbulent sea with the object of rowing to the nearest destroyer and pleading the case of the helpless.

It took two hours for four men to row to the nearest warship, held all the time in the searchlights' glare, but when they were almost within touching distance the destroyer abruptly danced away. Time after time this astounding game was repeated, inexplicably cruel and cruelly inexplicable, until suddenly one of the destroyers loosed six rounds into the *Giang Bee*. She glowed red from stem to stern and sank within minutes with all who were in her.

Two hundred died from this one ship, a dreadful augury of the ways of this unique enemy for those who were approaching an enforcedly close relationship with him.

Chapter 5

The arrival of the women on the beaches of Banka Island was an extraordinary event, a total reversal of the normal process of war. The enemy on the shore were not called upon to deal with a rampaging assault from the sea, but with a bedraggled, helpless influx who actually regarded the sands as safety, or at least a respite from the dangers of the Strait.

Those who struggled in the water could not remember considering the sort of reception they might receive on landing because the last lap itself was so consumingly difficult to achieve. One of the first groups to reach the shore, either by swimming or in a leaking lifeboat from the *Vyner Brooke*, consisted of some servicemen, some civilian women and twenty-two of the Australian nursing sisters. A number of the group were wounded.

It was the existence of the wounded which reinforced an instinct, natural even in these circumstances, to seek out some kind of authority even if it were, as seemed most likely, the dreaded enemy. After a day and a night on the beach it was decided that a naval officer in the party would most suitably represent the group and he set off on foot for Muntok to contact the Japanese. The feeling was that the Japanese would respond with at least some compassion to a combination of female non-combatants and wounded, and presently the civilian women set off too, intending to meet their captors half way. The sisters were left to follow with the wounded on makeshift stretchers. The nurses were sufficiently naïve, as it was to prove, to fashion a rough Red Cross flag.

The naval officer eventually returned with a Japanese officer and ten soldiers, and all those on the beach were ordered to form two lines, the men in one and the nurses in the other. There was no sign of heat or anger among the Japanese beyond the fierce, staccato bark which was the standard military mode of speech. Nevertheless, the men were immediately marched away around a small headland and bayoneted or shot, and when the Japanese returned, wiping the blades of their bayonets on rags, the nurses were ordered to walk into the sea and were machine-gunned from behind. The wounded, too, were despatched where they lay. This massacre was only to come to light later on so that the droves of survivors still making their way towards the island did so in continuing belief that it was at least some kind of sanctuary.

The group who had hitched a lift in a Japanese invasion barge were set down in the middle of a working party on the beach and, at first, aroused little interest among the soldiers. Shelagh Brown best remembered from these first moments the relief of lying at last on warm sand. Presently the soldiers gathered around to look dispassionately and briefly at these strange remnants on the shore before resuming their work, but to gaze back at them was to meet a sight as barbaric as any in the womens' worst imaginings of this savage enemy.

All were naked except for the white loincloth which was the customary undergarment of the soldiery, and their glistening olive bodies were slung about with rifles, bayonets and knives. We now know that they were quite as fierce as they appeared. They were part of the astonishingly small force, some thirteen divisions, which accomplished most of the initial conquest of the Orient on behalf of the Emperor. The same front-line troops who had been blooded first in the invasion of China were shipped on to assail the European enclaves one after the other so that they were to become professional fighters of the highest order. At the same time they were almost certainly experiencing that diminution in the capacity for humanity and emotion which seems to arise from long exposure to war.

It is hard to think of a more daunting species for the women to have encountered, and it is still difficult to assimilate that, for all their martial excellence, this was primarily a peasant army, drawn from the masses of Japan rather than some race of supermen. Mrs Brown evidently had no difficulty in divining that this was so. Her troublesome bag, vital in that it contained all her money and valuables, remained on the raft where Shelagh had tied it, and was now floating in the shallow water at the stern of the barge. Responding to a lifetime's habit, she attracted the attention of the most readily available Asiatic, a Japanese soldier in this case, and indicated that she would like it fetched. The Asiatic trotted away, as obediently as ever, released the bag with a slash of his knife and brought it back. Now, however, he opened it, examined the contents, then put it under his arm and walked off down the beach: a clear indication of the New Order in Asia. It was in this way that Mrs Brown's spectacles disappeared, together with other valuables she would sorely miss.

There were more desperate matters in the offing. More near-naked

Japanese appeared, this time distinguishable by their swords as officers, and there was a fresh outbreak of the snarling and snapping in which they conducted their verbal exchanges. The discussion was with the crew of the barge, and it can now be assumed that it was on a matter of life or death. Those on the beach seemed to be arguing for the quick despatch of what were now authentically useless mouths. The Japs on the boat, apparently pursuing the same quixotic impulse which had made them pause for a rescue in the first place, were opposed to the motion and their opinion finally prevailed. It was a crucial resolution, because once the decision was made it seemed to be acknowledged that the women were somehow in a different category from the ordinary, disposable run of captives. The two men, Stan and the Malay sailor whom Shelagh thought was called Johnnie, were separated from the females and they were set to work, a solution that was soon to be seen as an accepted remedy for the nuisance of male prisoners. A Japanese also approached Elizabeth Simons, whose hair had been cropped in Malaya and was now sealed even closer to her head by sea-water, and peered down the front of her slip as though to be sure there would be no mistakes in gender. The women were at last provided with some succour. They were given coconut milk to drink and when, to compound an astounding day, a flight of Allied planes attacked the bridgehead they were hustled into the scrub which edged the beach. After the raid, which added what could be seen as friendly bombs to the tonnage of high explosive so liberally strewn on them for so many weeks, some food was provided: a handful of dirty rice, some tinned meat and a tin of milk. But after the long swim, the women's mouths were too sore even for the liquid.

The only real comforts were warmth – although at the height of the day the heat was near-intolerable – and the possibility of rest after so much torment. It was not for long. In the late afternoon, as if their captors were searching for some formula for the treatment of such peculiar prisoners, they were escorted to covered quarters to spend the night.

It was a pigsty, not figuratively but literally: a low-roofed, ramshackle building with a cracked cement floor and a rickety partition down the middle beyond which, unmistakably, were its regular inhabitants, a family of pigs. The feeling that they were now no more than human livestock was unavoidable and, as if to indicate their complete acceptance into the animal world, a hen sat on a sack of meal and quite unconcernedly laid an egg. This event so impressed Shelagh Brown that in the diary she put together of the whole experience, predictably full of extraordinary occurrences, it was one of the few entries to which she awarded an exclamation mark. The diary, set down in Shelagh's own clipped, English style, conveys by its understatement the utter squalor in which these formerly immaculate ladies found themselves.

'Find water in stream. Wash a bit . . .' Shelagh records from the pigsty. 'All smelly with crude oil – seaweed etc in hair.' She produced the diary one winter day in Wiltshire before serving tea, and it was quite impossible to visualize her blackened and reeking with crude-oil and with her tidy coiffure tangled like the head of Medusa.

That night on Banka Island, trying to sleep on the cement floor and beset by hordes of black beetles, the women were troubled too by Japanese gawking at them with detached curiosity. Or so it had to be assumed from their impassive faces, for who then knew anything of the conquerors in their leisure mood, beyond the appalling whispers which had seeped from Hong Kong to Singapore? Shelagh retained ever afterwards the horrific image of a Japanese flyer who stood above them shining a torch on their distress. The Japanese airmen wore high boots and flying helmets lined with shaggy fur which ringed their faces and gave them the ferocious look of the hordes of Genghis Khan. But this nightmare figure, when he had completed his inspection, went and brought some coffee, perhaps in recompense for having showered these strangers with bombs. In spite of this small kindness the women were relieved when Stan and Johnnie, having finally reached the end of their labours, were brought to the shed as well. The belief that the presence of men in some way spelt security, even in these circumstances, was not one that could be dispelled in a day.

Not that the women in their reactions to stress were any more predictable than the Japanese in their attitude to mercy. The infinitely practical Mavis Hannah, clinging to a raft after the *Vyner Brooke* sank, heard another nurse who was a Roman Catholic gabbling Hail Marys on an obsessional rising note which conveyed growing panic. 'I told her to be quiet,' Mavis said. 'There was no time for that. What she had to do was to get a hold on the raft and try to get to shore.' With time to reflect, down the years, Mavis clearly still wondered whether she had been quite right to deal as brusquely with a matter of religious faith, but plainly her own equally strong credo was that, *in extremis* self-reliance was a virtue in its own right.

Mavis herself was actually very frightened because she couldn't swim and, indeed, was never to learn. 'On holiday my family always think I'm a great joke in my water-wings, but I have a little laugh to myself because to see me today nobody would guess what I went through forty years ago.'

Mavis and her group were rescued by a Malay fisherman who came out to them in his canoe and towed them in, clinging to its sides, a service for which she rewarded him with two soggy dollars. Her knees buckled when she stood, at last, on the sand but, ever reluctant to let events dictate to her when they should be seized by the scruff of the neck, she decided that the best course was to seek out the Japanese and surrender formally. Her decisiveness convinced the others, who were reluctant. A walk of several miles to Muntok followed and the first Japanese encountered had bandy legs and a long sword and looked, Mavis said, like a monkey. 'I thought: "Oh God, what have I done?" '

On the other hand, there was one nurse – a tall, Junoesque Australian – who had lost her uniform in the sea and come ashore wearing only her corselet. An officer provided her with a man's overcoat, yet another example of the curious thoughtfulness which existed alongside the cruelty. It was never long, though, before the Japanese came up with some reminder that they could be lethal and that their business in the islands was that of professional war-making.

The group that included Norah Chambers, her husband John and sister Ena, who had found a raft together, had spent a day and a night in the water and were steadily losing the battle with the off-shore currents when a small launch crewed by three young RAF men picked them up. There were numerous individual attempts at escape, employing eventually almost anything that would float, and the risks of the open sea were such that the people who set out in this way had more than enough to contend with in merely looking out for themselves. It was therefore an act of considerable charity as well as courage for the airmen to offer to land the surviving occupants of the raft at Muntok, even though it meant delivering them into the hands of the enemy. At this point, too, the murderous hazards of the shore could not be understood by those still at sea and, anyway, seemed less than those inherent in pressing on in the cockleshell launch. At any rate the prime object of Norah and her party, suffering from the extremes of exhaustion, was to get to land and to land they were taken.

The launch came alongside the pier at Muntok and waited gallantly while the survivors climbed a ladder up to its planking, a horrendous ascent with limbs that no longer functioned coherently, and the pause was sufficient to attract the attention of a squad of Japanese sailors. With practised speed these men fell into their killing role, throwing their rifles to their shoulders and pouring fire on the launch which shyed and sped off like a startled deer. 'We owed our lives to those young men,' Norah said, 'and I shall never forget them. I pray that they got away.' It was possible to confirm that the young men did on that occasion, but only to be captured further down the coast (see page 272).

The pier at that time stretched about a quarter of a mile into the sea, and had become a kind of staging post for survivors. In the years to come it was to take on a profound significance for the women since it punctuated the seemingly motiveless movement of the prisoners from place to place between Banka Island and the mainland of Sumatra. On each occasion, as the women weakened, it seemed to grow longer and more bleak.

On this day it was receiving, principally, the passengers from the *Mata Hari* for whom the Japanese sent launches as she lay surrendered in the Strait. This was by far the most conventional method of reaching the land, and it was also an indication of a further quirk of the Japanese. The human contents of a ship formally taken in war and with proper ceremony were evidently regarded in a different light from those who crept untidily ashore from the sea.

The Japanese told Captain Carston that he could take all his personal possessions ashore with him, including his servant, and the Japanese politely stood aside when all the passengers had gone so that he could pursue the tradition, as Captain, of being the last to leave his ship. This degree of courtesy didn't quite extend to the passengers who were told that they could each take only one piece of luggage ashore. This was no additional hardship to Phyllis Briggs, who had already left one of her suitcases behind in the chaos at the docks, but Christine Bundy who had two, both packed with clothes, was obliged to make an agonizing selection. She gave the surplus away to whoever was in need. Phyllis, whose surviving case was mostly filled with a travelling rug, thus acquired a black satin dressing-gown with long sleeves. A glamorous garment. It was never to fulfil its seductive potential. 'I hung on to it for the next three and a half years and always slept in it,' Phyllis said. 'It was protection against the mosquitos.'

Mamie Colley, who had so filled her suitcase with sensible English woollies that she could scarcely lift it, now left it behind altogether and took only the hat-box which accompanied it. This was to prove a crucial decision but was made at a time when Mamie was not at all well equipped to make it. Since leaving Singapore she had witnessed events through the painful haze of a terrible migraine which accompanied her period.

When she came to open the hat-box in the evening chill on Muntok pier, Mamie was appalled to find that it contained only her golf shorts, one pair of shoes and one dress, the rest of the space being crammed with sanitary towels. This was providential for the moment and made her the best-equipped female in this respect for some time to come, but even that good fortune petered out. Menstruation ceased among nearly all the women at an early stage in their imprisonment and did not resume until it ended.

The special tribulations which females carried into the experience were even more acutely expressed by a survivor of the *Vyner Brooke*, Olga Neubrunner, who was obliged to endure all that took place with the additional burden of being heavily pregnant. After a long immersion in the Strait she too reached the pier but there miscarried, as terrible a variant on an already tragic occurrence as it is possible to imagine.

The launches from the *Mata Hari* simply unloaded the women on to the pier like any other cargo and there they were left under guard. Through all that long, hot day they were given neither food nor water and, as night fell, the only attention they received from their captors was a foray by a guard for the purpose of removing rings and watches. Phyllis Briggs took off such jewelry as she had, knotted it into a headscarf and tied it under her hair, an early example of the quick-witted deviousness for which nearly all the women showed an instant flair.

The night was pierced by a cold wind and provided the prisoners' introduction to the animal intimacy which was to become a part of their lives. On the crowded boards of the jetty they huddled together for warmth as cattle do, clearly a natural instinct, but for those from such a civilized existence this was an oddly important barrier to overcome.

In the morning, again like cattle, they were watered from a bucket. Phyllis had brought a small metal sugar basin from the ship, which she used as a mug, and this was important too in the transition from ordinary existence. The significance of utensils was a major discovery only made possible by the lack of them. In that moment the cheap little sugar bowl was every bit as valuable as a silver chalice.

Whatever the discomforts of the pier for those who had already landed, it had a momentary appeal for Betty Jeffrey and her group because it seemed that they might make a landfall there in a progress of exceptional difficulty amid the currents. Their raft, however, was carried away yet again by the fierce, unseen energies which coursed through the waters; eventually, in extreme fatigue, it was decided that to lighten the raft Betty, another sister and two Malays would swim alongside it instead. In this manner they were making progress shorewards when yet another capricious current missed the swimmers but snatched the raft which fled away seawards again taking, among others, Matron Paschke to an unknown fate.

The Malays, too, were presently carried off in the same way leaving just the two nurses to reach a mangrove swamp which formed an ill-defined perimeter to Banka Island at this part of the coast. The mangrove swamp was every bit as repugnant as the name suggests, the very stuff of awful dreams with its myriad slithering, crawling and scuttling life-forms. Of these, the alligators were the least unbearable, their bulk and recognizable appearance making them preferable to the nameless things which squelched and plopped and were hideous when they touched the flesh.

As the tide went out the pair sank to their thighs in mud and now made the acquaintance of the mangrove roots which were hard and spiked and cut their hands as they waded or their bodies when they crawled. Both girls hallucinated at times, Betty clearly recognizing her father in a familiar pose: asleep in his armchair with the newspaper over his face. At night, marooned on a dead tree-trunk, they were brushed by the wings of huge birds or, more likely, bats. In the midst of all this the pair, who were from different units and had not met before, introduced themselves to each other rather formally, even exchanging home addresses much as tourists might if they were thrown together in some God-forsaken foreign place.

They were rescued from this particular hell by Malay fishermen who took them to their village. There Betty counted thirteen sharks laid out on the ground, a further peril of those waters which, so far, they had not even had the opportunity to consider in a marine marathon which had lasted from Saturday until Tuesday. The villagers were kind and even produced an English-speaking Chinese, but this blissful respite ended when a lorry full of Japanese drove into the village. The nurses walked out to give themselves up, and as soon as they were spotted the soldiers hurtled off the truck and raced towards them, fixing their bayonets as they came. They surrounded the exhausted nurses and one Japanese jabbed the point of his bayonet precisely on to the button on Betty's bedraggled uniform belt. 'The shank of the button stuck into me,' Betty remembered. 'It hurt quite a lot so I moved the bayonet down a bit.' The uniform buttons were to have their value. Amid the torrent of angry bawling which added to the fears of the moment only the word 'Americano' was distinguishable, furiously repeated. Since this was clearly a dangerous thing to be, the girls indicated the embossed map of Australia on their buttons. Australians were apparently marginally less unpopular at the time because they were bundled on to the truck and driven to Muntok.

By comparison the immediate history of the party which included Molly Ismail and her mother was relatively tranquil, perhaps some small recompense from fortune for the shocking end of the *Giang Bee*. There were fifty-six people in all in the lifeboat in which they made their way shorewards, but there was some water aboard and some ship's biscuits. Molly's mother's lips swelled terribly through the combination of sun and sea-salt but she remained bright and cheerful and, in Molly's words, an echo of that carefully mannered existence back in the colony, 'Put up a good front.' The vitality of Mrs Ismail emerged so strongly in all that Molly recounted of her that it came as a surprise when one day she mentioned that her mother was sixty-five at the time of these events.

When the survivors stepped ashore after nearly two days at sea they were met by some native children who led them to a little hamlet where they were sheltered until the inhabitants grew afraid of harbouring them. They then sailed up a river and some more children found them. It must have been a fascinating discovery for these little Malays out at play beside one of those small rivers which lace their way across Banka Island. In peace they had the lush effulgence of streams in a botanical garden and only war could have made them seem sinister.

The men in the party parlayed with the headman of the village from which the children came and it was arranged that two houses would be put at the party's disposal. A large group of Eurasians took over one and the Europeans the other, the division coming about quite naturally because, freed of the pressures of bombs and shipwreck, the old order of things reasserted itself easily. Both groups bartered what little jewelry they had for food and a week passed with so few alarms that Molly, a gently compliant lady to this day, began to think that this is where they would remain until the war ended.

It was a terrible shock when a lorryload of Japanese arrived – 'It was the *reality* of coming face to face with them,' Molly said – and once again they stormed around the captives poking them with their sharp bayonets, although bawling at the same time, 'No fright! No fright!' They counted their prisoners carefully and left, informing them that they would return the next day, which they did and herded this party also towards Muntok. Their confidence in leaving the group as if they were tethered made it plain that they were now the masters of all the land around. And, indeed, in that week the Japanese had established themselves sufficiently to start to come to grips with this peculiar accretion of unclassifiable human material in what was otherwise a routine annexation of one more segment of the white man's possessions in Asia.

Even the remnants in the pigsty began to receive some official attention. When they rose, stiff and aching from a night on the fractured cement, they were given a little milk which they mixed with the providential egg, the result being shared among the seven of them. An English-speaking Japanese officer arrived and laboriously wrote down their particulars – name, age, origins, rank in the case of the service personnel. The ever-active mind of Elizabeth Simons had already been bent upon finding some way out of this plight and she tried pointing out to the Japanese that the women were non-combatants and should not be imprisoned at all. She got no reply but the officer led them to a native house nearby and told them that they could take anything they required.

The house had already been thoroughly looted, since the Imperial Army itself habitually lived off the land, but the women found sarongs and *badjus*, a type of native blouse, at which even these locust-like acquirers had drawn the line – or rejected as too tatty since what was left was really not much more than rags. Mrs Brown, who was clearly not intended by Nature for this sort of circumstance, was altogether too large for sarongs meant for the small, slender indigenous females, but she found that she could put a *badju* to use by wearing it back to front.

Some fragment of the housekeeping instinct also led the women to seize any utensil that presented itself, although they had no idea then what their future would hold, and they left with a tinker's collection of empty tins and other dejected receptacles, broken spoons and a battered kettle. Such rags as were left were torn into strips by those who had lost or abandoned their shoes for the swim and used to bind their feet.

They returned to the hut, where a herd of goats had joined the pigs and added their contribution to the shocking smells which abounded, and there found that the hen had laid two more eggs. Shelagh recalled that it was Stan and Johnnie who made a small milk pudding, using the new kitchenware, but after this domestic interlude they were rediscovered by the Japanese and hauled off to work again.

At what would have been tea-time in Raffles Hotel if this monstrous cataclysm had never occurred, the women too were rousted out of the pigsty and told to march, which they did, over a rough track and uphill, an astonishing procession in their hand-me-down sarongs and carrying the junk they had collected. Mrs Brown found the going very hard. She told Shelagh that she was determined not to stop in case she couldn't start up again. The rags on her feet came undone but had to be allowed to trail pathetically behind.

They passed a bombed compound in which corpses still lay, and in a jungle clearing they found some limes and a whole hand of bananas. It was remarkably heavy and, without thinking, they gave it to their guard to carry. He accepted it uncomplainingly, in coolie fashion, and for a moment it seemed that the old ascendencies had been restored, but at the end of the march he walked off with it as well.

Their destination, after several miles, proved to be a large building in the centre of Muntok, formerly the town's cinema they later discovered. For all they knew, those in their party were the only survivors of the whole exodus from Singapore, but inside, the place turned out to be packed to suffocation with more than a thousand prisoners: soldiers, sailors and airmen lumped together with women and children, and a whole new element to add to the mélange – numerous Dutch who had been seized as their colony too was overrun. What had seemed to Shelagh's group to be a unique experience turned out to have been repeated again and again about the island. There were other women in ragged sarongs and with their feet bound and, like an emblem, all those who had been in the water were deeply sunburnt and bore the raw scrape of the lifebelt beneath their chins.

There were delighted reunions. The Australian nurses found more of their kind. Mrs Brown and Shelagh found Dorothy MacCleod, the wife of Mr Brown's partner in Singapore and last seen on the canting deck of the *Vyner Brooke*. Olga Neubrunner, another friend from Singapore, was there, still in dire distress from the miscarriage, and Shelagh did what she could for her which, in that place, could be no more than acquiring for her one of the limes found on the journey.

When night fell there was no room to do other than sit on the concrete floor. As there were doctors and nurses a dressing station was set up at one end of the cinema and worked all night to deal with the flood of wounds. The medical supplies came from a variety of sources. Some of the doctors had drugs with them and the nurses had remnants of their stock in trade. Mavis Hannah contributed her morphia and syringe. Invaluable bandages were made from the tablecloths and napkins and the like which many of the servicemen had bought in Singapore to take home as presents after they had completed the job of hurling the little yellow men back in to the sea.

A dim light hung over the dressing station in which the shadowy figures of the doctors and nurses could be seen as they tended the wounded. Sleepless, Shelagh surveyed the scene: 'It suddenly came to me that this is how it must have looked in the Crimea.' It was an important insight, the first detached realization of an involvement in an experience that belonged with such set-pieces. Nothing could demonstrate more clearly how ill-prepared these women were for suffering and deprivation of this kind. It was something that belonged to another century, and only small touches separated it from its historical antecedents. A Royal Navy medical orderly puzzled over a bright red outbreak on Elizabeth Simons' hands when she took her turn for treatment. She had smeared her rope-burns with lipstick, the only salve she had. In the course of the night a British sailor gave Shelagh and Mrs Brown the gifts he had intended for home: a box of face-powder and a handbag. The men were doing their best to atone to the women for their terrible failure at arms.

Norah Chambers and her sister Ena, who had been engulfed in the worst of the oil from the *Vyner Brooke* and had also lacerated their hands, were so disgusted with the stinking stuff that during their wait they attempted to cleanse each other using their feet, a contortionary exercise of such absurdity that Norah laughed heartily as she described it all those years later. On the Muntok pier that same night the prisoners there shivered away the long dark hours.

Margaret Dryburgh, the missionary, produced a diary in the camps illustrated with delicate pencil sketches and containing hymns and poetry, the sort of profusion of little creative skills that were cultivated by Victorian ladies of breeding, and there is a Victorian flavour to her account of night on the pier: 'Our Captain strode up and down looking out for possible interference with frightened girls on the part of the soldiers.' Quite what he could have done to prevent such a thing is not made apparent, but there was clearly still some comfort in the presence of an authoritative male.

At daybreak the prisoners were herded down the pier, which seemed about two miles long to Miss Dryburgh, staggering, like the rest of the *Mata Hari* group, under the burden of her luggage. On a grassy plot at its shorewards end the men were separated from the women and children who were ordered to form a column four deep and were then marched off behind a guard. As they moved towards the town there was a fresh version of the astonishment which struck the newcomers at the cinema when they discovered the existence of a whole other tribe of survivors.

'We noticed,' Miss Dryburgh recorded, 'another procession of women converging to meet us. Some wore the grey uniform of Australian nursing sisters, others presented a motley appearance, wearing Malay coats and sarongs, men's uniform and army socks. Some had rags bound round arms and legs and strange red sores under their chins. Our amazement changed to commiseration when we learned that these were victims of bombing and shipwreck who had just succeeded in reaching land by rafts, lifeboats or even by swimming.' Miss Dryburgh was the sort of person who would always find other people's hardships more striking than her own.

This other column, of course, had come from the cinema. When day came the men there had been assembled and taken off to repair bomb damage, but not before the women had made a discovery which seemed to remain in their memories at least as vividly as the bombings and sinkings. In daylight it became plain that the toilet facilities, a few crude latrines among some oil drums at the back of the building, had to be used in full view of the guards and passers-by. Back in Singapore, now fully occupied by the Japanese, the remaining population was learning that in this respect, too, the new masters were quite unlike the old. A lucid and humorous Chinese schoolteacher, N. I. Low, wrote a book about the occupation called *When Singapore was Syonan-Io*, which is what the conquerors renamed the city to stress their total domination, and he speaks of 'the unashamed way of the average Japanese soldier of discharging the minor obligations of Nature'. This, translated from Low's elegant English, meant that a Japanese relieved himself more or less where he was at the time, quite unimpressed with the stately surroundings of Raffles Place or the environs of the Cricket Club. 'He had none of our prudishness. Like the Greek of classical times, he was not ashamed of his body and his concerns.'

Nevertheless, to the women it was a distinctly alarming statement about their situation, touching deeply upon that invisible protection which their status as Europeans had always given them among the natives and suggesting untold indignities to follow. For the moment, they too were formed up in lines and set off on another march which Mrs Brown found especially taxing as she was still trying to recover after her brave effort of the previous day.

The combined column stopped, after nearly an hour, in front of another unlovely building. The Japanese, in this small town, had clearly had difficulty finding a structure large enough to accommodate so many people, but it was peculiarly apt that it had formerly been used as a kind of clearing station for the coolie labour arriving to work in the Dutch tin mines. Next door, as if at some time a decision had been made to keep all forms of servitude in the same location, was the old Muntok prison, although that had now become a pepper warehouse, saving the women at least from the additional disgrace of going to jail.

The coolie barracks were a U-shaped structure and the women were put in one arm, the other being given over to the men when they returned from their labours while the guards occupied the section between. Inside, the arms were divided into dormitories; these normally housed twenty coolies each but were occupied by forty of the women and, on the other side, up to sixty of the men. Margaret Dryburgh's Victorian style is well adapted for the Gothic gloom of the dormitories: 'The first sight struck dismay into our hearts!'

In each of the dormitories the only furnishing was a sloping cement slab on either side, which left a narrow passage down the middle. The slabs were so reminiscent of the display facilities for cod and haddock and the like, back in Britain, that the women christened the place 'The MacFisheries'. Those sleeping on the slabs predictably tended to slide slowly towards the floor, a progress they tried to arrest by stuffing their clothes and possessions at their feet. 'Shall we ever forget those nights?' Miss Dryburgh wrote. 'Babies howled and whimpered while distracted

77

mothers tried to prepare food for them in the dark. Exasperated bed-fellows expressed their thoughts loudly and forcibly. Heavy-footed sentries stamped along the passages through the dormies, flashing their lights on us. Rain pattered in from the roof and unsavoury whiffs floated in from the back premises.'

The lavatory accommodation was again dire, a matter of squatting over a drain in plain view of anyone who cared to look. The culture shock of this alone is conveyed by an incident which Shelagh Brown remembered. A Mr Roberts, who, in that other life, had carried the cross in front of the choir at St Andrew's Cathedral approached her one day and said, very confidentially: 'I've been thinking it must be difficult for the elderly using the drains. I've found a chair and I know where there's a saw, so I could cut a hole in the seat.' It was clearly a good idea but Mr Roberts required some specialized information. 'How big do you think I should make it?' he enquired. Shelagh awarded this exchange another exclamation mark in her diary: 'I thought back a few weeks and how impossible to imagine this conversation then!' On a diet consisting principally of small amounts of rice which, even then, the ravenous could not always bring themselves to ingest, the chair was valuable, but it was not overemployed until the first outbreaks of dysentery began, which they did before even this short phase of the imprisonment ended.

Miss Dryburgh, who was sleeping on the slab opposite Shelagh and her mother, quickly became concerned to find other forms of sustenance. On the very first morning in the barracks, equipped with her Bible and a prayer-book borrowed from young Phyllis Liddelow, she announced that each morning and night she would say prayers and read from the Bible and invited anyone who wished to do so to join her. This was the first indication of some form of leadership emerging among the women, although another Presbyterian missionary, called Ann Livingstone, clearly felt that it should exist. Her early contribution was to take the dwellers in her block in pairs to demonstrate the best method of using an open latrine, which amused some but vexed others considerably. For those with a high regard for the goodness of humanity the barracks were not encouraging.

If the camps were eventually Hell, the two weeks which were spent in the barracks were purgatory. Shocked, uncertain, crammed together in a doleful place where the sun never penetrated and the greater world was visible only as small patches of sky above the blocks, the worst aspects of human nature became evident. Ablutions were performed in a native *tong*, a rectangular bath about twelve feet long surrounded by a low wall. To use it the women stood outside the wall, scooped up water and threw it over themselves, but the small amount of water available was usually already dirty from previous bathers and further fouled by prisoners washing their clothes in it. Washing festooned the communal paths, constantly wet from the rains and closely observed because possessions disappeared if they were left unguarded.

'There was a terrible clash of nationalities,' Miss Dryburgh recorded sorrowfully. 'Chinese girls were upset at being classed with "dirty" Asiatics. Eurasians showed antipathy to Europeans.' The guards displayed no such xenophobia. They bashed everyone's feet with their torches, regardless of racial origin, as they passed between the slabs on their rounds at night, and if anyone got in their path they were kicked with the curious Japanese military boot, which had a separate compartment for the big toe. Otherwise their attitude was one of indifference to this squabbling, noisy, evil-smelling anthill. At first they would go to watch the women making their pathetic toilettes at the *tong*, but after a time they lost interest and drifted away.

To add to all this was the considerable burden of wounds and sickness. There were the conventional ailments which arose from exposure and immersion, tonsilitis and heavy head colds. There were the complaints which people had brought with them, long-standing ills of the flesh which, now they had a little time to reflect, they assumed would need the attention they had always been given. Norah Chambers' husband John would, in any other setting, have been a convalescent requiring careful nursing. Olga Neubrunner would have been propped up in bed, surrounded with flowers and visited by solicitous relatives. This was scarcely an environment in which to cope even with the psychological effects of a late miscarriage. There were old people, beset with routine aches and pains, but with no hope of receiving those small palliatives which ease the grumblings of age. Then there were the injuries associated with the violence of shipwreck and its aftermath, a spectrum ranging from the wounds of the bombing and shelling to broken limbs and the raging epidemic of lacerations to hands and feet. Nurses were rendered helpless by their torn hands and had to be nursed instead, amputees effectively. Shelagh Brown noted that she provided 'feet' for her mother, who could barely walk when the after-effects of the marches set in, and 'hands' for Dorothy MacCleod, who was dreadfully rope-burned. Among her duties Shelagh was obliged to wash the sole sanitary towel of her father's partner's wife in this place where all normal fastidiousness seemed abruptly to have disappeared.

There were five doctors in the barracks, two of them women, and a pool of trained nurses, but the chronic shortage of medical supplies and equipment, even of a ready source of clean water, reduced their ministrations to not much more than an advanced form of first-aid. When major surgery was required, the only arrangements the staff could make hurled medical science back by centuries.

The condition of an RAF lieutenant whose feet had been shattered deteriorated to the point where the removal of one of them became necessary to give him a chance of life. Pleas to the Japanese for his transfer to a hospital were refused by captors so callous that when a male prisoner who had been bayoneted in the stomach was laid on the floor of the makeshift hospital to await a fresh dressing a passing guard ground his heel into the wound. The Japanese also refused to send instruments in, so that when amputation became crucial it was decided to proceed with whatever was to hand. This amounted to a little morphine as an anaesthetic and the makeshift saw which Mr Roberts had devised to make the lavatory seat. It was made by cutting a section from the metal hoop round a barrel, heating and straightening it, then filing in the teeth.

The lieutenant was tied to the top of a table and the operation went ahead. 'It was just as well,' said Phyllis Briggs, who was one of the nurses in attendance, 'that this poor man was too ill to know what was happening.' Within a few days the other foot had to be amputated and the lieutenant subsequently died, to be buried in a coffin made from a door. Another male prisoner died of dysentery in this same awful two weeks and, an astonishing stroke of ill fate, the little Russian boy, Mischa Warmen, who had bobbed smiling from the water in the arms of a stranger beside the stricken *Vyner Brooke*, was reunited with his mother only to be orphaned entirely when she died of pneumonia in the barracks.

The deaths of these Europeans cast among the captives the gloom that its presence always occasions in a culture which, even in normal life, tries to hide from its omnipresence. Yet very close by, and known only to the men at first, a torrent of dying was in progress. Shelagh Brown's diary for this time records her puzzlement at blood-curdling screams and groans as of souls in torture coming faintly through the night, and all were aware of a dreadful stench overlaying the pervasive local smells of the barracks.

In fact, in the adjoining jail, strewn among the pepper sacks, was another human detritus. Some six hundred Chinese coolies had been scooped off the streets of Hong Kong after its fall and transported to Sumatra as slave labour, an early rationale in the working of the Co-Prosperity Sphere. They had spent six weeks battened down in the holds of ships, and when they were dumped off at Muntok they were useless from starvation and disease. The fresh male captives from the barracks were made to do their work and the coolies were left to rot in their own filth until they died.

It might seem that this place could not offer any more tales of misery, but all the survivors of Singapore had not yet been brought together. One night Phyllis Briggs was on duty in the hospital area when a girl was brought in, her skin so blackened by the sun and her eyes so sunken into her head that it was some minutes before her nationality was divined. This dehumanized mask belonged to Margot Turner who, with other QAs, was among some seven hundred who had taken ship in the *Kuala* at Singapore. When the *Kuala* was bombed and sunk, Margot had spent three days on a little islet before an island trading steamer, the *Tanjong Penang*, also crammed with women and children, had taken her off. In the course of the night the *Tanjong Penang* fell foul of Admiral Ozawa's fleet and was despatched without warning by gunfire. Amid the terror-stricken spillage in the sea Margot and another QA tied two rafts together and swam about until they had brought sixteen people together, six of them children and two of these babies under one year old.

By dawn two women had gone. The other sister, Beatrice Le Blanc Smith who had concealed a terrible wound, died in the afternoon and by the next dawn still more had slipped away. On the second day, waterless under the blazing sun, the children went mad and one by one died. 'I examined each of them with great care before committing their small bodies to the sea,' Margot has recorded. 'The last one was a very small baby and it was difficult to know when it was dead. I thought: "This is some woman's precious child; I must not let it go until I know it's dead." But in the end there was no doubt and it had to go with the others.'

On the third day only Margot was left. Miraculously, from a parched sky, rain fell and she was able to collect enough in the lid of her powder-compact* to sustain life. On the fourth day, clinging like a terrier to her wits, she was spotted by a large Japanese warship and hauled up its side on the end of a rope to be taken, inevitably, to Muntok.

On board was a Japanese naval doctor who had been trained in America and spoke English, and he was remarkably gentle in his treatment of her. Her tattered dress was removed on the ship and replaced with a sailor's shirt and trousers. On each of the days the warship remained in Muntok harbour the doctor came to visit Margot, and on one occasion he brought the remains of the dress washed, pressed and on a coat-hanger.

Of the other late arrivals at the barracks in Muntok, there was one which chillingly underlined the murderous aspect of the conquerors' nature. Vivien Bullwinkel of the Australian Army Nursing Service

* Now on show in the QARANC museum

walked unobtrusively into the barracks one day with a water-bottle slung over her shoulder and pressed to her side. It was covering a hole which a bullet had made in her uniform. This was not a vanity but an important precaution.

She was the sole survivor of the slaughter of the nurses on the beach and hence the only witness, a fact which, for the safety of all of them, became a closely kept secret among the women and remained so until Vivien's appearance as a witness at the War Crimes Trials in Tokyo in 1946. In fact, a bullet had passed clean through her side just above the hip. She fell and floated, to all appearances dead, until the Japanese went away. She had then managed to crawl ashore. In the jungle she found a British serviceman who had been bayoneted and left for dead and she cared for him for ten days, begging food from a village and taking water from a stream. They were picked up by the Japanese as they were making their painful way towards Muntok, which had become so much like the centre of a spider's web. There the soldier died a few days later.

It was a bad place. Only an individual with the dedicated optimism of Margaret Dryburgh could see any merit in what had been discovered there:

> . . . the gaunt spectres of disease and death hovered near. Mental anxiety tended to fray nerves. We felt to the full the blow to our national pride, anxiety about the future, uncertainty about the fate of friends and the state of the outer world.
>
> Contact with our captors was not pleasant as it meant close proximity to naked bayonets . . . Yes, Muntok spelt misery. Yet in the horrors there were flashes of light – self-sacrificing service, a new sense of values, a determination to try one day to share in repairing weaknesses in our social and political structure so ruthlessly exposed by the war.

A harsher view of this first phase of the imprisonment would almost certainly be possible, though difficult if preferred by anyone who wasn't there. And there would be years ahead in which to test Miss Dryburgh's judgement and further examine the ways of these women who had been pitched so brusquely together.

Chapter 6

It is intensely difficult, so many years later, to attempt to decipher the logic of the Japanese in their disposal of their prisoners in what was then something of a backwater among the host of glittering new possessions they had seized. If the 'useless mouths' washed up on Banka Island were of no great concern to them, why were they not left to rot like the Chinese coolies in Muntok Jail? If they had some significance, why was the pattern of their movement from place to place so apparently arbitrary, of no discernible value to either the prisoners or their captors?

It is necessary to speculate because it was not possible to find any formal record relating to these captives from the Japanese point of view. If it existed it must have been of the order, certainly in the early stages, of a pencil and the back of an envelope, the hasty accounting of a busy army anxious to move on to its next assignment. To approach the Japanese officially about this powerfully controversial aspect of their war of aggression, is to encounter an impenetrable obliqueness, the acme of Oriental inscrutability. There is no equivalent to the German attitude towards the examining of old wounds, which is either clinical or rueful, a little like looking for familiar names in the Punishment Book on revisiting the old school.

The erasure of unpalatable events clearly runs deep among the Japanese. There was a patriotic song called 'O Great Pacific' which was played relentlessly throughout the whole period of Japan's aggressive ferment and conveyed their militaristic ambition as clearly as the Nazis' 'Horst Wessel Lied'.

Chrysanthemum crest on our warships shall show
Who can rule the blue furrows of the sea here below.
O great Pacific! Shine Rising Sun!
Let thy crimson illumine the lands we have won . . .

So ran one verse in translation. The song was proscribed by the Allies on the occupation of Japan but it had been so relentlessly played from 1937 until the ending of the war that it seemed likely that a recording would exist somewhere and one turned up, surprisingly, in a Japanese gift shop in London. The shop assistant was able to identify the song as one she had played as background music until two elderly Japanese customers had entered and visibly recoiled. 'Bad song,' they had told the girl angrily, 'No play, no play!' It was a strutting little tune, blared by a big brass band to make it sound more arrogant and it was topped and tailed by the snarling of warlike slogans in harsh Japanese. Even among the lacquer boxes and the paper parasols it was possible to imagine those same hectoring voices goading the prisoners out when a move was in prospect.

At the start of March 1942, the Japanese abruptly decided to separate the women and children and the few civilian men from the Servicemen, and they were told to be ready to leave the coolie barracks at three o'clock the following morning. There was scarcely any need to worry about packing but the old and the lame dreaded the prospect of another march, having barely recovered from the last one.

Twenty-three of the women, those who were gravely ill, were to remain behind, and to provide some medical care for these and the five hundred or so servicemen, six civilian nurses stayed, among them Phyllis Briggs and Christine Bundy, and a few civilian volunteers, including Ruth Russell-Roberts who wanted to be with Christine. Theirs was one of the first friendships to prosper, and Ruth's decision to remain at Muntok when almost anywhere else must have seemed more inviting, indicates the value of a good friendship in the camps. It was a commodity that was to become ever more valuable.

Possibly to get the prisoners moving more briskly, or more likely as a tacit admission of the chronic food shortage which existed on Banka Island, an English-speaking Japanese repeatedly said of their new destination, 'Bread there, bread there', which those staying behind heard with considerable wistfulness. The diet in the past weeks had been so inadequate and repetitive that Phyllis Briggs had already sold a ring from among the hoard she had hidden under her hair, hoping to be able to buy some food. In fact she had only succeeded in swapping a blue handkerchief for two bread rolls in a deal with an Indonesian watchman, one of several brought in to supplement the Japanese guards. It was a nerve-racking transaction at a stage when the encouragement of a black market had not been tested for its potential in attracting retribution. There were other, much more alarming responses to the craving for food. One day the Japanese threw scraps of bread through the fence around the barracks, as if feeding the animals in a zoo, and laughed uproariously as some of the men scrambled for them, monkey-fashion. Phyllis turned away: 'I just couldn't bear to watch such a degrading scene.'

The women picked the barracks clean of utensils before they went, making off with the litter of broken rice bowls and the like that even their predecessors in the place, the Chinese labourers, who were some of the most frugal people on earth, had not felt were worth keeping. The likelihood that rice would continue to appear, assuming that anything at all would turn up on a regular basis, meant that spoons were at a premium. One lady found a treasure, a scooper of Brobdingnagian proportions. It was a shoe-horn.

Those departing were given a handful of rice wrapped in a banana leaf as rations for the journey and another bizarre procession got under way. An elderly woman with badly damaged hands believed that they hurt less if she held them up in the air and she kept them there still, lending a faintly religious aspect to the column as it struggled up yet another long hill. It was raining, besides being dark, and Mrs Brown's difficulties returned at once. Miraculously a lorry appeared, prepared to carry the most handicapped, and Shelagh experienced another stab of bleak anxiety over her mother. If Mrs Brown accepted the lift they would be parted in circumstances as uncertain as when they were drifting in the ocean, but there was not really any choice. Mrs Brown was boosted aboard and Shelagh trudged on, wondering if she would ever see her again.

It was dawn by the time they reached the pier and there, suddenly, colour began to transform the leaden sky and continued to build with theatrical generosity to become the most beautiful sunrise that anyone present had ever seen. As a final flourish a perfect rainbow formed. Everybody looked upwards with awe as it arched above their squalor. Miss Dryburgh received it as a sign and was later moved to poetry:

> We captives left the pier before dawn
> To meet a future dark with threatening fear.
> 'What lies ahead?' Our anxious spirits sighed.
> A wondrous rainbow arch with vivid glow
> Proclaimed the answer. 'Hope on, hope on' it cried.
> 'Hope on,' reflected colours echoed low.

Launches ferried the prisoners out to a group of stinking old freighters lying off the pier, and they were packed on to the deck of two of the ships, there to be belaboured by the sun which was now burning down with scorching intensity. Sun and torrential rain alternated during the journey producing intense discomfort, but there was an element to contend with which was even more excrutiating. On the ship which carried Margaret Dryburgh and her Muse the only lavatory was a box with a hole in it, projecting over the stern. The propellers threshed and churned alarmingly immediately below and anyone who ventured to sit on the box had to hang on grimly to the flagpole of the ensign at the stern. All this was in plain view of the rest of the ship and, like a threatening lavatory attendant, a Japanese guard stood by with his rifle and bayonet fixed. The majority baulked at the box, but those suffering from dysentery had no alternative.

After some twenty-five miles of open water a new coast loomed, the Sumatran mainland. The ships entered an estuary and began to negotiate the Moesi River, a waterway which, like the Muntok pier, was to come to seem longer each time it was traversed. The swamp-land which forms the south-east coast of Sumatra is riven by snaking waters, cold, green and lonely-looking, and the Moesi itself is to this day not a lovely river. Its waters are oily and sullen from the outpourings of the industry which had proliferated along its banks and even then, during the '40s, according to the women, was showing the wear and tear of what we have now come to call pollution. The prison ships covered fifty-four miles of it before they arrived at a wharf in the dock area of Palembang, the capital of Southern Sumatra, and those who disembarked first were obliged to wait while all four ships involved were tied up. Hours passed, then a fleet of battered trucks arrived and the prisoners were packed in, so tightly that they all had to stand, avoiding as best they could the yawning holes where planks were missing in the back. The Japanese intention soon became apparent. The trucks were driven in convoy through the heart of the town and the natives lined the thronged streets to jeer and wave Rising Sun flags. It was the recreation of an age-old practice of barbaric conquerors, the parade of dejected captives before a triumphant populace, but this time with a special edge. Who there could ever have expected to see white women brought together like coolies, their fair complexions ravaged by sun and dirt and their fashionable clothes exchanged for rags? The humiliation might have been greater if the women had not been distracted by the hair-raising driving of the Japanese. Presented with a vehicle they seemed to know nothing else but propelling it hell-for-leather without the slightest regard for obstructions, a style bequeathed to the Tokyo taxi-drivers of today.

The trucks stopped at what had formerly been a Chinese school and here the prisoners encountered the only charm of what had otherwise constituted another appalling day. They were given a meal that included such wonder ingredients as meat and vegetables, a treat which even made it bearable to lie straight down on the cement floor in their clothes to sleep.

This was effectively the end of the first phase of the imprisonment. The impression gained is that the Japanese had recovered a little from their bewilderment at this bizarre legacy from what was in other respects a tidy and thoroughly successful military operation and had given some thought to what would be necessary to handle the influx, if it was not simply to be eradicated. The existence of the Dutch, in a major seat of their own colony, was also important. Palembang was a Dutch city in the same way that Singapore was British, had fallen more or less intact to the invaders and was therefore going about much of its customary business but under new management, so to speak.

The large Dutch population of the Indies could not be rounded up and incarcerated *en bloc* instantaneously, so that although the Japanese clearly intended to deal with them in due course many were still free. This made for an approximation of normality after the chaotic nightmare of Muntok, and the following move of the prisoners from the school was to quarters that were more akin to a civilized internment than a POW cage or a concentration camp.

The Japanese had selected a group of bungalows in a suburb of the city and emptied them of their Dutch occupants, except for two households, so that the transition was rather like the shifting of a slum population to a council estate. The location was called Bukit Besar, which means Big Hill, very much the kind of carelessly chosen name that local authorities tend to give to low income housing projects. But before this chance to regain at least some respectability, the captives' poverty had to be paraded again. Their route lay down a main road and once more the population stared amazed at their condition. They were supplemented this time by Japanese photographers who recorded the march in that absorbed, obsessional way that the Japanese devote to their camera-work to this day. The object then was evidently to make the sorry end of the vaunted whites known to an even wider Asian audience and the women were well aware that they could hardly have looked worse. A British schoolteacher called Dorothy Moreton had acquired a pair of men's leather lace-up shoes, many sizes too big for her, and she remembered that she slopped along rather in the manner of Charlie Chaplin.

At Bukit Besar the conventional problems of moving-in day were dramatically diminished by the lack of possessions among the new-comers, but other confusions took their place. The houses seemed palatial after what had gone before. They were comparatively clean, contained oddments of furniture in some cases, and the electricity was still connected. The Australian nurses found that one of the two allotted to them contained an electric stove, and this was greeted with a delight that no simple stove can have engendered before or since. The major defect was that there were many more people than the houses were ever meant to contain, and the question of who should go where assumed crucial proportions. After the experience of ultra-communal living they all had their own version of the particular pitfall they would like to avoid in what looked likely to be a fairly permanent situation.

Those with well-defined views on matters of race did their best not to fall amid some ethnic grouping that was not to their taste. Those who had found the squalling of babies unbearable sought to dwell among the childless. Families and married couples were determined to remain together. No proper leadership had yet emerged, nor at that time been sought, since nobody so far had been able to tell what the next day would hold. Such group decisions as had been necessary had been dealt with by the worst possible method, which was everyone talking at once at the tops of their voices. Once again the already established cohesion of the Australian nurses gave them an advantage in this respect. They regarded themselves as a military unit, still in being though much depleted, and their determination to have their own sector was strengthened, it is possible to judge, by a growing irritation with the ways of pommies seen at such close quarters. The surviving thirty-two of them went into a pair of houses separated from the rest by the two Dutch homes still containing their original inhabitants.

Elsewhere there was confusion, little helped by a Japanese compulsion to count heads, an exercise that was always to produce untold discomfort and was characterized by a form of innumeracy that made them habitually forget the total, which obliged them to start all over again. Eventually a form of grouping emerged which was more or less dictated by caste: service officers' wives was one distinction, nationality another. The distribution was roughly seventeen people to one small house.

Once inside, the prisoners surveyed their new domains and the scavenging instinct which had developed so rapidly led them to much of value. The previous occupants, in clearing out, had thrown the unwanted contents of their households into the yards at the back and there were treasure troves of the kind of comestibles that accumulate in larders; half-empty sauce bottles and the like with sticky lids and labels showing the wear and tear of months, if not years. These were mined for their last drops and smears of familiar flavour, now grown impossibly remote and desirable. The Australians found a nanny goat and its kid in the yard of one of their houses. They gazed at the nanny with homicidal intent but settled for milking her, feeling that between themselves and the kid, theirs was the greater need.

The group that included Mrs Brown and Shelagh were denied any of these treats until much later. The keys to bungalow Number 5 where they were to stay were missing, and pleas to the Japanese were met with a snarl of '*nanti, nanti*', the Malay word for 'wait' and for the Japanese a local equivalent of '*mañana*'. The Dutch inhabitants proved excellent neighbours, turning up with hot soup and coffee, but when they finally gained entrance to the house the Browns were too exhausted to do any more than sweep the floor and lie on their limited expanse of it.

The next day there were further signs of at least a partial return to normality. Mrs Brown's legs had given up the struggle with the relentless new demands made upon them, and she was also suffering from a fever. Her request for medical attention was not only met but a rickshaw was sent for her; she left the house wearing a kimono over the pyjamas of a captured clergyman called the Reverend Wardle and a pair of black socks. She was to be detained for two weeks in the Charitas hospital in Palembang.

This Roman Catholic institution, run by Dutch nuns of the Charitas order, was to be central to the lives of the prisoners for many months to come. It was in fact no longer a proper hospital at all. With the arrival of the Japanese, a new building, opened by the nuns in 1940 was promptly seized for Japanese sick and wounded. The nuns were given five hours to clear out and return to what became known as Old Charitas, and had been converted into a school. They were allowed to remove no equipment from the new hospital except the beds and a single operating table. These devout ladies, however, also showed an immediate flair for devious conduct, using the inviolable recesses of their habits to transfer considerable quantities of drugs, medicines and even surgical instruments. Much had already been hidden before the Japanese even reached the hospital. In their turn the Japanese secreted a bomb-proof bunker for the military in New Charitas to take advantage of possible Allied squeamishness over attacking a target with both a religious and a medical significance. In that building, an unremarkable structure in view of its history, the present-day nuns exhibit this example of the enemy's deceit with many of those signs of suitably muted profound disapproval which they always convey so well.

In the houses at Bukit Besar, those who were fit enough – Shelagh had a delayed reaction, a heavy chest cold which kept her in bed, that's to say on the floor, for four days and left her very weak – strove to bring some order into their daily lives. They washed their clothes and swept and dusted, coming to grips with all the jobs that servants had spared them in the days now lost. By a great irony the Malayan women who had been servants to the Dutch now became the Ladies Bountiful, bringing food and cast-off clothing which they bequeathed with their charming smiles.

The Dutch, at the risk of Japanese wrath, were also generous, and the pattern of eating reverted to the form of that other life, though the meals were always meagre. Breakfast was a small piece of bread or banana and coffee or tea; lunch consisted of rice and a vegetable, with duck or pork sometimes and a concocted pudding or pancake; and for dinner there would be soup as well, to sketch the impression that the meal could retain its significance as a major ritual of the colonial day. Another device of this kind was the establishment of elevenses, only the unyielding nature of the issue biscuit providing a powerful reminder that mid-morning interludes in Robinson's restaurant belonged to another existence entirely.

With this degree of conventionality restored, the question of money also began to assert itself. Besides the charitable offerings, there was food to be bought from natives who were not yet receiving any visible benefit from the loosening of Asia's colonial chains. Such money as survived the bombs and the sea and the precipitate nature of the retreat from Singapore was mostly in Straits currency which nobody wanted. If a slightly suburban ethos was developing in Bukit Besar, the housewives were distinctly embarrassed when it came to paying for the groceries. It was this situation which produced a response when the Japanese asked for anyone with the ability to sew, the promise of a small payment being offered to volunteers. The work proved to be the making up of the loincloths first revealed on the beach at Banka, an oblong of white cloth which had only to be hemmed and have tapes attached at its corners. The pay reflected the simplicity of the task, but Dorothy Moreton, who was one of those to take up the offer, remembered how a fellow seamstress, a classic colonial matron, looked at her wages with a certain fascination. It was the first money she had ever earned by her own labours. Another of the volunteers was a large, bluff Canadian nurse called Mrs Layland who had an unquenchable sense of humour. One day, amid the inevitable tedium of the job, she suggested to the worker sitting beside her, a Frenchwoman called Mrs Gilmour who had left her English husband behind in Singapore, that she should embroider some forget-me-nots on one of the endless succession of white oblongs. 'Thistles might be better,' Mrs Gilmour replied with some venom. The notion of some such sabotage, it was whispered, was taken even further, with a number of women placing pins inside the hems and concealing them with neat, ladylike stitching.

The workroom was in the city, a lorry collecting the women early each morning and returning them in the evening. Sometimes they were given a little bread as a bonus, which they took home and shared with the rest. Another gleaning from this contact with the world outside the suburb was a host of rumours, which anyway circulated in riotous profusion among the prisoners. The crop from without had a particular edge because the longing to know what was going on among the rest of humanity was intense and, merely by being imported, a story assumed a degree of credibility that the home-grown variety could not match. The local population, of course, had access to the Japanese-run radio, and although Japanese propaganda was exceptionally wild, a broadcast rumour somehow seemed to have more dignity than one delivered from the corner of someone's mouth.

One tale which a number of the locals carried was that Singapore had been razed to the ground and that no white person had been left alive. It was just possible that this could be so, especially to those who had last looked back at that livid scene so much like a funeral pyre and were still tormented by the thought that they had left loved ones behind. Besides Norah Chambers and John there was one other married couple, Andrew and Marguerite Carruthers, living in the household to which Norah's sister Ena belonged, and this brought home to her agonizingly the fact that she had no means of knowing whether her own husband Kenneth, from whom she had parted on the dockside, was alive or dead. (Andrew Carruthers, as it happened, a lively young announcer with the Malayan Broadcasting Company, had been obliged to pass over the radio in the colony a great deal of the optimistic propaganda which had done so much to make such severances inevitable.)

The same kind of misery assailed Molly Ismail, who was sharing a room with her mother and a friend of theirs from Singapore, an Austrian lady called Claire Sammy. Their anxiety was about her father, of whom she was presently to be further reminded in a most sinister way. Molly was still carrying shrapnel in her head from the bombing of the *Giang Bee*, and was also suffering from another legacy, a persistent visitation of nightmares about the ship's terrible end. The frayed state of her nerves and, probably, the exceptional tranquillity of her young life in Johore Bahru, made the worst of Bukit Besar impinge on her, marring the small virtues that the move had brought. The overcrowding grated continually and the squabbles that for some were a valuable escape-valve, a flare-up that released innumerable tensions, were to her a source of misery. Several large families formed little power blocs in arguments over the distribution of rations or the apportioning of jobs around the houses. In Molly's group there was an Irish family, a mother with two sons and two daughters, all with a fiery temperament, and the mother would challenge anybody on behalf of her brood.

Amiable Molly, so many years later, still felt uncomfortable about her lapse from equability in Bukit Besar: 'What a responsibility she had! She *had* to fight for her family to survive . . .'

The Liddelow sisters had a curious situation to face in terms of family unity. A Dutch-Indonesian among the local people who helped the captives wanted to offer a home to Phyllis, to adopt her in effect, because she reminded him of a niece who had been killed. Phyllis insisted that Doris would have to come too and the idea foundered, but this was anyway a piece of remarkably mature diplomacy because the girls felt that their fate, for better or worse, lay with the women: that they belonged in the society of their upbringing and would share their travail. Later, when conditions were much harder, a Japanese official who became aware of their mixed parentage asked them if they would like to be repatriated to Thailand, but they stuck by their first decision.

In Bukit Besar the Japanese were beginning to take an interest in the women that was anything but paternal. The indifference or savagery with which they were greeted on the beaches of Banka had been replaced by what was evidently a growing curiosity born, perhaps, of the fact that the invaders too were enjoying a respite from action in conquered Palembang.

The guards moved freely among the houses, like over-zealous landlords, and rode roughshod over privacy. Once, when an Australian nurse was standing nude in the washroom, a Japanese walked in, peered at her for a few moments then laughed loudly and walked out again, leaving her torn between relief and vaguely affronted vanity. They would appear abruptly at windows and leer encouragingly if there was anything intimate to be seen, their Grecian detachment about their own bodies and functions seemingly not extending to other people's. And, indeed, there must have been a fascination in observing the nakedness of these female beings so remote and mysterious to a peasant soldier from Japan.

For Molly Ismail there was an encounter rather more explicit. A badly poisoned foot was added to the wounds in her head, the combination being sufficiently serious to earn a visit to the hospital, where the shrapnel was finally removed. On the return journey to the houses the lorry which functioned as an ambulance stopped at a large bungalow, on the verandah of which were a number of Japanese officers. The women were ordered into the building and, once inside, Molly was singled out by an officer and told to accompany him to another room.

He was a fierce-looking man with a single eye, unusually tall for a Japanese and wearing the inevitable sword. He was so alarming in appearance, in fact, that another woman volunteered to go with her. Once in the room the Japanese went behind his desk and shuffled a sheaf of papers in the official manner, then asked Molly for her name. When she gave it he said, 'Yes. Your father is a barrister and you lived in Johore Bahru.' He provided some more details. There was a little school which Molly had organized at home for the young children of Europeans and he showed interest in that. There was then a pause which seemed to be a prelude to something important, and Molly could only think that in some way her father was involved. 'Can you dance?' the Japanese said suddenly. An instinct made Molly say that she could not, even though she could, rather well, and that ended an interview which felt as if it had gone on for hours. When the women were put back on the lorry Molly found that she was the only one who had been questioned, which was deeply uncomfortable, but now, to stretch the tension even further, the one-eyed Japanese emerged from the bungalow and got into a limousine with a soldier at the wheel. When the lorry started on its journey back to the houses the car followed.

The lorry stopped, its tailboard was dropped for the women to jump down, and as Molly was poised to do so the tall Japanese suddenly appeared and held out his arms to catch her. 'I froze,' Molly said, 'I simply couldn't bring myself to move,' and it was in that moment of acute embarrassment that one of the young sons of the rowdy Irish family stepped forward, with considerable courage and sensitivity, and helped her down instead.

This curiously callow attempt at courtship by a senior Japanese officer with the power of life or death over the women was part of a kind of crablike approach to a matter which was clearly becoming increasingly important in the captors' minds. After the preliminary skirmishing in and around the houses the notion must have flourished that here, among the other valuable resources that were by-products of the conquest, was a fruitful and securely anchored source of physical gratification. Sex, in short.

That the possibility should have taken so long to dawn is probably more remarkable than the fact that it did, but its progress from the vague to the specific was no less disturbing. Already there were a number of women who would disappear with Japanese and return with money and food. The upending of a big city and the pouring out of its contents had brought, besides the elite, the other elements of a metropolis to cohabit in this strange society. Girls like the 'hostesses' who catered for servicemen in the dance-halls of Singapore had no great inducement to be stoical in adversity. Having brought a kind of profession to the camps it must have seemed logical to pursue it, much as the nurses automatically continued theirs.

The respectable, amid so much that was quite unlike their normal world, did not dwell much on the activities of those who exchanged themselves for comfort. The collaborators became known in the camps as 'free women', an ironic double entendre which expressed both the privileges of co-operation with the captors and the moral connotation, but in such general adversity the strong condemnation of others was already a luxury that few indulged in. The free women got on with their kind of life and the rest did likewise.

At Bukit Besar, however, the Japanese blurred this distinction and there now began an episode which combined high farce with discomfort and danger, adding a whole new element to the experience. Whether by instinct or via a tactical conference of military exactitude the conquerors must have divined that the haughtier element among the strange parcel of women they had inherited required a different approach.

The first manoeuvre was to order the Australian nurses out of their secluded quarters and to announce that these two houses would now become an officers' club. At the same time canvassing began among the women for those who would be willing to 'entertain' the officers in their leisure hours. A Mrs Chan, in fact an Englishwoman married to a Singapore Chinese, conducted this operation. She was a tall, statuesque brunette with a loud voice who could scarcely have been less suitable for such a delicate mission. As she moved among the houses she had something of the effect of a wolf in a dovecote. The missionary ladies were particularly anxious about this development and tried to hide the more attractive young women in the washrooms during a visitation. Shelagh Brown was one of these and she found their tremulous response annoying: 'I felt I could fight my own battles.' She and another spirited young lady in her house enquired, out of both defiance and morbid curiosity, about the precise rate for entertaining. It turned out to be one dollar per attendance, in Japanese military currency, thirty cents to go to Mrs Chan as commission.

This precision seemed to take care of any lingering possibility that the Japanese envisaged a sort of geisha role for women at the club, a matter of the tea ceremony and flower arranging in the Japanese manner. More explicitly still the Japanese now commanded the Australians to clean up another pair of houses on the far side of the suburb. The purpose of these was so apparent that the nurses promptly christened the area Lavender Street, after a well known thoroughfare in the red light district of Singapore.

Disagreeable as it was to be turned into charwomen, an even less appealing role now awaited the nurses. Following the poor results of Mrs Chan's campaign among the varied contents of the other houses, the Japanese simply ordered them to provide twelve of their number to report to the club on its opening night, a classically military solution to an intractable problem. At this point even the gallows humour that had sustained the Aussies through most of their trials could not hold the misery and dread at bay. They held a council of war and decided that safety, if anywhere, would lie in numbers. Rather than select their martyrs they would all go.

It still remained for each to consider alone how she could cope with this appalling new development. Mavis Hannah, with her brisk practicality, came to a conclusion: 'I wasn't going to fight because I knew I didn't have the strength. I thought, "If this is to be, it's to be", but I would never let it hurt the real me.' Betty Jeffrey remembered a girl who made up her mind that she would select the least repulsive Japanese and concentrate her energies on him. But to delay, or hopefully deflect entirely, the Japanese intention, they all now set about putting their femininity into reverse and, much as they might have competed in cosmetic skills before some social evening in the colony, they now vied with each other in making their appearances as unappetizing as possible. Those who had remnants of the slightly severe AANS uniform put them on. Those whose wardrobes had been reduced by shipwreck to a potentially fetching scantiness borrowed anything that fitted nowhere. Footwear seemed to lend a usefully unattractive element and the houses provided men's hobnail boots, plimsolls, and even a pair of Wellingtons. Some decided to go barefoot and smear their feet with dirt and, at the other extreme, they tangled their hair into messy beehives or dragged it back into schoolma'm fashion. There was one girl so incurably pretty that the more she tried to subdue her curly hair, the better she looked.

All thirty-two set off for the club at the appointed hour in a dreary straggle that was by no means an artifice. The only shred of comfort was that two English male prisoners had volunteered to act as waiters, one in each house, to keep an eye on the girls, but this was no more than a pyschological prop to do with ingrained beliefs in masculine protectiveness. Once again, the men were effectively as helpless as the women themselves.

In fact the evening was to develop in a way that nobody could quite have visualized: at once lurid and quaintly respectable as if the hosts had garnered their notions of the seduction of young ladies from some faded Victorian handbook, imperfectly understood. The device of descending *en masse* was immediately valuable because there were only six officers, two in one house and four in the other, and they could have no way of telling whether this large attendance showed enthusiasm or the opposite.

There was liquor, served with biscuits by the waiters, and on the tables sugar and little cakes. The attempt at conversation was hideously lamed by the barrier of language and the nurses' determined failure to comprehend, even when they did. They refused the liquor and the Japanese, perhaps mentally cursing the handbook, struggled to enquire what, then, Australian girls drank. 'Milk,' they answered straight-faced. A compromise was reached with soft drinks. The Japs were distressed that Australian abstemiousness extended to make-up, although that could be explicable in a desert of shortages of every kind. Would they like to go into the city to get some cosmetics? No, they would not. In the longueurs of this conversation the nurses took every opportunity to steal the cakes and the sugar in case this Mad Hatter's Tea-party should ever end.

The near-insupportable tension on the nurses' side, since at any moment the creaking attempt at charm on the part of the Japanese could have turned into snarling savagery, may also have existed in their hosts for different reasons, but if it did it evinced itself as a growing boredom and after two hours the visitors to one of the houses were dismissed.

In the other house, where there were four officers, much the same pantomime was enacted to the same conclusion except that four of the girls were told to remain. One of them was Mavis Hannah and she now faced the reality of the scenario she had put together before this episode had begun. It was not at all as she had visualized the denouement. The officer who had selected her as his quarry took her outside and began to lead her inexorably towards Lavender Street.

He was so small that he only came up to Mavis's shoulder and she remembered him as if he were in caricature: thick glasses, little cap, big boots, the inevitable outsize sword. When they reached the house he had selected in Lavender Street Mavis refused to turn towards the doorway: 'We walked on and got further and further away from the place and I thought, "This is rather ridiculous. I don't know where I am and I'm frightened", so I stopped in the middle of the road. He put his arms round me and kissed me on the cheek and he said, "I love 'oo, I love 'oo".' Mavis mimicked his attempt at English as if this particular grotesquerie was indelible. What happened next was at once more daft and dangerous than any other moment in her life. She pushed the armed conqueror and he sat down in the road, his glasses falling off and his sword clattering on the stones. 'I thought,' said Mavis, 'My God, he'll kill me.' She meant it literally. As the Jap scrambled up, grabbing for his glasses and straightening his cap, she instinctively turned towards the lights of the houses, expecting the rush of his boots behind her and the descent of his razor-sharp sword on her neck. Instead he followed her meekly and ten minutes later she was back with her friends.

It was both the first and last evening at the club in Bukit Besar. There was a former representative of the Red Cross in Palembang, a tirelessly helpful Dutchman called Dr Hollweg who, although he now had no official standing with the conquerors, constantly nagged them until he too was imprisoned, and he got word of the club to the civilian Japanese Resident already installed in Palembang. Relations between the armed forces and their civilian counterparts were never cordial. Some knuckles must have been rapped among the military because the débâcle was followed by every sign of frustration and anger among the officers.

They slammed the doors of the houses, banged the shutters, tore down notices from the walls and slapped the faces of the guards with greater regularity than even normal Japanese discipline seemed to demand. Rations to the camp were cut and those of the nurses stopped altogether for days on end so that they were reduced to eating tapioca root from a plant in the backyard of one of their houses.

It was a reaction as ridiculous and inconclusive in its way as the episode which brought it about, except that for women in so helpless a plight, none of it could be seen in perspective. The charm of absurdity, like so much else, could not survive for long in an environment dominated by such capricious masters. It was an abyss of humiliation which had been avoided for the moment but could open again at any time these strange and most foreign of men might choose.

Even the jaunty and resilient Australians suffered an aftermath that perhaps can only be fully understood by those who were there. 'I really think,' said Betty Jeffrey, looking back on this clumsy village wooing, 'that the mental strain was far worse than being bombed or ship-wrecked.' 'For two weeks after,' wrote the normally irrepressible Elizabeth Simons, 'we were under enormous tension. Any sound, at night especially, set our hearts pounding.'

It was two weeks later that the dwellers in the houses were roused at dawn and given half an hour to collect their goods and assemble at the *padang*, an open space a mile away. Yet another mysterious migration was clearly in prospect but it was greeted this time with relief as much as foreboding.

Chapter 7

It is not possible to say to what extent the events of Lavender Street affected the conducting of the move from Bukit Besar, or even if they brought it about in the first place, but the incident bore all the signs of rancour. The dawn start and the urgent hectoring of the guards caused a confusion in which painfully acquired remnants of food and possessions got left behind. Too late, Shelagh Brown remembered a whole duck still hanging behind the door of Number 5.

In the event, having reached the *padang*, the prisoners were made to wait right through the morning as the sun climbed higher and beat down on them while they stood, many of them bare-headed, in the scorching heat, and endured repeated countings by that Japanese method which never seemed to produce a total. The guards, either responding to some vindictive order or merely expediting a further ramification of the slowly evolving rules for the management of prisoners, conducted a search for sharp instruments: knives, scissors and the like. Some also took jewelry and watches from those still not sufficiently attuned to the new life to hide them. Mrs Ismail had shown resource. In the houses she had made up a purse attached to a long tape and, when the move came, she put the diamond ring which Molly and her fiancé had defied an air-raid to buy in the Orchard Road, her own rings and both their watches inside and tied the purse round her waist beneath her skirt.

For those deprived still further of their worldly goods, there now came an addition to the throng that was to underline their lack and would continue to do so for a long time to come. The Dutch had at last been rounded up and they walked into captivity in a comparative state of affluence. On their home ground, and with time to consider what might be involved in an imprisonment, they had been able to prepare themselves and arrived bearing treasures of unimaginable value: real pots and pans, bedding, sewing machines, typewriters. They were properly clothed, had their own shoes on their feet, hats, sunshades. As a final touch a large Dutch lady came with a small dog on a lead, the dog looking grumpy as if unwilling to join this disreputable company.

It was impossible for the survivors of Malaya not to feel a pang, however unreasonable it was to gaze sideways at the seeming good fortune of the new arrivals. Nobody, however, was prepared for a fresh deprivation which, at 2pm, was visited on everyone. Without warning the guards moved, snarling and prodding with their bayonets, into the crowd, separating the men from the women and forming them into a column which was marched away as soon as it was assembled.

The shock, to the women, was almost insupportable. 'The suddenness of it made you feel a kind of blind panic,' said Marguerite Carruthers. 'There was no time to assimilate what was happening, even to divide possessions.' With a mindless urge to press something on her husband before he was gone, she gave Andrew a tiny bottle of brandy she had treasured. The goodbyes were brutally brief, a scene of terrible anguish as fathers were torn away from children, husbands from wives, brothers from sisters: a repetition of the partings on the docks of Singapore, except that this time the hazards were even more diverse. Nobody knew what fate the Japanese proposed for the men as they marched them away, but nobody could now believe that it would be in any way benevolent.

A numbness settled on those left behind, even the women who were already alone, because the presence of men had been of high importance psychologically, some kind of inwardly understood protection against the violent potential of the Japanese even if, in practice, they had no means of defence against their weapons. The men had not taken easily to imprisonment. Back in the Muntok coolie barracks Phyllis Briggs, surrounded by some 750 servicemen after the departure of the main body of her fellow-captives, had been aware of the deep gloom among them and their incessant grumbling about the rations.

The women had responded to the adversity with more resilience, although this may have been due to the novelty of the experience, the absence of a subconscious conditioning to wartime imprisonment of a kind that men possibly inherit along with their duty to fight. It is also true that, by the nature of their role at that time, the women had much less of a distance to fall than the almighty *tuans*, the military custodians of an invincible fortress, all of whom had failed to accomplish what was expected of them. If Margaret Dryburgh, Presbyterian missionary, felt 'a blow to our national pride', the men of the Empire certainly suffered accordingly. One day, Phyllis remembered, a Japanese officer rode on a horse through the squalor of the coolie barracks, looking disdainfully about him, and she sensed the misery and humiliation of the men around her.

At the *padang* there was no opportunity to dwell on such matters. During the morning rumours had abounded. 'A sea voyage was planned which explained why no time had been allowed to gather belongings. The British had recaptured Banka Island and it was now a matter of awaiting their arrival in Palembang or being taken deeper into the interior.' In the event, when the Japanese came, snapping and nudging like sheepdogs to move the women, they marched for no more than a mile, finally up yet another hill, to a place very similar to Bukit Besar.

In another not unpleasant Dutch residential suburb there were fourteen bungalows arranged in two adjoining streets and they seemed to be new. When the guards gained entrance by smashing the locks with their rifle-butts the women saw that they were probably intended to house three or four people each. Somehow they would now have to accommodate some four hundred between them. They were devoid of furniture so that feet echoed on the tiled floors, and the water and electricity supplies were disconnected.

But even with these defects the bungalows were to seem attractive to the Browns who, once again, had some difficulties in getting housed. Mrs Brown was late arriving and, as Shelagh helped her over the last lap, the bungalows filled and there was nothing left for them but a bare garage into which fifteen British women eventually packed. The Browns actually thought back wistfully to their previous quarters. 'We could see Number 5 and the duck hanging up,' Shelagh said, 'not to mention the flour, rice, soya bean sauce and our utensils.'

Here there was no stove, no fuel, no beds and, more important, no food after a day without eating but, once again, the Australian nurses rallied and when some rice arrived at midnight they acquired water, smashed up the back door of one of the two houses they had moved into for use as firewood, borrowed a match from a guard and began to cook. Their only vessel was a Mobiloil tin which they emptied of a horrid mixture of ancient oil and spiders' webs so that the rice tasted most pungently of its former contents, but they delivered a meal for which Shelagh and Mrs Brown were certainly very grateful.

Entirely by coincidence Betty Jeffrey made her return to the bungalows exactly thirty-seven years after that memorable moving day, which was 1 April 1942. The suburb was still intact, although, with the Dutch long gone, it was now the home of Indonesian families. Betty found the very bungalow that she had shared with twenty-four people and its present occupants, an Indonesian couple and their child, stood aside polite but puzzled as she examined the place in the absorbed manner of a house-buyer. She tapped the walls because, in the seventeen months that the prisoners had spent there, the endless quest for space or privacy had led some to knock partitions down and some to

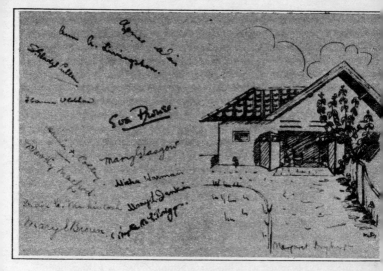

A Margaret Dryburgh birthday card for Shelagh Brown, signed by the other
occupants of Garage 9

create more. She swung the back door on its hinges to see what kind of
job had been made of replacing the one that had gone for firewood. The
bathroom remained exactly as it had been before, the simple stone *tong*,
a powerful reminder to Betty of those days when some Japanese guard
would come wandering in with his rifle and bayonet on his shoulder to
observe the women as they bathed.

On that first night in the bungalows the prisoners slept on the cold tiled
floors, using anything that would serve as a pillow. Some of the
shipwreck survivors had kept their lifejackets, the residue of a phobia
that sometime, somewhere in this extraordinary experience they might
be cast into the water again, and they laid their heads on those.

The garage dwellers were not even as comfortable as this, lying on a
dirty cement floor and with no toilet except a hole in the ground outside.
They mentioned this to the Japanese who said, 'Nanti, nanti' – everybody would be moving away in two days' time. Instead barbed wire
entanglements were set up around the suburb and a guardhouse was
organized. Besides these signs of permanence the women now had a
postal address. The main road was rather prettily named Irenelaan
and, for official purposes, the suburb was now The Womens' Intern-

ment Camp, Palembang. Not that either of these facts seemed of great significance when, as far as anybody there was aware, their existence was either unknown or a matter of supreme unimportance to the outside world.

It was clear, however, that the camp was the centre of the weird universe of women in southern Sumatra. Those left behind in Muntok were now called in and arrived with fresh tales of even more bizarre hardship. Margot Turner had been detained there, not as a nurse but a patient, because her days on the raft had left her with what was diagnosed, possibly in the absence of any comparable condition, as 'sea-water boils' – huge, red, intensely painful swellings all over her legs. The Scottish doctor among the men at Muntok was sufficiently alarmed by her condition to decide that they would have to be lanced if she was to stay alive, and he went about it with the only scalpel available, which was blunt, and with no anaesthetic. The operation sapped Margot's remaining strength so severely that when she was shipped to Palembang she rated a place in the Charitas hospital and was kept there for a month.

Phyllis Briggs had a story of the continuing peculiarity of the captors. Muntok was plagued with flies, in addition to its other shortcomings, and the Japanese decided that their numbers would be diminished substantially if the prisoners caught fifty each, their corpses to be delivered to the guardhouse. Phyllis, in a rare moment of good fortune, found a pile of dead ones behind a door, which almost met her quota. This was a considerable bonus because Phyllis felt deathly from a mysterious fever, perhaps an early onset of that ruthless killer of the women when they returned to Muntok.

There was another story of how the Japanese libido had exerted itself in even more repugnant circumstances. An order had been put in for six of the best-looking women to be provided three days hence, the euphemism this time being that they were to serve at table in the officers' mess. The move to Palembang had come before the three days had elapsed.

The sexual motif, of which this was a further example, was disturbing not least because, in the ugliest fashion, it might give some kind of logic to the otherwise erratic behaviour of the Japanese. Daily, in both its restraint and its excesses, there was a possibility that all could be explained as a cat-and-mouse game of the kind which, at that time, was widely played between the sexes even in their normal exchanges. If the men found their masculinity affronted by imprisonment, it was femininity which found itself degraded here.

Almost every variation on the female species made its way to the camp where, eventually, it was computed that no less than twenty-seven nationalities were represented. Presently there was a fresh influx which added its own particular flavour to the mélange: twenty-five Dutch nuns, headed by their Mother Superior. It was in this group that Sister Catherinia made her appearance in the saga.

These were teaching nuns of the Dutch Order of St Borromeus who had come out from Holland to set up a school at Lahat on the western side of Sumatra, and they had managed to iron out the strangeness of a notably unfamiliar country and impose their conception of a useful and suitably disciplined life. In four years they had built a convent, a guest-house and a boarding school for four hundred pupils which had come to have a high reputation for learning.

Catherinia herself had come to Sumatra in 1936, having just taken her vows, and a photograph of her taken in 1932 on the occasion of what was known as her 'solemn promise' showed her to be an attractive and lively girl, not at all subdued by her newly acquired nun's habit. It was possible to imagine, even meeting her so many years later, that she would have put a lot of zest into setting up a High School for young ladies on a jungle-ridden island in the South China Sea.

When the Imperial Army reached Singapore it was deemed wise to evacuate the pupils, but the nuns stayed. It was only when Palembang fell that they were ordered to evacuate, too, but in the enduring muddle that everywhere preceded the Japanese advance, it was not made clear exactly where they should go. Their wanderings constituted a small unworldly saga in themselves! They left the school with suitable meekness, taking the minimum of personal necessities and leaving everything there open for a greater authority to decide what its fate might be. The railway station at Lahat seemed at least a commonsensical starting-point for a journey to nowhere in particular, and they were perhaps divinely guided to the extent that they caught the very last train, consisting of open coal-trucks. At every small halt the train stopped and the railwaymen got down and smashed up the station. Sister Catherinia's English, though imperfect, was often telling in its brevity. Of this exceptionally nihilistic progress in the coal-trucks she said, 'It was raining and desolate and nobody knew what was going to be next.'

Some direction at least was injected by the fact that at Loebok Linggau, a remote place which one day was to mark the very nadir of desolation to all the women, the train could go no further, and the nuns took a bus to Benkulen, where there was a convent of their Order. At Benkulen the nuns in residence were so totally unacquainted with the situation in the world outside that after a few days the Mother Superior, Mother Laurentia, decided to consider a reconnaissance. She took five nuns, including Catherinia, but when they failed to establish a more rewarding direction to pursue, she led them back to Lahat again. This was an even more taxing journey, lacking a train this time. At a mountain village before Lahat they were warned that it was too dangerous to continue and they stayed there for a month, receiving the kind of unquestioning hospitality that nuns are sometimes offered in return for dispensing it so often themselves. This passage ended when the Japanese, having established themselves firmly in western Sumatra in the meantime, scoured the mountains for aliens, rounded them up and took them to Benkulen. It was as a staging post on their way to their final imprisonment that the sisters actually reached Lahat and were allowed briefly to return to the school. There they found that the Japanese had taken everything of value that they needed and burnt the rest. Catherinia was dearly tempted to elaborate the destruction of those years of work, but checked herself sharply. 'Never mind that!' she said, chiding herself, not her listener.

It now remained to be seen how these singular women would fit into the *modus vivendi* of the camp at Palembang, although in terms of poverty and the mortification of the flesh it had much in common with the more extreme rigours of the religious life. Humility was certainly insisted upon. The meat ration, if there was one, was hurled off the back of a truck into the roadway at the entrance to the camp, and ladies who had been fastidious even about buying from Chinese foodstalls in Singapore had to watch a horde of native dogs tear at it because they were not allowed to drive them away.

This was the privilege of the Japanese, one of whom would emerge from the guardhouse in a leisurely fashion, put his boot on the hunk of meat to hold it still and give a purchase on its toughness, then with his knife, or sometimes a sword, he would hack off lumps and throw them on a separate pile. This was not to be touched until he gave the word. The whole performance had, again, the air of the feeding of animals, which some people accomplish as though a little contemptuous of the creatures' slobbering anxiety.

Eating habits, among powerfully differing cultures, seem invariably to arouse a profound reaction on one side or the other and red meat may have revolted the Japanese in the same way that the Japanese predilection for raw fish is unbearable to many Westerners, but this ritual always appeared to be designed principally for the purposes of humiliation. Betty Jeffrey, who remembered it in detail and could even point to the spot in Irenelaan where it was conducted, also recalled that it was all for a portion, usually of wild pig, which would not cover the palm of a hand – this to be shared, in the case of her bungalow, between twenty-four people. The discovery of a fragment of pork in one of the endless stews became a moment of genuine excitement.

It was also very early in the history of this camp that the Japanese introduced a feature always regarded by the military mind as being an integral part of proper discipline: the parade. Shortly after the arrival at Irenelaan the women were rousted from their unyielding beds and bullied outside into two ranks, in the approved fashion, house by house as if each were a barrack block. There they were inspected by a guard who could not have helped but be appalled by the standard of turn-out. They were also counted with great deliberation, the forerunner of a further ritual that was to remain a thorn in their lives for years to come.

The first emergence of the practice proved to be the prelude to the arrival of a Japanese General, come to examine this exotic fruit of the conquest at first hand. At his passing all were to deliver an especially low bow, a type of salaam, bending right down from the waist, which they were now obliged to rehearse, their muffled mirth being briskly checked by a savage outbreak of snarling and snapping. A representative of each bungalow was to call a greeting, 'Kiri', politely to the General as he processed, and this caused a little difficulty as no formal hierarchy existed at this stage. The denizens of the Browns' garage – Garage 9 – a fascinating group which now included Phyllis Briggs, the newly orphaned little Mischa, the Russian boy, and the four missionaries, put forward one of these, Miss Cullen, chiefly because she had become the head cook.

This kind of makeshift organization clearly could not continue now the barbed wire gave such a grim air of permanence to the imprisonment. Even if there were to be a repatriation, the thought of which sustained everyone even when the possibility became utterly remote, it was evidently not going to happen very quickly. It was apparent that some sort of structure should exist to present a united front to the Japanese.

The women were now forced to face squarely a central fact of the female condition at that time. Among the men taken prisoner there were natural rallying points based on eminence acquired before the blow fell: Bishops, Generals, senior administrators, panjandrums of the business community of a thriving colony, a ready-made infrastructure of the kind that has developed historically in the world of men.

The women were the product of an era that gave little of high importance voluntarily to females and tended to make no more than interesting oddities of those who insisted on power or influence. In the camps there were women with a ready-made status inherited from the life which preceded the Fall but it was mainly based on class or money or the reflected glory of an important husband: in one way or another, secondhand. Here that was not sufficient. Respect seemed to be accorded most naturally to those women who had shown some independence of mind.

In this regard the military nurses had already made their mark, much helped by their strong *esprit de corps*, although that could be seen, then, as the borrowing of a male code of conduct. All nurses, since they possessed a professional skill, had a certain status. The lady missionaries were demonstrably willing, even eager, to accept responsibility, but theirs was a curious calling, inevitably associated with the directing of poor and ignorant natives down paths which they might not entirely want to follow, and perhaps that was a little too close to the women's present situation. Nuns came into the same category, although a Mother Superior would be an honourable exception, the role having emerged from the otherwise largely mysterious world of nuns as one requiring practicality as well as dignity and even goodness. What is significant is that among this polyglot and divergent community there seemed to be an unspoken agreement that the dowagers of the colonies were not to rule again, at least as formerly, by a form of divine right. They would have to prove themselves just like everybody else in this cataclysmic levelling.

The instinctive processes involved in the tricky business of investing authority in anybody in a situation as fraught and unfamiliar as this drew many of the women towards a lady doctor as the most viable proposition. All doctors, in an environment where injury and illness were endemic, occupied a more than usually god-like position, but a female doctor, at that time, could justifiably be judged as having shown particular determination and intelligence, if only to remain in a profession so dominated by men.

As early as the coolie barracks a Scotswoman called Jean McDowall had exerted that curious magnetism which makes one person apparent among others as a leader. She was a diligent doctor who always carried a satchel about with her, filled with what medical paraphernalia she had been able to salvage, but there was clearly some other aura as well. 'A fine woman,' Norah Chambers said of her, and could clearly recall the curls piled on the top of her head. Her curls remained in the memories of other women there as if they were a symbol of optimism and unquenchability. She had a soft Highland voice and a calm, direct manner that was very effective with the Japanese.

It was Jean McDowall who enlisted the help of Dr Hollweg after the Lavender Street crisis, managing to convey the camp's deep concern in a comprehensible way to a man beset with what must have seemed more critical problems, and more or less by unspoken agreement she became the first Camp Commandant on the British side.

Her deputy, expressing the new democracy, emerged principally on force of personality alone. She was called Gertrude Hinch, although everyone spoke of her later as *Mrs* Hinch, as if it were a title denoting special respect, just as Margaret Dryburgh was nearly always *Miss* Dryburgh. Mrs Hinch was an American married to the English

Principal of an Anglo-Chinese Methodist school in Singapore, now an inmate of Changi, and she had spent twenty years in Malaya. It was largely her unshakeable serenity which distinguished her from the crowd. Addressed to the Japanese in the form of a calm and tolerant smile, even at the height of their angry ravings, it deflected them miraculously, and it is interesting that both she and Jean McDowall got results with the captors by methods that would probably have worked equally well with disturbed children.

As their spokeswoman the Dutch appointed Reverend Mother Laurentia soon after she arrived, not least, perhaps, because she embodied so many of the characteristics of fictional Mothers Superior. She was tall and held herself erect, was grave but kindly, and she, too, had a memorably enchanting smile. The common denominators among the three women who first emerged may have something to tell us about the way women select their representatives when they have no outside influences to affect the choice.

In the second echelon of leadership, a Captain was appointed among each of the groups delineated by their occupancy of the bungalows and garages. The pressures of this post, in the overcrowded dwellings, were so complex and intractable that the job was rotated, the sloppy and incompetent having to amend their ways as best they could when their turn came around and the domineering being obliged to cede their power before they became impossible. The experience, shared by so many there of English boarding-schools and their Prefects may have had its effect in bringing this arrangement about.

It was now possible to form a camp committee where some kind of consensus could be sought on the innumerable problems of an everyday life which, in these circumstances, conformed to that description only inasmuch as each painfully constructed day was followed inexorably by the next. Such government as the camp possessed was in fact presiding over a life that had been reduced to its most basic terms. Each morning brought the same preoccupations as those with which animals fill their day: the quest for food, the elementary grooming, the search for others of the same species, made rather more complicated by the fact that these were human beings who had once very successfully constructed a notably sophisticated existence.

Garage 9 – which contained such a wide cross-section of British women – was a case in point. Here there was a variety of skills and intelligences that were eventually to make it an important address in Irenelaan although Shelagh Brown's diary of a day in June 1942 conveys the bleak regimen of some nineteenth-century poorhouse.

Get up 6am. Chop firewood. Bath. Breakfast 8am: porridge and coffee.

Morning duties: sweep rooms and drains etc. Wash clothes. Fetch rations.
Pick rice and prepare veg. for lunch. Lunch 12.30pm. Wash up. If cooking
loaf, watch fire. Bath. Tea. Prepare veg. for supper. Supper 6.00pm.
Prayers 8.00pm. Porridge. Bed.

Contained in this terse resumé, however, there was such a range of
endeavours that the diary requires interpretation as if from another
language. The question of firewood, for example, apparent as a problem on the very first night in this camp, was to continue as such until the
end, coming to compete even with food as a major preoccupation. The
camp actually began to consume itself in its hunger for wood. More
doors followed the first one, and the scraps of furniture that existed were
whittled down as if they were succumbing gradually to woodworm.
There was a child's cot in one of the Australian houses and a tiny nurse
slept in it at first, but later she sacrificed it bit by bit until only a side
piece was left on which she lay at night to keep herself off the floor
tiles.

One of Dr McDowall's early functions as Camp Commandant was to
approach the Japanese daily for more wood and eventually she succeeded, except that it arrived in unmanageable fifteen-foot lengths,
already badly charred, the roof-beams from bombed buildings in
Palembang. A fresh round of talks then had to begin to acquire two
blunt axes for the use of hundreds. The expression 'chop firewood'
masked the ceaseless effort of struggling with these blackened monsters,
like ants trying to carry off a beetle.

'Bath', another word which sounded grand, was merely a stand-up
splashing at the *tong* in bungalow Number 9, which meant competing
with the occupants there for space at the trough. Those whose sheltered
lives had left them unaccustomed to being naked in front of others took
a long time to develop what eventually became a total lack of inhibition,
although the heat of Sumatra in summer provided a powerful motiva-
tion. Palembang is only two degrees below the equator, and although
the winters brought incessant rain and cold nights the pervasive
recollection of the women was of a craving for long, leisurely bathing
and ice-cold drinks of the kind that contributed so much to the charm of
the colonial way of life.

The acquisition of water for these ablutions was another Herculean
labour. There was a single tap for the camp which was located,
inevitably, beyond the guardhouse because the Japanese had a shrewd
understanding of all the basic necessities and kept them in their hands
with peasant cunning. There was an endless queue for water that
might, under other circumstances, have been amusing to observe,
because the utensils for carrying it were so makeshift and inadequate. A

tin hat had survived among the military nurses and even that saw service as a bowl.

The breakfast 'porridge' was another survival of a familiar and comforting word, in surroundings that left only its previous association intact. In fact it was a rice gruel, and the morning coffee, with its suggestion of aroma and invigorating flavour, was rice again, burnt this time and with boiling water poured over it to produce a liquid the colour of coffee but with no other lineal connection. Once again the fundamental commodity was acquired only by prodigious effort. When Shelagh refers to 'picking' rice in her diary the inference is that it was freshly picked, as from the paddy, but in fact it was precisely the opposite: rice at its furthest extremity from its growing. In a hemisphere where rice was a staple food, consumed by billions, the women must have received the utter dregs that even the most poverty-stricken of the population would not have tolerated, literally the sweepings of the warehouse floor that had to be picked in the sense that rags are picked by paupers. In the rotting sacks of the discoloured stuff there was dust and grit and insect-life and even broken glass, so that it had to be disinterred from the debris literally grain by grain.

It required an especially dedicated, unselfish and painstaking person to pick the rice to a standard that reduced the possibility of severe intestinal damage without sacrificing any fragment that was edible. In Garage 9 Miss Dryburgh therefore graduated naturally to the job, or perhaps couldn't bear to see other enduring a task as terminally irritating, and she was assisted by Mrs Brown who had suffered a variety of setbacks ranging from carbuncles to dysentery and took on a contribution to community life that would actually benefit in a way from enforced immobility.

For those who were not so beset by physical disabilities there was a job so revolting that it had to precede any relationship to food, even among the ravenous. The 'drains etc.' in Shelagh's account of 'Morning Duties' was actually the management of the effluence of the hundreds of prisoners, a torrent that overwhelmed the septic tanks of the packed bungalows and caused them to seize up. Catharsis, so to speak, was achieved by manual intervention but then it was the open gullies that served as drains alongside the buildings, which baulked at the flow. The camp was situated on the top of a small hill, which should have helped its descent, but even gravity seemed to be dumbstruck by the volume of matter and it had to be helped along by the only suitable implement available, a large heavy native hoe called a *chungkal*. It was possible to become a heroine merely by persisting in this endeavour and in Garage 9 the small, attractive and vivacious Dorothy MacCleod, who was once again rooming with her friends the Browns, received special mention from two of the other ladies for her consistent devotion to the duty.

The washing of clothes after such an episode is self-explanatory, but here the hurdle was not only the shortage of water but the total absence of soap. Laundering consisted of no more than wetting clothing and leaving it out for the blazing sun to cauterize the dirt. The morning, as described by the diary, was still not yet over. 'Fetch rations', a simple-seeming chore, was in fact among the most demanding and disagreeable tasks of the day.

The vegetable truck was heralded by a smell of decay even before it reached the camp, and its contents, as with the meat, were merely tipped into the road: old Chinese cabbage, rotting green beans, and kangkong, or water-spinach, which, the women discovered, grew in the gutters and puddles of Palembang. Yet regardless of their paltry nature the arrival of the rations stirred powerful instincts among famished people. Tempers frayed more easily at the distribution point than anywhere else, and it required a magisterial figure of impeccable probity to preside over the apportioning of what, elsewhere, might be regarded as garbage so that no one got either more or less than their share.

Garage 9 provided just such a judicial eminence in another of the missionaries, Miss Livingstone. It was she who had tried to institute a late form of toilet-training in the coolie barracks for those unused to the Asian method. She had been thwarted in that ambition but now, equally unprompted, she took over the supervision of the food distribution. She was a tall, thin, bespectacled lady with a military bearing who invariably wore a pith-helmet, the standard headgear of missionaries in the Victorian era, and she was highly successful at governing the division of rations, mostly because nobody could conceive of her ever being unfair.

The civilized-sounding 'Lunch, 12.30pm' of the diary was the consumption of the unappetizing items already mentioned, and washing up was certainly not an elaborate operation in a community in which one member was still eating with a shoe-horn. Equally, the loaf of the afternoon's activities was by no means the delicious-smelling home-baked bread that might be imagined, but a concoction of more rice, this time pounded into flour, and mixed with coconut water. To cook the unsalted, unappealing dough which resulted, the fire had to be tended constantly and, indeed, 'fire-flapping', the attempt to keep the tired wood of the fuel ration alive, was consistently a major form of industry.

'Tea' was tea only in that it was a drink taken at the hour when tea, in that other life, was customarily enjoyed, and the evening prayers were the continuation of Miss Dryburgh's offer to any who wished to join her in her daily devotions.

THE SANCTUARY

Within the camp's confined domain
No great Cathedral reared its walls,
No pointing spire tried Heaven to gain,
No church bell sounded welcome calls,
Not e'en the smallest meeting place
Did offer us the means of grace.

A little company did dwell
Within a garage, scarce supplied
With furnishings of prison cell
So bare it was! Each eventide
They met for simple family prayers
To God commended their affairs.   M.D.

This, if it had no other appeal – and religious observance became sufficiently important for Garage 9 to be turned over every Sunday for use as a chapel – brought respite from a day otherwise dedicated entirely to grubbing, literally, for existence. It was a period in which, as the women struggled to come to terms with what had befallen them, their precise recollections were of singular incidents that made them raise their heads for a moment from the drudgery.

The bungalows, having acquired barbed wire to give them the appearance of a conventional POW camp, now rated a Commandant of the Japanese variety. His name was Miachi and the women noted unwillingly that he was rather handsome for a Japanese. He wore his hair in planter style, neatly brushed and with a parting, and he had a military moustache. There was a possibility that he might be an army officer of the recognizable type that all there understood, rather than another peasant soldier, mainly distinguished by the wearing of an ungainly sword, and this impression was increased by his command of English. He had lived in Singapore before the war and, perhaps by his exercise of the Japanese gift for imitation, was polite and solicitous when approached, furthering the remote chance that he was an Oriental version of those mannerly products of decent schools who had tended to run the British colonies. His greatest defect, and sadly this too may have been copied, was that having listened to representations from the inmates, with much nodding and taking of notes, he would then do absolutely nothing about the problem.

One day he bustled into the camp and supervised the distribution of some important-looking forms which had to be filled in by all, providing a comprehensive account of each prisoner: besides relevant details like names and ages and birthplaces there were spaces for details of cash and valuables and even a space for the nationality of the wife of each. Everybody was convinced that this must be the first stage towards repatriation, or at least an exchange of prisoners, but the forms disappeared into the mysterious maw of the Japanese administration and their true purpose never came to light.

Soon after, there was another visitation of notables which caused more buzzing activity among the guards. The Japanese arrived, much more impressive-looking than the ones the women were used to, and in exceptionally grand cars. The limousines drew up, providentially, shortly after the ration truck had shot its contents into the roadway, and the women were able to contrive the bursting of a sack of rotten beans so that these lay in the path of the visitors like a horrid green stain. A high-powered conference was held in the middle of the road with the Japanese casting glances at the stinking heap out of the corners of their eyes, and everyone hoped that they were properly shocked and would now amend the diet. But they got back into their shiny cars and everything remained exactly the same.

The notion that the Japanese were ineffectual little fellows, strong on pomposity but short-sighted, muddled and distinctly inferior, the stereotype which had caused them to be so dangerously underrated in the first place, did not survive because it was so constantly spiked by examples of their terrifying savagery. One night a shot rang out in the darkness and in the ensuing flurry of noisy activity among the captors it emerged that a sentry had shot and killed another Japanese who had been moving about the camp too stealthily. Even the kindest of the ladies found it difficult to feel as appalled as they might at the tragedy, but the incident restored the deadly threat of the ever-present rifles and bayonets and made stepping out of the bungalows at night a nerve-tingling experience.

If any further proof were needed that a devil lurked in even the most mild-seeming of the Japanese, their treatment of the natives was chilling in the extreme. A Malay caught trying to sell food at the wire was tied to a post by the gate in an excruciating way that made his every move a torment. He was left there for two days receiving, by way of attention, only off-handed kicks and clouts from the guards, and was then taken away to some unknown fate.

This public punishment, and there were to be more examples, engendered an atmosphere of brutality that lingered over everything, and there was now a new method by which the Japanese could impose themselves as masters of the women every day. This was the ritual of *tenko*, which came to be so called by the prisoners because it was the word shouted by the guards as they rampaged through the camp driving the women out to be counted. In addition to the early morning count there was often a *tenko* at noon, so that the women caught the full blast of the midday sun, and indeed at any hour one of its most objectionable aspects was its unpredictability. As soon as it was called everyone was obliged to drop what they were doing and hurry out into the roadway where the counting process would begin at the whim of the Japanese guards and continue endlessly until the total met the curious necessities of their mathematics.

It was a very personal imposition: a peasant-soldier could strut and posture as much as he pleased while the women wilted before him in the heat. Perhaps in subconscious counter to this arrogance some of the Dutch women drew on their comparative affluence to turn out for *tenko* looking their best, including a dash of lipstick but there was one guard, pursuing who knows what strange private phobia, who would grow infuriated at the sight of it and hit the offenders across the mouth.

Tenko was never a true contest between the fuming women and their oppressors, because the Japanese had the trump card in terms of humiliation. Before the count began the women had to bow. No single gesture could more graphically have expressed submission in the Western mind, and there were innumerable devices for lessening the sting. 'We would tell each other that we ought to do much more of it because it was so good for the figure,' Shelagh Brown said, still ruffled all those years later, but the bow was so bound up in the Japanese order of things that to refuse was to risk a tempest of wrath. Margot Turner, restored to health and back in the camp, described the bowing, as 'very irksome', which could be translated from her understated style as totally infuriating. Margot took the view, like the Australian nurses, that she was a military prisoner who should not have been placed with civilians anyway and one day, when the indignities felt unbearable, she failed to offer the bow. She was promptly punched in the face, hard enough to knock out one of her front teeth.

There were other, rather more subtle indications of who now held the whip hand. The women found themselves obliged to celebrate the Emperor's birthday – not the King-Emperor, who was the only one the British then considered the authentic Ruler of a proper Empire, but Hirohito, Divine to the Japanese as the direct descendant of the Sun-goddess, but to all others merely the shy little man in Tokyo. It was a bittersweet occasion because the Japanese, in their turn, had to find some way of marking the day and improved the rations to the remarkable tune of four prawns and a banana per prisoner, and a pineapple per house; the dividing of the latter into the tiny portions necessary being treated in the camp as an indication of this Emperor's standards of hospitality.

The Emperor's birthday, in terms of events that would stay forever in the memories of the women, was probably the nadir. At this stage the true dramas of the imprisonment were internalized: the struggle, now it was unmistakably apparent that they were all locked together in a variety and proximity that none, in their previous lives, could ever have imagined, was with demons other than the Japanese. Human nature had to adjust itself, and it was to prove that this vast collection of women were not miraculously free of the customary mixture of good and ill.

One significant tension initially was race, which not even a shared antipathy towards the Japanese could entirely eradicate. The complex distinctions which had set those of mixed blood apart in the society of the colonies could not be disregarded immediately.

The term Eurasian covered many permutations of intermarriage and accounted, in fact, for a high proportion of the twenty-seven nationalities represented in the camp. Besides the mixing of Malays and Chinese and Thais and Malaya-domiciled Indians with the major colonial interlopers of the area – the British, the Dutch and the Portuguese – there were exchanges of blood within these principal groupings. The complex distinctions were of interest, if not importance, to the owners of such family trees and, predictably, the mixing often produced people of striking appearance and temperament.

The generic description of all these people was Eurasian and this term placed them in a certain category, particularly in the arrangements of the British colony: not a submerged society, but certainly not the elite. For better or worse the two species co-existed in a not unbearable imbalance, much helped by the tacit agreement of the Eurasians to remain in the secondary position.

The Japanese had jammed these two elements together so suddenly and in such close proximity via the imprisonment that the readjustment was inevitably difficult. The situation was further complicated by the fact that, in such a profound upheaval, the Eurasians could no longer see any reason for leaving the *status quo* intact. Having shared bombing and shipwreck and capture on an equal footing, and observed the imperviousness of all three to social distinctions, they clearly decided that in this unique new environment their position was as valid as anybody else's.

As a result the Eurasians were often seen by others as noisy, assertive, over-sensitive to the possibility of unfair treatment, clannish and frequently unco-operative. From a more sympathetic viewpoint this meant that they were distinctly more extrovert than the British and Dutch; that they often failed to agree that a job like clearing drains was important and left it to those who did; and that they diverged generally from the English public school ethos laden with such codes as 'duty

Sister Catherinia in 1932.
The occasion: her
'Solemn Promise', the
taking of her vows
(courtesy Mr Liedmeier)

Norah Chambers in
Malaya before the war
*(courtesy
Norah Chambers)*

The Liddelow sisters, Phyllis and Doris *(courtesy Phyllis Liddelow)*

Presbyterian missionaries in Singapore before the Fall. All four *(l to r: Sabine Mackintosh, Gladys Cullen, Margaret Dryburgh, Ann Livingstone)* were to fall into Japanese hands *(courtesy Norah Chambers)*

Ena Murray in
pre-war Malaya
(courtesy Ena Murray)

Phyllis Briggs in a break
from hospital duty,
Penang 1939
(courtesy Phyllis Thom)

The Brown children,
Shelagh in the centre,
with their Chinese amah
Ah Chow *(courtesy
Shelagh Lea)*

A dance at the Seaview Hotel, Singapore. Molly Ismail *(2nd from r)* stands
with her parents *(courtesy Molly Smith)*

Colonial chic: Major Brown *(far left)*, Shelagh and Mrs Brown attend a police fête in Singapore in 1936 *(courtesy Shelagh Lea)*

Part of Singapore docks

Raffles Hotel, Singapore

Singapore Harbour before the Fall *(Popperfoto)*

The end of an 'impregnable fortress': Singapore reels under Japanese attack before the surrender in February 1942 *(Imperial War Museum)*

The last days of Singapore: the long-delayed evacuation of women and children gets underway *(Imperial War Museum)*

The evacuees still display the fatal optimism that contributed to the tragedy
(Imperial War Museum)

Flanked by senior officers of his staff, General Yamashita accepts
General Percival's surrender at 7pm on 15 February 1942 *(Imperial War Museum*

Squalid living conditions at Tjideng Camp, Batavia *(Imperial War Museum)*
No photographs were taken of the camps described in this book

Margaret Dryburgh's drawing of the Men's Camp, Palembang

A POW camp in Thailand which was very similar to the Men's Camp in Palembang, of which no photographs exist *(Imperial War Museum)*

Portrait of Mrs Brown in Irenelaan featuring her celebrated sun-shade hat, her dress made from a vicar's pyjamas, and a shipwrecked sailor's shoes

Dame Margot Turner in 1979, outside the cell in Palembang Jail where she spent the longest six months of her life *(courtesy Lavinia Warner)*

Lavinia Warner with Dame Margot Turner and Betty Jeffrey in Palembang Cemetery in 1979 *(courtesy Carol Akillian)*

Margaret Dryburgh's drawing of the kitchen in the Women's Camp at Muntok

Sister Catherinia in 19?? revisiting the well in the camp at Muntok, the only surviving landmark *(courtesy Lavinia Warner)*

Communal life continued after the Japanese surrender. These women were photographed in their camp in Java just before repatriation, when the Allies had brought in renewed supplies *(Imperial War Museum)*

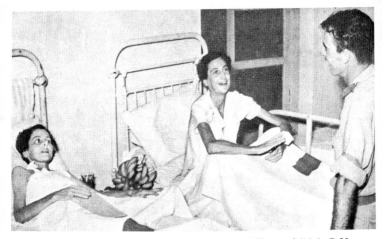

A cheery visitor for Sisters Jenny Greer and Betty Jeffrey at 2/14 A.G.H., Singapore *(Netherland Indies Government Information)*

The Reid family reunited in 1946 (*standing, l to r:* Dirk, Jane and James; *seated:* Mr and Mrs Reid with Roy) *(courtesy Jane Elgey)*

Reunion in the grounds of Charitas Hospital, Palembang, 1979: Betty Jeffrey and Dame Margot Turner sing 'The Captives' Hymn' with the surviving nuns and Sister Catherinia *(3rd from r) (courtesy Lavinia Warner)*

Dame Margot Turner with Netta Smith

With Christine Cleveley

With Jennie Taylor

With Mavis Allgrove, Jenny Pemberton and Maudie James

done' and 'pulling your weight'. When rations were apportioned they made quite sure that all that was due to them became theirs and, family-orientated, usually arrived in numbers to state their case. At close quarters, in fact, they were visibly a separate strain from the colonials, which of course they had been encouraged to be in the first place. Some of the most notable abrasions arose from those small differences of behaviour which seem to become so grossly inflated when separate cultures first become neighbours.

Prisoners were still arriving in the camp and seven very dark-skinned indigenous Malays, three women and four children, were squeezed into one of the now impeccably organized houses of the Australian nurses. The Malays had scabies and fleas and turned the backyard into a compound where they did their cooking, pausing occasionally to relieve themselves in the freshly scoured drains, but what seemed to impinge most as an expression of their alien ways was that they peeled their vegetables by moving the knife away from themselves, rather than towards in the Western manner.

The other Australian house had inherited the fiery and combative Irish family, which brought more familiar divergences of conduct and, apart from the problems of the minorities there were certain strains between the larger national groups. The Dutch – and indeed the Eurasians – brought up with a belief in Great Britain's invincibility in the Far East and schooled to accept that the impregnable naval base of Singapore guaranteed the security of all the European colonies in that hemisphere felt betrayed by the incredibly swift collapse in Malaya. It was clearly somebody's fault that women and children had ended up in squalor and to all appearances abandoned by the world. The events that had precipitated this disaster had not been in the hands of the women, but as the only available representatives of the fallen Power the British in the camp had to bear the resentment.

The opportunity was there, perhaps, for all the women to combine in their condemnation of men and their high-handed ordering of the globe on both sides of the conflict, but it was not a time when women thought in that way. The outside world's way exerted itself at another level, even in this peculiar environment, because the Dutch were so notice-ably better off than the rest. Later on, when living or dying became the currency, even a fortune could not stave off disease but at this stage the penniless felt their position very keenly.

The Dutch were almost invariably generous to those in need, but they were giving, frequently, to women who had never known poverty and to whom charity was a matter of donation, not of receipt. It was reasonable, perhaps even graceful, for the Dutch to exchange money for labour, and those who went to work for them were grateful that there was a source of earnings, but first there was a psychological barrier to overcome.

Some time later, when the intense hunger came and even the Dutch resources were at an end, it took them much longer than the rest to accustom themselves to the very worst of the camp diet, having previously leavened it in various ways, and they found kangkong particularly hard to deal with. As with normal spinach they would only eat the leaves and then throw the stalks away. Phyllis Briggs noticed that the stalks would collect under the rough trestle-tables where the Dutch prepared their vegetables, and she would crawl along beneath them on her hands and knees, picking up these leavings to put in the soup.

Phyllis was quite at ease in recalling her scavenging, because the camps eventually took care of all pretensions, but in that first phase of the existence in the bungalows life was not as uncomplicated. The British were considered a stiff-necked lot, reluctant to unbend, and the Dutch, too, stood firmly on their dignity. They preferred to be known as Hollanders and would say so without any hesitation.

It was in Bungalow No. 9, at this time, that a useful symbol of the general unease could be found. The large lady Hollander with the small dog that had made its distaste so apparent at the padang was now installed there and she was proving to be just as imperious herself. The dog, which was no longer young, was distinctly smelly but he had his own little bed in the crowded quarters and there was no dislodging him. Nobody even tried after a time. Like so much else in the Women's Internment Camp, Palembang, it was something that you had to learn to live with.

Chapter 8

From time to time, a curious echo from that great world outside the camp which was daily receding into a kind of never-never land quite unconnected with the enclave behind the wire, a Chinese funeral would pass on its way to the cemetery which adjoined Irenelaan. From the highest part of the camp there was a view of the road and a funeral would announce itself first by a discordant racket like fairground music run suddenly wild. Presently its source would come into sight, the mourners armed with cymbals and drums, tins and rattles, producing the greatest possible volume of clangs and clatters and brazen shrieks that they could extract from this paraphernalia.

It was an authentically foreign sound, expressing the vast expanse of the Orient in which the camp stood marooned. But for those who used the road, and the Japanese sentries who sat nursing their rifles and thinking of home, the darkness of the evenings would now often contain an element just as foreign to them. On the night air there would come the tinkle of a piano and then women's voices raised in songs that could only have found their way to a small corner of Sumatra by means as unlikely as this herding together of hundreds of beings from far-distant lands.

Music seems to survive, and even flourish, amidst the most terrible privations. In Palembang it marked a distinct turning point in the dissonance which existed between the women as they struggled to come to terms with each other and with their new environment.

In House Number 7, one of the two which the Australians occupied, a piano, remarkably, remained like a beached whale. The surrounding circumstances were so different from those in which pianos are usually found that one of the nurses used it as a bed, preferring it to the tiles. Stray pianos, however, exert a magnetism which draws somebody, one day, to sit down and play them and then, Pied Piperish, others gather around and once someone begins to sing the activity spreads like a bush fire.

So it was at House Number 7 where Saturday night sing-songs got under way among the nurses. The familiar and happy noise they made, the first of that kind to be heard in this place, gradually attracted others until the gatherings grew to the size of concerts and wafts of the whole compendium of great old British, Australian and Dutch songs rang into the dark, alien trees around the camp. Music of one sort or another was so important to the prisoners that we shall return to it, but here it was the catalyst that made all kinds of blendings possible.

It was in the months in Irenelaan that the women earned respect for doing more than surviving a variety of hazards which might have killed them: bombs and shells, shipwreck, bullets and bayonets, and all the ills that arise from hardship and hunger. The questions of how women, bereft of men and all their normal systems of living could cope and adapt, combine and govern and even prosper, were answered in Irenelaan, and the results were heartening and demanding of sincere admiration.

Uncertainty and anxiety never left them, because their imprisonment was conducted so haphazardly that right to the end nobody knew what each fresh day would bring, but when the first shock was absorbed, those with an existing skill rallied briskly and put it to use. The doctors continued their work unquestioningly in that long tradition which puts them eternally at the beck and call of the sick. If lady doctors had ever been considered as second-class citizens in medicine, a concession on the part of their male colleagues in a deeply conservative profession, there was no suggestion now that they were limited in what they could undertake.

The nurses, too, rose to their duty. Lacking a designated leader they each had to find their own way to the decision to serve the community in addition to meeting their own needs in the daily battle for survival.

Phyllis Briggs fell ill again, passing blood fast enough to be given an injection of the precious morphia that, like most of the limited medical supplies in the camp, came from the Charitas hospital. At that time not enough experience had accumulated of the correlation between deteriorating general health and routine dosages and the cure nearly killed her.

Another nursing sister called Alice Rossie paid a visit to the garage which was serving as an isolation ward and found Phyllis unconscious. Alice massaged her until circulation returned with a sensation like pins and needles in its most cosmic form, and Phyllis could remember a voice coming from a great distance, which proved to be that of her rescuer as she came back to the land of the living. Still weak and giddy, in an environment where gentle convalescence was an impossible luxury, she was restored to the garage she was obliged to call home.

Then Alice Rossie became ill, and so did Jennie MacAlister, whom Phyllis had first encountered preparing methodically for her wedding in Seremban as Malaya fell apart around her during the long trek southwards down the Peninsula.

'Alice undoubtedly saved my life,' Phyllis said, and the imminence of a lonely death in a garage raised the possibility that in circumstances like these more people might have wilted unnoticed: not the drastically ill whose distress was immediately apparent, but those who, in a climate of sickness and with the medical facilities hopelessly overstretched, might bravely conceal their condition or wait too long to seek what specialist attention there was. Following Phyllis's experience the British nurses decided on a daily round of house-calls to deal with anything short of the chronic and to seek out those cases which should properly be sent to the hard-pressed doctors.

Once a duty-roster appeared the other nurses, as if it were a familiar bugle-call, automatically offered their services and, in conditions that made their disciplined natures wince, they began to get to grips with the various legacies of all that had beset the women. There were innumerable complaints that, in normal life, would have filled hospitals and doctors' surgeries but here rated only the attention of what was, in effect, the District Nurse.

The overcrowding and the enduring difficulties with the sanitary system caused infections to flourish riotously in the summer heat. Dysentery spread and was joined by malaria, heralded by a blinding headache which was followed by shivering cold and then by a soaring temperature and a deluge of sweat. There were countless varieties of sores and skin conditions. Bites from the omnipresent mosquitos turned septic and there was a generalized irritation of the skin that was of such mysterious origin that it was known simply as The Itch. The Itch possibly arose from the lack of vitamins in the diet, because certainly the dependence on rice brought a whole range of side-effects.

Swollen legs and distended 'rice-bellies' added to the distress of those brought up to care a great deal about their personal appearance, and at a more basic level the rice played havoc even with the processes of elimination. Shelagh Brown remembered the appearance of what was known as the Penny Trots, as the bladder became overactive, followed by a more dramatic reaction which was known as the Twopenny Trots. Debilitating as these conditions were, and it was possible to suffer from them all simultaneously, they had to flare to chronic proportions before it became feasible to consider them as major complaints and made a bid for hospital treatment, so that the nurses were invaluable in sketching at least some system of care. This could only be primitive because the available pharmacopoeia was so limited and often unfamiliar. Rock sulphur was said to be efficacious against The Itch, but was so unassimilable in its natural form that it was pounded into a powder and sprinkled on food. Nobody knew the correct amount to use and it was a matter merely of sprinkling and hoping for the best. The Dutch, with an experience of the East Indies stretching back over 350 years, believed that cold weak tea was a help in the treatment of dysentery and that was tried in the absence of anything else.

There was a limited supply of quinine tablets for the treatment of malaria, and a little morphia for pain relief, but thereafter it was largely a matter of trying more simple methods to reduce the discomforts of the afflicted. Phyllis Briggs' daily round included washing the sick, piling covers on those who were in the shivering stage of malaria, and sponging down those who were at the fever stage and awash with sweat. She rubbed the backs of those immobilized for long periods on the hard floors of the bungalows and pounded the charcoal remains of the firewood because mixed with water it was good for relieving stomach pains.

At this medieval level of nursing the sun was also put to use, this time to lave sores. The sufferer would be put out in the sun, charged with the task of preventing flies from settling on open wounds, while the rags that served as bandages were washed and put out to bake before they were replaced. The nurses also provided the invaluable service of listening patiently to tales of worry and distress, even when they could do nothing to remove the source of them. The problems of eyes and teeth, which are given a lot of specialized attention in sophisticated societies, were ignored by the Japanese at first, so that the agony of toothache, and the difficulties of the myopic whose glasses had not survived, were added to all the rest.

It was in this phase, too, that the specialized functioning of females became a factor again. It was now obvious that the absence of menstruation was more than a temporary matter. For many its disappearance was a relief in a place offering such limited facilities for hygiene, but some of the women looked back to the emotional leave-taking from their menfolk in Singapore and wondered if pregnancy was to be added to their difficulties.

Not least of the torments of the departure from Singapore was the decision on whether women already pregnant should go or stay. At the time the chance of reaching some place of safety where proper care would be available seemed clearly preferable to the unknown rigours of Japanese occupation. The fruits of that error became apparent in July when an English expectant mother came to full term. The guards showed a profound lack of interest in her condition. The other women in her house pleaded for her to be taken to Charitas but were met with a stony refusal, the act of childbirth, perhaps, being regarded together with teeth and eyes as being given an undue importance in the Occidental world.

To add to the mother's anxieties over what was, in fact, a first confinement it was now necessary, as a last ditch device, to act out a sort of melodrama of child-bearing: groans of agony and rolling eyes and female helpers gathered around. It was sufficiently convincing to earn a ride in the lorry to the hospital, but only for the grim denouement of a still-birth.

Another mother-to-be was unaware of her condition until the seventh month of the pregnancy, blaming rice-belly for the untoward distension of her stomach. This child was delivered successfully to join some half a dozen other babies in arms in the camp, wan little creatures whose infant ailments included dysentery and skin rashes of terrifying virulence. One mother circumvented the poverty of supplies by producing breast-milk for two years, but for other babies there were only inadequate substitutes invented out of desperation: a little powdered milk was available at first but thereafter the ubiquitous rice was boiled over and over again until only a milky gruel remained, and soya beans were pounded and strained for their liquid content. In a climate of such persistent improvization Phyllis Briggs found a most useful straining material. It was the gusset of a pair of pale blue French knickers.

The babies lived fretfully but at least they were blissfully ignorant of the sad accident of their earliest surroundings and, in spite of the trials of motherhood combined with the difficulties of life in the camps, the patience and tolerance of the mothers was remarkable. 'You hear and read of battered babies today,' one of the women said, 'but in those conditions I never knew of any parent showing the least sign of cruelty of that kind.'

For those growing up in such an environment the difficulties were predictably complex and varied. There were some thirty-eight British children and a larger number of Dutch and, in the early days at Irenelaan, they ran about within its confines in noisy packs, seizing on the small incidents of camp life and turning them into vivid events. The arrival of the first consignment of charred firewood was the signal for an excited rampage among the bungalows, shrieking the tidings. The weekly arrival of the truck that carried the sick to Charitas was treated as if it were a visitation from another planet. All the women could remember the rush of young feet and the ear-piercing yell: 'Am-ba-lans! Am-ba-lans!'

In Singapore, in 1979, it was possible to meet one of these small savages whom the years had transformed into a successful lawyer in that thriving city. Impeccable now in a dark-blue suit of tropical weight and a club tie, confident and precisely-spoken, Harry Dyne was ten years old when he and his mother set out on that fearful voyage of the *Mata Hari*, and he spoke of the time with a curious detachment as if it were not a part of his childhood but the recollection of a disturbing dream.

The camp was, in fact, a turning point for a little boy whose life had previously gone along in a calm, protected and normal way in the city. His first recollection of fear was not the bombing of Singapore, even though his home was hit and a servant was killed. It was the aerial attack on the *Mata Hari* which made him afraid, still not of the high explosive but of the response of the adults around him. 'They cried out and prayed as the bombs fell,' he said, 'and I had never known grown-ups to behave in that way before. I knew that something must be terribly amiss when I compared their conduct with their confident ways on land.'

That was the beginning of Harry's enlightenment about the wider world, and in the first weeks of imprisonment he stayed close to his mother for reassurance. In Irenelaan, though, he ventured out timidly, as quiet children do, drawn to other youngsters but a little unsure, and he found those in the camp to be a particularly boisterous breed. Harry permitted himself his attractive smile: 'At the beginning I needed protection even from the bigger *girls*!'

The camp was divided into rival gangs, loosely aligned as British versus Dutch, and the British were led by two tough, flaxen-haired brothers, James and Dirk Reid. There were five Reid children in the camp, the offspring of a Scottish father and a Dutch mother who had met and married in Johore Bahru, and their upbringing had been of a different quality to Harry Dyne's. Via Harry's recollection of the brothers when he first encountered them, they emerged as fully-formed, invincible men-of-the-world, and it came as a surprise to discover that James was only eleven and Dirk eight.

An example of the sort of fearless exploit that they led involved the Japanese sentry-boxes and the foul-smelling leaves of a plant that the Dutch called *kuntut*, which can only be translated as 'fart'. The game was to wait until the guards' backs were turned, then rub the leaves on the inside of the sentry-boxes, making their interiors highly obnoxious in the heat. One finesse was to time the application to take place immediately before a rain-storm so that the guard would be left with the choice of a soaking or going inside the box to sit amidst the shocking whiff.

It was not an authentic act of sabotage against an enemy so much as against adult authority in general, of which the Japanese were no more than a part, just another species of the irrational, irritable, repressive tyrants which grown-ups appear to be to children who have created a society of their own – or are 'running wild' as many of the ladies would have seen it, as their nerve-endings were riven by the shrieking and the squabbling of the young pack.

Harry Dyne remembered a Malay caught in some forbidden dealing with the prisoners who was roped to a crucifix outside the guard-house and left without water for two days. But that, too, belonged to the remote and inexplicable sector of adult behaviour much like the alarming demonstrations of distress during the bombing at sea. The Japanese, in fact, were consistently kind to children, perhaps as a necessary respite from the consistently harsh code they applied not only to others but to themselves. The same guard that would strike women in the mouth for wearing lipstick gave one of the two Reid girls, Jane, a cheap little ring one day, telling her that she reminded him of his daughter in Japan.

The game which came to dominate the children's play was a game of war, the British against the Dutch, and with the girls pressed into service as Red Cross nurses. 'Forts' were defined for each side and assailed in turn, the ammunition being mud pellets fired from cata-pults. The ferocity of these wars increased – there was even a three-day official 'armistice', which was greeted with gratitude by the other inmates – and one day, to counter their numerical inferiority, the British hit on the masterstroke of baking their pellets to a flinty hardness. In the ensuing exchange a boy was hit and temporarily blinded in one eye and at this even the Japanese responded. The children were called together and told that there was enough war in the world already. Coming from such a source, this had a certain irony about it, but showed yet again how strangely the Japanese concern evinced itself. For Harry Dyne, though, what was important was that at the height of the battles he had learned enough of rough and tumble to stand now as Number Three in the gang dominated by the Reid brothers, a position to stand comparison with his captaincy of the Rugby XV when he came at last to a school in England.

The gang warfare was precisely the situation which, in normal circumstances, would call forth mention of 'the need for a father's hand', but there was no such commodity here and once again the women set about repairing the omission by their own efforts. It was Miss Dryburgh, ceaseless in her concern for others, who convened a meeting in her garage to bring together another seam of expertise in the camp. Some form of schooling was a trusted method of bringing the young under control and there were schoolteachers to hand.

In the inexhaustibly valuable Garage 9 itself there was Mamie Colley, who had kept the banner of education flying for so long in battered Singapore, a Miss Prouse, Plymouth Brethren and former teacher, and her colleague and co-religionist Miss Glasgow. From the other bungalows there was Dorothy Moreton, of the over-large men's shoes, and Mrs Ward, an archetypal English schoolteacher who with a single stern glance could command instant discipline among unruly children.

Between them they apportioned the noisy tribe: Infants to the care of Dorothy Moreton; Juniors to Mamie Colley and Mrs Ward; and Seniors to Miss Prouse with Miss Glasgow assisting. Miss Dryburgh became a combination of supply teacher and School Inspector, lending her aid wherever necessary, and to complete the picture of the kind of facilities that some enlightened Borough Council in England might consider suitable for the welfare of young people – save, perhaps, for the lack of pencils, paper, blackboards, books, and all else necessary to a formal education – a 'youth club' was set up to function every Friday night.

It was in a youth club rendering of scenes from *Twelfth Night*, produced by Molly Ismail, since each initiative in the camp brought forth fresh talents, that Doris Liddelow played Malvolio. For both the Liddelow sisters the introduction of schooling was an event of some importance. Miss Prouse's classes and the club restored a little of the cocoon of the convent boarding-school in Penang where life had been a great deal less complex than it was for two adolescents of mixed parentage in the camp at Irenelaan.

In Penang the girls had had no reason to dwell on questions of race and social status but here, where Eurasians constituted a distinct grouping, they had to fit into a mould and they couldn't do so easily. At first they were accommodated in a bungalow with two large families and there was the unspoken assumption that they would act as maids of all work. 'To have been *asked* to mind younger children or to wash clothes or to fetch water, or to have had the chance to volunteer, would have made the difference,' Phyllis said, in trying to explain the struggle that faced them in their new surroundings where they were alone with no buffer against a world where subtleties had been ironed out by hunger and need.

Their desire for the independence and dignity they had thus far been taught to cultivate as convent young ladies, Phyllis conceded, must have made them seem aloof. They were unused to the informality of the Eurasian community and yet not quite at one with the British, and the Women's Internment Camp, Palembang, was not the best place to meet this familiar and uncomfortable by-product of colonialism. It was to take more hardship of every kind before the camps disposed entirely of such man-made difficulties and came to the simpler verities of living or dying.

The prisoners were to look back wistfully, when those times came, to the comparative effulgence of Irenelaan, but at this stage, when rations arrived at least with reasonable regularity, a different sort of adjustment had to be made by everybody. The strong memories of a better existence still remained and were a source of weakness. There was an actual repugnance towards the sameness and tastelessness of the food in the camp, and for some, rice, especially, became almost impossible to ingest, even in extreme hunger. Prodigious efforts were made to introduce a variety by cross-pollinations between the basic ingredients. On the rare occasions when fish turned up the bones were kept, dried, powdered and sprinkled on rice to make a suggestion of flavour. Duck eggs appeared sometimes, one to be shared among half a dozen people and often already bad, and their shells were powdered and used in the same way. For those, like the doctors and nurses, whose anxieties extended to a deep concern about the long-term effects of the diet, there was the hope, too, that here was a slender source of calcium. Prodigies of dissection went on whenever there was meat, a single chop divided among a dozen people so that each received an equal morsel. Novelty was no bar. Waterlily roots were chucked into the camp one day, luridly coloured in pink and mauve and white, and they were eaten appreciatively because the taste was new. Coconuts took on the dimension of one of those multi-faceted boons that scientists are always promising for some rosy time in the future. Its milk was prized, of course, and its pulp made a flavouring. Its oil cured shiny noses and lifeless hair, its husk became a pan-cleaner, its fronds, tied together, served as brooms, and the shells were ready-made feeding bowls. Margaret Dryburgh was moved to verse:

> O coconut, our trusty friend,
> Though from the East we may depart,
> Thy praises we shall ever sing
> With thankful heart.

Not everyone could feel as grateful for such a small mercy. The craving for the flavours that the Western palate grows used to remained and, tantalizingly, the location of Irenelaan meant that somewhere in the city beyond the wire many of them could still be found. One day some of them, at least, came to hand. A Chinese trader was allowed past the guardhouse with a bullock-cart containing unimaginable luxuries: bananas, limes, curry powders, herbs and, more astounding still, sugar, butter, coffee and tea.

All these last commodities were in miniscule quantities and everything that the Chinese, who was called Gho Leng, sold was of the poorest quality: tiny, bullet-hard green peas, brown beans, a good proportion of the weight of which was made up by weevils.

Nevertheless, when Gho Leng made his first visit he was mobbed by customers and his stock was snapped up immediately, the greatest prizes, as at a January sale, going to the most ruthless and dedicated among the buyers. The other drawback of what came to be known as 'the shop' was that Gho Leng's prices, in what was literally a captive market, were astronomical. A smallish tin of Klim, an American dried milk that the mothers in camp eyed with desperate longing, cost the equivalent of three English pounds. The supplier of routine rations was paid only about £25 a month by the Japanese for all that he brought for the feeding of hundreds.

The existence of the shop brought into sharp focus the gulf between the haves and have-nots and, as if an emaciated Serpent had made its appearance in this threadbare Eden, it was now even harder to go without, knowing that there were some who could enjoy such elixirs as tea and sugar and stew in which curry powder masked the taste of the dreadful ingredients.

It was a juncture at which women who had never had to fight for a share of the good things of life were obliged to decide if they had the energy and ingenuity to compete, and in this respect, too, they were to show their mettle.

'Mother,' Shelagh Brown's diary records, clearly itching to award another of those rare exclamation marks, 'is now the breadwinner', and in fact Mrs Brown, after such an exceptionally sheltered lifetime, went briskly into business to earn the cash Gho Leng required. She acquired two well-to-do Dutch ladies who wished to alleviate the tedium of camp life by improving their English and gave lessons regularly. She also began the production of mattresses and pillows for sale, a shrewd choice of merchandise given the enduring hardness of the bungalows' tiled floors.

The mattresses were hard work. They were made from rice sacks, washed and dried in the sun, and had to be put together like air-beds in separate compartments, so that they could be folded and carried if another trek was ordered. Their filling, at first, was the kapok from old mattresses that had given up the struggle, but when that ran out dried grass was used.

Mrs Brown also successfully pioneered the making of sun-hats, fashioning hers from an old Chinese silk umbrella by removing the handle and somehow stitching a crown into its centre. The effect, when worn, was similar to that of the shade on a standard lamp, but a thriving sun-hat industry now got under way. The Eurasians, especially, made a fashion out of them, having not worn hats at all as a rule in that other life before the camp.

Mavis Hannah went into partnership with Elizabeth Simons in the Australian bungalows, making straw hats out of *soempits*, the native baskets in which fish were brought to the camp, or the woven grass native bags. Customers provided the materials, which were in short supply like everything else, and a hat cost the equivalent of four shillings and sixpence, although Mavis remembered that she had to pay a Dutch woman ten cents an hour for the loan of her sewing machine.

The Australians, by nature competitors, also went into food production using the comparatively plentiful but totally unappetizing soya bean – which as an additional source of unpopularity induced a most embarrassing form of indigestion – as the basis of a milk substitute and for small cakes, both items benefiting in taste from the investment of some capital with Gho Leng to buy flavourings. Any qualms which might have arisen over the sale of items of such poor pedigree were quelled by the fact that the cakes, at least, were rich in vitamin B in a form which could be easily assimilated.

'You learned', said Mavis of the money-making activities, 'that *everything* in the place was important in some way – a bit of wire was something you grabbed and treasured until it came in useful, even a stick or a stone was worth a second look.' It must have been thus with the cavemen as they slowly found the uses for all that littered the world they were discovering. Those who had not yet reached the evolutionary stage of manufacturing primitive goods and comestibles, sold their labour, chopping wood for those who could afford to pay for the service, or undertaking some extra part of the daily grind, like fetching water or washing clothes.

There was one other method of acquiring the money which, in the primitive economic structure of the camp could only, eventually, equate with food, and that was by the sale of valuables. A watch or a ring, a pendant, a brooch, a necklace took on an entirely different significance from its former function as adornment or token of sentimental regard. It had to be evaluated for its contribution towards survival in this ruthlessly practical environment, but most important, it had to be brought to a marketplace and that meant, inevitably, seeking contacts beyond the wire.

To the list of novel activities presented to women with no previous experience of the by-ways of existence there was added that of shady dealings, clandestine meetings, hard bargaining and all else that is involved in the formation and administration of a healthy black market. The initial contacts with the world beyond Irenelaan were helped by the presence in Palembang and its surroundings of many of the former servants of the Dutch settlers, and a sort of grapevine existed via the natives who occasionally came into the camp at the behest of the Japanese.

In this way it became known that for those who were prepared to risk a foray outside the boundaries a rendezvous with food sellers could be made each night at 6pm in the rubber trees behind one of the rows of bungalows. A small gap magically appeared in the wire and it remained to be seen who would have the nerve to pioneer this route with all the risks that it involved.

Ena Murray was one of the first to decide that the need was sufficiently acute. She too was living in a garage, together with her sister Norah who was ill with malaria and badly needed proper nourishment but, most crucially, Ena had 'adopted' a five-year-old girl called June Bourhill, whose mother had died in the sinking of the *Vyner Brooke*. Among the several such adoptions in the camp, the surrogate mothers invariably proved totally devoted and, with June to care for too, Ena decided on a sortie.

It was an episode every bit as fraught as it appeared in contemplation and in this case was nearly to prove fatal. At the appointed hour she took her fellow garage-dweller, Marguerite Carruthers, to keep watch at the wire, crept through in the gathering dusk and made her way to the prearranged spot among the trees. She waited for a few moments, looking anxiously about her, then a Malay appeared carrying a basket of food. He was nervous, too, and the difficulties of the transaction, carried on in Ena's halting Malay, were compounded by the fact that as she spoke he kept backing away. The moment of actually parting with her diamond engagement ring was acutely uncomfortable as she half expected the native to dart away with both food and ring, but the basket was handed over. Ena turned back towards the camp and as she did so rifles cracked from the perimeter and bullets tore branches from the trees as the Malay hared away.

Ena regained the wire in panic and the alertness of the guards to these intruders and the savage punishments offered to those they caught eventually made the black-marketeering an heroic form of endeavour rather than the disreputable activity which the term normally implies. Just as in the other areas of life in the camps, necessity brought forth individuals with the heart and skill to tackle the job, and among those who became adept secret negotiators on behalf of all the women was Zaida Short.

Zaida, born in Baghdad and married to a British soldier who was also a prisoner after Singapore's fall, acquired the sort of unimpeachable reputation that an English family solicitor might enjoy, although her transactions were conducted amid the gloom of the rubber trees and in the imminent expectation of being shot while going about her business. Her daytime respectability was established by her membership of the rationing committee, where her scrupulous fairness was also invaluable; she had in fact previously worked in the office of Harry Dyne's solicitor father in Singapore. Now in the vastly changed circumstances she lived in the same crowded bungalow as her former employer's wife and son, and was relied upon implicitly by those ladies who decided that the time had come to swap their valuables for a square meal and required not only the best price possible but the certainty that some nameless native would not be allowed to vanish amid the trees, taking the precious item with him and giving nothing in return. Molly Ismail eventually entrusted the Orchard Road engagement ring to Zaida in a particular crisis when her mother fell ill. As a special finesse when her skill increased, Zaida even successfully played the dangerous game of selling to the guards. Fountain pens were popular with them, even though the ink with which to fill them was as scarce as a square meal.

In Singapore, thirty-seven years later, Zaida was still the round-faced, smiling, energetic little woman that everyone remembered from the camps but was now ensconced in her own luxurious office in one of the ultra-modern buildings of the commercial quarter where her business was dealing with the legalities of patents, a prosperous activity in that thriving city and an earnest of the changed status of women since the days when the *tuans* dominated all. She had been obliged to make her own way because when she returned to Singapore at the end of the war it was to find that her husband, a Staff Sergeant, had died in the building of the Burma railway and her brother had been tortured to death by the Japanese.

The gold rush initiated in Irenelaan by the appearance of Gho Leng was controlled to an extent by the formation of a Shop Committee, the task of which was to see that the benisons of the bullock-cart did not go entirely to those with the longest purses and the sharpest elbows. A quota was set which no one was allowed to exceed: an extraordinary refinement of rationing but one which ensured a wider distribution of the goods.

Now, however, a fresh pressure appeared from the outside world in the shape of an Indian cloth merchant called Milwani, who was allowed to bring cheap materials and thread, the textile equivalent of Gho Leng's low-grade foodstuffs, to the camp. In the parlous state of the women's wardrobes his stock was hard to resist. For those who had reached the camp by the immersion route the question of clothes was particularly acute.

Mrs Ismail, who clung doggedly to the notion that 'a good front' remained important even in Irenelaan, routinely bathed and changed for dinner every night even though the bath was a sluice-down at the *tong* and her evening wear, for one who had favoured silk dresses in Johore Bahru, meant replacing the knee-length men's khaki shorts she wore during the day with a threadbare skirt. She was always able to find from somewhere a dash of make-up and, thus titivated, would settle down to the evening repast of rice and rotting vegetables with a dignity that was as much a help to those around her as to herself. Mrs Brown's best outfit remained Reverend Wardle's pyjamas, which she had worn on her rickshaw ride to hospital and she also had a pair of shoes, formerly the property of a sailor, to complete the ensemble.

Small Phyllis Briggs's evening wear was the black silk dressing-gown which had belonged to the tall and elegant Christine Bundy, because the sleeves and hem covered her hands and feet and gave protection against the mosquitos which swarmed at sunset; she also got a remarkable amount of mileage out of a long-sleeved, blue shirt which she bought from a Dutch lady, the lady's husband having been marched away from the *padang* on that fateful morning too briskly to sort his possessions.

From the sleeves, elbow to cuff, she made two sun tops for herself, and from the tail a garment for Mischa who, in the loving care of Phyllis's friend, Mary Jenkin in Garage 9, had even been fixed up with a little suit and his own small, hand-made mattress as well. What remained of the blue shirt was Phyllis's 'best' wear for two years until, in some fresh crisis, she sold it to another Dutch woman receiving, she recalled with pride, the same amount that she had paid for it.

Milwani, in this situation, took on the aspect of a saviour, and even his flimsy tea-towels were snapped up for conversion into the universal sun-tops. His arrival, however, possibly even the reason for it, co-incided with what the women called 'the modesty campaign' on the part of the Japanese. In yet another of the inexplicable workings of their strange mentality they decided that sun-tops, which had very much the ambiguous impact of fig-leaves in drawing particular attention to that which they were meant to conceal, were not sufficient and that 'coats' should be worn as well. But there were no coats and so another conundrum of the imprisonment gained ground.

The Japanese, perhaps fearing a mass descent on Milwani by women maddened even more than in normal circumstances by that ceaseless craving for clothes which men attribute to them, kept him beyond the gates of the camp and would only let the inmates go to visit him in twos. Shelagh and Phyllis made up a twosome at the height of the modesty campaign and Phyllis, arriving in a sun-top, was roundly berated and sent back to the camp empty-handed as a punishment. Shelagh, demurely clad in her only frock, was allowed to remain. 'But what they didn't know,' she said, pouring tea politely in her drawing-room in Wiltshire, 'was that I was wearing no knickers!'

The advent of Milwani and Gho Leng, for all the turbulences that their presence caused, made a valuable difference to the quality of life, not least because the miniscule luxuries they added went some way towards meeting what was evidently an important human need. It was now possible to mark special occasions and show personal affection or gratitude by small gifts, a meaningful alleviation of the sense of utter poverty and deprivation, even if the present amounted to no more than a lime or a banana or a reel of cotton thread.

Previously the gestures of this kind which had been possible had subtly underlined the women's plight, although the spirit of them was never in question. On Betty Jeffrey's birthday, shortly after the arrival in Irenelaan, she received the sort of tokens that children might put together in a game of let's pretend. She woke up to find beside her on the tiles a tiny cucumber from the rations, placed on an even tinier piece of red georgette which Maudie James, who was responsible for this surprise, had later to explain was to be thought of as a handkerchief. There was a little bouquet of jungle flowers picked from the Chinese cemetery and an oil painting of a rice-field, of all impalatable topics, presented as a 'valuable antique' to explain its coating of dust and spiders' webs, this from Betty's companion of the mangrove swamps, who had found it in a shed. Birthday tea was served on proper plates, borrowed from the Dutch, but in fact consisted entirely of rice dressed up in true dolly's tea-party style with funny descriptions: 'Ack-ack puffs', 'Parachute-drop scones', 'Palembang pasties'. There was a birthday cake, decorated with flowers and a strange wild fruit from the cemetery which looked like strawberries, but when Betty was made to cut it, it proved to be no more than an empty tin, upturned.

With more substantial treats to hand birthdays and anniversaries grew in elaboration and were eagerly seized upon as milestones in the drudgery and sameness of the passing days. Miss Dryburgh enhanced the occasions with home-made cards, their verses tailored to each recipient's known history and virtues and thus obliquely reflecting the life in Irenelaan. Phyllis Briggs was to treasure a memento of her birthday in 1942 right through the camps and was able to produce it in Bournemouth on its thin, yellowing paper, in Miss Dryburgh's neat hand. (*See overleaf*)

For decoration Miss Dryburgh had drawn the unwieldy saw and an intractable log and even the garbage with its attendant cloud of buzzing flies. The little offering powerfully evoked the magnificence of restoring

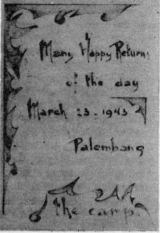

The greetings card industry in Palembang: examples of birthday card
manufacture in the camps.

Who visits dwelling in the camp,
Looking for garbage, filth, and damp,
And hopes the power of germs to cramp?
 'Tis Phyllis.

Who often wields the borrowed saw,
And its whole length with toil does draw
Through logs that call for firm-set jaw?
 'Tis Phyllis.

Who tends the sick upon the floors,
In bottles tea, milk, water pours,
With rice and porridge health restores?
 'Tis Phyllis.

Our birthday greetings now we send,
Trusting that soon the times will mend,
And your true love his way can wend
 To his Phyllis.

some kind of civilized order in an environment so inimical and with such temptations to despair. The customs and manners and attitudes of a lifetime could not be quenched by squalor and, except on closer inspection, the camp resembled a busy village in the English shires rather than the alien and poverty-stricken place that it was in reality. There were Jumble Sales, which were no more than the redistribution of the pathetic minutiae of the camp's worldly goods. There were Coffee Mornings to raise cash for the sick, tiny amounts inevitably, but an echo of those charitable activities which ladies had always considered a part of their duty. The little pool of money came to be known, from habit, as the Red Cross Fund, since even the Red Cross, that powerful institution which has overcome so many barriers to bring succour to the needy, could not penetrate to this lost community. There was the Lending Library, the name conjuring up a vision of some municipal building in stolid Gothic supervised by a stern lady librarian; in fact this was a small collection of dog-eared volumes that had somehow survived the holocaust – Galsworthy and Dickens having shown great stamina as they always seem to do when literature is under stress – and located in one of the garages.

It was possible to attend Mrs Mamie Colley's Country Dance classes, or go to church, Protestants to Garage 9, Roman Catholics to the quarters of the Dutch nuns. There was even an equivalent of those discussion groups beloved of Women's Institutes, the titles of the weekly lectures reflecting a wistful preoccupation with all that had been lost: 'Life on a Malayan Rubber Plantation', 'Life on an Australian Sheep-station'. Angela Kong, the Chinese nurse who had remained so mystically immaculate in her cheongsam as the soot of burning Singapore fell on the decks of the departing *Mata Hari*, gave a lecture on Chinese customs which was long remembered as much for her remarkable personality as for her tales about the use of cockroach paste as a cure for fever and pounded tigers' toe-nails for mumps. Betty Jeffrey remembered, besides the appreciative mirth that Kong engendered, the extra dimension that was given to her talk by her sparing use of English. 'You had to fill in the spaces for yourself to keep the thread,' Betty said. 'She knew all the words but couldn't be bothered using them.'

Phyllis Briggs also recalled Kong clearly: 'She was short with funny little sparrow legs and a broad face, always smiling unless she was in one of her moods. She would do anything in the world for people she liked but if she thought they were trying to boss her or take advantage of her she would sulk for hours.' Phyllis divined that she liked being made a fuss of and joked with and they got on well, so that she learned a little about Kong's background which included both a family shop and a gold mine in Kuala Lipis in Malaya, where the Kum Kiews had been settled for a number of years.

Kong's knack for impeccable cleanliness had survived surroundings in which perhaps the greatest luxury of all was soap, and although her favourite garment was a man's waistcoat on special occasions she would turn out in a spotless *baju* with a string of really good jade beads, a perk presumably of having a gold mine in the family. This was the outfit she wore on the evening of the lecture.

There was much to be learned about the intricacy of human beings in the camps, as well as about their decency and their faults. In this comparatively halcyon period Mrs Gilmour taught French and you could also learn Dutch and Malay, and even how to draw, from a Dutch nun who gave lessons. All these activities were recorded in the Camp Chronicle, which represented a considerable achievement in itself.

The Irenelaan newspaper, with a joint British and Dutch editorial board, sprang up largely to meet a craving for news which came almost to compete with the hunger for food. In the barbed-wire bubble of the camp, so comprehensively severed from the rest of the world, rumour had reached the proportions of a disease, an insanity even, which the wiser members of the community, like Dr McDowall, Margaret Dryburgh, Mamie Colley and Mrs Hollweg, wife of the valuable Dutch doctor of Bukit Besar, all members of the editorial management, were

THE CAMP CHRONICLE. march 6th 1943

ENGLISH EDITION.

Editorial Staff: Dr. McDowell, Miss Dryburgh, Miss Glasgow, Mrs. Coley.

A MORNING IN MARCH.

The cock is crowing,
The stream is flowing,
The small birds twitter,
The lake doth glitter,
The green field sleeps in the sun;
The oldest and youngest
Are at work with the strongest;
The cattle are grazing,
Their heads never raising;
There are forty feeding like one!

Like an army defeated,
The snow has retreated,
And now doth fare ill.
On the top of the bare hill
The ploughboy is whooping—anon—anon;
There's joy in the mountains;
There's life in the fountains;
Small clouds are sailing,
Blue sky prevailing;
The rain is over and gone!

William Wordsworth.

Page One of a hand-written edition of the camp newspaper

determined to counteract. Each day, as people met and talked, the fortunes of the war would swing wildly between total surrender by the Allies or the Japanese; capital cities changed hands almost hourly or were totally eradicated; Mussolini was in London; the Americans were landing in Sumatra; and the Pope seemed to have abandoned all his other onerous duties to concentrate on the plight of those locked up in Irenelaan. Repatriation to a variety of destinations including, for some reason, Lourenço Marques in Africa, was to be accomplished via the Vatican, and there was even a verse in circulation which related to this elaborate development:

> There are some young women who hope
> To travel by sea to the Pope,
> And there be exchanged
> As this good man arranged,
> So back to their homes and some soap!

The Camp Chronicle did not compete with the riot of 'news' in circulation, but bravely set about making the world of Irenelaan as interesting as possible with the aid of the camp's one working type-writer and a supply of paper that allowed for the production of only two copies each month which were passed from house to house. In the issue of 5 September 1942 there was a Patience Strong poem – 'Keep on hoping though skies look grey today; keep on looking for sunshine on the way . . .' – a recipe for making soup out of fish heads; a word-game competition and Part Three of a rather taxing series of articles about a Dutch system of child care: 'Up till now, we have talked about the Mensendieck System chiefly in connection with pupils suffering from a bad posture . . .'

Local 'news' was contained in an item called 'Miss Know-All's Diary', and in this issue had buried a considerable scoop half-way down the page after a paragraph about a jumble sale for the children. On the 24 September twenty Eurasian women and children, evidently of a racial mixture that the Japanese had decided did not place them among their official enemies, were actually to be released. 'Great excitement . . .' is Miss Know-All's only comment, 'about 10 o'clock twenty women and children were set free'. The caution was due to the fact that the Chronicle was censored by the Japanese and it was a matter of reading between the lines to extract the true juice from its tidings.

Another item referred to a round-up of dogs in the camp by the Japanese, 'Bello' from House Number 1 and 'Beertje' from Number 17 being among the victims. 'Beertje preferred camp life and escaped after a few days,' Miss Know-All records carefully. 'He was welcomed back with cheers.' In fact Beertje's snub to the conquerors was a source of immense glee to the ladies, heightened by the mention in the Chronicle.

One excellent item denied the paper because it only became known after the war was that Margaret Dryburgh's astonishing creative output actually found fame beyond the camp. Her master-work, 'The Captives' Hymn', was first sung at the Sunday morning service in Garage 9 on the 5 July 1942, passing instantly to an immortal status in the memories of all who survived, and when repatriation came it was carried by a Eurasian girl to Singapore to be sung by the prisoners there.

THE CAPTIVES' HYMN

Father in captivity
We would lift our prayer to Thee,
Keep us ever in Thy Love.
Grant that daily we may prove
Those who place their trust in Thee,
More than conquerors may be

Give us patience to endure,
Keep our hearts serene and pure,
Grant us courage, charity,
Greater faith, humility,
Readiness to own Thy Will,
Be we free or captive still.

For our country we would pray,
In this hour be Thou her stay.
Pride and selfishness forgive,
Teach her, by Thy Laws, to live,
By Thy Grace may all men see,
That true greatness comes from Thee.

For our loved ones we would pray,
Be their guardians, night and day,
From all dangers, keep them free,
Banish all anxiety.
May they trust us to Thy care,
Know that Thou our pains doth share.

May the day of freedom dawn,
Peace and justice be reborn,
Grant that nations loving Thee
O'er the world by brothers be,
Cleansed by suffering, know rebirth,
See Thy Kingdom come on earth.

Norah Chambers' transcription of the music to the 'Captives' Hymn', dictated
to her by Margaret Dryburgh

This was the closest that Miss Dryburgh would come to a wider
acclaim, but in Irenelaan she had the status of authentic genius,
making possible a positive explosion of musical talent that immeasur-
ably leavened the dark, empty evenings in the camp. Among her
endless abilities she had an infallible memory for both music and
words, perfect pitch and an instant command of harmony. 'You could
go to her, hum a tune and straight away she could write it down and
harmonize it,' said Norah Chambers, alumnus of the Royal Academy of
Music.

Norah had a facility for copying musical manuscript at great speed
and, in a minute hand to take account of the shortage of paper,
produced the sheet music for a thirty-strong choir to add to the Sunday
morning devotions in the garage. For secular occasions the choir
transformed itself into a Glee Club, and the sing-songs pioneered by the
Australians took on the stature of concerts. Soloists emerged, with,

among others, Ena Murray, Margery Jennings and Dorothy MacCleod becoming star performers.

'In foreign land we lived interned,
The depths of bitterness we learned,
As days and weeks crept by.
Hunger, o'crowding, sickness, pain
Humiliation, nervous strain,
Made life sheer misery.
A sudden thought the mind did cheer,
"Much music that Thou once did hear
Is stored in memory.
It lives for ever. Bring it forth.
Use your own instrument of work
Sing! Thou wilt happier be."
The admonition struck a spark
From souls till then both cold and dark,
The mind's ear heard again
Old songs of schooldays, college glees,
Ditties of home, gay comedies,
Anthems of nobler strain.
The airs to paper were transferred,
A search was made for many a word,
With harmonies we played.
A willing scribe the live long day
The part of printing press did play,
And scores for singers made.
Then music lovers formed a choir,
As music makers did aspire,
To concord of sweet sounds
As blended voices filled the air
The soul could soar to worlds more fair
Escape from prison bounds.'

The Saturday night gatherings grew so large and loud that they could not be ignored by the guards, and after some preliminary suspicious prowling, peering in at the windows and climbing on to the dustbins for a better view, they took to inviting themselves, sitting in the front row on cane chairs while the women sat on the ground. One of the ladies realized with some astonishment at the end of the imprisonment that she had not sat on a chair for three and a half years, but among the creative endeavours of the camp was the manufacture of little cushions which were worn slung from the waist at the back because, as flesh fell away through the increasing degree of starvation, they gave some relief to bony bottoms.

As a finale, since National Anthems might have seemed a bit out of place to those in the front row, 'Land of Hope and Glory' was frequently sung, best given its full stirring resonance by a Dutch singer called Mrs Vandenhoot, and always wildly applauded by the women. The Japanese, for all the song's rampant nationalism, evidently missed the point. They liked it a lot and would often call for an encore, at which the women clapped and yelled more energetically than ever.

Like all jailers the Japanese were obliged to share some of the deprivations of their charges and, aside from occasional fits of disapproval in one of which all laughing was banned, they seemed to be generally appreciative of these breaks from the grinding repetitiveness of life in Irenelaan. Shelagh Brown remembered being part of a group which presented an entertainment in one of the houses and attracted the attention of a drunken guard who was determined to hear a repeat of 'Ingrish song "Long Way"'. 'Tipperary' was sung again and much appreciated, except that the guard's rifle had slipped round his neck on its sling and, as he tottered back and forth, the bayonet narrowly missed impaling all of the entertainers.

On another night a guard settled down on the dustbin outside the window of a house where a little show was going on and derived so much enjoyment from a rendering of the monologue 'Albert and the Lion', of which he could not understand a word, that he gave the performers a small tin of bully beef, this being at least the equivalent of a rave review in the civilized world. It was through yet another initiative from Garage 9 that a sort of touring company existed, drawn from its remarkable occupants, which would turn up at houses for occasions like birthdays and anniversaries and perform charades and monologues and other diversions of the kind that used to amuse Victorian drawing-rooms but were now given a new lease of life in this extraordinary setting.

Once again others were inspired, and the musical concerts expanded into a cross between revues, comic operas and variety shows. Ena Murray, who had a stage training, showed particular flair as a producer of these spectaculars. When one was mounted, the largest room in one of the houses was cleared and a tiny stage set up. The audience, when it overflowed the auditorium, which it usually did, clustered round the windows and doors. As well as the musical entertainment there was an inexhaustible supply of those local jokes which are only comprehensible in the dreadful circumstances which spawn them.

A typical Variety Show 'bill' from the Palembang camp

One night the acerbic humour of the Australians turned up a hit: a fashion show by that well-known couturière 'Paula of Palembang'. There was a display of creations made up of everything from dishcloths to rice sacks, absurdly elaborate and romantic for their label, 'Camp Possibilities'. This was followed by something a little more practical for everyday wear, yet another outing for the shorts and sun-tops to which the women were opposed as firmly as the Japanese, though for different reasons. They were heartily sick of them rather than peculiarly prudish. The highlight of the show was Madame Paula's prediction for the fashions of 1945, given the current trends in camp. This took the form of three girls wearing nothing but three paw-paw leaves apiece, and was to prove almost a prophecy.

Another show-stopper was a parade of the camp's personalities, hilariously guyed. The tall and willowy Ruth Russell-Roberts, ex-mannequin, was sufficiently alarmed by the effect of an incessant rice diet on her impeccable figure to become an early example of the jogger,

Mrs Brown's birthday tribute from Margaret Dryburgh

adding an evening run round the perimeter of the camp to the trials of a day in Irenelaan. It was merely necessary for a slender impersonator to run determinedly across the stage a couple of times for the mirth to make the rafters ring. Then a large figure, fattened by cushions, walked into view with her feet at a quarter to three, and that was Mrs Brown coping bravely with her outsize sailor's shoes. For any who might have missed the joke the figure was topped off by a Chinese sunshade hat – Mrs Brown's own, as it happened, lent for the occasion. Mrs Brown, after so many years spent as the consort of that important colonial gentleman, Major Brown, had come most definitely into her own. As Madame Pêche Melba in a dress worn back to front with a pink fichu, with chillis for earrings and a necklace of pumpkin seeds, there came a night when she stole the show herself.

Chapter 9

Ken, my darling,   October 1942.   Palembang.

This is our anniversary, eight years ago today since we were married.
Never did we think that our eighth would be spent apart in such
circumstances as this. You don't know where I am and I can only hope
and pray that you are safe in Singapore. Today I think of you all the time,
dear, and hope you are thinking of me, and I make fresh vows to you and
we shall start married life again in such a burst of happiness when we
meet. When I think of that day I just tremble all over with joy. When will
it be? Please God it will be very soon. In spite of the misery that the war
has brought us, and this hated internment, I am surrounded by very dear
friends for which I am very grateful. Our garage room is fêted with wild
flowers for our day today . . .

This was a letter written never to be sent, a most poignant way of
assuaging loneliness. Ena Murray was to write to her husband
Ken on each of their anniversaries until the war ended, but her
letters were set down in the little notebook that was given to her as a gift
on that day in Irenelaan. She wrote never knowing if he were alive or
dead, but there were women in the camp who were now spared at least
that torment. Although in practical terms the gulf was immense, the
men who were so brusquely torn away from the women at the *padang* at
Bukit Besar were actually imprisoned only three miles away from the
Women's Internment Camp.

They were marched from the *padang* to an authentic prison, Palembang Jail, from which the native transgressors had been removed. The
jail survived into the late 1970s and it retained that morose and
hopeless air which hangs about houses of correction. In a forbidding,
blank wall there were heavy wooden double doors and, inside, a
courtyard surrounded by cells enclosed by iron grilles like animal
cages. Its bleak functionalism clearly appealed to the *Kempei Tai*, the

Japanese secret police equivalent of the Gestapo, as an ideal workshop for the terror and brutality which they practised.

Connoisseurs of environments which would cause the heart instantly to sink, even before any precise distress was applied, they must have briskly ear-marked the prison for their own purposes because the men were put to building a fresh camp on the outskirts of the city. As this would provide considerably more amenable surroundings than the old jail, the *Kempei Tai* were instrumental for once in making a contribution to human happiness rather than the pain and degradation they inflicted all over Asia.

One day in August, down the road where the women watched the Chinese funeral processions, a silent column was seen trudging under armed guard. Even at a distance the column was unmistakably made up of Europeans and, when it passed Irenelaan at its closest point, some four hundred yards away, the women recognized them as the missing men. For those straining desperately to pick out their own menfolk it was a moment almost too tantalizing to be borne, but the next morning the column passed again and the following morning as well. Tentative waves were exchanged and then shouts of greeting, and with that much contact established it was as if the men had come back from the grave. In fact, their route to and from the site of the camp they were building lay along the cemetery road, and both they and the women fell furiously to considering how this fingertip reunion could be extended.

At around the same time the Japanese, working as ever like some mysterious deities whose decisions could only be divined by mortals through the interpretation of signs and portents, had withdrawn many of the soldiers who guarded the camps and replaced them with Javanese police. The move seemed to coincide with the switch from a military to a civil adminstration in Sumatra. The Japanese war-machine had rolled on to the South-East and the early conquests were now evidently seen as permanently settled areas of the Co-Prosperity Sphere.

The Javanese guards were called *Hei Hoes*, and indeed they proved certainly as insouciant as their name suggests by comparison with the Japanese. They were armed only with revolvers, which provided an immediate relief from the threatening presence of bayoneted rifles, and the women found their dark-skinned faces far more mobile and comprehensible than the frozen, alien countenances of the Japanese. Attractive, even, though this judgement may have been much influenced by the fact that the *Hei Hoes* were slip-shod and incurably idle, sleeping in the sentry-boxes for much of their spells of duty or delousing each other in an amiable way if they managed to remain awake.

They were detachedly friendly to the prisoners and very much open to bribery, which was a boon to the black-marketeers, but their temperament was of most use when it came to making more overt efforts to get in touch with the men. With *Hei Hoes* on duty it was possible to make a daily ceremony of congregating at the point of maximum proximity to the road and cheering the marching column past as if it were a victory parade. In the same way the men could dawdle and respond without the goad of bayonets in their backs and the yapping of commands.

On the birthday of Queen Wilhelmina of Holland, 31 August, the Hollanders in Irenelaan found a riposte to the misery of being obliged to observe the birthday of the Emperor of Japan, by celebrating Her Majesty's anniversary with as much ostentation as the circumstances would allow. The anniversary fell on a Monday, but there was a church service in the morning with flower arrangements in the national colours, and as the men passed on their way to work that day they were astonished to see the Dutch flag waving triumphantly from the roof of one of the houses behind the Women's Camp wire: a sight of eye-rubbing unlikelihood in a place which probably never elsewhere saw that emblem from its fall to its liberation.

The flag was flown from the roof of House Number 17, whose occupants included three young Dutch girls, Antoinette, Alette and Helen Colijn, the daughters of a Dutch oil-man; they had already made the roof a landmark to the men by sitting astride it and yelling at the tops of their young voices every morning in the hope that their father, a prisoner in the men's camp, would be able to identify them.

The exploit with the flag and its attendant dangers, of which falling off the roof was probably the least, paled beside the hazards of the Colijns' journey to the camps. Helen, the eldest of the sisters although she was only just twenty at the time of Irenelaan, was to make her home in California eventually and had yet another saga of shot, shell and sinkings to recount.

The girls were in Java when their father was captured in the oil port of Tarakan off Borneo and sent under guard to another port, Balikpapan, to warn the authorities there not to raze the oil installations before the Japanese took over. In fact he escaped to Java and with the girls embarked on a ship bound for Colombo which was bombed and sunk in the Indian Ocean. Helen and her father, in one lifeboat, became separated from Antoinette and Alette in another and had no real hope of seeing them again as the boat struggled for six days to make a landfall in southern Sumatra. The survivors began to walk north along the shoreline and after three days came across another beached lifeboat and were reunited with the two younger Colijns. In the inevitable strafing which followed the sinking of a ship a bullet had slashed

Antoinette's arm from the elbow to the wrist and in the three weeks that the march continued her wound could be treated only with salt water and bandaged with rags.

After all this they remained, as Miss Dryburgh noted in her diary, 'three bright young things who persisted in looking on life as an adventure', an attitude much to her taste, and the buoyancy of the women's camp generally managed to convey itself to the men, even at a distance. The effect was highly beneficial. Down the road past Irenelaan there passed many times with the men's party an American prisoner called William H. McDougall who had been a journalist in China before his capture and was to produce a brilliant account of that parallel existence which the men pursued, so near and yet so far from the women.

What emerges from his description is that the misery of defeat and subjection did not leave the males. The glumness which the women had observed before their separation from the men persisted, unleavened by the sort of absurdly optimistic gestures which the women contrived. The displays of cemetery flowers, the tea-parties, the exchange of little, impractical gifts would anyway have been a little out of place. It would scarcely have been in the mould of ex-Empire builders, oil-men, planters and District Commissioners to display the kind of hilarious skittishness that led the cockney Maudie James to visit her friends in the Irenelaan bungalows one day, dressed as a bride. Her veil was an old mosquito net and her outfit was complete down to a bouquet made from the ghastly water-spinach and marred only by the ragged bandages round the tropical ulcers on her ankles and the ungainly lump of wood, known as 'trompers', which those without shoes wore on their feet.

There were many acts of kindness and selflessness among the men but broadly the imprisonment, as it continued, drew the men away from each other into a dogged, solitary battle with their circumstances whereas it drew the women more closely together. It was therefore distinctly heartening to the men to be made aware of this other tribe, clearly keeping intact their womanly gift for making human existence less dour. The women were never to be as devastated as the men by the outward signs of their subjugation, perhaps from having been cast in a more acquiescent role long before this dramatic oppression occurred.

In nearly all material matters, however, the men had proved themselves better equipped. Their traditionally superior manual practicality had allowed them to fashion implements like saws and hammers and screwdrivers, from which they could build other appurtenances such as tables, chairs and beds. Their black-market dealings were infinitely more elaborate and productive, extending to long and dangerous nighttime forays beyond the camp. Their transactions, and indeed their whole economy, was much helped by the existence of more money among their numbers. The Japanese haul of males at the conquest was richer not only as far as the former status of many of the prisoners was concerned, but in actual cash, in an era when money was so much a male concern. Men tended to be the ones who carried it about physically in their wallets and pockets rather than entrusting it to the handbags and purses of females who, the legend insisted, might either spent it importunately or have it snatched from their frail paws.

Now, however, they usefully resumed the convention that women should be cared for and did their best even in this fractured version of the interplay between the sexes. One day in August Marguerite Carruthers heard her name called from the other side of the wire and looked out to see a group of young Malays who told her that they were carrying a letter from her husband. She could only receive it if she would come outside the boundary because they were too scared of the fate that befell native interlopers in Irenelaan to bring it in. This time it was her friend Ena Murray's turn to wait anxiously while Marguerite made the trip into the trees behind the bungalows, that short but harrowing journey into uncertainty. She got back without event and had her first news of Andrew since they had been parted. He told her that he had paid the Malays for their delivery service and that she should look out for further communications.

The combination of the means to offer bribes, the laxity of the *Hei Hoes*, and the men's better access to illicit food supplies was ideal from the women's point of view. Shelagh Brown's diary for 20 August records: 'Yesterday parcels came from the men . . . bully beef, butter and marg . . . feast day in Garage 9.' These delicacies actually arrived hidden among the routine contents of the ration truck, the driver having been bribed. The lorry which brought the wood to Irenelaan in its elephantine form performed the same service for the jail first, and the men arranged that they could employ their better technology to chop the women's supply to manageable size before it passed on, a fabulous advantage to the wielders of the women's two blunt axes.

The wood lorry, too, became a treasure trove, messages being hidden among the timber and even inscribed on the wood itself. With such excellent channels of communication established, it was possible now to make the daily exchange of waves and shouts between those on the road and those at the wire infinitely more meaningful. By pre-arrangement it was possible for a prisoner on one side or the other to wear a brightly coloured garment or a distinctive hat that was readily identifiable to one who knew to look out for it and, once the connection was made, to wave and shout so furiously that it was almost as good as shaking hands.

Actual physical meetings were clearly the summit to aim for, and here the change in the management of the camps was also valuable. The civil administration did not seem to be as acutely disdainful as the military towards the weaknesses of the flesh, even recognizing that teeth and glasses – the faulty existence of the first and the handicaps caused by the absence of the latter – were a problem of some magnitude. It thus became possible to achieve a trip to the Charitas hospital in a condition short of illness or injury grave enough to make the cemetery the only other alternative.

Mrs Brown, whose somewhat high-handed behaviour towards a Japanese infantryman on the beach at Muntok had resulted in the loss of her spectacles, had now become not only considerably more self-reliant but had amended her technique for dealing with the enemy. She achieved her trip to Charitas in this period by a subtle combination of the manners of the old order and the new, approaching Miachi, the Camp Commandant, with a respectful inclination of her Chinese sunshade hat but simultaneously announcing herself in a most confident voice as Mrs E. A. Brown 'of Singapore'. At the same time as she graciously presented the Japanese officer with a bowl of flowers, she asked firmly for a new pair of glasses and the bewildered Japanese found himself agreeing before she withdrew with as much dignity as was possible in her jumbo shoes.

Shelagh chuckled with boundless affection as she remembered this exchange. Under this new regime she was able to accompany her mother for an eye test of her own, with some leg-ulcers thrown in as a make-weight, on the Wednesday outpatients run which became a routine. She also remembered that the journey into Palembang was a considerable health hazard in itself, due to the kamikaze Japanese driving style, but there was an atmosphere of barely suppressed elation among the group of women in the ambulance as they were hurled about at every corner.

Charitas now had a significance quite apart from its status as the only source of proper medical aid in the shrunken world of the prisoners. The hospital served not only the women's camp but the men's, too, as well as dealing with Servicemen patients from two POW camps in the area and the Dutch oil-men who were imprisoned separately among the Shell and Standard Oil refineries they had once run at Pladjoe on the outskirts of the city.

In terms of the narrow horizons of each of these groups in separation, this made the hospital into a metropolis and indeed, beneath its calm surface, Charitas was a hot-bed of intrigue to compare with the underworld of any notorious capital city. The Dutch nursing nuns, gliding impassively about in their white habits, were the key to smuggling operations on a grand scale led by the hospital superintendent, Mother Alacoque, a lady of most gentle and pious appearance. It was she who masterminded trafficking in letters, parcels and messages between the various camps, and secretly got vital medicaments out to the doctors struggling in isolation in their makeshift clinics behind the wire. Three of her nuns who were midwives provided a vital link with the outside world because their duties took them into the city without close supervision; through them Mother Alacoque, made wary by what had gone before, established hidden caches of drugs and medicines against the day when Charitas might be closed down on some sudden whim of the conquerors. In this she proved herself to be a prophet as well.

The senior medical staff at Charitas consisted of a Dutch surgeon, Dr Tekelenburg, an Indo-European, Dr Ziesel, and one woman, Dr Goldberg, who was German. This was a plus in view of the Japanese partnership with the Axis, but she was also Jewish which seemed to cancel out that advantage and eventually made her qualify to be interned. Amid this much ambivalence, Dr Goldberg preserved a careful neutrality, going about her duty of attending the women patients with a brisk detachment that could not be considered as partisan.

The two men, however, were deeply immersed in underground activity. Since he was on constant call, Dr Tekelenburg lived in a house across the street from the hospital and, as he was effectively imprisoned by the pressing need for his surgical skill, he was not closely guarded, which made his home ideal for concealing the radio that was another by-product of the men's superior constructional abilities. To disseminate the news received in this clandestine and infinitely dangerous fashion another figure of seemingly impeccable probity was involved: the Bishop of Palembang, who used his religious offices at Charitas to pass on bulletins to trusted prisoners returning to the men's camp.

Dr Ziesel, whose racial origins were not unacceptable to the Japanese and who was allowed to live away from the hospital, was in close touch with a useful segment of the native population: the Ambonese colony in Palembang. These immigrants from the island of Ambon in the Molucca group off New Guinea had a strong antipathy to the Japanese and an equally powerful loyalty to the Dutch and, through the doctor, they became an invaluable source of commodities which the prisoners needed, and at their true price rather than the inflated demands of such as Gho Leng.

As a money exchange Charitas was as busy as a High Street bank.

Cash passed from husbands to wives, and from both men's and women's camps out to the city in exchange for supplies. The Servicemen made a donation to the destitute women in Irenelaan and this, too, was channelled through Charitas. The volume of items that had to be transported to and fro inspired prodigies of concealment.

Among the mementoes which Mavis Hannah preserved was a wan-looking sanitary towel, whose history almost certainly qualified it for a place on show in a war museum. She explained in her matter-of-fact way, holding up the object like a talisman by one of its tapes, that she had found it in a chest in her bungalow at Irenelaan and had kept it 'just in case', since her period had not evinced itself for such a long time.

While the women were racking their brains for fresh ways of concealing contraband – one Dutch matron had even had her corset ransacked by excited guards convinced that this garment, quite novel to them, was custom-built for carrying mail – an excellent notion occurred to Mavis. Henceforth, on the trips she engineered to Charitas, she carried letters and money by a method which gave genuine meaning to the expression 'personal delivery service' since both were hidden in such profound intimacy inside the towel.

Of all the many ramifications of Charitas, what was of central importance to the women was the chance to meet their menfolk face to face, and one of the greatest conspiracies centred on contriving to have both halves of a relationship as patients at the hospital on the same day. It would sometimes take weeks of message-carrying and unexpected setbacks before a pair could manage to coincide, and even once they were there it was scarcely a matter of greeting each other with open arms.

The low-lying Charitas buildings were divided into three sections, one each for the civilian men and women and one for the Service personnel, and guards patrolling the wards and corridors with no other duty than to keep these categories apart. There was a secluded garden, a place of meditation for the nuns where they could sometimes, in their endlessly humane way, juggle events and the Japanese to allow a couple to meet, but the only consistently common ground, unguarded and available to both sexes, was the solitary toilet given over to visiting patients.

It was there that months of separation and fretting and longing and fears were resolved in the brief moments of reunion that were feasible in such a trysting-place. Probably nothing in the whole experience expressed as vividly the fall from grace of the white elite of the Empire as these encounters of once-proud men and women in a lavatory. Nor, more optimistically, could anything match the resource and adaptability of these people.

In the more relaxed regime of the civilian administration, a period when the Japanese were visibly daring to wonder if their lightning conquest had actually altered permanently the order in Asia, as in their original dream, it must have occurred to them that there was some practical value even in the captured women. The suave Miachi, honing his impression of a British military type and exuding persuasive charm, called the nurses in Irenelaan together and asked for volunteers to go out and nurse some two hundred American and Dutch men at the Pladjoe oilfields, putting it to them as a means of 'going free'. Betty Jeffrey was one of the women involved, and she conveyed well the deep and chilly suspicion that was extended towards the Japanese commandant as he sat with studied nonchalance on a wall of the camp to put his proposition. Their attitude was clearly a version of that stern disbelief which, in normal life, nurses are good at extending to visitors who creep in after visiting hours with some feeble reason for special admission.

The issue was rather more grave here, however, because Irenelaan, for all its defects, now represented a cohesive society with certain systems of support and protection, and to leave it meant a further foray into the unknown and the abandoning of the unexpected strengths which the women had found in each other's company. When Miachi left, all the nurses, British, Dutch, Australian and Chinese, pooled their considerable weight of practicality to discuss this latest development. They decided to temporize until more information was forthcoming, and there the matter rested for some time until Miachi returned to elaborate. When the nurses learned that the requirement was in fact for nurses to work in the Japanese military hospital, the response was a unanimous negative.

In a more brutal phase, presumably a refusal would not have been possible and now, as both a punishment and a further inducement to leave Irenelaan, three of the bungalows were emptied and their residents crammed into the already packed rooms of the rest. House Number 17 was one of those which were evacuated, putting an end to the defiance that had been expressed from its roof, and one of the few advantages of the reshuffle was to the Liddelows who were displaced from the house next door. It was yet another of the curiously benign by-products of this awful experience that the move actually affected the development of the whole of their young lives, as well as providing them with some immediate happiness. From an environment where their fragile confidence had left them vulnerable and uncertain, they now found themselves in the company of a group of women with such distinct personalities that it was literally an education to be crammed together with them day by day in a crowded bungalow.

The sisters shared a bedroom with Mrs Layland, the Canadian of the

G-string sewing episode, Mrs Ward, the teacher, and Maudie James, who between them provided a fascinating spread of attitudes and origins. As an example of how to encounter hardship with humour and cockney cheek Maudie was impeccable. Mrs Ward was a great deal more staid but just as resolute in refusing to let the environment conquer her, and Mrs Layland was clearly totally indomitable: a unique lady whom Phyllis cast in her mind as a Red Indian chief in her youthful need to assimilate such a powerful individual. She was tall and big-boned with a prominent nose and chin and penetrating blue eyes which in the Liddelows' recollection could make the strongest individual quail at a glance. What these women had in common, for the two girls, was an ability to draw them along as if they were part of a lively sisterhood rather than two lonely youngsters who didn't fit. 'From an early age we were conditioned in the attitude of colonials to Asians,' Phyllis said once, 'and that was that there were only two kinds of people – the privileged and the unprivileged.' These women made the Liddelows feel for the first time that they belonged among the privileged, and in return they received the kind of hero-worship of which only teenagers are capable. Phyllis had a vivid memory of a moment that belonged totally to adolescence, that time of mystification and endless questing. Only the setting made it into a unique vignette: 'I had a mosquito net,' Phyllis said, 'and under it, seemingly fast asleep, I used to tune in to conversations between Mrs Layland and her visitors. One particularly fascinating exchange was of past experiences. Women have been liberated for ages without drawing too much attention to themselves, you know! Occasionally they would discuss some rumour that was circulating and one that stayed very much in my mind was that the married couples were to be reunited in a new camp. Much as the women desired the men they dreaded the thought of pregnancy, and while they were discussing that someone suggested an old Javanese form of contraception. At that moment I couldn't prevent an untimely cough and the volume was turned down . . . how frustrating!'

There were other memorable women in that house: Zaida Short and her sister, Hilda; and a stout Dutch burgher called Mrs Gardener, with a fondness for *risqué* music-hall songs which drew a certain schoolmistressy disapproval from Mrs Ward when sung in the presence of young people. 'Life was so much more *interesting*,' Phyllis said. The sisters at last began to take a full part in all that went on. They were shown how to chop wood by an Australian nursing sister called 'Shorty', a mistress of the art who worked with a cigarette butt constantly in the corner of her mouth, a smoke she made from dried leaves wrapped in pages torn from her Bible. The girls found wood-chopping therapeutic, a release for those nervous turbulences of adolescence.

It is possible that problems were not totally confined to the inmates of the camp. In October Miachi, perhaps responding to continuing pressure from the administration to meet some directive pertaining to the employment of interned persons, returned to his quest for nurses. This time his tactics changed and he approached individuals: Olga Neubrunner, now recovered from her miscarriage, Jennie MacAlister, and the two QAs in the camp, Mary Cooper and Margot Turner.

How the Commandant made this selection is not known, but the suggestion was that they should nurse in the native hospital now run by Dr Hollweg and an Indonesian, Dr Gani, with the inducement that they might later on be allowed to nurse their own people in Charitas. Miachi had learned from his previous encounters with the nursing breed. 'We were given no time to think things over,' Margot Turner recalled. 'We were told that we must make our minds up there and then and the move from the camp was to take place the next day.'

All four agreed to go, a decision which proved to have appalling consequences, extending far beyond the unease they felt at leaving the women's community for an isolated existence in a city which had become like the very edge of the known world. At first, though, it seemed a distinct move for the better, largely because the native hospital required the whole gamut of professional nursing skills. Margot became the theatre sister and, although the conditions were primitive, and Dr Tekelenburg would arrive like a plumber carrying the instruments from Charitas to perform surgery, there were major operations ranging from big abdominals to amputations. The out-patients ward provided a crash course in tropical medicine and even a language school since it was vital to acquire enough Malay to communicate with the patients.

The nurses lived in the hospital untroubled by guards and were given passes which allowed them into the city and to make visits to Charitas where, inevitably, their freedom of movement drew them into the smuggling network, another step on the road to the fate which awaited them. For the moment, however, they could walk on the streets of Palembang and shop in the markets protected still by the mantle of their European inviolability, even in what was now an intensely alien city. It is an odd comment on the way that the world has gone that nearly four decades later when Margot was back in Palembang she, like other visitors, was repeatedly warned about the dangers of the streets, the muggings and purse-snatchings that made it unwise for women to go about on their own.

Back in Irenelaan the prisoners had taken a further step towards the proper organization of their society by holding a formal election for the job of Camp Leader, with a home-made polling booth, ballot slips and some mock-serious campaigning on behalf of the candidates. Dr McDowall was confirmed in the post with Mrs Hinch as her deputy on the British side, a very peaceable conclusion by comparison with the intensity and considerable bad feeling which accompanied similar events in the men's camp.

A great deal more of the women's energy went into the preparations for the Christmas of 1942. The output of care and ingenuity expended was no more than a conventional response to the season, but it can be seen now as a remarkable demonstration of all that the women had accomplished in retrieving their lives from the ruin of that year.

In November one of Dr McDowall's first executive acts was to commission Dorothy Moreton to organize the secret manufacture of toys for the children. 'I was very thankful', Miss Moreton noted, 'that one of the compulsory courses during my teacher-training was handi-work contrived from "waste" materials and even more thankful that I could remember it.' She could never have imagined that she would put the knowledge to use in such peculiar circumstances.

Milwani, the cloth merchant, was invaluable. He sold some of his books of material samples – probably something *he* would never have expected – and they became the basis for a whole range of gifts: needle-cases, bags, purses, rag dolls, stuffed animals. The silk samples were made up into brightly coloured balls and the most intricate of the creations was a Victorian nursery stand-by, nursery-rhyme rag books. For these Miss Moreton drew the original pictures in pencil on double samples of white shirting material and then coloured cloth was appli-quéd over them and the rhyme supplied for each scene. Mrs Gilmour used her exceptional skill with a needle to sew up the pages with stitches of exquisite neatness.

For the older children there were home-made games: stand-bys like Ludo, draughts and chess, and some innovations such as a motor-racing game which Shelagh Brown invented and Miss Moreton's master-stroke, a game called Rescue. It showed a firm grasp of the psychology of children that this game actually allowed them to extract some fun from the horrors of the flight from Singapore. If you landed on a square which denoted a bombing, you had to go back five spaces.

The classic children's card games also made their reappearance in this bizarre setting: Snap and Happy Families, the cards decorated with skill and loving care. There was even a football, destined for the tough little Reid brothers, who would otherwise have had to go without such an essential component of their boyhood. It was carefully made from canvas sections, piped with colours and filled with coconut fibres, a use for the bountiful coconut that even Miss Dryburgh had not visualized in her poem on the subject.

As Christmas drew nearer even the Japanese caught a little of the excitement, although they tempered their concessions to the season with the sort of parsimonious strictures that might be found in a workhouse. Husbands and wives were to be allowed to exchange gifts, but on the condition that nothing must appear on the present except the name of the giver and receiver. The Charitas grapevine made short work of that. The message system was working overtime, much as the Post Office does at the same time of year. The Camp Committee decided to spend some of the internal Red Cross Fund on a gift for the Servicemen and enquiries were made via the underground route. The message came back that clothes were a serious problem: lacking anyone who could sew well they were reduced to wearing skirts when their shorts wore out. It was resolved that some material should be sent to them. Back came the query: 'What's the fashion this year – above or below the knee?'

By Christmas Eve the spirit of the occasion had fought its way even through the sweltering heat of Palembang, and William McDougall's account of that morning's march down the road past Irenelaan belongs among the great set-pieces of Christmas fable:

> As usual the working party began to wave and shout when in sight of the Women's Camp. But the women were silent, standing motionless in the open space. Their stillness silenced us. We slowed to a halt and asked each other, in whispers, what was wrong.
>
> The answer came in song. Across the no-man's land which separated us sounded the melody of 'O Come All Ye Faithful'. Our guards were as astonished as we and let us stand there listening. The music softened on the second song, 'Silent Night, Holy Night', and grew stronger on the third, a Dutch carol. Leading the singers was a woman in the habit of a nun. Her arm rose and fell, as though waving a baton. The guards finally asked us to move on. 'Please walk,' they said in Malay. 'Japanese may come.' We walked, moving quietly and slowly in order to hear those voices as long as possible and we were silent during the rest of the hike to the new campsite.

The nun who conducted the singing was Mother Laurentia, who had been rehearsing a combined Dutch and English choir for weeks. No detail of the festivities that could be contrived in such circumstances was left aside. The traditional hanging of a Christmas stocking by the children was made a little difficult by the absence of such refinements as socks in the camp, but a variety of substitutes were found. Little Mischa in Garage 9 hung up his tiny, home-made trousers and awoke delighted to find them filled with presents.

On Christmas morning there was a combined British and Dutch church service with two choirs. A Salvation Army lady from Lancashire gave a sermon which included, Betty Jeffrey remembered, a reference to having been saved from sin some thirty years previously, although Betty and the other Australians were a little disappointed that the precise details of her previous history were not forthcoming.

Shelagh Brown's diary for the day is like one of those records of Yuletide feasting that survive from the days of arrant gluttony, except that the plenty is on such a miniature scale: 'Back to Garage 9 for a super breakfast. Rice porridge and ginger sauce. Toast and butter. Coffee with milk and sugar and a banana.' The women had been scrimping for weeks to be certain of eating well on this day of days and the men's camp had produced a gift of princely munificence: a large piece of beef, onions, potatoes and fat which allowed for a Christmas dinner for the whole camp beyond the prisoners' wildest expectations. It was eaten in the middle of the day, in Garage 9, on a table made up of the four planks which comprised Shelagh Brown's bed but covered with a white cloth and suitably decorated with a home-made Christmas tree and even a cracker or two. The women sat on the floor, teasing out the meal to six courses, the last an authentic Christmas pudding, concocted by the Australians out of ground brown rice, peanuts, beans, cinnamon and the sweet substance, *gula*.

The company did not rise from table until 3pm, Shelagh remarks with wonderment, as meals were normally such brief affairs. In the afternoon there was a children's party in one of the Dutch houses with a present-laden tree and sweets for each child. In the evening the children walked in procession round the camp with lighted candles in their hands, forming a circle at the top of the hill to sing carols, a strange and touching tableau in that foreign dusk.

At night, for the grown-ups, there was a party with everyone in their 'best' clothes – 'a gloriously mad party', Shelagh notes. 'Play silly games. One causes so much noise that a guard rushes up to ask if it's a snake or a rat we're killing and can he help . . .' As an example of the possibilities of a party lacking two such major ingredients as alcohol and men the gathering was fascinating. The women had sent reciprocal gifts to the men's camp, hand-made mah-jong and chess sets, and a sweetmeat for everyone in their camp. On Boxing Day, as the work-party passed, the men acknowledged this outlay of such slender resources by singing as they marched. It made the women weep. 'It was so lovely to hear male voices,' Shelagh said.

Boxing Day was otherwise somewhat marred by the cutting off of all water except for one tap at the guardhouse. This meant that much of the day was spent queueing there for a minuscule amount, although in the afternoon Mother Laurentia conducted a rendering of the Magnificat by a British and Dutch choir of all denominations, a truly ecumenical event that all who were there remembered as a high-point in the submergence of differences, by no means only of religion. It was a valuable assertion of unity because with the passing of Christmas there was a subtle but distinct change in the attitude of the Japanese which, within a very short period, was to make the freedom and gaiety of those days seem as remote and unlikely as a fable.

On New Year's Eve there was a concert party in House Number 12 which was interrupted by the Japanese with the order that only half the programme could be completed, the remainder to be presented the following day. The reason for this, which was barked with the awful fury of the Japanese issuing instructions, was that 'Japan is at war!'

This simplistic assertion, and the curtailing of the enjoyment of the prisoners, was in fact almost certainly a strange and oblique admission that in martial terms 1943 was not beginning in quite the all-conquering manner of the year before. The Japanese had boasted to the Australian nurses that they had overrun Australia and were already growing rice there, but in mid-1942, quite unknown, of course, to the women, they had been stopped in their surge across New Guinea and by the year's end were being forced back to the northern coast and on the point of a disastrous reverse. The awakened might of America was making itself felt, and on the borders of India the British had rediscovered that gritty ability which had seemed lost to them at the time of the fall of Singapore.

How much of this was known to the simple soldiery who guarded the camps is not clear. On New Year's Day, which was also her birthday, Mrs Brown, in skittish mood at having survived so adequately thus far, and perhaps also at having slimmed down to some ten stones from the fifteen that she had weighed the year before, had a highly amusing encounter with a Japanese guard. When she went out to get the coffee grinder which was used to turn rice into flour she found a guard lounging in a chair waiting for a cup of tea, a recognised perk of the duty. As Mrs Brown turned the handle of the grinder she began, on an impulse, to sing 'God Save the King' as if accompanying herself on a barrel-organ. The Japanese thought this was extremely funny. 'Bagus, bagus,' he said, which is Malay for 'good', and he guffawed immoderately. But in the higher echelons of the jailers a far graver attitude prevailed towards Nippon's enemies.

In the second week of January an official arrived who was rumoured to be of such elevated importance that he had come all the way from Singapore, and he inspected the camp with every sign of boiling anger at its inmates and their insolent ways. There was to be no more waving to the men, and no more exchanges of the Churchillian V-for-Victory sign which had found its way even into this wilderness as a gesture of defiance and solidarity among the women. The official, whom the prisoners dubbed The High Lord Executioner, announced in scalding tones that severe punishments would follow any infraction.

In true Japanese fashion the ill humour of the mighty seemed to be passed down in shock-waves to the lower rungs of the hierarchy, and the guards responded visibly to the tightening of the reins. Over the months they had graduated from threatening facelessness to some kind of individuality and many had been given nicknames based on their appearance or their known temperament. There was Grumpy, who was both bad-tempered and small, like one of Snow White's dwarfs. There was the Fifth Columnist, a tall *Hei Hoe* who habitually wore dark glasses giving him a sinister and conspiratorial look. There was Egg Face, who had one of those perfectly oval bland Japanese faces which made his head sit on his collar just as if it were an egg in an egg-cup. There was Heart of Gold who seemed to be permanently drunk and conducted *tenkos* with such beaming bemusement that it was impossible to be angry with him as he struggled with the counting over and over again.

It was a great mistake, however, to lose sight of the Japanese capacity to turn in a moment from amiability or impassive detachment to wanton cruelty and, as if limbering up for an increased harshness towards the women, the guards abruptly set about the dogs. The dogs that wandered the camp could scarcely have done so in search of scraps, since the prisoners themselves were living on the sort of remnants that are usually fed to stray animals, so it must have been principally for company that they remained, in their gregarious fashion.

The women, in their turn, found their presence comforting, enjoying vicariously their freedom to come and go but more importantly, finding in them an outlet for the sort of uncomplicated affection that is a good antidote to loneliness. As an appealing side-effect the dogs were also generally hostile to the Japanese, barking when guards approached and rejecting the quite considerable efforts the Japanese made to make friends with them.

There were therefore sinister undertones when a Japanese guard, after gazing broodingly at a dog the women called Karzan, suddenly unslung his rifle, put it to his shoulder and shot the dog twice through the neck. The bullets missed the windpipe and Dr McDowall was able to stitch up the wounds with a needle and thread so that Karzan survived, but the shooting seemed to be a signal for the persecution of the dogs and it was impossible not to feel that it stood as a threatening symbol for what could be visited on the women themselves.

This deeply disturbing possibility gained ground through an incident that Norah Chambers found as horrifying, in its way, as anything that befell her in the whole experience. One day a Japanese officer singled her out with the instruction to take a particular dog, which had allied itself permanently to one of the families, outside the camp and there to kill it and bury it. When Norah recounted this story at her home in Jersey the recollection of it still made her anguished and her response at the time must have been dramatic because she recollected that a whole group of guards gathered about her as she pleaded with the officer, pointing continually to the pistol at his belt as the obvious way of despatching the doomed dog. It was to no avail. The officer was remorseless and eventually Norah had no alternative but to comply. She led the dog into the trees. 'I put a cloth over it and hit it on the head. It was the most terrible thing I have ever done.' The killing was to remain with her in nightmares for the rest of her life.

In a kind of escalating turbulence after the period of calm, the Japanese military presence in Palembang and its environs began to stir like a disturbed hornet's nest. There were air-raid sirens at night, followed by the all too familiar bark of anti-aircraft guns, but the faint hopes that this raised among the prisoners were dashed by the discovery that these were no more than rehearsals for the day when at least some of the rumours of the Allies' return might become uncomfortable fact. The Japanese pressed more Javanese auxiliaries into service as air-raid wardens and they practised for the evil day by rushing into Irenelaan armed with long staves and herding all the women into two or three houses, causing near-suffocation among those whose lives they were presumably learning to protect.

The *Hei Hoes* were shaken out of their habitual sloth by being set to bayonet practice alongside the Japanese soldiers. Stuffed effigies were impaled with blood-curdling cries within sight of the camp, then a mock attack would send them all skirmishing through Irenelaan with camouflage branches thrust into their helmets and showing a ruthless disregard for anything in their way, from precariously balanced cooking pots to the inmates themselves if they were unwise enough to venture out.

The peaceful existence of the *Hei Hoes* was certainly at an end. Shelagh Brown remembered a night-time rumpus accompanied by screams and the sickening sound of repeated face-slapping which proved to be the discovery by a Japanese of a Javanese sentry asleep at his post. The following morning, when Dr McDowall reported to the guardhouse on some official business, she found the Japanese in charge deep in slumber, but the women had learned not to mistake the absurdities of their masters as a sign of feebleness or laxity when they could so quickly uncoil and sting like vipers.

Dr McDowall herself had her face slapped at *tenko* when there was a savage outburst at a discrepancy between the number paraded on the road and those permissibly absent through inclusion on the hospital list. *Tenko* was a useful barometer of the deteriorating temper of the captors, and there were many indications that they were becoming increasingly displeased.

Shelagh recalled one day of particularly nightmarish fractiousness out in the roadway when a Javanese, catching the prevailing mood, deemed himself insulted by one of the women. He called the Japanese guard, Grumpy, who slapped the woman's face repeatedly before casting about for some fresh affront to fuel his anger. He remembered that in the heat of his arrival one house captain had omitted to bow, so that all had to begin again, including the relentless counting. At this the Javanese became confused and had his head brutally punched for his incomprehension. Three women fainted before the seemingly endless ritual at last drew to a close.

Even Miss Dryburgh permitted herself a complaint – 'Our guards were horrid,' she wrote of those first weeks of 1943, which can be taken as a scream of agony from any other source – and throughout this time the seasonal rains of the South-Eastern monsoon fell with a virulence that in itself was a cause of major misery. By turns chilled and sweating in sticky dampness, the women whose health was already poor were easy prey to fresh surges of illness: the first case of typhus was identified, and malaria, dengue fever, dysentery and chronic bronchitis all flourished.

On New Year's Day the women had wished each other a happy New Year and exchanged the catch-phrase that was half a wry joke and half a prayer in the camps: 'It can't be long now.' But in fact, in the months ahead, it would be necessary to reach for new reserves of endurance. 1943 was not to be a good year at all.

Chapter 10

For the inmates of the men's camp the year began with an important change. On 16 January 1943 they were moved out of Palembang Jail and into the barracks that they had built for themselves. The jail again became a prison for native malefactors, but it had an infinitely more sinister function in prospect.

William McDougall, a shrewd analyst of such information as percolated from beyond the wire, believed that the *Kempei Tai* had a presence in Palembang from the middle of 1942 although, in their sly and secret way, they were not apparent for nearly a year.

Of all the threats to the existence of the prisoners in Japanese hands the *Kempei Tai* was the most pernicious. 'To give an accurate description of the misdeeds of these men,' said the prosecuting officer at the trial of a number of *Kempei Tai* operatives in Singapore in March 1946, 'it will be necessary for me to describe actions which plumb the very depths of human depravity and degradation. The keynote of the whole of this case can be epitomized by two words – unspeakable horror.'

There was a baroque quality to the cruelty of the Japanese secret police which even the Gestapo could scarcely match. There was the water treatment in which the victim was bound in a prone position and had water forced through the mouth and nostrils until unconsciousness ensued. The water was then expelled by jumping on the abdomen. Burns were inflicted with everything from cigarettes to hot irons, oil and scalding water, the heat being applied to the nostrils, eardrums, navel, sex organs and, for women, the breasts. There were other complicated methods of inducing agony in all the joints of the body, using ropes and wooden stakes stout enough to receive the weight of a *Kempei Tai* officer as he jumped upon them to apply the pressure necessary to drag joints from their sockets. Kneeling for hours on sharp objects was a variant, a flogging being added as a punishment for any movement. Finger- and toenails were pulled out with pliers or nails and bamboo slivers were hammered under them into the quick.

A woman accused by the secret police in Malaya of helping Resistance workers there in 1943 was subjected to a selection of these tortures during her interrogation. She refused to give information and described what followed to the court trying the *Kempei Tai* sergeant in charge of the investigation at Ipoh in February 1946:

My young daughter was hung from a tree about ten to twelve feet high, under which there was a blazing fire. She remained suspended there while I was tied to a post close by and beaten with a stick until it broke in two.

Sergeant Yoshimura kept shouting to me to speak out, but speaking out, as I and my daughter well knew, meant death for hundreds of Resistance people up in the hills. My child answered for me. 'Be very brave, Mummy, do not tell. We will both die and Jesus will wait for us in Heaven above.'

On hearing these words I told the Sergeant that he could cut the ropes and burn my child. I told him that my answer was 'no' and that I would never tell. All I can remember is that as they were about to cut the rope God answered my prayer. A Japanese officer who had arrived on the scene took pity and ordered the Sergeant to take down my child. She was sent home and I was sent back to my cell.

Since terror was an officially sanctioned method of exerting dominion over the lands which the Japanese had conquered, it was not necessary to wait until the war's end to be aware of the methods and proclivities of the secret police. They were common knowledge to all who were held in the thrall of the Japanese and, indeed, the country's wartime Prime Minister, Tojo, was a former *Kempei Tai* man himself, who had served before the war in the captured Chinese territories.

With such a leader it is probably not surprising that there was even an Army training manual detailing modes of bending prisoners to the conquerors' will, which is of some significance in trying to comprehend the erratic behaviour of the womens' jailers at Irenelaan in the months ahead. In this document, which appeared at the War Crimes trials, there is a passage on physical torture which is followed by a note on the use of threats towards the achievements of the same ends:

Threats
(1) Hints of future physical discomforts, for example, torture, murder, starvation, solitary confinement, deprivation of sleep.
(2) Hints of future mental discomforts, for example, not to be allowed to send letters, not to be given the same treatment as the other prisoners of war, to be kept back to the last in the event of an exchange of prisoners.

Once aware of this blueprint it is possible to see a pattern in otherwise apparently haphazard acts by the Japanese soldiers. At the end of January a Japanese officer called the Australian nurses together and told them that the Australian Government was aware of their presence in Sumatra and had sent a Christmas message – allegedly 'Keep your chins up', which drew suitably disrespectful comments from the Aussies. He added that they would all be receiving parcels and would be allowed to write a letter of not more than thirty words to their next-of-kin. The sting in the tail of this encouraging news was that the nurses were to provide a full list of their names for transmission to Australia which implied unmistakably that in nearly a year of imprisonment nobody at home had been made aware of whether they were alive or dead.

At about the same time the other women were told that official cards were to be provided which they would be allowed to send to relatives but it was three months before they actually appeared and then in insufficient numbers to supply all who needed them. The effect of all this was to counteract the apparently benign gesture of permitting some contact with the outside world, merely serving to underline the prisoners' growing belief that they were living in a vacuum and totally at the mercy of their captors.

The astonishing Margaret Dryburgh, without benefit of hindsight, was able to discern an actual technique of disorientation at work and expressed her discovery in a remarkably sapient pastiche of Lewis Carroll which she called *Alice in Internment Land*. An abridged version of this survived of which the following is an excerpt:

Alice turned and saw a scholastic figure at her side. 'Are you a professor?' she asked respectfully. 'Correct,' replied the gentleman, 'I am Professor Toromento, LMT.' 'That degree is quite unknown to me,' said Alice. 'I daresay,' said the Professor. 'It means Licentiate of Mental Torture. I specialize in experimenting on the emotions,' he swaggered.

'In what way?' asked Alice. 'Various ways of course,' he replied. 'I have tried the effect of a Mental Vacuum on the internees. Formerly news used to leak through from the hospital but I have put a stop to that and now rigidly exclude all news of the outside world. . . . I shall explain another of my experiments, known as Delayed Action. I announce that something will happen shortly and then postpone the event at will. After a fortnight they relapse into uncertainty!'

'But how wearing to the nerves,' said Alice. 'Why should they have nerves?' asked the Professor. 'When they are listless I use the other method of Precipitation. Without warning I give orders for sudden action. It is funny to see the commotion, like an anthill being disturbed.'

The Professor laughed heartily. 'Oh yes, and by the way there is another little form of torture I use. I have allowed no communication with friends and relatives overseas except one postcard.' 'In two years!' gasped Alice. 'Of course,' chuckled the Professor, 'These insignificant women can mean nothing to their kinsfolk. . . .'*

As if to hold at bay the sense of ceasing to exist for everyone else on earth, the time, and date, and day of the week became a matter of central importance to the prisoners. Betty Jeffrey remembered that among her group there was eventually only one functioning watch left. Its owner was asked repeatedly for the time but supplied it punctiliously even if there were half a dozen queries in quick succession.

These sources of mental distress were soon to be supplanted by more tangible manifestations, because tailor-made for the attentions of the secret police were the subterfuges of the Charitas hospital.

The skein of intrigue at Charitas had grown increasingly elaborate and, inevitably, those involved in it had become less cautious through their success in circumventing the activities of the guards. At its height the Charitas operation was a masterpiece. Marguerite Carruthers, when her meeting with her husband eventually materialized, felt that she was taken up by a smooth-running machine which accomplished the miracle as casually as if the Japanese did not exist.

A whispered message from a patient returning to Irenelaan provided her with the date when Andrew was due to be at Charitas. Dr McDowall briskly fixed her up with sufficient symptoms to merit a trip to the hospital and once there the organization was impeccable. There were more whispers: a certain corridor, a certain time, a certain room within the corridor. 'I was absolutely terrified,' Marguerite said, 'More for Andrew than myself because I thought that if we were caught the Japanese would be harsher with the man.' The Carruthers had the luxury of a tiny office for their meeting, a five-minute encounter that was like one of those long-distance phonecalls which strike both parties tongue-tied as soon as the connection is made. 'There was so much to say that we never got beyond the trivia,' Marguerite remembered. 'What we were getting to eat, had Andrew heard from Singapore or home. He was more concerned for me, how he could get rations to me and messages, and I could get no idea of what his life was like in the men's camp.'

Andrew arranged a signal with a handkerchief so that she could identify him on the work march past Irenelaan, then it was all over, leaving Marguerite more anxious than before, because her husband's attempt at cheerfulness was at odds with his drawn appearance, caused

* See Appendix II

164

by attacks of fever and malaria. It remained a wonder to her that they had met at all. The message-carrying was as smoothly contrived. Whenever the Japanese set up a thorough search of those entering hospital, anyone known to be in possession of contraband was edged to the back of the line and, as the search drew near, was primed to stage a collapse so that nuns lurking nearby could bustle forward and insist on carrying the sufferer inside.

With such safeguards to hand it was too easy to become complacent and more ambitious about what might be achieved. One day in January 1943, a planter's wife called Mrs Curran-Sharp was caught carrying no less than sixty-two letters and messages. The flagrancy of this crime must have stunned even the Japanese because Mrs Curran-Sharp went unpunished, but it was made known that the volume of material she was carrying established that many were guilty and from that moment Charitas was doomed.

The first consequence was that attendance there was drastically reduced again to those with serious complaints. The vigilance of the guards noticeably increased but, like ripples from a stone flung into a muddy pool, there were incidents and attitudes visible throughout the small world of the prisoners which, pieced together, suggested that a new element was at work among the Japanese. By its sluggish and crab-like functioning it seems certain that that element was the *Kempei Tai*.

On New Year's Eve Margot Turner and the other three nurses who had gone out of camp with her enjoyed a most civilized evening. Dr Gani, the Indonesian doctor at the native hospital, invited all four to a little party at his house which was even, Margot remembered, adorned by the unlikely presence of an English dentist. At midnight, to compound the pleasure of the occasion, the doctor gave each guest a wine glass containing – miraculously, in the course of this otherwise teetotal existence – a tot of neat whisky.

It seemed a promising beginning to the year and, later in the month, emboldened by such normality, Margot suggested to Mary Cooper, her fellow QA, that they should take a walk in the direction of one of the Servicemen's camps which was not far from the native hospital. Close to the camp a Japanese car passed them but stopped and came back and two Japanese in civilian clothes got out and asked them what they were doing. Margot insisted that they were simply out for a walk but the Japanese ordered both women into the car. Margot, whose commanding physical presence must always have been unnerving to the Japanese, managed to stand her ground, but the girls' passes were taken away and were not returned for some time.

There the matter seemed to rest, a tame performance if these were indeed the *Kempei Tai*, but thereafter when the nurses went out they had the sensation of being followed and shortly afterwards, with no explanation, their visits to Charitas were banned. A month later a Japanese doctor was put in charge of the native hospital and, although he was unfailingly polite, there was something in his manner which Margot and her companions found disturbing.

In Irenelaan, too, it was as if, in addition to the pique of the military at the battlefield reverses of the period, some other more pernicious influence was at work. There seemed to be a positive directive to remove any fragment of comfort from the women as though to restore in full that bleak and charmless existence which, to professional jailers, is the proper condition of prisons.

There was even a bureaucratic rendering of this. Escape had barely been considered by the women, marooned as they were by vast expanses of sea between them and the nearest friendly lands, and trapped too by their white skins amid the native population. The Japanese, nevertheless, obliged them at this time to sign a declaration that they would not try to break free, a curious document in the circumstances which seemed somehow to underline their helplessness.

The water supply remained cut off for long periods, a simple method of increasing the prisoners' distress although this gave some value at least to the incessant rains, which were trapped for drinking and cooking or to provide inpromptu shower-baths as they coursed off the bungalow roofs. The rations, another obvious pressure point if a malevolent new authority was now guiding the conduct of the camps, decreased sharply. One day, when the prison population was standing at more than four hundred souls, there were only sixty cucumbers and the same number of worthless *kang-kongs* to be distributed among all of them. Meat became more rare than ever and sugar disappeared altogether, even from Gho Leng's cart, which continued to appear but with increasing prices: a large tin of Klim now cost the equivalent of £10. Even the quantities of rice were reduced and were sufficient to fill only a cigarette tin for each person. The poverty stricken were in even greater distress than before. In March 1943 Shelagh Brown's diary notes: 'Poor Mrs Anderson asks if she might feed with us. She is living off the Red Cross Fund and her garage cannot support her.' Translated into terms of parish relief and other humiliations of the poor there is a Dickensian ring to the entry. On another day in March one of the ladies saw some cabbage leaves on a garbage truck making a call at the camp and she removed them and served them for lunch.

The crack-down at Charitas had grievously marred the flow of extras from the men's camp, although Olga Neubrunner at the native hospital managed to smuggle Mrs Brown a bath towel, she and Shelagh having coped for nearly a year on a quarter each of a towel removed at some time from the ownership of the P & O Steamship Company as the worn initials thereon made plain to all.

Astonishingly, given such a dearth of material goods, the camp was plagued at this time by thieves from outside who evidently found it worthwhile to circumvent the guards and the wire to steal anything from washing left out to dry to the prisoners' possessions. The most spectacular coup in this respect was the suitcase of Ruth Russell-Roberts, preserved since the *Mata Hari*, which contained a silver-fox fur intended, when she packed it in Singapore, to maintain her elegance in England when the flight from Malaya reached its natural conclusion.

The thieving, not unnaturally, infuriated the women to the extent that one night a prisoner gave chase to a shadowy figure slinking towards the wire at 3am. The disturbance brought out the guards who, in their temper at being aroused, immediately rousted out the rest of the camp and conducted an interminable *tenko*. Only Margaret Dryburgh could derive some benefit from such an incident and in fact turned out one of her best lighter works, 'The Thief of Palembang', which was based on her recollection of the score of 'The Thief of Baghdad':

> *A thief to our camp on a certain dark night*
> *Came creeping, came creeping, came creeping.*
> *He said, as the sentries were nowhere in sight*
> *They're sleeping, they're sleeping, they're sleeping.*
>
> *With cunning quite daring he laughed at all locks*
> *From the house all asleep dragged a trunkful of frocks*
> *And shouted when females protested, this box*
> *I'm keeping, I'm keeping, I'm keeping.*
>
> *The angry internees to tell of their loss*
> *Went leaping, went leaping, went leaping.*
> *The sentries when summoned quite frightened and cross,*
> *Came peeping, came peeping, came peeping.*
>
> *They looked o'er the fence and they bellowed quite loud;*
> *They dragged us from bed and with gestures quite proud*
> *They counted our number, now a weary vexed crowd;*
> *We're weeping, we're weeping, we're weeping.*

A fresh offering like this from Miss Dryburgh was greeted, in the wretchedness of the camp, with the sort of enthusiasm that Gilbert and Sullivan used to receive on turning out a new operetta, and her value was now inestimable. The return of hardship and repression after a period in which life had been not unremittingly grim tested to the full the relationships between the women, and where some abrasions still existed they now became distinctly inflamed. Margaret Dryburgh recalled a *tenko*, ordered at the punitive hour of 5.30am when even the sick were obliged to turn out. 'While waiting in lines,' she wrote, 'one could not help noticing the universal camp attitude of scratching. This was due to "Itch", a nervous irritation. With scratching the little blisters went septic and were very unpleasant. . . .' It could have served as an analogy for the discord.

Of a day in February when the Camp Committee stepped in to reallocate houses so that certain warring factions should be separated, Shelagh Brown noted, 'Yesterday was the worst day yet. Everyone seemed snappy and crotchety'. After detailing the new housing arrangements she added, most untypically in a record distinguished by its willingness to remain hopeful and humorous and determined to make the best of things, a very glum aside: 'After all who really cares – this is a queer life anyway . . .' She wrote out a list of church services in Garage 9 to try to forget the friction.

Even the Australian sisters, whose unity and buoyancy were usually remarkable, must have been feeling the strain because two of their number constructed what became known as 'The Flat' at the rear of one of the two packed Australian houses. It was a grandiose title. A little space was retrieved by surreptitiously moving the barbed wire backwards by a few feet, and a crude roof was strung between the bungalow and the trees. The furniture comprised a table and an old sink retrieved from the Chinese cemetery, but unquestionably the best amenity of The Flat was the relief it brought from the endless press of other people.

In April, a year after the arrival in Irenelaan, the Japanese were still finding new prisoners from their possessions to swell the numbers in the camp, but in this same month there was an exodus that once again demonstrated the chilling absence of human feeling among the captors. On 11 April the guards rampaged through the houses in the self-important fashion in which they carried out any assignment likely to cause shock and distress to the prisoners and rounded up the biggest boys among the child population. A group of them were herded into the guardhouse, their mothers trailing after them anxiously, but only to be excluded roughly so that they could do no more than stand in silent fear in the street outside. Within, the Japanese followed what was to prove their normal method of deciding whether a boy had passed on to manhood, which was by lowering his shorts and examining the genitals for the signs of the onset of puberty. Nine of the boys were deemed sufficiently mature no longer to be left in the company of women, and at two o'clock that day they were marched away to the men's camp. Young James Reid was among them and his sister, Jane, said that the scars of this brutal separation remained with him for long afterwards, besides leaving their mother heartbroken. The family knew nobody in the men's camp and James, at just twelve years old, would be obliged to fend for himself.

But the fate of all the prisoners was to seem preferable to what now befell those at the native hospital. The vague portents of the previous weeks suddenly, one April morning, materialized into a terrible reality. All four nurses and Dr Hollweg were ordered to report at the offices of the Gunsiboe, the Japanese civilian administration, at 12 noon, and when they did so they found that Mrs Hollweg was also there. There was an unnerving wait of two hours during which all kinds of possibilities passed through their minds – even, remotely, the chance that this summons might in some way be connected with repatriation.

Instead the group was suddenly bullied to their feet and hustled into an office which, from its coldly implacable atmosphere alone, was unmistakably a lair of the *Kempei Tai*. There were several officers present, but the only words addressed to the nurses were abusive. 'You blue-eyed English,' Margot Turner remembered one of the policemen snarling, and then he spat.

Their attention was concentrated on Dr Hollweg. They asked a flood of questions, the purpose of which was not discernible, and then suddenly they began to beat him up. His wife went to his aid but was held and beaten too, then, just as abruptly as the interview had begun, it ended and the doctor, Margot and Mary Cooper were sent back to the hospital, leaving Olga Neubrunner, Jennie MacAlister and Mrs Hollweg in the *Kempei Tai*'s hands.

The following morning Dr Hollweg was taken away but the Japanese doctor, amiable and courteous as ever, asked Margot and Mary if they would like to continue working in the hospital or be returned to the women's camp. Badly shaken, they naturally chose the camp and the Japanese replied smoothly that they would be picked up at 1.30pm and taken to Irenelaan. The transport arrived at the appointed hour but took them instead to Palembang Jail where they were searched and put in a cell from which some native prisoners had been ejected.

It was an extraordinary moment to return with Margot thirty-six years later to those same forbidding gates and to hear them slam behind us as we stepped into the courtyard that had been her daily vista for six appalling months in 1943. It required a sheaf of Government permissions to make our visit so that the present-day warders received us in that cautious, wooden style which descends on officials in the presence of those bearing documents signed by unimaginably lofty powers, adding much to the gloomy emanations of the place.

The present-day jailers were crisply-uniformed and peak-capped and showed us about as if we were a visiting deputation, clearly having no idea that the tall and commanding Englishwoman, who gazed so keenly at everything and seemed to know the lay-out of the prison at least as well as they, was in fact a former inmate, the occupant of one of those cells, from the barred doors of which expressionless brown faces stared back at us.

As Brigadier Dame Margot Turner, Matron-in-Chief of Queen Alexandra's Royal Army Nursing Corps, Margot had conducted innumerable official inspections of one sort or another and she carried off this singular tour well but at the end, when we were beyond the gates and free again she was very shaken. It was there that she had come face to face with the repertoire of the *Kempei Tai* and that was something that could not be forgotten.

Inside the jail on that first day thirty-six years before she and Mary Cooper found that their cell was on one side of the central courtyard, and that on the other side Olga Neubrunner and Jennie MacAlister were also together with Mrs Holweg next to them in a cell on her own. The nurses entered the prison in the white muslin dresses they had made for themselves to wear in the native hospital; these were now their only earthly possessions. The sole furnishing of the cell in which Margot found herself was a rush mat on the stone floor. There was just enough room to take four paces consecutively before coming up against one of the three blank walls, the fourth providing the only air and light between the bars of the padlocked door.

The dirt of the prison bred bugs and fleas, and flies abounded in maddening profusion. The sanitary arrangements were a filthy cooking pot which, by mutual consent, was never used in the cell so that relief had to be reserved for the two spells of about five minutes a day which, for two months, was the only time the prisoners were allowed outside the cell. There were two meagre meals each day and either a little cold tea or water to drink.

The jail had by this time resumed its function as the civil prison of Palembang so that all around them were Malay and Chinese criminals, the thieves and murderers of a city which, through industrialization, even then had a tough reputation, but it was these desperadoes who provided the only comfort the newcomers received. 'Whatever they had done to deserve imprisonment,' Margot said, 'they were kind to us. They would sometimes pass black coffee through the bars in a cigarette tin or, if they had been out on working parties, a banana, perhaps, or a bit of bread.'

For the first two months Margot and Mary did not see the other three women but the convicts would carry messages between them. These were the only indications that the world continued to exist outside the cell. In the paralyzing emptiness of the days, held in this Kafkaesque vacuum with no knowledge of their crime or when, if ever, their mysterious punishment would end, they collected stones on their brief excursions outside and marked the floor to play draughts or noughts and crosses.

At the end of this period the routine was changed to allow the women to exercise together for half an hour each day, back and forth between the walls of the jail, but they had to remain in single file a yard apart and were not allowed to talk to each other. Who made such decisions, or why they were made, was a further mystery, but in the second week of July there was no mistaking the fact that there was a fresh influx of prisoners and to accommodate them the nurses were taken out of their separate cells and locked up together in another one only slightly larger.

The new arrivals were Ambonese and Dutch and the women had no way of knowing what had brought them there. In fact, the secret police activity that William McDougall had suspected towards the end of the previous year had run its course. The probings and ferretings of the *Kempei Tai*, of which the arrest of the nurses was almost certainly an offshoot, came to fruition in a sudden and violent descent on suspect elements in Palembang.

It was the Ambonese and Chinese populations which bore the brunt of the fury and they died in their hundreds. The Ambonese, traditional allies of the Dutch and suppliers of some of their toughest colonial soldiers, rather as the Gurkhas have long stood in relation to the British, were suspected of operating a Dutch-sponsored underground movement, ready to rise if the Allies should return, and of spreading damaging propaganda in the city. The Japanese became aware of the existence of an illegal radio, and the trail led inevitably to the Charitas hospital.

One after the other the leading figures of the hospital were arrested: Mother Alacoque, Dr Tekelenburg and Dr Ziesel, joined Dr Hollweg. Dr Tekelenburg and 171 Ambonese were manacled in long chains and taken to a camp on Banka Island. Only seven of this group survived and the doctor was among those who died. Dr Ziesel was beheaded in November 1943. Mother Alacoque was sentenced to seven years in a military prison after days of interrogation spent kneeling with her hands behind her and her head bare and bowed before the *Kempei Tai*. There were searches and interrogations in the men's camp and one prisoner taken from there was beheaded.

These details were not known to the women in Palembang Jail but both Dr Tekelenburg and Dr Hollweg endured their preliminary beatings and torture there, and it was clear that the place had become a torture chamber for the secret police. Margot's eyes filled with tears at the recollection of the shocking sounds that filled the prison day and night: the screams and cries and the choked gurgling of those subjected to the water treatment.

Each day, lacking any notion of what their fate was to be, the nurses had to consider that their turn would come to suffer in the same way and imagination ran riot. One day, Margot remembered, some planks appeared by the wall of the jail and Mary Cooper was seized by foreboding. 'Mary said to me: "You see those planks?" I said, "Yes." She said "You know what they're going to do? They're going to tie us to those and they're going to shoot us." I said, "No, I don't think that's what they're for. They're for something else. . . ." ' Margot clearly marshalled all her authority to make this sound convincing, because for all she knew this might have been precisely their purpose.

The minds of the women escaped as far away as possible from the nightmare around them. Cramped in their cell for day after day, in utter deprivation, they would go for 'walks' in their heads. 'Jennie was from Scotland, Mary from Ireland, and Olga and I from England, and as we paced the few steps each way up and down the cell Mary, say, would take us for a lovely walk in Ireland then we'd come back and have a glorious meal. The next time Jennie would talk about a walk in Scotland, then home for a magnificent Scottish dinner. Then we'd go for a walk in England and come back to a high tea. . . .'

Memories provided remarkable sustenance, particularly memories of families and childhood. Margot thought that the happiness of her childhood was centrally important to her survival of the whole experience of imprisonment.

I was the only girl among three brothers so I had to be a tomboy. They'd make me play cricket but always to field, never to bat. I liked school. Games and gym were the things for which I got 'Good' on my school reports. Everything else was 'Could do better if she tried'.

I went on and did my hospital training and I was terribly happy again. We worked long hours but I enjoyed the leisure time, little as it was. My father died when I was young but I had a delightful stepfather and I was enormously fond of my mother. I was determined that I would see her and the rest of my family again and I'm sure that was one of the most important things that kept me going.

It must have been extraordinary to return from a reverie to the reality of the cell. Olga Neubrunner found her escape in poetry, which she scratched on the wall of the cell with the point of a nail. Margot treasured some of her verses, which she wrote down on paper later on. This is from a poem called 'A Prisoner's Thanksgiving':

Though weary weeks just come and go
And oft the lamp of hope burns low,
While Freedom's but a word
There's ne'er a day that ends but we
Can raise our hearts in thanks to Thee
For little mercies, Lord.

In Irenelaan, too, it was the simple verities which seemed to survive best in the awfulness, and the uncomplicated memories which were most sustaining. Shelagh Brown's diary for the 14 April 1943: 'Yesterday had an awful bout of "past sickness". Think of the lovely evenings when Army friends would come and take me out. How good they looked in their Mess Kit and how nice I felt in my evening dress, clean and lovely. And how they did appreciate my looking nice. And the little dinner parties we would have at home, and the tennis parties and all the fun. Oh dear! However it is good to have had such good times so that we can remember them.' It would have been hard, then, to believe that anything in Irenelaan would serve the same purpose in the years ahead, but memories are clearly a most remarkable commodity.

When Margaret Dryburgh's birthday came along she was delighted with her present from Mrs Brown: a patchwork apron made from fragments of the dresses of all the women in her choral group and the church choir. It is some indication of the ragged state of the prisoners by now that all of them could afford to donate an adequate piece of material without greatly harming the appearance of their outfits. This apron left the camps in Shelagh's possession and, when Phyllis Briggs saw it thirty-six years later, she recognized her own contribution with a distinctly nostalgic pleasure, having known the dress from which it came so very well.

Civilized events, birthday parties, concerts, the services in the garage church, and anniversaries like St George's Day, which the English in camp elevated from its normally muted status in the homeland in order to have at least something to set against the birthdays of Queen Wilhelmina and the Emperor of Japan, continued in brave defiance of the worsening circumstances but the trend was steadily downwards.

A plague of rats made the nights even more unbearable. The problems of drains and garbage were becoming insuperable so that the menace of typhoid grew. The water supply was not restored so that the acquiring of it became a daily Herculean labour. In June even the determinedly humorous and optimistic tone of Shelagh's daily record flagged: 'Life is truly grim. People seem to be cracking in our house . . . our rice ration is cut down and the Japanese have given us tapioca chips (cheap food given to the poorest coolies) and some very hard beans which are hard to digest. . . . Oh for a rest, cleanliness and someone to take care of me!'

Throughout these months the conduct of the guards deteriorated as if some poison were eating away at their souls too. The gaucheries of Lavender Street seemed to have left a mark because those in Irenelaan who were prepared to accommodate the Japanese lived out of camp in the 'free' houses of Palembang and, apart from occasional leering intrusions into the bedrooms of the bungalows, the women were not much troubled by the sexual ambitions of their captors. 'It was impossible to see them as men,' Mamie Colley said of them, 'they were just cyphers', and perhaps the guards, too, had come to the same debilitated conclusion about the women. In the empty houses of Irenelaan, though, they now held binges attended by the 'free' women, which left them drunk for days on end and concomitantly ill-tempered and aggressive. In terms of the relationship between the prisoners and their guards the analogy is acutely with some awful, soured marriage of endless standing.

At this point, the camp suffered the first death of a woman in her prime. It was the big, ebullient, humorous Mrs Layland who died. At first she had been delighted when she began to become more slender by the day, Phyllis Liddelow recalled, but then the flesh began to hang from her large bones in folds and she was taken to Charitas in the last stages of her illness.

Her death was of sufficient significance then for special arrangements to be made. The Reverend Vic Wardle, donor of Mrs Brown's pyjamas, was brought from the new location of the men's camp to Irenelaan to conduct the obsequies, and two mourners were allowed to accompany the coffin to its resting place in the Chinese cemetery. The major official response to her passing came after the funeral. Mrs Layland had left her possessions to her friend, Maudie James, but when Maudie went to the guardhouse to collect her bequest she found that a new mosquito net which Mrs Layland had acquired was missing. Her reaction to its disappearance elicited yet another of the infinite quirks of the Japanese. The notion that they might appear to have stolen it threw them into a frenzy of activity. Even the *Hei Hoes* were galvanized as the camp was ransacked for the missing net. Led by the Commandant, a house-to-house search was conducted with guards trampling over the women's beds and possessions, turning out their luggage. '*Susa*', a commotion, was another of the many Malay words which passed into the language of the camps, and this was a *susa* of memorable proportions.

When no net could be found the Japanese accounted for their loss of face, or whatever aspect of their complicated honour was in question, by deciding that it was in fact a towel which was missing, clearly quite another matter. 'Fools,' Shelagh fumed to her diary. 'It is really just like a comic opera to see these men in action!'

But William McDougall, in his reflective way, observed that for all the seeming stupidity, inefficiency, contradictory conduct and evident disorganization of the Japanese they would invariably reach their goal in the end by sheer persistence. Recalling his years in the Far East he remarks:

> Foreigners often laughed at the incredible stupidities of the Japanese; at their endless bureaucratic rivalries and quarrels. The army jibed at the navy and the navy at the army and both at the government. Like scorpions, government bureaus stung themselves with their own tails. Definite answers on anything were usually impossible to obtain. Yet their trains ran on time, their merchant ships maintained clock-like schedules and their armies swept over Eastern Asia like a storm. In time we would win it all back. We would give them an awful pasting; smash their cities, seize their conquered territories and write the peace in Tokyo. We would squash them so thoroughly they could never rise again. But they would. . . .

McDougall made that final prophecy long before the Japanese did precisely as he had predicted but, in a small corner of their lands in September 1943, there was another example of their bewildering methods.

The harassment of the Charitas hospital produced some classic absurdities as the long investigation ground on. A patient coming out of the dentist's room put a hand to her mouth and was promptly set upon by a guard who accused her, in the prevailing atmosphere of acute suspicion and elaborate watchfulness, of swallowing a secret message. She was made to say 'ah' by an infuriated soldier with his bayoneted rifle digging into her midriff, then she was felt all over and even obliged to remove her shoes as if, mysteriously, the missing message might have emerged at her toes.

Mavis Hannah had the experience, ridiculous if it had not been so terrifying, of coming face to face with the *Kempei Tai* for an interrogation on the subject of her sanitary towel. She believed that an informer told the Japanese of her unique method of secreting money and messages and she was arrested at the hospital and taken to a house nearby where, in mortal fear of the hard-faced secret policemen ranged round the table at which she was made to stand, she was questioned over and over again about the uses to which she put the article. 'I was shaking all over but I stuck to my guns,' Mavis said. 'But every time I told them something they didn't want to hear I was slapped in the face.' It was the brave intervention of Dr McDowall, proferring strong medical grounds for the wearing of sanitary towels by females at certain times, which brought the interivew to an end on that occasion but, in the way of the *Kempei Tai*, Mavis was kept on tenterhooks for weeks before she learned that this investigation was at last at an end. 'The waiting', she said, confirming the efficacy of at least this part of the police technique, 'was in some ways worse than the interrogation.'

Part of the guard duties at the hospital were taken over by Sikhs, formerly of the Indian Army, whose allegiance had now been transferred to the Japanese. They still wore the uniforms in which they had served the British, producing an odd feeling of security and familiarity among the women when they first appeared, but in fact the Sikhs were even more strict and watchful than the Japanese. Patients were relentlessly searched, both arriving and leaving, and contact between the men and the women was now virtually impossible, although Mrs Brown was involved in one exchange which properly belonged to a pantomime.

At the hospital for treatment for the appalling carbuncle which had added itself to her problems, she helped a Dutch lady whose husband was also there but strictly forbidden to speak to his wife. Mrs Brown sat with the wife as close as they could get to the husband who was sitting beside another man. The women appeared to be talking to each other and so did the men, but the real conversation was between the husband and wife, with Mrs Brown merely throwing in a 'yes' or a 'no' or a 'really' for the benefit of the prowling guards.

In the second week of September the whole strange existence of this most remarkable hospital came to an end. Charitas was closed down completely as the Japanese, presumably, had all along intended, and its nuns and the sole survivor of the medical staff, Dr Goldberg, were sent to the Women's Internment Camp. The days of Irenelaan, it was to prove, were numbered too. On 14 September a terse message from the men's camp was found hidden among the firewood: 'We are leaving tomorrow. We think you will be moved too. Prepare for journey.'

It was the final flourish of the prisoners' underground network. The Japanese were about to succeed in severing the women's last lifeline.

Chapter 11

The men's informational system was not infallible. Before their move there was a strong rumour that they were being taken to Java where the food shortage was not as acute as it had become in Sumatra. Infinitely more hopeful was an item in the Japanese-controlled Malay newspaper of Palembang which stated that a repatriation ship would be leaving Batavia at the end of the month. If this was intended for the prisoners' consumption as part of the psychological pressure applied by their jailers, it was a great success.

After a dawn march through the city the men were put aboard a ship which set off down the Moesi River. As it approached the river mouth, there was high excitement from the belief that it would turn southwards and set course for Java. Instead the ship ploughed steadily across the Banka Strait and by mid-afternoon their destination was apparent: Banka Island. They were to continue their imprisonment in Muntok Jail.

They left behind them in their former quarters a shambles that was intended to express their view of the conditions in which they had been kept. They removed everything which might be of use, not only because of the prudence gained from previous migrations but because they wanted to leave the place looking as much like a desert as they could. Yet another confident assertion by those who knew all was that the camp was to become a barracks for Japanese troops. It was on the grounds of this possibility that they used the wells, which were the principal source of water, as rubbish tips and left an overlay of filth everywhere else.

It was an absurd stroke of fate that the men's camp was in fact intended to contain the women when their move came, a few days after that enigmatic message in the wood. The rumours that burgeoned as this message was passed from mouth to mouth were even more ambitious than those among the men. For some, the war was undoubtedly over. Life in Irenelaan had become so immutable that nothing else would justify a move. The more cautious assumed that the Allies were now very close and that the Japanese were withdrawing, taking their prisoners with them. The customary wild speculation over repatriation, via ever more elaborate routes, redoubled.

All of the women, however, from past experience, prepared themselves for movement, assembling bundles and packages of the bizarre apparatus which supported life in the camp: more tin cans and wire and rags; nails and wood and bricks for fireplaces. As ever, the departure, when it came, was at a moment's notice with the maximum *susa* from the guards, who yapped and prodded as if the Allies were indeed thundering towards the gates. Betty Jeffrey managed to get a lift, standing up in the back of a native truck which appeared at the Australian bungalows, and as it was about to move off another of the nurses ran out with a pudding wobbling in a flower-pot. This Betty was obliged to carry in her hands, regardless of where the journey might be leading.

In fact, profound anti-climax, the new destination was only about a mile away from Irenelaan. The men had called it Barracks Camp but to the women, from long habit and the force of association, it was 'the Men's Camp' and remained so until it, too, passed into their history. It was an awful place. Molly Ismail, who walked there with her mother, well remembered her first sight of it: 'I felt utterly desolate. At least, in the bungalows, there was some semblance of a home and a community. This seemed totally a prison and somehow final, as if this is what had been awaiting us all along.'

And, indeed, custom-made for no other purpose but incarceration, the camp could scarcely have been more forbidding. Built in a low-lying, swampy area so that even its atmosphere was damply unhealthy, it was roughly a hundred yards long, sixty yards wide at one end and thirty at the other, and its walls were formed by the backs of the wooden barrack buildings which enclosed a central open space, in local terminology the *padang*. Where the backs of the barrack blocks ended the gaps were filled in with a solid fence and surrounding all there was barbed wire. It was a stagily authentic prison, completed by four tall sentry boxes, one at each corner, overlooking the whole area.

Inside the long, windowless blocks which constituted two sides of the *padang*, and were roofed with the palm-thatch known as *atap*, the appointments belonged to a cattle shed rather than a domain for human beings. In each of them there was a central walkway of beaten mud flanked on either side by a raised platform for sleeping purposes, in Malay a *bali-bali*. Here the women would sleep side by side in rows. The only accommodation for personal belongings was a narrow shelf above their heads.

In the centre of these pens, one on each side, were the camp's only toilet facilities: a cement trough for washing, and a lavatory that was no more than a long, cement drain, the effluvia from which ran out to a primitive septic tank just beyond the wire so that its presence remained a daily feature of camp life. The water supply consisted of a single tap and three wells sunk into the *padang*, the shortcomings of which were rapidly to become apparent.

The other buildings of the prison were an open-sided cookhouse at one end of the vague rectangle and, at the other, a guardhouse by the gate with sleeping accommodation attached; on the other side of the entrance there was a hut which was to be designated as the hospital, given the demise of Charitas.

It was immediately apparent that the camp would be grotesquely overcrowded, but now there was a fresh injection of prisoners. Following the purge in Palembang, all the Dutch who were still at liberty were rounded up, many of them the German wives of Dutchmen, the Japanese friendship with Nazi Germany having cooled considerably as the war in Europe became progressively less of an Axis victory parade. Even the 'free' women were recalled from their comparatively sybaritic existence in the city, and when the prison population had climbed to around six hundred Betty Jeffrey made a note of the nationalities that were represented in the camp. They were English, Scottish, Irish, American, Canadian, New Zealand, South African, Dutch, French, German, Russian, Austrian, Swiss, Latvian, Icelandic, Indian, Singalese, Chinese, Siamese, Malay, Javanese, Balinese, Indonesian, Indo-Dutch, Eurasian and, of course, Australian. 'And we all', Betty remarked, 'have the same enemy!'

Among the new arrivals were the five women from Palembang Jail. As abruptly as they had been arrested they were released by the *Kempei Tai* with the warning that if they repeated their misdeeds they would be brought back again for a longer sentence, a terrifying addition to their ordeal, as Margot Turner pointed out, since they left the jail still unaware of the nature of their original crime.

Betty Jeffrey, who had seen Margot limp into the camp at Muntok only half alive and burned black by the sun after her days alone on a raft in the Banka Strait, now witnessed her return from the nightmare of six months in a *Kempei Tai* prison. 'All the girls looked terrible,' Betty remembered. 'They were pitifully thin and there was a wild look in their eyes. Amazingly enough, they were quite sane.' But one of the five, Jennie MacAlister, who had almost died of typhoid in the jail, had to be hospitalized immediately and neither Mary Cooper nor Olga Neubrunner ever fully recovered their health after the experience. Margot's recuperative powers, however, remained extraordinary. 'What a strong, healthy girl Margot must be!' Betty, no weakling herself, exclaimed to her diary.

Even Margot, though, was sufficiently shaken by what she had encountered in the jail to burn the diary which she had been keeping in Irenelaan (Betty sewed hers into her makeshift pillow until she felt it was safe to resume), and the fierce breath of the *Kempei Tai* which the nurses brought with them had its effect throughout the camp. Vivien Bullwinkel's terrible secret, her knowledge of the massacre on the beach of Banka Island, seemed potentially even more lethal, and the presence of the 'free' women, known collaborators, brought an element of fear and suspicion that had not existed before. The secret police had done their job well.

Their divisive technique may also have dictated that in this camp the British and the Dutch should be separated, the British occupying the long pens on one side of the *padang* and the Dutch the other, with the nuns, now fifty in number, forming their own small community in the sleeping quarters next to the guardhouse. The continuing Japanese belief that the British were too stiff-necked and 'proudful' – a memorable linguistic lapse – may also have helped to determine this arrangement because it made the relative affluence of the Dutch more apparent, rather as a better-class suburb points up the shortcomings of a neighbouring slum.

For days on end, though, on first arrival, all of them were united in trying to reduce the squalor left by the men. The only ray of pleasure in this process, involving not least the tortuous excavation of the rubbish from the wells and the cleaning of the awful latrines, was the discovery by Mary Jenkin of a small, wooden stool on which her husband had carved his name. She was overjoyed and kept it like a talisman.

Mary, still the faithful guardian of little Mischa, had managed to remain with her friend Phyllis Briggs and, of the former inhabitants of Garage 9, Mrs Brown and Shelagh, although Miss Dryburgh and the other missionaries had been redistributed in the upheaval. Everyone slept side by side on the *bali-bali* and, with some sixty souls in each of the barrack pens, the sovereign space of each worked out at a strip twenty-seven inches in width apiece on the long slabs.

When the men had slept on this same *bali-bali* a savage territorial imperative had manifested itself. William McDougall tells of frequent and bitter quarrels over who was infringing on whose space. 'Some men protected their rights by erecting tiny fences of sticks and wire on either side of their spaces. . . . A few rugged individualists, using saws, cut their bed spaces from the bench and then elevated them like platforms above the bench level. Those who could built lean-tos against the fence outside and slept there.'

The women seemed far less prey to this type of mania but suffered much in the communul bathroom, not only from its murkiness and the proximity of the hideous latrine. 'The sight', Phyllis Briggs recalled, 'of so many naked women of all ages made one feel one never wanted to see another nude body.' By now most of the prisoners were showing the signs of all they had undergone: 'The women were either very thin and scraggy or else had swollen rice tummies and legs and most of them had septic sores and mosquito bites.'

Vermin and insects proliferated to a degree that, even many years later, the women squirmed involuntarily as they spoke of them. 'Rats, rats, rats,' Shelagh's diary for a day in late 1943 bursts out as if barely suppressing hysteria. 'They eat our clothes, bananas etc on shelves, and lay their young in our luggage. There are bugs in our dorm. Mrs Colley finds them in her net. Bugs, rats, the trots – life is not such fun. When we go to the lav. the mossies bite our bottoms. It is all very ghastly. . . .'

There was a species of tiny ant, known to the natives as 'fire ants', which earned its name by finding its way to every part of the body like a consuming flame and setting up an itching and a burning that brought its victims to paroxysms of wriggling and scratching. The bugs were so virulent that at night it was sometimes necessary to rise and pace the floor barely clinging on to sanity.

The rats, too, won a victory over the infinitely larger species, womankind. They would appear boldly, walking over food and clothes and bedding while the watchers looked on, horrified and mesmerized. One prisoner re-stuffed her mattress with straw and, when she lay on it, heard squeaks from within and found she had sewn two baby rats inside. Mary Jenkin woke up to find a rat on her chest and lay there dreading the moment when either she or it would move. The rats in the men's camp were unmistakably of an especially shrewd and arrogant breed. The men had taken them on as adversaries, determined to beat them, although losing just the same. William McDougall offers a set-piece:

Dentist Harley-Clark, the English dentist at Dr Gani's New Year's Eve party who with Dr Hollweg had been taken away from Palembang Jail to work in a hospital for natives, was returned to us in Barracks Camp. He moved into the eight-foot-square hospital staffroom occupied by Allen [another prisoner], myself, a New Zealander named Wilson and numerous rats who lay low by day and frolicked around at night.

The dentist brought with him two small sacks of green beans which had to be protected against the rats. We decided the safest place would be hanging in mid-air, suspended on a wire from the ceiling. Careful calculations showed that if the beans were hung in the exact centre of the room they would be four feet from any wall, too far for a rat to jump. We retired that night feeling sure the beans were safe. But next morning holes had been gnawed in the sacks. Rats had proved they could not only reach the wire but shinny up and down it. Harley-Clark fashioned a conical tin guard around the wire and we retired the second night, certain they could not get around that rat guard. They did.

We greased the wire before going to bed the third night. Strange noises awakened us. I switched on the electric light we were allowed to burn in the clinic. There was a rat crouched on the tin guard. Frightened by the light he had paused for a moment in his frantic efforts to go back up the wire. Then he resumed them, but the grease was too thick and slippery. He would start up and slide back, start up and slide back. He tried again and again until finally, either baffled or exhausted, he stopped, clung to the rat guard and watched us. Perhaps it was my imagination, but I fancied his sharp features were wrinkled with bewilderment. Now was the time for us to act.

'He's yours,' said Harley-Clark, 'I can't reach him.' I grasped a club we had made for this specific moment and stood up to swat the rat. He must have read my mind. In one enormous leap he sprang from the tin, cleared the four feet of space to the wall and scuttled out of the window. Harley-Clark took his beans to bed with him after that.

The women's best, indeed only, protection was the cats which were to be found in numbers in this camp, as dogs were in Irenelaan, until the guards, in a fury of dislike shortly before the end, bayoneted them all leaving many, Phyllis Liddelow vividly remembered, to wander the camp with their intestines trailing beneath them. There was one cat, called Hitam, the Malay for 'black', which was not only a rat-catcher of tremendous prowess but became a pet, especially of the children. The Japanese, observing the prisoners' attachment to Hitam, one day kicked him to death.

The early months in the Men's Camp, however, were principally bedevilled by the rains which set in with a violence which suggested that even Nature was joining the campaign to break the women's bodies and spirits. In its hollow below sea-level the camp was effectively a pond, the poor drainage of the swampy land on which it was built retaining the floods of water which fell from the heavens and turning the red earth underfoot into the consistency of tomato soup. 'Trompers', the wooden clogs which were now worn by almost all of the women as their other footwear gave up the ghost, could scarcely have been less effective for moving in mud, which sucked them down and brought their wearers headlong, often hurling whatever precious cargo of food or water they might be carrying into the slush.

The rains filled the wells but the water was dirty and unhealthy. The most accessible of the wells was some sixty feet deep, unlined and surrounded by such a quagmire that it had to be approached with considerable care. The only means of acquiring the water was by lowering containers on rotting ropes which from time to time broke, sending the container, in itself a valuable commodity, to the bottom with a distant and heartbreaking splash.

When so many of the makeshift buckets had been lost that the whole system was grinding to a halt, it became necessary to send someone down to retrieve them, relying still on the mouldering ropes that had caused the problem in the first place. It required a particular kind of courage to undertake the descent but, as ever in the camps, there were those who possessed whatever quality was needed. In this case the heroes were a large and remarkable Eurasian girl called Rita who, in addition to a strange ability to defy gravity, could paint, sing, dance and draw portraits, and young Dirk Reid who, if Fate had allowed him a conventionally mischievous boyhood, would probably have been punished for attempting something as dangerous and foolish.

Water for the big, cement *tong* in the middle of the washroom was supplied by the simple expedient of tearing a hole in the roof above the trough, but in the sleeping quarters the rain coursed in almost as liberally because the *atap* did not meet properly at the crest of the roofs. The mud walkway between the *bali-balis* became a swamp which was agony to negotiate and splattered its surroundings with muck. Other defects in the design of the blocks were thoroughly tested by the seasonal gales, known as 'Sumatras', which blew violently two or three times a week. The winds lifted the *atap*, letting in sheets of water; Elizabeth Simons offers a typically vivid recollection of the peak of one Sumatra: 'One stormy night when I went outside my short hair would have stood straight up if the wind had permitted. Illuminated by a flash of lightning I saw a witch, long black robes fluttering wildly in the wind, sitting astride the ridge of one of the buildings and fiendishly trying to tear off the roof. At least that is what it looked like at first; actually the figure was a nun, soaked by the deluge of rain beating upon her, who was trying to restore to its place a slab of thatch which had been wrenched free in the storm. From below her room-mates called damp advice. . . .'

The witch, in fact, was Sister Catherinia, who conducted a personal war with the soaking, intractable *atap*, coming to the aid of any who were suffering in this way, like a one-woman fire brigade. Norah Chambers climbed up to help her once when she was at work on top of one of the British huts and had an equally unforgettable recollection of her, barefoot and with her habit hitched up round her waist, straddling the roof with her veil blown out at right-angles by the wind. 'At one moment,' Norah said, 'she lost her balance and slid down the roof and I had to catch her and hoist her up again. She muttered a few things that were rather surprising to hear from a nun but, as ever with Catherinia, she ended up laughing. She had a philosophy of life that nothing could beat.'

Sister Catherinia was also talented as an electrician. The electrical system of the camp was in keeping with the primitive nature of the place and the storms repeatedly fused the lights. A fuse would send the Japanese busying about self-importantly – principally, it seemed, in order to obscure the fact that they knew very little about electricity. Eventually the nun's reputation for fast and efficient repairs around the compound led to her being called, shamefacedly, to the guardhouse to deal with the aberrations of the main fuses. 'I used to like that job,' Catherinia said, with her marvellous smile. 'Sometimes the guards would give me a tin of milk, which of course I would give to the babies.' 'One of the oustanding personalities,' Betty Jeffrey said of her. 'She once told me she would have given her boots to be in the Navy. Instead she entered a convent. . . .'

The difficult, dirty and dangerous jobs acted as a kind of yardstick for character, drawing respect and admiration in more or less reverse proportion to the view taken of such tasks in normal life. Another of the by-products of the rains was a persistent overflowing of the cesspools, which brought a disgusting tide back into the camp to mingle with the mud. This constituted a major health hazard and, once again, lacking any assistance from the Japanese, the women had to attack the task of reducing the volume of effluvia by hand.

Two of the first volunteers were Norah Chambers and her best friend in the camps, a New Zealander called Audrey Owen. Their friendship began, just as it might have done in normal circumstances, because both of their husbands had served in the Public Works Department in Malaya. Back in Singapore they might well have been among the women who peopled Robinson's restaurant at the coffee hour, exchanging news and views and Department gossip when a shopping trip brought them to the city from their stations up-country.

Here they went out of the camp before breakfast each day carrying two kerosene cans on either end of a pole, which sat across their shoulders like a yoke, and a halved coconut shell apiece. With the shells they patiently filled the cans from the vile contents of the cesspools and, using the yoke, carried them a safe distance from the wire to empty them. They then returned to repeat the appalling process until the job was done.

As so often in the friendships of the camps, the awful surrounding circumstances brought a depth of communion that might not have been possible in any conventional environment. Both women were creative. Norah had her music and Audrey wrote poetry and the bond they had formed in the weary months of captivity helped them now to keep at bay the unspeakable nature of their daily chore. 'Audrey taught me a great deal,' Norah said. 'She knew a lot about the stars and on clear nights we would sit outside and she would point out the constellations to me, a wonderful escape from everything around us. She was a very intelligent, gentle person and sometimes, to take our minds off our sanitary forays, she would recite her poetry to me as we worked. And even in that ghastly mess we found flowers, beautiful passion flowers which we would pick and take back and give one bloom to anyone who had a birthday.'

It was an extraordinary triumph of mind over such repugnant matter but reality could not be held entirely at bay. One day, with an awful inevitability, Audrey, who was tiny, only just over five feet tall, lost her balance and fell into a cesspool. 'I regret to say,' said the tall and elegant Norah, 'that I stood and roared with laughter before I pulled her out and took the poor soul back into camp where we somehow got together enough water to clean her up.'

The pair took on the job through an attitude of mind that is invaluable to humanity – 'Somebody had to do it' – and whatever needed to be done tapped the same response somewhere in the camp. Lacking the help of the men, the eternal problem of firewood reasserted itself quickly and painfully. The supply now consisted of huge rubber-tree logs, sopping wet and running with latex. The only implement for reducing them to manageable proportions was the one blunt axe which had survived from Irenelaan, its head now loose and prone to flying off with lethal violence, and it required both strength and iron determination to belong to the wood-chopping squad. Margot Turner gravitated naturally towards it as soon as she recovered.

When a small group of women combined to achieve some specific aim it was known as a *congsie*, this being the Chinese word for family, and the growth of the concept of *congsies* was an important stage in the development of camp society. There were practical reasons for their existence. As the women's health deteriorated so that even minor chores became exhausting the members of a *congsie* could lean on each other for assistance.

In this camp the Dutch continued to cook on a communal basis, using the big kitchen, but the British found that it was too taxing for one or two women to cook for a whole household, as in the bungalows, and they now prepared food in *congsies* of two or three, each with an individual fire outside the huts of the British side of the compound.

There were drawbacks. The wet wood meant that fire-flapping was a ritual that consumed most of the morning and the line of smoky fires added to the mess, but in this way the sharing of food was easier and it was possible to experiment in its preparation without risking the wrath of all if the experiment went wrong.

But perhaps more importantly the *congsie* was a definite statement of trust and reliance between its members, the submerging of the sometimes unyielding individuality with which many women began the experience of the camps. The concept of a family was accurate and all the women remembered fondly those moments when they found strength from having cast in their lot with others at a time when such trust could literally have made the difference between life and death.

The question of money for extra food was now acute. The Red Cross Fund, lacking the inputs which the Charitas network had provided, was almost exhausted and, certainly among the British, the range of items with a saleable value had dwindled dramatically. Ruth Russell-Roberts had parted with almost everything that, at the time of the flight from Singapore, had seemed of such sentimental value that it would have to accompany her to whatever end was in store: a pair of earrings which were an engagement present from her husband, her engagement ring, her charm bracelet, a diamond wrist-watch which she treasured. Only an emerald, ruby and diamond eternity ring, Denis's wedding present, remained because she could not bring herself to sell it.

Lacking any contact now with the outside world, the black market could only be continued through the Javanese guards, and the problems of those with nothing to sell increased through the shortage of money in circulation and the continued inflationary spiral. But here, too, the *congsie* system helped. The team of Mavis Hannah and Elizabeth Simons found that sales had dropped off in their millinery business but they added a cooking service and hired themselves out to do other people's chores. The clothing situation was even more acute and Mavis made some money for the firm by miraculously retrieving fragments of clothes too far gone to be of any further use to their owners. Milwani, the cloth-vendor, no longer called, but Mavis and Elizabeth had made a shrewd capital investment in some reels of cotton in Irenelaan and, *in extremis*, sold it off at ten cents a yard.

The recycling of clothes was an area for development. Mother Laurentia gave her nightdress to Norah Chambers' *congsie* as an act of charity, and it was transmogrified into four pairs of shorts and bras. Another *congsie* somehow contrived seven pairs of black shorts from a nun's habit. The *congsie* made up of Betty Jeffrey and her companion of the mangrove swamps on Banka Island, Iole Harper, existed on hairdressing and cooking. Betty was obliged to double the price of a

186

haircut with the curved nail-scissors which had accompanied her from Irenelaan in order to counter inflation, but more profitable was a soup which was much in demand among convalescents and those with severe hunger-pangs late at night.

Mrs Reid, who had a totally authentic *congsie* in the shape of the three children who remained with her after the removal of James, took all the burden on herself of protecting them from want as best she could. 'She worked her fingers to the bone for us,' her daughter Jane said, having subsequently realized far better than when she was a twelve-year-old in the camp the full extent of her mother's self-sacrifice. 'She was wonderful. She made sure even in the worst times that we children never had the burden of wondering where our next bite was coming from. We were shielded totally, from the harsh realities so that we were not even really aware that it was she who made sure we survived.'

Mrs Reid tirelessly took in washing from Dutch families, a gigantic task bearing in mind the laundry facilities of the camp and the final disappearance of anything even resembling soap. At night, with what remained of her energy, she sewed and cooked and, using her command of both Malay and Dutch, acted as a go-between in black market deals for a small commission. When even the Dutch money ran out she accepted IOUs, payable after the war.

The Liddelow sisters, another natural *congsie*, earned their living by making and selling 'bread' – pounded soya beans and tapioca root mixed with water and salt and steamed in old bully-beef tins – but their real gains derived from contact with their new neighbours in even closer enforced proximity than Irenelaan, yet another stage in their unique education. 'These were women', Phyllis said, 'who could open new windows on to the world for us through the places that they talked about and the people that they knew. They extended our knowledge in a way that a school or a university never could.'

What the Liddelows were seeing at close quarters, in circumstances that would otherwise almost certainly have been denied to them, it is possible to judge, were those forbidding elderly Colonial ladies who might not otherwise have revealed so much of themselves to two young girls of mixed blood. The sisters were much taken with a nearby resident on the *bali-bali* called Mrs Langdon-Williams who took a great interest in their welfare and even first suggested their bread-making activities. Mrs Langdon-Williams must have been equally impressed with the Liddelows, having grown to know them, because she often told them that they must keep in touch with her after the war, at which time she would be able 'to open the right doors' for them. Sadly she was never able to perform that valuable service because she was dead before the war ended and, anyway, the society that she had known was not to restore itself in quite the same negotiable form.

Another neighbour, a planter's wife called Mrs Maddams, had the kind of ebullient personality that commended her to crowds of people rather than individuals, but she included the sisters unhesitatingly so that they never felt left out. Mrs Maddams had travelled far and met many luminaries of the literary and theatrical worlds. She sang Noël Coward songs in much the manner of the maestro, her rendering of 'Mad Dogs and Englishmen' leavening many an ordeal beneath the selfsame Midday Sun. She did an immaculate impression of Maurice Chevalier, complete with gestures, accent and even, from somewhere, a straw hat, which she also wore for water-carrying. It was her rendering of Stanley Holloway's monologue, 'Albert and the Lion', which had charmed even a Japanese in Irenelaan.

Even the critical shortage of food could not entirely suppress Mrs Maddams who, at especially hungry times, would recount stories of how the famous but initially low-born had coped with poverty. One story which impressed the sisters was of Charlie Chaplin who, according to Mrs Maddams, had the habit in his impoverished childhood, of sucking a sweet for a minute or two before putting it back in its wrapper for another time. The Liddelows actually paid this story that high compliment of youth, which is emulation. When they bought themselves some black market biscuits from the profits of the bread-making they would eat only a quarter of a biscuit a day until they were all gone.

In terms of better human exchange and understanding emerging from the mud and misery, this camp was to provide one great example that was nothing less than theatrical in its symbolism and, once again, music was the magic ingredient. The 'orchestra' of women's voices was founded.

When Margaret Dryburgh was ill with dengue fever, the choir languished without her dynamism, and Norah Chambers felt that something a little different was needed to provide an impetus amid the squalor. She hit on the inspired notion of using voices in place of instruments to present an orchestral piece.

'We started,' Norah said, 'with what we thought was the simplest piece to begin – Tchaikovsky's "Andante Cantabile for Strings", which was only for four voices and we used first and second sopranos and first and second altos. We hummed to get sounds and used consonants to get rhythms and light and colour from the voices. We would practise the first line, then the second, then the third and fourth, then put them all together.'

These early experiments were conducted in the Dutch kitchen, in the dusk, another of the remarkable vignettes in which the camps abounded. In that dark and dirty place, blackened by smoke and hung with the sinister cobwebs of the tropics Norah would stand before her musicians, conducting with her hands, and all who were there were totally wrapped up in the sounds and oblivious to their surroundings. 'We clean forgot where we were during those rehearsals,' Norah said, 'and, you see, that was so important.' The prisoners would gather round to listen. 'To sit on logs or stools or tables in the crude old *atap*-roofed kitchen, with only one light, and then to be lifted right out of that atmosphere with this music is sheer joy,' Betty Jeffrey wrote. 'It is so easy to forget one is a prisoner.'

The orchestra was like a seam of pure gold running through the mire and was to involve some forty voices at its zenith, many of them, like Betty, never having sung seriously or read music before. The miraculous musical memory of Miss Dryburgh went to work on producing the scores of each piece of music in the repertoire and Norah would make a copy for each voice, in that tiny hand which conserved paper. Norah's copies survived the camps and there was a distant echo of those far-off nights at the home, now in Buckinghamshire, of her friend, Audrey Owen, herself one of the original 'instruments'. 'Here's the Dvorak – the Largo from the "New World" Symphony, remember that? Here's the "Unfinished" Symphony where dear old Jeff came in too soon. Do you remember? She came in with that C-sharp there right at the wrong moment and we all burst out laughing. She never lived it down. She wrote to me after the war and said "I'm sure I didn't do it, it must have been someone else. . . ." '

Some of the brightest and strongest spirits in the camp gravitated to the orchestra and, as their confidence and growing wonder at their skill

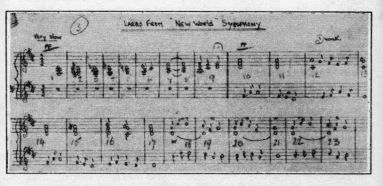

Part of Norah's musical score of Dvorak's 'New World' symphony, written from memory for the female 'voice' orchestra.

increased, their ambition was to give a concert for the men when the war was over. It was never to be. The 'orchestra' dwindled rapidly in numbers when death came at the end.

Illness, the stalking-companion of hunger, was beginning to take a firm hold by the last months of 1943. The hospital hut could house about thirty patients and it was always full, and there were usually about fifty women sick in the blocks at any one time. Long-term malnutrition surfaced first in the form of a hopeless lassitude. Betty Jeffrey described a day when she and Iole Harper were trying to recover from an attack of dengue fever: 'Today I was so hungry that I could hardly walk. The first time it has hit me like this. Iole and I literally hadn't a thing we could eat. All our tins were empty – rice, sugar, corn, all gone. Iole spent the morning lying on her bed-space and I just flopped on my part of the table outside and prayed for death or something to eat. At midday my prayers were answered and along came rations, all in tiny quantities but it is food. We felt better very quickly after cooking a little rice. . . .'

Nourishment of any kind had a remarkable reviving effect. A single kerosene tin of red palm oil shared among six hundred people was the first fat the prisoners had seen in months, perhaps a tablespoonful each for a few days, but it worked like an elixir while it lasted. The vague skin complaints which afflicted so many responded particularly well to it.

Even food that was virtually worthless served a purpose in keeping at bay the hopelessness which set in when there was none at all. Banana skins were stewed, turning them an ugly purple colour and producing a very bitter taste, but they served a psychological purpose. Having gone to the lengths of crawling under tables to retrieve *kang-kong* leaves which the Dutch had rejected, Phyllis Briggs was not surprised to notice that some people were acquiring their coffee grounds and giving them another lease of life. Shelagh Brown remembered a more substantial second bite. One day a dog arrived in camp with a mouthful of liver, stolen from the Japanese quarters. The ladies of an enterprising *congsie* retrieved it, washed it and ate it.

It was in this climate that a sort of mania for talking obsessionally about food swept the camp. Everyone conjured up the meal of their dreams and took turns at regaling a salivating audience with the details. Their imaginings were not always of Lucullan feasts. Mrs Ismail longed for a plate of ham and eggs and Ena Murray craved thinly sliced bread and scrambled egg. Talking about eating proved to be curiously satisfying, rather than sharpening the pangs and, so that the delicious reveries could continue in private, people began to write down recipes ranging from simple, country fare to *haute cuisine*, according to past experiences and tastes. It was a logical step then to exchange these recipes with others and a furious traffic began between the women, sheaves of scribbled ingredients and methods of preparation changing hands around the compound.

Dorothy Moreton collected these fragments assiduously and contrived a sophisticated index system, a cookery book effectively, which was much in demand because of the ease of finding some favoured dish. In the scarcity of paper Phyllis Briggs utilized an item she imagined might never be needed again for its proper purpose: her cheque-book from the Chartered Bank of India, Australia and China, which had survived all that had befallen her. It eventually made its way out of the camps as well. When Phyllis produced it, the very handwriting on its crowded leaves gave an impression of feverish enthusiasm to cram ever more mouth-watering dishes into the safekeeping of the imagination. There was something there from the cuisine of half a dozen nations, from Pavlova Pudding, the national delicacy of Australia, to a Dutch dessert called *road groat*, an ambrosial concoction of raspberries and redcurrants garnished with cream and blanched almonds.

Even at the time it struck Phyllis as curious that the preparation of food had actually not engaged her very much in her life before the camps. Ena Murray was another for whom domestic chores, even though she was married, had been of little importance in the servant-laden bungalows of Malaya, but she collected recipes with even greater vigour. In this utterly unlikely setting she spent days on imaginary domestic duties. She wrote down detailed household budgets which also survived the camps and were touching to read in the knowledge that they were written so far from the comfortable normality which they represented: 'Ken's Season Ticket – £5; Lunches at two shillings and sixpence – 15/-; Post Office Savings – £1; Newspapers – 2/6; Butcher – 10/-; Baker – 3/6.' Totally absorbed and insulated for the moment from the life around her she went on to design the house in which she and Ken would live and furnished it and chose the curtains, the seat covers, the carpet and all the rest. She was even prepared for guests and put together a week's dinner menus, one of which must have been almost unbearable to write down with an empty stomach: '*Hors d'oeuvre* – sardines, olives, hardboiled egg, mayonnaise, *pâté de foie gras*, soused prunes; *consommé*; baked lobster dish; roast duck and apple stuffing; Green peas, roast potatoes; Meringues, ginger and cream; Coffee; Nougats, chocolates.'

The Christmas of 1943 might have been designed to bring fantasies of food to a brutal conclusion. The Christmas dinner consisted of a small amount of pork, hardly enough to flavour the rice, although the women's tastebuds were by now so acutely alert to meat that even a fragment placed in rice and removed again for another time was detectable to them as if it were a full-bodied sauce. There was also a 'plum pudding' made from beans but, although the children provided a carol concert again, it was such a pale ghost of a Christmas celebration that Mrs Ismail, for the first and only time in the camps that Molly could remember, wept.

1944 began with the same wave of depression that had swept Irenelaan in the previous January, the New Year seeming less of a fresh start than the writing off of yet another twelve months to oppression and want and the absence of loved ones. The overcrowding of the camp worsened even further when about twenty-five trainee *Hei Hoes* were moved into the hut where the Australians still stuck together in their indomitable allegiance to their version of 'mateship', that special Antipodean form of unity. The hut was boarded up across the middle to accommodate the newcomers, so that the nurses were squashed even closer together down at one end, a searching test of their camaraderie. Their bed-spaces were reduced to a precise twenty and a half inches each, and the *bali-bali* was now marked out to assist arbitration in demarcation disputes.

The Japanese treated the Indonesians as inferiors who were little better than women in their conception of the ordering of species. One day a Japanese NCO savagely and repeatedly punched a *Hei Hoe* in the face in front of a crowd of women, fastidiously knotting a handkerchief round his fist before he did so. Then, in the ungovernable rage which seemed to seize the little men, as if their initial sense of outrage was somehow fuelled by their violence, he forced the young man back against the wall by ramming an enamel plate between his jaws.

There was never long to wait before the other aspect of Japanese cruelty manifested itself: the bleak heartlessness with which they would casually kick a cat to death, bayonet a dog, or leave human beings to wither. The impression is of a kind of yawning boredom at the inconvenient amount of time the humans took to dwindle and depart. Phyllis Briggs used a chilling phrase when she referred to the transfer of the hospital from Charitas to this place: 'From now on the dying remained in camp. . . .'

The British and Australian nurses continued their daily rounds helping those not yet committed to the hospital and, in March 1944, Phyllis was nursing a prisoner called Mary Anderson who was clearly sinking fast. 'I had known her in Penang. She had been a large woman with a booming voice and she was a very keen golfer.' She was also highly intelligent and a voracious reader. When she had exhausted all the books in English in the camp she learned sufficient Dutch in six weeks to make a start on the Dutch supply. 'I used to wash her and try to make her comfortable. She was desperately thin and frail now.

Nobody would have recognized her and she was pathetically grateful for anything one did for her.'

Mary Anderson died on 4 March 1944; this happened to be a Japanese holiday and no guards would come to move the body or even provide a coffin. An open-sided shed had been built in the middle of the compound, what the Dutch called a *pendopo*, and it was used as a school and playroom for the children during the day, for church services on Sundays, and the orchestra's concerts. Now, with the hopeless over-crowding of the blocks and the tropical heat taking effect upon an untended corpse, it became a mortuary. Mary Anderson lay for a day and a night in the *pendopo*, covered only by a sheet, until late the following day when, their holiday and its aftermath over, the guards allowed her to be taken to just beyond the guardhouse where there was another long wait until a coffin came. During the night, against the depredations of rats and dogs, the prisoners went in pairs to watch over her. This is part of Margaret Dryburgh's commemorative poem, 'The Vigil':

> 'Tis night, and in the camp's wide square
> Unwonted silence fills the air,
> For now the central open shed
> Acts as a shelter for the dead.
>
> How slowly time doth pass!
>
> A tiny lamp with a steady glow
> Lightens the darkness and doth show
> Where watchers solemn vigil keep
> Beside the dead while others sleep.
>
> How slowly time doth pass!
>
> 'Why do you use this public place?
> Within the walls is there no space?'
> The living scarce have room to lie
> There is no spot for those who die.
>
> How slowly time doth pass!
>
> But, watcher, in this tropic clime
> Death brings decay in little time.
> Why, therefore, do you think it meet
> To use nought but a winding sheet?
>
> How slowly time doth pass!

Through this requiem Mary Anderson's sorry end did not go quite unremarked, but like so many of those who died she would have no permanent memorial in Sumatra.

Chapter 12

One day I killed a Jap,
Killed a Jap.
I hit him on the head
With a bloody lump of lead.
Blast his soul,
Damn his eyes,
Bloody Hell.

Where the verse came from nobody knew, but it was muttered under the breath like an incantation and vented a little of the loathing and frustration of utter helplessness. The most significant change in the prisoners' lives in the early months of 1944 was the transfer of responsibility for the camp from the civil administration back to the military, almost certainly a response to the setbacks which Japanese armies were continuing to suffer all over the Pacific.

There was a theatrically brisk indication that the true masters of the Orient had resumed their sway. Once again 1 April proved to be a significant date, the new Camp Commandant arriving with a strong whiff of fire and brimstone, like the Demon King. His name was Captain Siki and physically he was well cast for his role. His features were brutal and dominated by a hard, staring brown eye, the other being hideously bloodshot and evidently useless, and accounting perhaps for the fact that such a truculent-looking warrior had been relegated to the command of a prison camp for women.

On April Fool's Day, as the prisoners wryly noted, he had a table and chair set up in the *pendopo* and sat regarding his new subjects as they were paraded, in groups according to nationality, out in the compound under the blazing sun. Each one of them, including the children and even the infants, was presented to him individually by his second-in-command, an overweight Japanese with a face like a pig who was promptly christened Ah Fat.

Ah Fat announced the name of each inmate, in the manner of a toastmaster, and the person called had to step up to the table and bow. There was a patch of wet and slippery clay at the point where this obeisance was made and a number of women skidded or lurched over the table, which produced a muted hysteria in the ranks and a sort of solemn fury in the Japanese. As ever, though, the captors at their most ridiculous had some fresh unpleasantness in store. Siki, through an interpreter, now made a long speech.

It began with a résumé of Japanese military successes, which aroused scepticism in inverse proportion to its optimism, but the message which most concerned those listening, and seemed to contradict altogether the notion of an approaching Japanese victory, was that all of them would have to work to survive. Captain Siki made a crude attempt to tailor his remarks to his new audience. 'After the war women will have to work hard for the men, who will be so tired,' the interpreter translated but in fact, at this time, all over the Japanese possessions an even harsher regime was being enforced.

Post-war investigations have established that as early as the end of 1942, Premier Tojo issued a directive to all Camp Commandants that prisoners' rations were to be cut in order to conserve more food for Japanese workers and the armed forces. This was followed a year later by the positive dictum, 'No work, no food', and it seems likely that this was the order now percolating through to the least regarded of Nippon's captives, the women prisoners in this far corner of its domains.

It was announced that the women would begin by cultivating the land within the compound and its surrounds with the object of growing their own rations – a bleak prospect to those already weakening fast on what was doled out to them. Siki's lecture, when the women discussed it afterwards, seemed designed to indicate that life under military government, which was presently to be restored all over Sumatra, was an altogether tougher and more business-like matter than sloppy civilians could contrive. As if even the paperwork of a possession governed by a Japanese Resident rather than a General were not to be trusted, another of the endless lists of prisoners' personal details was prepared. (The eagle-eyed Elizabeth Simons noted that even after two years of captivity the ages of a number of ladies remained the same as when their imprisonment began!)

There were several ways in which it was possible to trace an effort at this time to follow some more conventional path in the treatment of the prisoners, as if at least a few rules had been laid down and, in military fashion, the captors were trying to obey them. But, as usual with the Japanese, there were strange anomalies and the customary signs of an ineradicable callousness, a mindless pursuit of orders in which humanity had no place at all.

The quality of the rice improved immediately under the new management. Sugar and salt were provided, and tea, curry powder and maize. The maize proved usefully filling and diminished the sharp pains in the stomach where the hunger bit. But the supply of vegetables promptly dropped by half and overall, though supplies became more regular and better organized, there was actually less than before: three quarters of a cup of rice per person per day, a half a cup of tea-leaves per person per month.

It was starvation put on a tidier footing. Each month now the prisoners were carefully weighed and their weights written down by the guards so that there was a formal record of their deterioration, a statistic which existed totally for its own sake. Shelagh Brown's method of keeping account was rather less detached. 'Mother has lost 1ft round waist and 1ft round hips in the last year,' her diary noted. Mrs Brown's weight was now down to seven stone, less than half what she had weighed when the ordeal began.

It was in this ebbing condition that the women were put to work. They were divided into working parties and set first to the breaking of the ground of the compound into small growing plots around the huts. For this purpose they were provided with *chungkals*, the native hoe which, with its iron head and thick wooden handle, weighed about 22lb. The *chungkal* was so heavy and intractable, so difficult even for women's hands to grasp, that it became a sort of emblem of servitude as the yoke did to peasants in the Middle Ages or the oars to galley slaves.

The burning sun which followed the rains had turned the mud of the compound, trodden constantly by hundreds of feet, into a surface like concrete. The *chungkals*, at this stage, had to be used in place of pick-axes to break this surface into clods. They had to be raised as high as possible and came down with a thud that jarred every bone in the body. As a finesse to this distress, the Japanese insisted that the hoes should rise and fall in unison so that the spectacle of a working party under its languid taskmaster, rifle and bayonet on shoulder, had the authentic appearance of ancient slavery. The working hours were from 5am to 6pm with a three-hour break in the middle of the day.

A profusion of seeds and cuttings arrived and there was more toil under the relentless sun to plant them, but the completion of that task brought no respite. There was a shortage of coolie labour in Palembang and an order went out that parties of six women from each block must be provided to cut the grass verges of the road around the camp and keep them swept. Phyllis Briggs's first day at this job was not a conspicuous success: 'The first *parang* [a type of native sickle] I was given broke and then one of my trompers fell into a filthy drain. Getting it out I got covered in mud. Praise be, there was some water in the washroom when I got back into camp so I was able to bathe and wash my hair and clothes. I felt,' Phyllis concluded, with memorable understatement, 'very weak for the rest of the day.'

After weeks of the work, however, Phyllis was clearly arriving at that attitude of uncomplaining stoicism which is often visible in those who perform the hard and unrewarding tasks of the world. 'Am getting used to being a road coolie,' her notes on the period remark, 'and now understand why they spend half their time sharpening their *parangs*!' On the day when she was afforded this insight into a way of life that she could justifiably never have expected to comprehend in such detail, another of the prisoners had a sudden moment of clarity about the plight that had befallen these daughters of the Empire: 'Poor Maudie Hilton cut three blades of grass and then her finger. She stood up on a pile of dried mud and said very solemnly, "This picture will go down in history. It will not be forgotten in a hundred years."' It was a slim grasp at immortality. Maudie Hilton was dead within a few months and among all those who kept day-to-day records their accounts are now dappled with deaths. Mrs Curran-Sharp, whose indiscretion in the matter of letter-carrying had gone unpunished at the Charitas hosptial, had only a few months to dwell on that good fortune. She died on 11 May 1944.

But there were still recruits to this unlovely place. On 6 April there was a rumble of trucks on the road outside which sent the prisoners rushing to the cracks and knot-holes in the back walls of the blocks which gave them their most expansive view of the outside world. There was immense excitement when it became apparent that there were women in the vehicles. The Australian nurses, who had never given up hope that some of their missing numbers would one day turn up to join them, felt sure that the moment had come, but in fact the newcomers were British and Eurasians, transferred from a camp in Northern Sumatra, called Djambi.

As ever there were fresh tales of survival to recount. Netta Smith, the Scottish nurse who had followed Margot Turner's example and ducked beneath the waves as the Japanese planes strafed the survivors of the *Kuala*, was in this party and she was able to continue her story for Margot from the time that they had bobbed together in the Banka Strait.

Netta had graduated from a floating wooden box to a ship's boat and had reached a small desert island already crowded with survivors. They had neither food nor water for three days and nights except when a sea bird flew over with a fish in its mouth. Those below made so much noise that the bird dropped the fish. They divided it into tiny morsels and ate it raw.

A Chinese junk rescued them and took them to a Dutch island where they existed in reasonable comfort for several weeks while the wounded and sick recovered. As they did so they were sent over in small batches to the northern shore of Sumatra, where some were picked up by friendly vessels which took them to Ceylon and even Australia. The fortunes of war among those who fled from Singapore were quirky indeed, and there are many stories of escape as well as of imprisonment.

Netta was on the way to Sumatra when the ship broke down and was forced to return to the island. This was when her luck ran out. The Japanese appeared at last and she spent the next two years in Djambi jail, suffering the standard brutalities and hunger. The clothing situation in Djambi was even worse than among the women in Palembang. Netta, who had stepped over the side of the *Kuala* immaculate in white uniform and shoes had watched this outfit fall to pieces and was reduced to a pair of briefs and a bra, as were a number of her fellow prisoners. 'The *Folies Bergère*,' Netta said, with her sweet smile, restored to proper decorum at home in Aberdeen, 'were simply not in it!'

There was a doctor among the new arrivals, Dr Thompson, who had been very roughly handled by the Japanese in Djambi, and she now joined Dr Goldberg, Dr Smith and Dr McDowall in the hospital. Dr McDowall had by this time been succeeded as British Camp Commandant by Mrs Hinch, who had a particularly good technique for dealing with the Japanese.

Ah Fat proved to be a fussy individual who was often gripped by the cares of his job while he was off-duty, a neurotic impulse which would send him waddling through the camp in his reclining garb, which was yellow pyjamas worn with slippers. As he went he would scream at the top of his voice for Mrs Hinch, whom he insisted on calling 'Inchi', this being by useful coincidence the Japanese word for the number 'one'. Betty Jeffrey described this absurdity: 'Inchi! Inchi! Mrs Hinch emerges serene and calm and with a most dignified, bored expression on her face asks him what he wants. Everyone who hears this can hardly keep a straight face until he has gone.'

If he had not been vicious as well as porcine and ridiculous, Ah Fat could be seen as belonging to that breed of overbearing seaside landlady who used to make their boarders' lives unbearable by constant and imperious commands relating to domestic matters. As an example of the kind of brooding that would suddenly impel Ah Fat from his quarters and send him yelling through the camp there was his dislike of the line of British cooking fires smoking untidily beside the blocks.

One day 'Inchi' was obliged to provide six of the stronger women from each of the huts to lug huge iron cooking-pots, known locally as *kwalis*, from the guardhouse to the kitchen, and it was announced that the British would henceforth prepare their food in the same communal manner as the Dutch. The insatiable *kwalis*, each with a capacity of ten buckets of water, represented a considerable new burden which only teamwork could surmount. The *congsie* system had to be set aside to provide cooking squads: rice cooks with attendant rice washers and sorters; vegetable cooks with vegetable choppers; water carriers and firewood suppliers; fire-flappers; servers and washers-up.

The menus were scarcely demanding: breakfast was a small bowl of rice porridge per person, one part rice and six parts water; at 10am there was weak black coffee or tea; lunch was another small quantity of rice with vegetables, a bland repast, flavoured only by a concoction of any scraps remaining mixed with curry powder and dignified by the name of *sambals*. Dinner was a repeat performance, meat by now having become a wondrous rarity, the first in months appearing as a dispensation from Captain Siki when Hitler's birthday joined that of the Emperor of Japan as an event which the women were required to celebrate.

That it should require so much organization to produce such pathetic fare is an indication of the mountainous and exhausting difficulties which were entailed. The *kwalis* in particular brought a fresh affliction: small painful blisters all over the unprotected flesh of those obliged to attend them by the hour. These were caused by the boiling water which the rice spat out as it cooked.

Once again, though, there were tiny glimmers of accomplishment that perhaps only these bizarre conditions could make important and rewarding and productive of something even more vital than the food itself, which was the will to continue with such an insupportable life. Ena Murray was put in charge of a cookery squad and proved very efficient. 'I found,' she said, 'that I was beginning to see the job of running a home in a different light and I felt that if ever I were to be reunited with Ken I could put this experience to use.'

French Mrs Gilmour, in surely the most searching test of the Gallic flair for cuisine, upheld her country's reputation by producing *sambals* that were sought after as if they were truffles and gave no hint of their origins among the leftovers of what had been totally inadequate in the first place. Audrey Owen found a gift for lighting fires and received the sort of satisfaction from coaxing the green wood to burn that an artist might take from an act of creation. She would rise at 3am to begin the task of bringing a fire to life. There were many other smaller rewards of the kind that are usually lost at the end of childhood. For the washers-up the grim chore of cleaning out the *kwalis* concealed the treat of access to the rime of burnt rice which accumulated round their insides.

Food nagged so imperiously at the psyche as well as the stomach that when the women tried to revive their flagging spirits with a concert in the *pendopo* the central item was entitled 'A Musical Market', with all the songs and recitations pertaining to food. Phyllis Briggs contributed 'Cockles and Mussels' and the item was so well received by the Japanese that they gave the performers a small tin of corned beef to be shared among the cast of eight.

The relationship with the Japanese that made such gestures possible can probably be best understood in terms of the recent phenomenon of seizing hostages and holding them prisoner for lengthy periods. A number of the women had noticed the modern parallel and found that they could perfectly comprehend the very complicated interplay between the captors and the captured in these incidents, the occasional cordiality which seems to emerge even when lives are threatened, as if no human being can remain either monstrous or utterly cowed all the time, however extraordinary the conditions.

At the end of May Captain Siki mounted a table in the compound to give him the necessary height to address the women and, in another long speech, he told them that there was now a possibility of Allied air-raids. In that eventuality they were to form themselves into groups and make for the cover of a nearby rubber estate. In a gesture that could have been intended either to enhance his reputation as a warrior or as another clumsy attempt to find some psychological footing with those with whom, in fact, he shared a danger, he announced that the Japanese would go with the prisoners 'and die with you if necessary!' He was afforded a loud cheer, the irony of which may have escaped him, because the harshness of the regime within the camp was tangibly increasing. Margot Turner, who right to the end was physically stronger than most of her companions, had a recollection of the sickening weight of the rice sacks which the women were now obliged to unload themselves from the ration lorry. It took hours to recover from such an effort.

In June Siki mounted his makeshift rostrum again to make another dramatic announcement. There would be no more supplies of rice after September and it would now be necessary to cultivate the land in order to eat at all.

Both this and the possibility of Allied bombs paradoxically raised the prisoners' hopes. For all their protestations the war could scarcely be going well for the Japanese. There were equally convincing signs, however, that the food shortage was truly acute, not only in the camp but in Palembang and possibly the whole of Sumatra. In fact the Allied submarine offensive was gradually eradicating the clockwork movements of the Japanese mercantile marine and paralyzing their supply lines, but the tactical situation filtered through to the women only by oblique portents. The sacks containing the rice, to which was now added, besides the customary broken glass, weevils and rat-droppings, many fragments of shrapnel, had often been tampered with before their arrival and even black market food was clearly the dregs of the local supply. Eggs were often so far gone that, in addition to their dreadful odour, the yolk would frequently contain a well-advanced embryo.

Most telling of all as a sign of their deteriorating fortunes were the forays which the Japanese led into the surrounding jungle, parties of twenty women being taken out each morning to be shown a trade secret of the exceptional mobility of the Imperial Army: a method of truly living off the land. Edible ferns, grasses, wild vines and even dahlia leaves were pointed out to the women, as on a nature ramble, but the further element here was that they were then obliged to collect these specimens and take them back to the camp to form a part of their diet.

Alarming as this was, it was the longer-term solution to the crisis which was to provide the greatest distress: nothing less than the order to cultivate the entire compound and all the open land beyond the wire. The small plots had proved remarkably fruitful, the soil of Sumatra at least displaying a generosity that had not been visible in any other aspect of the island so far. Betty Jeffrey and Iole Harper had put their energies into two plots some six feet long and three feet wide, which at first had the appearance, it struck Betty forcibly, of graves. Their fertility, however, was exceptional. The seeds or roots of vegetables, simply stuck into the ground, grew apace. Some rotting spinach retrieved from the kitchen burgeoned. The nurses had brought some balsam seeds from Irenelaan and they blossomed into flowers.

Now the pair trimmed the rough grass round the plots with a table knife to form a lawn and built a makeshift table. They bought a serviette from a Dutch woman as a tablecloth, filled half a coconut shell with balsam flowers, and ate their evening meal there alone as if it were the terrace of Raffles. Such luxury and seclusion could not last. In one of Ah Fat's rampages it was decreed that all small plots would be scrapped in favour of the bigger undertaking, and once again the women set to with the *chungkals* on the hard ground of the *padang* and beyond the wire.

The summer heat of 1944 matched the intensity of the rains which had ushered in the year so that now the shuddering impact of the hoes was even more agonizing, but the seriousness of the task could not be denied because the guards and even Siki himself joined in the work and helped to plant thousands of sweet potato and tapioca roots.

It was the next phase of this endeavour which brought the women to the absolute nadir of their coolie role. The plantation they had now created required irrigation and fertilization and the method of providing both water and manure was the same: by hand, and by the women. The water shortage was now acute, the camp tap no more than a home for spiders, offering only a painfully slow trickle for a few hours each day that had to suffice for washing, drinking and cooking. The ration was a single Klim tinful per prisoner per day. The wells were down to their last dirty dregs and the only properly functioning source of water was a hydrant half a mile away outside the camp near the street where the guards had their houses.

Betty Jeffrey described a typical outing for the inmates:

> At the hottest hour of the day, 1pm when even the natives sleep, we have to stand in the sun for half an hour and wait for *tenko*. Then, when it pleases the guard, we move off and out of camp to the road, carrying anything that will hold water. We walk a long way to the back gate of the camp. From there we turn into a street full of Jap houses, eventually getting into the main road. Down a hill on a very stony road we trudge, barefooted, until we come to a pump surrounded by mud and filth. A queue is organized to keep law and order.
>
> Back we come up the hill with the water and are forced to throw it on the sweet potatoes. I hate to think how many trips we make. If only we had protection for our feet! We can manage at odd times to get a little dirty water from one well. We asked Rasputin and Ito [two of the guards] if we could change it for the clean water we were carrying and so have the clean water for ourselves and put the well water on the potatoes. Absolutely no!

Margot Turner remembered the suppressed fury of the water-carriers when the filling of the baths in the Japanese houses and the watering of their private plots was added to the task: 'After all that labour we would be lucky to get one bucket of water in to camp.' Through the lack of bodily modesty among the Japanese the women were able to note that a Japanese bath consumed at least four buckets of water per bather, which they counted with loathing, having hauled each one at such a cost.

The spectacle of the prisoners labouring like oxen seemed to inflame the guards, as if at last the women's 'proudful' behaviour had been undermined and total humiliation should follow. An order was issued that all the prisoners should now bow every time they encountered a Japanese, and there were frequent outbreaks of rage when a woman, probably staggering with fatigue, forgot the obeisance.

Phyllis Briggs remembered a day that, in its misery and absurdity, could have taken place in some nightmare kindergarten. She and Mary Jenkin had been nauseated at the spot where they slept by an appalling smell which seemed to come from beyond the wall. It contained the now familiar element of decaying flesh and they thought that perhaps a dead rat was impaled on the barbed wire. They asked permission to go round to the spot on the outside to try to trace the source and, as they were searching, they failed to notice Ah Fat walking by until he had passed them in his yellow pyjamas. On their return they were stopped at the guardhouse, given an hysterical berating and made to stand bareheaded in the blazing sun for an hour, a punishment that left its victims drained and shattered for days afterwards. They had failed to bow to Ah Fat.

The slapping of faces was now a commonplace, only the amount of force used distinguishing one assault from the next. Mavis Hannah recalled a pathetic gesture of acceptance of this peculiarly unbearable affront. A British woman called to the centre of the compound by a guard to answer for some nameless crime waited passively while he climbed to the pinnacle of rage that always preceded a blow. But as he drew back his arm she called to him to stop, turned away to remove her glasses and false teeth and then faced him again resignedly.

Ena Murray was returning from a water-carrying trip with three other women when they were called to the verandah of the guardhouse by a vicious Japanese who was known as The Snake. 'Say you are sorry,' the Snake said in his fractured English. 'For what?' one of the women asked. 'Say you are sorry,' the Snake repeated. 'For what?' The Snake lashed out so forcefully that his victim went over the wall of the verandah and fell about four feet to the ground.

The whole group were made to stand out in the sun until darkness fell and both the British and Dutch Commandants went to plead for them, but they were ordered to return to the guardhouse at 6am and, although Ena was in charge of cooking, they were set to manuring the compound until noon. In some respects this was the most terrible trial of all because the only fertilizer to hand was their own effluent and this had to be retrieved from the cesspits and carried to the compound, the Japanese gardens and the cultivated areas outside the camp.

In the unremitting heat the women had to scoop up the filth in kerosene cans tied to sticks and travel with it in such awful intimacy that the stench permeated their hair and clothes and skins. Once spread the manure dried and the wind blew a reeking dust to every corner of the camp so that at no moment of the day, lacking now both water and soap, were the prisoners free of their own voidings.

Possibly to observe closely a health hazard of such comprehensive virulence, one day in June two Japanese nurses made a tour of inspection. They wore white dresses, almost to their shoes, and elaborate hats and, since they kept their handkerchiefs pressed firmly to their noses throughout the tour, they looked much like two stunted Edwardian ladies of quality visiting a slum in the course of good works.

Shelagh Brown was one of many who wondered if the bowing process was equally mandatory in the case of Japanese females, and out of a combination of irony and caution she produced an energetically exaggerated version as they passed. It was a waste of energy. The nurses swept by with their hankies clamped to their faces giving no sign of acknowledgement. Shelagh confided a doleful insight to her diary: 'What *do* we look like? And how we must smell!'

The Japanese may have acknowledged to themselves that they were creating a breeding ground for epidemics because, to the astonishment of all, they now provided the only positive medical care of the imprisonment: injections against cholera and typhoid. All the nurses there agreed that these saved scores of lives in the months ahead, but it was such an unexpected gesture that the administering of the needle was a very frightening experience. With no precise knowledge of what the syringe contained it was in the minds of many that they were now being used as guinea-pigs in some bizarre experiment of the kind that Nazi doctors are known to have carried out on concentration camp inmates.

There was certainly sufficient evidence for the Japanese to assure themselves that their regime was lethal. In June Sally Oldham, the missionary who had intrigued her listeners in Irenelaan with her confession of having been saved from sin, died, barely into middle age, leaving behind an impression of a rather hard and lonely life, ending with a unique flourish of deprivation. Phyllis Briggs provided her with a sad little epitaph: 'She was very Lancashire and although she had spent years with the Chinese in Singapore she could only speak English. She was a simple soul without much education, and she did not get on very well with the other missionaries.'

This death was one of four in as many weeks, and one of these brought a particularly ominous chill to the prisoners. Phyllis Liddelow was friendly with a pretty, popular woman in her early thirties, called Grace Gurr, who slept in the same block. She found her company enlivening because Grace was more vigorous than most and always full of plans for the life she would lead when she was released. 'Two days after we had had a long and interesting talk about many things,' Phyllis said, 'Grace called out to me from the *bali-bali* nearby: "Phyllis, I can't move my legs." She was clearly in pain and when I went over to her I saw that she could no longer control her bladder.'

Grace was taken immediately to the hospital but two days later she was dead. It was normal now for bodies to be left overnight, so that the ghastly vigil had to be kept against the rats, but in this case the girl was taken out of the camp at once, suggesting that the Japanese were alert for any mysterious outbreak that might spread, extending the danger, of course, to themselves. In fact, weeks later, word filtered through that Grace had died of polio.

The hospital was rapidly running out of the medical supplies which the nuns had brought with them from Charitas and, although the powerful Dr Goldberg, more or less by force of will, directed the best of the black market supplies towards the hospital hut to supplement the patients' diets, the battle against illness was slowly being lost. Malnutrition underlay all of the more spectacular sicknesses – malaria, dysentery, cholera, and the beginnings of the lethal and classical deficiency disease, beriberi. As if to parody the increasingly skeletal arms and torsos of women whose average weight was now around six stone, feet and legs began to swell, the first muffled warning of the hydropic form of the latter disease.

The prisoners met the unremitting setbacks with a courage that remains inspiring. In a life that was harsh, dirty, dangerous and endlessly debilitating there were only two known suicides among these hundreds of women in the whole of the experience. Faced with the removal of nearly everything that they would once have considered made living worthwhile, there were many who wavered, but the abiding impression is of a combative spirit. If women believe themselves possessed of qualities of endurance and adaptability and resourcefulness, there was ample evidence here that that is not unfounded.

They assailed the existence in various ways. Elizabeth Simons wrote: 'We lived in the present, having learned that the past could not help us and that there might not be another day.' Margot Turner said: 'In these conditions you just had to have a sense of humour,' by which, one judged, she meant that the women insisted on finding an absurdity in situations in order to vanquish the panic and horror.

In the camps, Margot created a reprise of her tomboyish girlhood among her three boisterous brothers. She and Netta Smith had become firm friends and small Netta followed tall Margot on what they called 'thieving parties', which meant the purloining of Japanese vegetables whenever the opportunity arose. One day they were caught and, after hours standing in the sun outside the guardhouse, they were taken inside for interrogation. Netta, whose height made her an ideal target for the Japanese, was threatened with a wooden tromper about the head – a severe strain on the sense of humour, but the episode could be seen as a prank if put in the right perspective, and Margot was always ready to supply the required rueful grin.

Betty Jeffrey had a story of Margot at her exuberant best:

A fowl, Palembang model, flew over the fence from the Jap guardhouse and there was a mad rush by a few Australian and English sisters. Margot Turner was first to get it. In two minutes the unfortunate bird was in our block and we were discussing if we should kill it or put it back over the fence. We also discussed whether we could cook it without the smell going round the camp.

Margot was holding it by the legs and keeping its beak shut to stop its noise, when suddenly the fowl closed its eyes and went limp in her hands. Margot's face was a study; she was sure she had killed it, so she let it go. The wily old bird flew under the bed-space platform and it took us ages to get it out. This time there was no delay; it was killed, de-feathered and into the pot in a few minutes. That night the Australian and English sisters had chicken soup and stew for dinner.

The New Zealander, Audrey Owen, was able to articulate a view that many arrived at when the experience was ended but which for her, even at the time, was a method of turning a negative into a positive. 'For all the hardships,' she said, 'without families and all the pressures of the real world bearing down, there was time to think, to work out what kind of person you really were, to indulge in off-beat or eccentric behaviour that would have been impossible in conventional surroundings. I found *myself* there.'

Norah Chambers was conscious of an expanding of her personality that only those bizarre circumstances made possible. She dwelt on the cosmopolitan circle of close friends that she had made as if they were jewels, which in many ways they were: from Australia, Betty Jeffrey and Iole Harper; from Holland, Sister Catherinia and the Colijn sisters; Audrey Owen; Sally Topps, a remarkable Dutch Eurasian who blended the Dutch and British sides of the camp with the skill and diplomacy of an Ambassadress purely, it seemed, because her nature thrived on harmony and kindness; and Maudie James. 'Maudie helped in the kitchens, in the camp hospitals – there was nothing she wouldn't turn her hand to. I had a very bad back after hoisting sacks of rice and she crushed some chillies and rubbed it with them. The burning was terrible but it took the ache away. Give me the Maudies of this world if ever I'm in a tight spot again. . . .'

Music was Norah's gift to the camp. When life was very harsh she lost herself in it and led others with her, as into an enchanted wood, away from the dross and the bullying and the smells. Rehearsals for the 'orchestra' continued twice a week in the Dutch kitchen and the music grew steadily more complicated: Beethoven, Chopin, Brahms. The fast interwoven rhythms of Ravel's 'Bolero' almost defeated the musicians. For once even Margaret Dryburgh was stumped: according to Norah, 'Margaret didn't know the tune so yours truly had a go and it really was very difficult getting that peculiar rhythm. But it was such fun. . . .'

The greater the absorption, the more complete the escape from the blackened, dreary kitchen. The Japanese must have sensed this and found it out of keeping with their cat-and-mouse game. Norah was made to stand in the sun for hours for refusing to include a Japanese song in a concert, then Siki upbraided the women for singing at all in the midst of war. They must be 'serious' while their friends were being killed. After June 1944 the orchestra's performances were sometimes cancelled for no visible reason beyond the Japanese need to make it clear that nothing happened without their will.

The women were not invariably a sisterhood, smiling and humming their way through the days. The hardship and the stifling proximity of others and the depth of squalor that caused Mary Jenkin to wake one night to find a rat nibbling at her toenails brought friction and lost tempers. The forthright Australians, not inclined to be over polite, and prepared to face the fact that this was rapidly becoming a survival

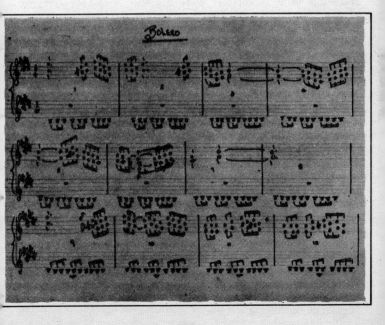

situation, had no illusions about those who preferred to conserve their energies. 'The same old hard-working few,' wrote Betty Jeffrey of a working party now set to excavate the unspeakable rubbish tip and empty its foul contents on to the plantations, 'The same old "passengers"!'

It was Miss Dryburgh who produced a panacea which was invaluable to all. Her advice to everyone, and an expression which became a catch-phrase, was 'Look up' – not a banality in the Victorian mould, but a literal re-direction of the attention from the sordidness below to the sky above. There, to the astonishment of many and the pleasure of even the most cynical, a whole new world existed. The sunsets of Sumatra once dwelt upon, proved to be unbelievably beautiful, changing colour by the moment as the sun fell, so that there was an excitement and a wonderment in watching the unique display. At sunset a single flying fox, a perfect symbol of freedom, would fly across the compound, path-finding for great squadrons of those delicate creatures that would wing their way towards the indigo horizon. At night the stars of the southern horizon were mesmeric to those who had had enough of the earth beneath.

> *A prison camp! A dwelling bare!*
> *Privations and discomforts sore!*
> *And yet a thing of beauty rare*
> *At our own door.*
> *A tree, a wealth of blossom bore,*
> *Its petals of a pinky hue*
> *With rosier buds. Each day it more*
> *Entrancing grew.*
>
> *It took the mind, in swift retreat*
> *To apple blossom in the spring,*
> *To lanes, where hawthorn hedges sweet*
> *Their fragrance fling.*
> *Ah! When, in future years we think*
> *Of sorrows we in exile knew,*
> *We'll also see the sprays of pink*
> *Against the blue.*   M.D.

In August 1944 the skies brought a more tangible reward. Shortly after midnight on 11 August the women woke to the sound of planes with an engine note quite unlike the high whine of Japanese aircraft, then the familiar, drawn out 'crr-u-ump' of falling bombs. The sirens wailed in Palembang and the anti-aircraft guns opened up – the full,

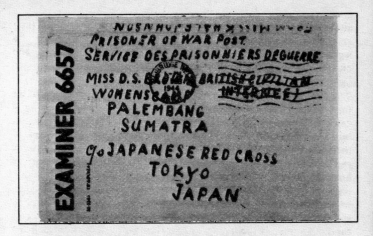

This letter to Shelagh was one of the few which finally reached Sumatra

familiar orchestra of the aerial assault on Singapore with the difference that this air-raid was welcomed like a deliverance. Even to be bombed by the Allies was better than being forgotten or ignored. One of the Aussies rose to fetch the old tin-hat which was used as a water bucket, but it was filled with water so she returned to the *bali-bali* and lay, like the rest, trembling with excitement that some sound had come at last from the outer world.

In the following week there was even greater cause for hope. 'Wild excitement!' Phyllis Briggs's diary erupts. 'Letters from the outside world!' They were fifty-word letter cards, some posted more than two years before, but somehow they had found their way to this place and, even more miraculously, been delivered. The Japanese could not contrive to do even this graciously. A queue was formed in the sun and Mrs Hinch was obliged to sign for each letter, a process that took more than an hour of appalling suspense. Betty Jeffrey: 'I looked over Mrs Hinch's shoulder and suddenly saw my mother's handwriting. I went cold and goosey all over. It was so familiar and to see it in all this awful mess and among people from all ends of the earth. It didn't seem real. I signed for it and walked away somewhere with it and for the life of me I couldn't open it. I just stared at that handwriting. After a while Iole came along and opened it for me . . .'

Betty learned that she had acquired two nieces and, all over the camp, there was some wonder to be shared. Mrs Brown found that she had become a grandmother via her elder daughter and that her son was also a prisoner, in Germany. Many years later Phyllis Briggs discovered that Alec Brown had been in the same POW camp as her husband-to-be, and that they were good friends. For some, equally, there was news of deaths, and the letters brought a strange, bitter-sweet atmosphere to the camp. The women were told that they could write replies of not more than fifty words and with no mention of food shortages or being forced to work.

A Japanese interpreter let slip the fact that the letters had been in the possession of the camp authorities for more than three months before they were handed over, and it was somehow these petty cruelties that stung even harder than the overt acts. These continued. An Australian nurse called Raymont was so weakened that she suffered from persistent fainting fits during hard toil and was reduced to sewing as her only contribution to the common weal. One day, as she was sitting sewing quietly at her bed-space, the Japanese guard called Rasputin stormed in and, pointing to a small piece of wood missing from the back wall of the hut, accused her of damaging Japanese military property. She was dragged out into the sun and, aware of her condition, another nurse took her a hat. Rasputin raced out of the guardhouse, threw the hat away and punched Sister Raymont to the ground.

Her friends watched in horror as she picked herself up and stood swaying as an hour passed. Mrs Hinch and Dr Goldberg were fetched to plead for her, but unavailingly until at last the girl crashed down unconscious. There was a concerted rush to pick her up, ignoring the Japanese, and she was taken to the hospital. She was never to recover fully and did not survive the camps.

This mindless punishment may have occurred because of a growing paranoia on the part of the Japanese. There was a complaint that the children had been making faces at them and otherwise showing disrespect, the parents to be punished if there was any repetition. Alerts and raids went on through August as the oil refinery at Pladjoe attracted more attention from Allied bombers. The guards reacted with that hasty lack of dignity often seen in silent comedy films at moments of stress, shouting among themselves and pelting to their dug-outs, leaving the women to their fate under the flimsy *atap*. A heavy, clanking metal box was always carried from the guardhouse to the shelters at these times. The women decided it contained the Japanese recipes, now the local metaphor for the most important objects in the world.

The reckless bravery that had sent these peculiar people spilling out into Asia to overwhelm their enemies could not have evaporated so suddenly, but if it was a kind of group hysteria that had driven them to conquer it was now evidently going into reverse. A visit to the camp by a

Japanese dentist provided a nightmare refinement of distress. He had called before and peered in various mouths but had always gone again, leaving behind even here that relief which dentists engender when they postpone the actual treatment to some other time. But he returned in September and removed teeth wholesale without anaesthetic. Teeth that broke were chiselled from the gum and patient after patient reeled away in agony, as in some picture-postcard fantasy of dentistry at its worst. Ah Fat was drunk that day and paraded the victims in front of the guardhouse for an hour to lecture them on good manners. Only one person, he bellowed, had had the decency to thank the dentist.

If this was a parody of concern for the prisoners' welfare there was worse to come. In October, perhaps the most tangible evidence yet that somewhere out in the void there was an awareness of the women's plight, a consignment of Red Cross parcels arrived. The women saw them first through their spy-holes in the walls, and they observed, too, their ruthless pillaging by the Japanese and *Hei Hoes*.

From a camp where, one night, a prisoner eating in the dark found a rat crouched on the other side of her plate and sharing her rice, the prisoners had to watch medical supplies, dressings, quinine tablets, unwrapped and taken away, tinned food opened and eaten and hundreds of American cigarettes half-smoked and thrown away. It was weeks before the remains were brought into the camp and divided between the British and the Dutch.

For each prisoner there were minute amounts of chocolate, already bearded with mould, a half cup of powdered milk, four tiny sugar loaves, a little tinned meat, salmon, some jam, and an inch of cheese. Enough only to awaken a sense of taste gone moribund and to underline the years of going without. But one day an Allied plane dipped briefly through the clouds in the middle of the morning and there were the buddings of a tremulous belief that there were now several portents of an approaching release.

It was to prove a false dawn and there were some who would not live even to see the beginning of the end. Since the start of the year Mrs Ismail had been in and out of the hospital hut with a variety of ailments, none of them of great assistance to a worsening heart condition. In June she was taken in and did not re-emerge. Through the strict regime which Dr Goldberg maintained, the visiting of patients was rigidly curtailed.

Molly Ismail had lived with this exceptionally lively woman hour by hour, more like sisters or best friends than mother and daughter, through all that had taken place for nearly three years. She missed her sorely and in her distress she wrote to her, only a score of yards away across the compound, as if she were in another land, sometimes two missives in the same day.

Molly kept those notes, on scraps of cheap and scruffy paper. They were heartbreakingly vulnerable, as Molly in her maturity could see for herself, but they were so close to the inner thoughts, rather than the brave or stoical exterior of a woman in the camps, that she gave permission for them to be quoted: 'My dearest, darling Mummy, I am longing to be with you daily. I am really so frightfully fed up here – I long to have a nice long talk with you . . .'

On another day: 'I am simply longing for the time when you and I can be together again. You understand and know me far better than anyone. I don't get much real love. People like me and are always very nice, but I want you . . .' When the first pangs of separation receded a little, Molly tried hard to dwell less on her own misery: 'Mummy darling, it was lovely seeing you this morning – I did so enjoy it . . .' 'My dearest darling Mummy, How are you today? I do hope you had a good night and that you are feeling stronger than you were. I do hope Dr Goldberg will let me spend a little time with you tomorrow. . . .'

The small, poverty-stricken details of life in the camp kept breaking through: '8 October 1944. Thank you for the note. I was so distressed to hear that you were in much pain. I am sending over my blue socks to you but I am sure you will find that the white socks are in your knapsack. If you do find them, Mummy dear, please send me back the blue ones. . . . I am sending over my curtain coverlet, which I do hope will make you feel warmer . . . Have just finished serving in the kitchen. Now *tenko*! All my love, your loving Molly.'

Food, of course, found its way into the notes: 'I have not sold my pink voile yet, but I am still trying. I want to purchase some oil. . . . There is a very small tin of Bear Brand milk going at 15 guilders. Would you like me to buy it for you?' There are no more notes after 13 October, which is the day that Mrs Ismail suffered a stroke. Molly was called to the hospital where her mother lay in the ward for the chronically ill, a little compartment in the hospital hut set aside for those nearing the end of the road.

'She never complained,' Molly said. 'She just murmured two or three times "Oh Molly, I'm so tired of all this nonsense. I'll be so glad when we can go home." ' Three days later Molly was sent for by Dr Goldberg at midday and told that her mother was dying. Molly was left alone with her and she held her mother's hand and tried to talk to her but she was not really conscious. A guard was posted outside the window of the little room because there was a strange punctiliousness among the Japanese about registering the precise moment of a death.

It was not long in coming, but once again the body had to be carried to the *pendopo* to remain overnight. Molly shared the watch against the rats. An inventory had to be made of Mrs Ismail's belongings and signed by Mrs Hinch. It amounted to very little for a lady who had once been welcome in the Sultan's Palace of Johore Bahru:

List of Effects of Mrs Ismail

1 knapsack	1 blouse (old)	1 small pr nail scissors
1 pr tennis shoes	1 dress	3 handkerchiefs
1 pr white sandals	1 felt hat	1 bed roll
1 pr white socks	1 handbag (straw)	
2 prs shorts (men's)	Passport + Drafts	
2 cotton vests	Hairbrush + comb	
1 cotton panty		
1 khaki shirt		

Four days after Mrs Ismail's death, on 20 October 1944, the women were told that they must prepare to move back to Banka Island. Molly would have to make that journey alone.

Chapter 13

A party of about sixty women went on ahead of the rest. 'The order came at midday that the first group were to get ready to leave by 2pm,' Phyllis Briggs recalled. 'We hurriedly packed our few possessions and had a meal – then had to wait for two hours before the lorries came to take us away. The rest of the camp cheered wildly as we drove off, sitting on our bundles with tin cans and other possessions tied to our backs.' Some of the most vigorous prisoners were chosen for this advance guard for reasons that would soon become apparent. Sister Catherinia and Betty Jeffrey were among the group, and seven other Australian nurses; it was the first time that tight-knit band had been separated since they emerged from the waters of the Banka Strait.

A vessel was waiting at the docks in Palembang and Phyllis Briggs was astonished to discover that it was an old friend, one of the ferry-boats which used to run between Penang and Butterworth on the Malayan mainland shore. 'I thought of the times I had boarded that ferry in happier days, sometimes on my way to a club dance or to play golf.' Even the ship's bell had a familiar sound as it signalled the boat's departure, but all the seats had been removed and there was nothing to do but lie on the deck.

The first part of the journey was brief. Across the river to a railway station where a whole new group of prisoners had arrived by train from Benkulen. There were more than a hundred Indonesians and Indo-Dutch women and children and a dozen Dutch nuns, and they were laden with possessions: heavy cabin trunks filled with household goods, books, china, even corn and rice. The Japanese now ordered the Palembang women to haul everything aboard the ferry, a striking reversal of that former arrangement of life whereby a European lady would walk languidly up the gang-plank of a vessel in Eastern waters while sweating coolies bent their backs to the weight of the baggage. This fact was possibly not lost on the Japanese. Some of the trunks of the Indonesians were too heavy to lift and had to be dragged on board, but when the women paused in their labours the Japanese officers drew their swords and brought them down sharply so close to arms and legs that they produced an involuntary surge of effort. The work continued until midnight and the last of the cargo taken on board was dozens of coffins. Sister Catherinia, rubber-legged with exhaustion, missed the gang-plank on her final trip and had to be hauled out of the river.

The ferry was now crowded and on the stretch of deck where Phyllis Briggs lay down to sleep a large Indonesian family appeared and spread themselves around her. 'A dirty little boy curled himself at my feet and spent most of the night scratching his head and, for some unknown reason, pinching my legs! Another woman came on board with two live chickens which she deposited by Dr Thompson, much to her annoyance. It was a miserable night . . .'

The vessel sailed at dawn and at least the air was fresh on the river passage after months in the fetid, low-lying camp. As the day wore on and the sea grew nearer the women had a moment of optimism: that this was a farewell to Sumatra for ever and somehow a step towards freedom. The sea, for all the perils it had brought, remained the road home if ever it were to come. The women had each brought a bottle of boiled water and a little cold rice to see them through the journey. Phyllis experienced one of those sharp pangs of longing for a little normal comfort which always seemed to accompany a lightening of the misery: 'How we would have enjoyed a cup of hot coffee! I took a spoonful of my precious sugar. This always did me good when I felt particularly weak and I used to keep a little store of it in a face-cream jar for emergencies.'

A distinct crisis was in prospect. The ferry set off across the Banka Strait, passing the spot where the *Vyner Brooke* had gone down in 1942, and anchored off Muntok Pier in the late afternoon. Darkness had fallen by the time the first transhipment of the prisoners into a lighter began. It was a small, filthy boat that appeared to have been a coal-barge. A narrow, iron ladder led into its hold, ending some distance above the floor and, as the women jumped, in pitch blackness, they found themselves landing up to the ankles in kerosene. The water was very rough and an air-raid siren wailed from the shore as the embarkation was completed, throwing the Japanese into a panic. They battened down the hold, leaving those inside stifling in the kerosene fumes and lurching against each other in the Stygian darkness.

'Some of the women screamed and became hysterical,' Phyllis said, 'and I felt terribly sea-sick and was trying not to faint. By the time we reached the jetty I hardly had the strength to climb up the iron rungs of the ladder but fortunately two Japs at the top caught me as I was about to fall backwards into the sea. They dragged me on to the jetty where I curled up in a heap for a few minutes.'

The pier at Muntok stretched out before them again, the Japanese barking at the women to march in threes, but they were staggering too much to keep a formation so the guards goaded them along as fast as they could go in an untidy, reeling straggle. The final exertion was to climb into trucks at the end of the pier, a particular trial for Betty Jeffrey who had been suffering agonizing pains in her chest ever since the hauling of the luggage at Palembang.

After such a dreadful journey the new camp, at first sight, was a revelation. Now no more than the anonymous open space that Sister Catherinia returned to all those years later, at that time it was a small village of wooden huts enclosed by a bamboo fence but there was none of the grubbiness of Palembang. The six main sleeping huts were large, there were three big kitchens and the impression was one of light and air and space after months in the dank hollow of the Men's Camp. The sleeping accommodation was luxurious by comparison, three feet on either side of each person and a brand new rush mat to lie on, free of the bugs and fleas and nameless creeping things of the previous *bali-bali*.

There were nine wells, clean and with cement surrounds, there were new cement floors in the communal washrooms and even, wondrously, a vast supply of cut wood, so plentiful that it gave the appearance of high walls around the kitchens. The newcomers, prowling suspiciously like cats in new quarters, tried to divine why there had been such an improvement in their conditions, and the most optimistic were prepared to believe that this was a kind of show-camp where neutral observers would be allowed access to the prisoners in order to arrange their repatriation. There was a touching willingness to find hope in the slightest recession of distress.

The major defect of the camp was the lavatories, which were no more than pits spanned by bamboo slats on which the user crouched with a foot on either side. They were built, with the Japanese flair for such juxtapositions, right alongside the kitchens and were to contribute much when the true horrors of Muntok revealed themselves.

For the first arrivals there were further indications that they had reached a comparative Valhalla. From their quarters in the coolie barracks which the prisoners had first occupied on Banka Island the men had sent over rice, fish and tea sufficient for a large influx of women so that the advance guard were faced with a plethora of food. 'Some people just stuffed themselves – and were ill the next day,' Phyllis remembered. 'I felt too tired for a big meal but took a good helping of rice and fish against less plentiful times. We had not washed for over thirty-six hours and were filthy but as there was no water we lay down on the *bali-bali* too weary to bother with anything.'

Adequate supplies and oblivion were to provide a very bearable respite in the life of the camp at Muntok. The main body of prisoners from Palembang arrived in three contingents – the Dutch, the British and the staff and patients of the hospital – and all of them had a passage which was in some ways worse than that of the first arrivals. One vessel, containing a hundred women, was so unsuited for the sea crossing that all aboard her were warned to remain as still as possible to prevent a capsize in the Strait. The boat which transferred the hospital had only three feet of freeboard, close enough to the water to give cool relief to those who were able to dangle their feet in the river. At night a tropical storm erupted, sending the vessel out of control and convincing the passengers that they were to meet their end, after all, in the same waters that had so narrowly spared them before.

Betty Jeffrey remembered the arrival of one of these groups at the new camp: 'They looked terrible when they finally drew up in trucks. They were standing up and clutching each other, most of them too weak to get down. Two of the AANS sisters jumped into the trucks and helped them while we others were trying to cope with those who fainted after they got out. They were cold, hungry and utterly worn out. It was a nightmare of a trip for the older women amongst them.' Mrs Brown was in this group, luckily still with Shelagh beside her, full of admiration for her mother's dogged determination. The only sanitary arrangements on the craft which had brought them over had consisted of a chamber pot, which one of the women habitually used as an eating utensil, and this was passed around politely. It was actually Shelagh who was hospitalized on arrival with malaria and, rather more mundanely, piles, while Mrs Brown carried on as the breadwinner, sewing to make a little money.

There was one further addition to the complement of the new camp. Just as the cooks already in residence began to distribute a meal of rice, vegetables, shark and tea to the latest arrivals, the Palembang Commandant, Siki, appeared and banned the giving out of all but the tea. An armed guard was posted on the kitchens throughout the night. The following morning, when the women came to examine their possessions, they found that they had been picked over by the guards during the journey. 'How those Japs hate the British!' Betty Jeffrey noted. 'We must be giving them merry hell somewhere . . .'

The Americans in fact were gaining a powerful foothold in the Philippines, a major stepping-stone towards the Japanese homeland, but as ever the women were ignorant of these developments and were obliged to devote themselves solely to the daily problems of existence.

Here, it was to prove, they had changed their form but were to remain besetting. There were now more than seven hundred women and children in the camp and the wells were dry within a week, leaving as the only reliable water supply a small stream in the jungle more than half a mile away. This stream ran in a steep gully, pretty and peaceful and adorned with wild flowers, if the labour of water-carrying permitted any attention to the surroundings. The constant passage of feet turned the area into a swamp so that falls were frequent and much of the precious water lost. It took constant representations to the guards before some of the *chungkals* were diverted from the fresh cultivation that had begun around the camp to be used to cut a series of steps down the bank. A line of women crawled up and down them, ant-like, throughout the daylight hours, providing yet another graphic picture of their servitude.

In the camp itself the latrine pit, lacking drainage, filled and became a crawling mass of huge maggots beneath the precarious bamboo slats, a spectacle that for those who dared to look down recurred in nightmares for years to come. The only means of reducing this appalling health hazard was to empty the pit with buckets as it approached overflowing, and once again there were volunteers to be found. The wood supply, seemingly boundless at first, was consumed very quickly by the demands of the cooking fires and the jungle had to be scoured for logs. An armed guard invariably accompanied women, and now even children, who barely had the strength to get their burdens back to camp. Every activity of this kind was visibly slowed down by weakness. The dramatic loss of vigour set in very quickly because, for all the light and air of the Muntok camp, the comparative prettiness of the surroundings and the occasional, pulse-quickening waft of the smell of the sea, disease had been held at bay for too long and was now rampaging in, past defences that were crumbling away.

The nurses could hardly help but take a professional interest in the forms of illness that were striking the women down and discerned that, inescapably, diet was the key: the lack of food compounded by the lack of nourishing properties in what food was available, the classic killing formula still visible where hunger exists in the world today. For all their trunkloads of rice and corn and their profusion of possessions, the Indonesians from Benkulen were riddled with beriberi to a much worse degree than the women of Palembang, and the Dutch nursing nuns in their company attributed this to their cooking methods. The length of time for which they customarily cooked their food still further diminished its nutritional value and, besides the deficiency disease, they were easy prey to malaria and gangrene. The mothers of families, who had stinted themselves to provide for their children, were at particular risk at this crucial point when other diseases hovered, waiting to move into the hungry void. Tragically, at the moment of their children's greatest need they were at their most helpless. In one Indonesian family of a mother and five children, four of the youngsters died within a week, to be followed soon afterwards by the mother herself.

It was a stark exposition of the cruel economics of survival, that those who could afford to supplement their diet improved their chances in direct proportion to the size of their purses, and the course of beriberi was a particularly obvious yardstick of an individual's worldly status. The two types of the disease, caused primarily by lack of Vitamin B and protein, both brought about profound physical changes. The hydropic form, in which fluid fills and expands the tissues of the body, caused the sufferer to swell to as much as twice the normal size. In its terminal phase death occurred from almost literally drowning in the poisonous fluid. In the case of the atropic, or dry, form of the disease, the process was reversed and the victim shrivelled in an equally dramatic way. The progress of the illness was from the feet and legs upwards so that the characteristic hesitant, drunken walk of a sufferer from it became commonplace, adding to the overall impression the camp gave of being a kind of ramshackle mechanism grinding slowly to a halt.

And if none of these fruits of long-term deprivation had existed, Muntok bred its own especial and murderous disease. Betty Jeffrey kept a note of its onset: '10 November 1944. Suddenly felt very ill and was carried over here to the hospital, hoping somebody could remove my head; it felt as if it were about to burst. In a week I was joined by Mitz, Shirley Gardham, Mickey Syer and Jenny Greer [fellow AANS sisters] all with this awful fever, raging temperatures and unconscious-ness, followed by skin reactions. It is such a mixture of things that, for want of a better name, the doctors have called it "Banka fever".'

Banka fever was to be the great scourge of the women. The feeling it created as it laid hundreds low was of a lethal mist which tainted the air, and the singing of the Death Bird in the jungle night as the illness raged compounded its mysterious nature, but it was almost certainly a form of cerebral malaria and its source most likely the pretty dell from which the water came.

The fever affected the life of the camp at every level, and it was as well that the camp hospital was bigger and better organized than in Palembang. There was a general 'ward' which could receive some twenty patients, lying side by side on a *bali-bali* made of woven rubber-tree branches which swayed and creaked at every movement. There was also a small children's ward, its equipment principally an old cot which could hold two babies. In another hut, designated as the isolation block, there were four compartments which could hold three patients each but leaving only enough room for one sister to work. Some fifty yards away, with more space and air, was the convalescent section, in fact one of the big sleeping huts made over, and this could hold about thirty patients.

Banka fever filled all these buildings and spilled over into the huts, and now it became necessary to call upon the nurses to function only in their primary role instead of also taking their share of the chores of the camp. Since, by both training and temperament, they were in the main practical and diligent women who applied themselves assiduously to any task before them, the decision to relieve them of water-carrying, cooking, wood-chopping and all else that had to be done to maintain the framework of existence was of considerable significance. The nuns who had laboured so unstintingly since the Charitas days were now becoming overwhelmed by the tide of illness and a roster was organized dividing the pool of civilian and military nursing skill between the hospital and the 'district nursing' system in the blocks.

The four doctors divided their duties in the same way, but the lack of equipment, and particularly medicines, drastically reduced their ability to make any profound effect on an epidemic. The Japanese contribution amounted to little more than quinine tablets – a consignment of perhaps a hundred, to be shared among the whole population of the camp, appearing about once a month. The tablets had to be reserved for only the severest cases of malaria, and it was made a rule that they should be swallowed in the presence of one of the hospital staff when they were administered. There was otherwise a great temptation to sell them on the black market, where they commanded a price equivalent to some three English pounds per tablet.

The black market, seemingly among the most indestructible of human endeavours, persisted at Muntok in spite of blood-curdling threats from the Japanese. Indeed, among those who could discover a fragment of hope in the direst darkness there was a strong belief that it was now principally an operation to benefit the guards who, sensing an end to their dominance, were lining their pockets with all speed. Its existence meant that it was still crucial to earn money. The long-established *congsie* of Mavis Hannah and Elizabeth Simons, in addition to their nursing duties, sold boiled water at ten cents a bottle to the affluent and also provided a cooking service which prospered sufficiently to oblige them to become employers. For a wage of two guilders a week and a small extra rice ration, they took on the English wife of a Malayan rubber planter to assist with the food preparation. Mavis remembered the guilty pangs they felt at offering this low reward, but this was life at an ebb which did not allow for such squeamishness.

Presiding over it all, the Japanese conducted themselves with a curious detachment. They were not as aggressive as they had been in the last stages in Palembang and seemed to have fallen into a kind of weary tyranny as if there was little satisfaction to be gained from the energetic persecution of their spiritless charges. There was one order, however, that they pursued diligently. This was the directive that each hut in a camp which was without electricity must keep a kerosene lamp burning all night.

After the war, when the Geneva Convention was cited as a yardstick in the assessment of the conduct of the Japanese towards their captives, it was noted that this war prisoners' charter included an injunction that their quarters should remain brightly lit. Although the Japanese had never ratified the Convention they may languidly and belatedly have read the document and come to the conclusion that a kerosene lamp was an adequate gesture towards the civilized management of prison camps. If this was so, the Convention was now of even less use to the women than it had been before because the guards insisted that a watch should be kept each night to ensure that the lamp remained lit. It was to become an onerous duty because the Japanese took one of their punctilious turns and insisted that the watcher must at all times remain on her feet and free of any encumbrance, such as a blanket or a mosquito net, enforcing the rule by regular patrols. The savage mosquitos of the Muntok night feasted on the women's bare limbs and, as a night's haul of bites inevitably turned septic, there was fresh work for the medicos.

To counter this hazard an hourly roster was established which further disturbed the rest of the exhausted women; there were many memories of drowsy vigil listening to the night sounds of the camp: the strange chatter of the jungle beyond the bamboo, the whirring passage overhead of the mysterious flying creatures of the darkness, fleeting shapes that passed across the bright stars. Closer to hand there was the vicious whine of the mosquitos, the creak of the *bali-balis* and the feverish, restless muttering of the uneasy and the sick.

The dying began in earnest in the last month of 1944. In late November there were 210 victims of Banka fever lying in the huts and, as December began, there were six deaths, all Englishwomen and hence almost certainly of slender means. Three nuns died in as many weeks and on Christmas Eve the tally stood at fifteen. Christmas, which had held out so bravely as a landmark for the past two years, could not stand up to this assault and served only to underline the descent into sickness and the beginnings of despair. Miss Dryburgh held a short, quiet service on Christmas Day. 'We couldn't even sing,' said Phyllis Briggs. 'Most of us had lost our voices but anyway there was an apathy that had never existed before.'

Besides a sinking of the spirit the physical toll of the long hunger left a blanket of inertia even among those who avoided the fever. 'Malnutrition', Mavis Hannah said, 'caused a lack of concentration, a deterioration of memory but worst of all a feeling that you no longer cared what was going on about you.' In Muntok even that dauntless lady faced a crisis that only her vast determination could hold at bay. After a period of sickness her body rebelled against the rice: 'I used to hold my hand over my mouth to force myself to swallow but it would take an hour or more to eat a very small quantity. I conquered the revulsion and was able to go on eating it but other people, who didn't conquer it, died.'

The Christmas fare was a hundred extra kilos of rice and a small amount of pork and there was a thin travesty of generosity on the part of the Japanese: the delivery of a few letters from Servicemen held prisoner in Japan. It was as if, having brought their prisoners to this pass, the captors allowed them only occasionally and indolently to flick across their minds. Ena Murray lay very sick with beriberi, filled with fluid up to her waist: 'The Japs used to come round that so-called hospital and look at the patients and take note of the ones they thought were on their last legs.' Ena, lying among a row of the dying, looked up one day to see herself being closely observed: 'I know I was written off and I don't think for one minute that I had the will to live or for anything else. I just happened to turn the corner so on that day the Japanese who had made up his mind about me just happened to be wrong.'

Ena's experience expressed the value of a life in Muntok prison as 1945 dawned, and there were to be further indications of its cheapness. Mary Jenkin had become so ill that, eventually and reluctantly, she had to turn over her care of little Mischa to Mamie Colley and go into the hospital. She recovered enough to rejoin the camp but was still very weak when, one day, the ration lorry which had called first at the men's prison arrived at the women's camp bearing an additional burden. The possessions of men who had died there had been sent to their wives by the Japanese. Mary was handed a pair of boots and a small suitcase and was able to divine only from this that her husband must have died. 'Mary was very brave,' said her good friend, Phyllis Briggs. 'She was quiet and unable to cry but she was determined to keep going for the sake of her son Robert, who was twenty-one by now and in England when she had last seen him.'

Death took on a different significance as it became a more likely eventuality than continuing life. Seventy-seven women died before 1945 was a month old and in the written accounts of this period the epitaphs become concomitantly terse. Dorothy MacCleod, of the sweet singing voice, died: 'Dorothy had been such a cheerful, hard-working little person – a great one for sweeping the drains.' Another missionary,

Sabine Mackintosh, died: 'Two days after Christmas she collapsed early in the morning and though the doctors did all they could nothing could rouse her and she passed peacefully to her rest early in the afternoon.'

Even the indestructible Australian nurses began to die and Elizabeth Simons whose sharp sense of the absurd had never flagged now wrote with a restraint that conveyed a terrible sadness: ' "Rene" Singleton, 2/10th Australian General Hospital, a Victorian, will always be remembered for her dry humour. Emaciated, almost beyond recognition save for her deep blue eyes, poor Rene was always hungry – on the day she died she kept asking for "more breakfast, please!" '

'Blanche Hempsted, 2/13th AGH, a Queenslander, was notorious for hard work; this assuredly hastened her end. She said she was sorry for the trouble her illness had caused and, when she realized that death was inevitable, that she had taken so long to die. Always frail Shirley Gardham, 2/4th Casualty Clearing Station, a fellow trainee of mine from the Launceston General Hospital, although very sick for some time, mercifully died quite quickly. During the three years of imprisonment she had received no letters. She did not know her mother had died in 1942. . . .'

THE BURIAL GROUND

How silent is this place.
The brilliant sunshine filters through the trees.
Their leaves are rustled by a gentle breeze.
A wild and open space,
By shrubs pink tipped, mauve blossomed, is o'ergrown,
A hush enfolds me, deep as I have known,
Unbroken save by distant insects' drone.
How silent is this place.

How awesome is this place.
The pageantry of death approaches nigh
But in strange guise. Two companies pass by
(With slow and stumbling pace),
Of women captives bending 'neath the load
Of comrades, journeying to their last abode
Amid the tinted shrubs up winds the road.
How awesome is this place.

How sacred is this place.
Among the flowers, beneath the sunny sky
The dear remains of two war victims lie

Each in a burial space,
By women's hands, filled in and beautified,
And women offered prayers for those who died,
Set up a cross of twigs so simply tied,
How sacred is this place.   M.D.

Death, in such profusion, might have lost its normal impact, but sorrow remained as poignant: 'After living for over three years with each other, we were like sisters of a family,' Elizabeth said of the Australian nurses. 'Of course we did not always see eye to eye but what sisters do? I many times heard people vowing they never wanted to set eyes on a certain person again, but when trouble came they were usually the first to rally round. . . .'

Those awful pangs of remorse that accompany the irredeemable continued. Netta Smith was nursing Dorothy MacCleod at the end: 'I remember I was feeding Dorothy with an egg and without giving it a thought I put salt on that precious egg. I can never forgive myself because her mouth was quite raw and she just couldn't take it. It was a dreadful, thoughtless thing to do because she was *so* hungry, really hungry, you know? It has always stuck in my memory as such an awful thing to do.'

These were individuals thrown together by fate and the links became profound, but the camp at Muntok had more and even crueller severings to offer. Shelagh Brown came out of hospital on the last day of the old year to find her mother alarmingly low in health, fever-ridden and palpably weak. Mrs Brown rallied on New Year's morning to celebrate her birthday with as much of her courageous spirit as she could muster, but by the afternoon she had sunk into delirium and Shelagh did not have the strength left to look after her.

Her mother was taken to the hospital block and lay sick for two weeks until Mrs Hinch, as yet another of her endless duties, came to tell Shelagh that the doctors were worried about her mother's condition and that she was to expect bad news. On 17 January 1945, Mrs Brown, her generous proportions restored by beriberi, died. The manner of her passing is described in a letter which Shelagh wrote to her sister Barbara, against the possibility of her own death:

MUNTOK, February 1945
  My darling Barbara, should anything happen to me, I hope this will reach you some time when this ghastly war is over. . . . Mother died on 17 January, in the camp hospital. She had put up such a gallant fight all the difficult years and we were lucky to have each other. When we came here I was ill and in hospital for three weeks, then came out and had a stupid

accident with an axe, resulting in a tropical ulcer on my ankle, and had to return to hospital for another month.

All this time Mother was on her own in the camp but happy as usual, though swollen with beriberi. . . . On Christmas Day she was very well and cheerful and seemed to have lost all her swelling. Then suddenly she went down with the fever. (It is a terrible fever and many are dying from it.) I came out of hospital and had a great shock at her condition. On her birthday she was better and had a happy day – and we thought so much of you all at home.

Mother was so looking forward to being at home and having Celia. She was in the middle of making her a Camp Doll – like the ones she used to sell. Then my fever got bad and I could not look after Mother. She was very swollen and she went into hospital. For two weeks I hardly saw her as I had fever and they are very strict about visiting. But then later she was moved into a small room on to a bed and I was allowed to see her every day. I knew her heart was bad and they were afraid of a sudden collapse. She was still cheery though very weak but was glad to see me. How I longed to be with her all the time.

She must have loathed hospital – and especially this one. Food was scarce and money also. I was trying to sell her old gold bracelet and had to keep waiting as these things are done in shady ways – it was sold the morning of her death. She had one egg the day before she died. She had been longing for it for such ages, poor dear.

I saw her on the evening of the 16th – a short visit but cheery but I thought she seemed weary and a little breathless and on the morning of the 17th I was sent for at 5.30am. She never spoke to me but I think she knew it was me. I stayed with her right to the end, which was peaceful. Miss Dryburgh came and had a short prayer with us. I don't know whether Mother heard. Olga Neubrunner came and stayed with me until Mother died at 9.30. As she died she gave a beautiful smile. I feel she must be happy with other loved ones away from this ghastly existence. And who knows what the future holds for us.

There was a quiet funeral in the evening, with a beautiful little service. Miss Dryburgh read her favourite psalm. 'I will lift up mine eyes unto the hills'; a few verses from a hymn she loved and that we had so often in the Cathedral at Communion: 'Just as I am'; a portion from Revelations and at the end the BBC prayer that Mother loved: 'When the busy day is done and the fever of life is over'. . . . The burial ground is not consecrated, just a clearing in the jungle but it is peaceful and overlooks the hill.

I was sorry for one thing. Sister took off the wedding ring on account of our captors perhaps taking it and I knew that Mother would have wished this to remain on. As nothing can be done as one would do it under normal conditions I had to take it. . . .

It was a terrible battle to bring some dignity to death. The business of burial had to take its place among the chores of the camp, just another struggle like the hunt for fuel or the management of the cesspit. Mrs Hinch and Mother Laurentia had to nag the Japanese for coffins and the guards reluctantly knocked the plain wooden boxes together with the help of the young boys, who were also made to deliver them to the hospital as they were needed.

Grave-digging was added to the burdens of the stronger women. There were no spades so the back-breaking *chungkals* were put to yet another use and, at the last, the women had to carry the coffins through the jungle themselves with a bored Japanese guard bringing up the rear and grumbling when they stumbled. The women would pick wild flowers for the grave as they went but when the path became so frequently trodden it was stripped of blooms on either side and permission had to be sought to detour into the jungle to search further afield.

The nuns or the missionaries sketched the funeral service, and it was such an insubstantial end to the long struggle – a rough wooden box in a shallow grave in an anonymous jungle – that the matter of some kind of memorial became paramount in the women's minds and Norah Chambers took it upon herself to make wooden crosses for each grave. With a screwdriver brought to red heat in the kitchen fire she burned the name and the date of the death of each victim into the wood and that served at least to delineate one small mound of newly turned earth from the next.

By the end of January 1945 there were two or three funerals every day, the deaths leaving voids in the skein of relationships that had sustained each difficult day for so long. The group of women who had contributed so much to the young lives of the Liddelow sisters simply faded away. Mrs Langdon-Williams died, and with her went her promise to guide them through the labyrinth of Malayan society when, quite inevitably as she believed, it was restored intact after the war. Mrs Maddams died too, her repertoire of impersonations also lost to her friends for ever.

Miss Prouse, the teacher who had been so concerned that the sisters' education should not suffer from the intolerable interruption of the camps, gave up the ghost in an excess of exhaustion. 'I'm too tired to live, too weary to die,' she told them one day as she lay mortally ill, but die she did. A Mrs Pennefather, a spirited lady whom the Liddelows much admired for her worldly chic, had sunk so far into sickness at the end that when they visited her in the hospital block she begged them not to come again. 'You must try to remember me as I was,' she told them and hugged them both as they fought the desire to weep. At each death the Liddelows helped carry the coffins into the jungle.

These were crushing bereavements for the sisters. Afterwards Phyllis said, 'Nothing mattered very much any more except preserving the will to live and to help each other survive. Everyone was now so terribly ill, Doris and I began to kiss each other goodnight as if in farewell, wondering whether we would awaken the following day.' Their early detachment returned, the sensation of watching a drama unfold without being part of it. Doris: 'I was fascinated by what the experience was doing to some families. There were terrible divisions, mothers and daughters refusing to speak to each other, or else the complete reverse: a very close, very protective drawing together as if the realization had come that relatives were all they had in the world, that there was nobody else.'

Elizabeth Simons: 'When there had been more hope there was more wrangling and struggle for what was going but in Muntok we were welded into a new solidarity by the relentless struggle for survival in which we were all engaged.' The presence of death as a daily factor, the reality of dying placed squarely before everyone as a precise likelihood rather than a vague spectre, enforced an appraisal of life as a commodity either to be fought for or surrendered. The solidarity existed between those who were in agreement that the fight should continue to be waged.

The rest, in a phrase that recurred constantly when the women spoke about the dying time, 'turned their faces to the wall'. The expression was never used pejoratively. There was no smugness in those who survived, merely a sort of wonderment that the will to continue had existed in them when it proved to be a crucial factor in keeping them alive.

The will to live seemed to manifest itself in several forms. Margot Turner's attitude was uncomplicated and she expressed it in simple terms: 'The thing was you had to keep going – I mean, you could have a very high temperature one day and have to lie down on your mat and if you didn't get up the next day you probably never would get up again. There had to be a determination to survive. I feel very strongly that quite a lot of people who died shouldn't have done so but they just gave up. I know I wanted to live. I wanted to get home and see my family. But there were people who could see no reason for continuing and that was very sad.'

For others religion played an important part. Ena Murray: 'As far as I am concerned my religion or my belief – belief I would rather use – became Number One in the camps. It was, and is, the most important thing in my life.' Mavis Hannah: 'I wasn't what I'd call a religious person, although I was always used to going to church and that sort of thing. I was in the choir when I was young, in fact right up to the war, but I never realized how you could feel you were not forsaken. That was the main feeling, I think, during the internment. I never felt forsaken. With Miss Dryburgh's help and our church services every Sunday there was a tremendous consolation. That and the comradeship of other people.'

Sister Catherinia, though professionally dedicated of course to 'that sort of thing', offered the same conclusion: 'You had not much time to pray because of everything that had to be done all day long. There was not much time even to think but something grew in you – some trust, some knowing that God was near, and in that nearness you found the strength to go on. Just to go on, hoping and trusting that things were going to be good again. . . .'

Norah Chambers found that fatalism served her best: 'Actually, to be quite honest, I didn't think of dying. I simply didn't think of it. There was so much work to do there just wasn't time to think and really I believe the point is you are either lucky or you are not. As far as dying goes it is meant to be or it isn't. You came to accept what happened from day to day. If it was your luck to get up in the morning you did and if it wasn't you didn't. That seemed to be the answer, if there was an answer there . . .' Amid the dying in the men's camp William McDougall, quite independently, came to the same conclusion: 'When all the chips are down it is the man with the will to live, and the ingenuity to use the will, who survives. And, in addition to will and ingenuity, he must have something else: some call it luck.'

There was infinite opportunity to review this most central of human conundrums. The death rate continued unabated through February and March. In an agonizing exposition of the capriciousness of fate, Ruth Russell-Roberts and Christine Bundy, who had stood side by side on the deck of the *Mata Hari* so long before and almost instantly formed an enduring friendship, now lay side by side on the hospital *bali-bali* suffering from Banka fever in equal degrees of virulence. Christine recovered but Ruth died, although to the very end there was a continuance of that romantic flair which gave a Maughamesque twist to everything about this beautiful girl.

In October 1944 Ruth's husband Denis, still prisoner in Singapore, was put to work on an airfield and made the acquaintance of a Japanese Air Force Sergeant who was keen to improve his English. He was shortly due to fly to Sumatra. Denis, combating a suspicion that the powers of the *Kempei Tai*, that the Sergeant seemed to share, persuaded him to take a letter to Ruth and it reached her, via endless adventures, as she lay drowsy with sickness late one night in Muntok. Christine Bundy read the letter to her and she indicated understanding and smiled. The next day Ruth died. She had sold the three-banded eternity ring which her husband had given her, but only at the last.

The camp was becoming no more than a species of slaughterhouse, but the strange detachment of the Japanese continued. The scales were brought over from Palembang and the women were weighed and their weights just as solemnly recorded even though many of them could barely stand steadily enough for the equipment to register. On a diet in which jungle grasses and ferns were now a central ingredient a weight of seven stone was a rarity. Who on earth could have called for these statistics which merely confirmed formally that the women were starving to death?

In the same lunatic vein the Japanese made their usual elaborate preparations for the visit of a dignitary, this time a representative of the Japanese Foreign Minister. Work went on for days before his arrival. The prisoners were set to removing every weed from the compound, little bridges were constructed over ditches and potholes and all those places in the camp where the women habitually slipped or stumbled in their variety of paupers' footwear. In a kind of conditioned response to an 'occasion', Nurse Kong produced from some mysterious hiding-place a pot of Pond's Vanishing Cream, as if that could rescue her complexion from the ravages it had received. She gave a little to Betty Jeffrey, who found that its scent was almost overpowering after the years deprived of any odours other than jungle, sweat, drains and boiled food.

Two days before the visit, in a flourish of absurdity, the Japanese furnished the camp with half a dozen goats, some fowl and some pigs, evidently to give the impression of having created a self-sufficient and contented rural community. The final deceit, in a place where even the wondrous 'orchestra' had been stilled by death and disease, was the appearance of a piano and a host of chairs, as if the morale of the prisoners was also a matter of great concern.

On the day itself the entire population of the camp was called to *Tenko* hours before the arrival of the cavalcade of resplendent cars that seemed indivisible from the on-progress of a Japanese personage. All the prisoners were obliged to bow as perhaps a score of Japanese officials stepped down and processed from one end of the camp to the other before leaving again some ten minutes later, having failed even to glance at the farm animals or the little bridges or even the piano and the chairs. Within an hour of their departure all but the goats were gone again. The goats being in such debilitated condition that one fell down dead on entering the camp, were clearly deemed to be beyond any consideration.

Generally the attitude among the women to affrontery like this was wry rather than outraged, the classic feminine response, perhaps, when the actions of men pass beyond comprehension, making the world seem not so much dangerous as insane. It is possible that this tractability of mind was eventually a factor in survival. Of life in the men's prison, so close by geographically but very divergent in other aspects, William McDougall writes of the same period: 'As a community we were disintegrating. We had forgotten how to play or study or relax. Worst of all we had forgotten how to laugh. In the struggle for self-preservation too many men adopted the attitude of survival at any cost and the devil or the grave take the hindmost.'

Theft and deceit became sufficiently prevalent for the men to draft a list of laws and punishments and even institute their own private jail within the prison, a room in which wrongdoers were locked for varying periods according to the gravity of their offences. Possessions came to be of such importance that it was necessary to appoint executors to administer the pathetic 'estates' of those who died, this to avoid the wrangling which often followed among those who felt they had a claim to the effects of the deceased.

There is cause to wonder if this disharmony among the men, and notably greater intransigence at many levels, affected the rate of mortality which was even higher in the men's camp than it was in the women's, although there the dying continued with a frequency that makes any debate seem irrelevant. Four more of the Australian sisters died in Muntok, their comrades turning out in the remnants of their uniforms to give a semblance of military dignity to their funerals. Olga Neubrunner died, having survived enough since her first sight of Banka Island to appear indestructible.

In some ways most tragic of all, children died having known almost no other life but that of the camps. The schoolteacher Mrs Ward, that stern disciplinarian of the junior class in Irenelaan, had a boundless regard for children and took care of a brother and sister when they became orphans in Muntok. Her sadness was almost insupportable when, within weeks, the little boy too was dead. Among those who still lived there was a tragic diminution of the energy that had fuelled their pranks and their noisy rampages of earlier days.

The children had adapted remarkably to a world so confined and peculiar that even the half-dead goats were a source of fascination: an intriguing novelty to those whose knowledge of animals was confined to vermin, a few dogs and an ancient bullock that sometimes dragged a cart containing the rations into camp. To the youngest, this was not a bullock at all but a 'Gho Leng', a curious linguistic memorial to that Chinese trader, otherwise remembered principally for his soaring prices and steadily diminishing stock in trade.

'When the children came into camp they were normal children, naughty of course but lively and very imaginative in their play,' said Sister Catherinia, by now the mother to a whole brood of orphans. 'But slowly all creativeness and inventiveness went out of them and they grew into seemingly old men and women with no strength but to sit down and wonder what they would have to eat that day.'

Chapter 14

Some special demon seemed to seize the Japanese when it came to the movement of prisoners. The hideous record of their cruelties that was compiled, when the war ended, to pursue the prosecution of war criminals is studded with journeys in which the barbarity of the captors reached new levels of wickedness in the treatment of human beings. It seemed that something in the sinister maze of the Japanese character was activated by the raw power placed in the hands of even the humblest of them when their task was to shift large bodies of helpless people from place to place. Again, the analogy is powerfully with the herding of animals: a stick in the hands of a simple cowman providing him temporarily with measureless domination over the creatures in his charge. Even the Japanese War Ministry was able to recognize the species of hysteria that gripped the armed peasantry under its command when this type of governance came their way.

In December 1942 the Ministry had issued a directive: 'Army Asia Secret Order No. 1504 – Recently, during the transportation of prisoners of war to Japan, many of them have been taken ill or have died, and quite a few of them have been incapacitated for further work due to their treatment on the journey, which at times was inadequate. . . .'

The Japanese flair for euphemism can rarely have been better demonstrated and, nearly three years later, with the Rising Sun in the descendant, there was little chance that in the farthest reaches of the Co-Prosperity Sphere much heed would be given to a memorandum from Tokyo counselling greater care. The women's last journey in the hands of the Japanese certainly surpassed all that had gone before, although, appallingly enough, the treatment of other prisoners in transit elsewhere in the East was infinitely worse.

Once again it was the month of April which brought activity. At the end of March Captain Siki assembled the prisoners to announce that they were destined for a move from Muntok to Loebok Linggau on the south-western extremity of Sumatra. It would involve a three-day trip by boat and train and all were to make ready for the journey. By this time the weariness and sickness had bitten too deep for the customary flood of hopeful rumour that attended a departure. There was only apprehension at what such a trek would entail for the sick and the dying and a sense of sorrow at leaving so many behind in the jungle graves.

The prisoners were divided into three groups for the journey, of which the first, which left Muntok on 9 April 1945, were to prove the most fortunate. They were packed on to a small steamer so tightly that there was no room to lie down, and they were forced to remain on the open deck in the blazing sun for a whole day and through the chill of the night. One young girl went mad and screamed incessantly, hour after hour. The subsequent train journey, in filthy, sealed goods wagons and with barely any food or water, occupied a day and two nights but all survived.

It was the following groups, including the hospital patients, who caught the full malevolence of the Japanese, to a degree that makes it possible to wonder if the weakest had already been deemed superfluous and left for Fate to decide if they should live or die. The order to be ready to move at 6am the following day was issued on 11 April in spite of protests from the doctors: it was obvious that a number of patients had only hours left to live and to move them seemed an absurdity that even the Japanese might perceive. But the pleas of the medical staff were rejected out of hand and, as dawn came up over the island in its customary splendour, the sick were placed on makeshift stretchers with the strongest of the women on hand to bear them. Among these were half a dozen of the Australian nursing sisters, who were about to prove their courage and fortitude as never before. The rest of the group comprised about a hundred women, none of them, by any normal standards, fit enough to undertake an arduous journey.

As usual there was no activity for hours but, at 11am, just as torrential rain was beginning to fall, the guards went racing through the camp, yelping and bullying in their cattle-market style, and loaded the prisoners into open trucks with liberal use of bayonet and sword. The trucks set off at their lunatic speed, causing the gaunt remnants of humanity on the stretchers to lurch and roll in the cold downpour, and they came yet again to the pier at Muntok.

There the sick were laid in the only semblance of shelter, the soaking grass beneath the trees, and one of the women immediately died. Norah Chambers: 'The rest of us were given hand carts and as the luggage, including the belongings of the Japanese, arrived by lorry we had to unload the stuff and fill the carts and pull them down that very long jetty. We did this all day without a break and without even a drink of water. At the end, worn out, we crawled into the lorries again and were

233

taken back to camp. Even the poor sick souls were taken back to camp after they had been left to lie in those ghastly conditions all day. Some of them were dead by the time we got back and had to be buried before we were herded out again the next day.'

The next day the stretcher cases had to be carried the length of that interminable pier, the bearers making trip after trip and heartened only by a telling sign that the world was closing in on their tormentors. At frequent intervals along the pier there were now camouflaged gun emplacements manned by heavily armed Japanese soldiers. They gazed at the long, straggling procession of the halt and the lame as they made their way past, but offered no morsel of assistance. It struck one of the women, looking back into the dull, unblinking eyes of the soldiers, that already they had lost the swagger of all-conquering Sons of Nippon and resembled, crouched in their lairs, nothing so much as rats in a trap.

It took several hours to assemble all the prisoners at the head of the pier and there was a further agonizing effort to get the stretcher cases into a small launch which bobbed and tossed in the swell. The launch was serving as a ferry to a tiny, wooden coastal vessel lying off, and painfully slowly it filled the ship with its cargo of misery. For even the bravest of the women that last, excruciating journey down the pier had been an effort sufficient to make the soul quail. Ena Murray walked its length on feet grotesquely swollen by beriberi, leaning on her friend, Marguerite Carruthers, but still holding her ward, June Bourhill, protectively by the hand. Little June, Marguerite remembered, was also coming to the end of her resistance, pitiably thin and with her eyes wide and staring listlessly ahead. 'In the last few yards,' Marguerite said, 'Ena's will wavered for the only time in all those years and she said over and over, "I can't go, I can't go. *You* must go but I can't." ' It was unthinkable that she should stay and I literally pushed both her and June into the boat and fell aboard myself.'

It was on the pier that Molly Ismail, walking alone in one of these ghastly migrations for the first time since the flight from Johore Bahru, reached a crisis too. For her the months in Muntok had largely been a blur of malarial fever that had run the days and nights together in exhaustion or restless delirium, but the fresh breeze from the sea cleared her head and the pain of the loss of her mother came flooding back. 'I could suddenly see all of the future without her,' she said. 'Even if this journey were to be a step towards release she would not be there. I could only keep going by making my mind a blank and simply putting one foot before the other until I got to the end.'

Aboard the coaster those who could walk were forced down through a small hatch into a hold lined with sacks of verminous rice. It was black, airless, stinking, and as hot as a furnace. The deck was packed with the stretcher cases, lying jammed together and staring upwards at the blazing sun. Although dysentery was rampant there were no toilet arrangements and this gave rise to a most arcane act of heroism. Betty Jeffrey: 'The Dutch nuns managed to get some bedpans with handles aboard and as long as I live I will never forget Iole Harper emptying them and dragging them in the sea to cleanse them. She would tie a rope through the handle then get out on a six-inch ledge that ran round the *outside* of the ship. Pat [Blake, another of the AANS sisters] would hold her hand and arm while she tossed the bedpan in the sea and the drag every time nearly pulled her into the water. I can't remember how often the girl did that. If ever anyone deserved a Victoria Cross she did.'

During the afternoon a young Englishwoman died, and in that burning heat there was nothing to do but lower the body into the Banka Strait to join so many others who had found their last resting place there. There was no means of weighting the corpse, so it floated in the vessel's wake. Strangely this girl had mentioned months before that if she were to die in captivity she would like to be buried at sea but it seemed now, at the very end, as if she were loath to leave her sisters.

The ship anchored for the night in the mouth of the Moesi River, those below continuing to suffocate in the reeking darkness, and those on deck, blackened by the day's sun, shivering instead in the cold which came with sunset. The only food had been a little cold, sour rice. At dawn the ship began the endless river passage to dock at Palembang in mid-afternoon. There an interminable *tenko* was held on the wharf, as though any there were capable of escape other than by death. The stretcher bearers were first made to carry the sick over a wide expanse of railway track to lay them on the grass, but when this exhausting endeavour was completed they all had to be carried back in order that they, too, could be counted. In such moments even the most forgiving of the women could feel only a cold hatred for their captors, the habitual woodenness of the Japanese facial expression fuelling the notion that they were a people possessed of an evil insanity.

Towards evening a train came in and the sick were loaded into goods wagons while the rest were packed into carriages filthy with coal dust. The floors of the goods wagons where the patients lay were thick with the dust. A container of water was acquired to mop the faces of the fever-ridden and when the train began its journey this would slop over to mix with the grime. The train in fact remained stationary all that night, sealed dark and stifling, the Japanese threatening to shoot if the women made any attempt to seek respite by opening the windows or even raising the blinds. The excreta of the dysentery sufferers could be ejected only through a small, sliding hatch which existed high in the walls of the wagons. It was a night of unmitigated horror which none who endured it could ever forget. In the morning six more of the women were dead.

The train set off at 7am, travelling south-west across Sumatra with only the minimum of ventilation allowed by the guards. When they passed stations or inhabited areas the blinds of the carriages were closed completely and the doors of the wagons shut tight, but whether to prevent those inside from seeing out or to hide the shame of the Japanese nobody could tell. The distress of the women on this stifling twelve-hour journey, with only a little hard, brown bread to chew and no water, reached a paroxysm of misery. In the carriages the over-crowding was such that it was possible only to sit bolt upright and, as the hours drew on and the women sank into a stupor of exhaustion, only the jolting of the train brought sufficient movement to assure an onlooker that they were still alive. In one carriage, which was arranged with two long seats along its sides, the Australian nurses made suf-ficient space for those at the end of their endurance to take turns lying down for an hour until they found the strength to resume their places.

It was dark by the time they reached Loebok Linggau. Those who could move jumped down and drank in the fresh air but they were herded back into the train and made to spend another night in its awful interior, the third without food, drink or sleep. The nurses and doctors on this journey had exerted themselves beyond praise to alleviate the suffering of their companions, but when finally the stretcher cases were lifted down and set on the wet grass, just before dawn, more were dead: twelve in all since the departure from Muntok.

The rest of the prisoners were harried out of the train at bayonet point as if a sudden, tremendous urgency had overtaken the lethal crawl from Banka Island. Instead there was another prolonged *tenko* at which the guards failed again and again to make their totals tally. Eventually they had to be reminded that they were failing to take account of the dead.

There followed a breakneck drive of some twelve miles through the cold morning air, the rough road winding through jungle in the foothills of the mountains of Sumatra's west coast. As they passed occasional clearings remote peaks were visible in the distance before the twilight of the trees and dense undergrowth closed in again. It was lonely and deserted terrain.

The trucks left the road to follow little more than a trail through serried, silent ranks of tall rubber trees. This was in fact a rubber estate, called Belalau, which had been the largest in the area until, following the scorched earth policy of the invasion time, its Dutch managers had wrecked the buildings and machinery of the rubber manufactory and allowed the jungle to riot again at the base of the trees. What remained, when the convoy stopped in a clearing, were the scattered huts that had housed the estate coolies and some long, wooden barrack blocks, clearly hastily assembled. A fringe of barbed wire formed an area roughly rectangular in shape, but the true perimeters were the rubber trees which cut off all reference to the rest of the world except for the sky above.

If it was here that the women were to be finally entombed and forgotten it was well chosen. A stream ran through its centre, the sight of running water gladdening many hearts for a moment. One of its banks was considerably higher than the other and very steep and a rickety bridge linked the two halves of the camp. Overall the atmosphere was one of dampness and neglect. 'I looked round our new home', said Phyllis Briggs of her first acquaintance with Belalau, 'and was not impressed.' Phyllis liked to keep a firm grip on circumstances and plainly chose to express herself in terms of rather lordly disapproval, but there were others who felt quite defeated as this latest prison revealed its defects.

There were deep puddles everywhere and the floors of the huts were of churned mud except where the grass grew in profusion beneath the leaky roofs. The coolie buildings had the comparative luxury of cracked cement floors but they were otherwise in poor repair. The hut designated as the hospital reeked of unhealthy dampness and the layout of the camp was clearly going to lead to untold new difficulties. The communal kitchens were on the lower bank so that supplies would have to be carried long distances through the mud and down the steep bank.

The years of living in the most basic fashion had equipped the women to assess such matters promptly and expertly, and made them deeply wary of any further drawbacks that might reveal themselves in due course. For the present, when their baggage arrived after a long delay, they found that their pitiful possessions had been rifled again en route. Clothing had gone and there were innumerable smaller miseries. Phyllis had lost her precious sewing needles, which represented not only a means of making clothing for herself but money from sewing for other people: 'I could have wept because I had only a few cents left and didn't know how I was going to manage. Like every time something turned up unexpectedly. Dr Goldberg never wore trompers like the rest of us. She was always well dressed and seemed to have plenty of money but she had only light sandals and with mud everywhere she was anxious now to buy a pair of strong shoes. Just before we left Muntok I had been given a good pair of shoes which were too small for their owner and I was able to offer them to her for a few extra guilders.'

Phyllis was obliged to sell the last piece of the jewelry she had cannily tied into her headscarf on that first awful night on the Muntok pier three years before. It was a gold bracelet which had belonged to her mother and fetched a hundred guilders. This was bitterly disappointing; the black market had taken a turn for the worse at Belalau where it was even more crucial to survival.

Phyllis recovered from these setbacks. Something of the optimism which was such a vital ingredient of remaining alive gleams through her description of her new living quarters. 'Ours was a small, one-room house of wood with a corrugated iron roof. The floor was of cement and so was the tiny verandah outside so really it was a better built place than we had been in for a long time. It obviously had belonged to one of the native workers on the estate who was slightly higher up than the ordinary coolie.

'Fortunately, the roof only leaked in one place.' This happened to be immediately over her bed-space but she was able to deal with that on the innumerable nights when it rained by curling up into a ball which allowed her to avoid the persistent drip. 'I always meant to climb up on the roof to try to mend it but somehow never got there. The noise during heavy rain was terrific and being a tin roof every little twig that fell from the trees sounded like a huge branch. The house was surrounded by rubber trees with foliage so thick that one could hardly see the sky and when the rubber nuts fell on the roof they sounded as loud as a pistol shot.'

Inside, the house was almost entirely taken up with the *bali-bali*. This was made of bamboo and was very old and dirty and reeked of must, but Phyllis and her companions even found the energy to attempt some improvements to this unlikeable dwelling.

For the first few days we roamed the camp keeping our eyes open for any treasures that might come in useful for our little house: pieces of wire, planks of wood, metal, the cups which the coolies used to catch the rubber from the trees, all sorts of bits and pieces that were left when the Dutch smashed things up before the Japs arrived.

Our greatest find was a large wooden table which was partly submerged in the river and caught by a fallen tree trunk so that it was wedged into the bank. It must have been in the water for months and was very slippery but we scrubbed it with coconut fibre and when it was dry we carried it in triumph and placed it against the outside wall by the fireplace. We made ourselves little stools to sit on. I'm definitely not a carpenter but I made myself a seat. Mary [Jenkin] was really clever at anything that required a hammer and nails. She spent hours hammering pieces of tin to make lids that fitted, kitchen utensils, all sorts of useful things.

I was better at lighting a fire, often with damp twigs and a little latex from our nearest tree. The latex was most useful. We used it for mending holes in tins and for sticking pieces of rag to the bottom of leaking buckets and the like.

All over the clearing similar feats of insistence on the positive were keeping the flame of life burning in the emaciated bodies of women for whom simply walking from place to place in the glutinous mud was a major physical effort. Betty Jeffrey, discharged from hospital the day after the journey and back on duty there as a nurse, was just as determined to make the best of her accommodation in one of the long coolie blocks: 'We are back on the sloping *bali-bali* again but this time we have boards instead of branches to lie on. This is much more comfortable although they are full of bugs and rats. We are packed in again, about twenty-two inches of bed-space each, but we do have a concrete floor and galvanized iron roof. We are in the prettiest little gully and the creek flows only ten yards away from the door, full of rocks and lined with ferns. We could almost believe we are up in the hills near Gembrook, at home, if we didn't have eight lavatories built over the creek and looking like tiny bathing boxes, right in front of our door. . . .'

To find any merit at all in that stream required almost superhuman powers of mental resource because its waters reflected so many of the evils of Belalau. The water which rose after heavy rains to flood the low-lying huts and cut them off from the rest of the camp was hideously polluted and undoubtedly added its lethal quota to the soaring mortality rate. Besides the effluent from the women's latrines there was a daily contribution from the Japanese, who were ensconced in the former manager's compound upstream. In place of a bath-house for the prisoners they had done no more than string *atap* screens from one bank to the other to portion off some fifty yards of the stream. It was as well that privacy was but a memory because the screens hid nothing, and as the women washed in the shallow waters the guards lounged under the trees perhaps a dozen yards away and watched in the impassive fashion that made their gazing even harder to bear. The women no longer bothered even to try to hide their nakedness, but the lack of a requirement for modesty was a daily reminder of their status in a world that had long ceased to care.

As a further underlining of that it was necessary to eat the ferns and grasses which grew on the banks of the stream to supplement a diet to which only the sweet potato had been added in any quantity in an area of great fertility and considerable cultivation. Various fruits grew in profusion in the gardens of the former estate, but they were proscribed by the Japanese as firmly as if they were the apples of Eden. The sweet potatoes were invariably dumped in the pools of dirty water which lay beyond the wire by the camp entrance and left for three or four days in alternate rain and burning sun until the women were allowed to bring them in. By this time they were a rotting mess.

But if this was a step in calculated murder by slow starvation it was more elaborate than was necessary. The terrible journey from Banka Island now brought about a death that, more than any other passing, shook the belief of even the strongest that courage and will and faith, if they could be maintained, would win through in the end. Miss Dryburgh did not recover from the trip and within a week of the arrival in Belalau was desperately ill. When she was sinking her faithful ally and helper, Norah Chambers, was sent for to come to the hospital. Norah: 'She was semi-conscious and it was obvious that she was dying. She should have recovered but she was so weak from starvation that she just couldn't. The last awful journey was too much for her. She wasn't a young woman. She recognized me and whispered something. The nurse beside her said to me, "She wants the 23rd Psalm." I climbed up beside her, held her hand and to the best of my ability said the psalm. It was so very hard. When I finished there was a silence then she looked at me and in a very confident voice she said, "That's what I wanted." She died shortly afterwards. We carried her body to a clearing and buried her. Before the coffin was closed I put a bunch of flowers in her hand. She looked so peaceful and content. She had done her job and done it well.'

Norah made a cross and burnt Margaret Dryburgh's name and the date – 21 April 1945 – on it in the usual way. Some flowers were planted on the grave because she had loved flowers so much, but this was a poor place to leave such a remarkable lady. The burial ground was on a hillside among the rubber trees above the lower camp and, as more and more women gave up the struggle in Belalau, it become dreadfully overcrowded. Eventually grave-digging became the job of the young people because they were the only ones with sufficient strength. One day when the Liddelow sisters were in the digging squad Phyllis stepped on an 'occupied' plot and found herself apologizing profusely to the dumb earth at her feet.

Shelagh Brown describes a burial of another of the victims of the journey just after the arrival in Belalau, with a thunder storm echoing among the motionless trees: 'We pushed the clay into the grave on our hands and knees because we were unable to wield the *chungkals* and afterwards I remember running straight down the hill and into the river hoping that the guards with rifles would not think we were trying to escape. It was the first taste of running water – bliss!'

Death was already sufficiently commonplace to make it natural to turn again as quickly as possible to the business of living, but the loss of Miss Dryburgh was sorely felt. Her grave and her little cross were to be swallowed up by the jungle, like all the rest, but her true memorial was indestructible. She was the vigorous and inventive spirit who made a large and disparate body of women coalesce to find strength against a common peril. If religion had been her only contribution she would have been invaluable. The church services she initiated, amid the doubts and impatience and even embarrassment of those around her at the start of the imprisonment, endured as a vital rallying point to the very end. But in fact she did more, fostering the tribal strength that became the foundation of survival when the desperate fight at Belalau forced each person there to call upon their last individual resources.

With Miss Dryburgh's death there was a distinct change in the ethos of the camp. The move from Muntok had redistributed the women in different patterns. For the first time the Australian nurses were split into two groups, the 'district nurses' living on the hill at the top of the camp, the hospital staff on the lower level and across the stream, close to their place of work.

The kitchen staff formed another unit, also living near their employment. This caused further separations: Norah Chambers, for example, who was a cook, lived down the hill while Ena Murray was at the top with an agglomeration of British and Dutch. There were many new alignments. Shelagh Brown and Molly Ismail with their awful loss in common, came together in a *congsie*.

The distances between the various locations and the taxing terrain left a number of scattered oases, often with little contact from day to day, and within them the women came to see very clearly the true nature of themselves and their companions. They had learned much in their long travail. Relationships were dramatically different from those which had prevailed at the beginning. They had been honed now to a fine edge in which exasperation and affection existed in almost equal parts but cold indifference seemed to have gone forever.

In the little, tin-roofed house which was officially the British sisters' hut but which its inmates had dubbed International Cottage because of its polyglot occupancy, Phyllis Briggs surveyed her companions with a breadth of mind and a tolerant acerbity that perhaps only these extraordinary circumstances could bring forth. She described some of them, one by one in their places along the evil-smelling *bali-bali*:

The best place in the hut was bagged by Mrs Rover – a German married to a Dutchman who was somewhere in Java.

In the early days in Palembang she was allowed comparative freedom and got the job of running the household for the Jap Governor and his staff. She evidently got on quite well with the Japs because when she was sent to join us in the Men's Camp, eighteen months after we had been captured, she arrived looking as fit and fat as if she had been through no hardship. She also arrived with stacks of luggage – a whole collection of saucepans and cooking utensils, a dog and even some of her husband's clothes. Fortunately the dog had been given to a Jap before we got to Loebok Linggau. She was a women of about forty, a trained nurse before her marriage, and she decided she would like to join the hospital staff when we moved from Muntok.

She had a deep voice and her English was very funny at times but she liked being the grand lady and as she had a much bigger mattress than anyone else she consequently took up more room. She hated getting up early but never minded doing late duty in the hospital at night. She loved her coffee and her cigarette and always had plenty of both as she was well in with the Black Market people. But although Mrs Rover was utterly selfish she was also kind and generous in many ways and lent her zinc bath, cooking pots and many other useful possessions. I don't know how we would have managed without them for our rusty tins were all developing unstoppable leaks and the little frying pan had two large holes in it . . .

Georgette Gilmour took the place next to Mrs R. She was a sweet thing with plenty of common sense and most capable in every way and with a sense of humour to go with it. Mrs Rover used to get on her nerves and it is no wonder that, being French, she had little time for a German woman, especially as when Georgette was a young girl she had been through a bad time in Lille all through World War One. Georgette used to get severe attacks of malaria and generally became delirious and talked all sorts of rubbish, sometimes in English but usually in French or Malay. She must have been very attractive when younger. She had pretty, wavy fair hair and big blue eyes and a slight French accent. She became very pale and tired looking but always did her best to keep cheerful and neat.

Mamie Mackintosh came next to Georgette: a little woman with a round face, always talking about the Highlands or her Grannie, although she must have been one of the oldest in our little hut. She was very nervous and easily upset over things and she used to worry about her health a lot, her swollen legs especially. At one time she used to tremble all over and become too frightened to go across the bridge by herself. Georgette used to try to calm her. Mamie struck me as the type whose husband had always been the boss. She seemed unable to make decisions for herself and got flustered very easily.

Mary Jenkin slept next to Mamie and I was next to her with Helen Mackenzie on my left. Helen had been in Malaya only a short time, as a nursing sister in Kuala Lumpur, when the Japs came. She spoke with a broad Glasgow accent which many people found difficult to understand. In ordinary times she was a really big girl but by now she was very thin and bony and was always falling over things. She had beriberi and found it difficult to lift her feet. Helen used to get wildly excited over the least thing and was always going off the deep end about somebody but one couldn't help liking her. She used to get dreadful attacks of vomiting whenever she had fever but as soon as she got over the worst of it she would be up and about again – although very depressed when she realized she had not got the strength she used to have.

Next was Nurse Kong. She, according to Phyllis, was always having trouble with Mrs Rover, who made the cardinal error of treating her in a superior manner, and with Mamie Mackintosh who could not tune in to the elaborate quirks of her personality at all. But when she was free of the fever she was generous, funny and endlessly entertaining, and much loved by those who could accept the labyrinth of such a singular character.

Next to Kong was a lady who was almost as unique: 'Miss MacKinnon had been assistant Matron of Penang Hospital. She came from Edinburgh but her mother was pure Icelandic. She was tall and thin with long, black, untidy hair – definitely the wrong type to wear shorts and suntops but she always did so. Mac nearly always had a cigarette drooping out of her mouth, made out of any vile tobacco she could get hold of and rolled in any old scrap of paper. Sometimes she got hold of native straws, which I think smelt worse. She was one of those people who, whenever they are not well, refuse to say anything about it until just on the verge of collapse. She used to nearly kill herself with work and in the end she developed tyhpoid and very nearly died. Her heart had been in a bad state for a long time so it was amazing that she pulled through.'

And so the fascinating catalogue went on. All over the camp, shining through the sickness and the exhaustion, there were similarly touching efforts to see other human beings in the round: to see the worst and the best of them without making the sweeping judgements by which society so often and so briskly pigeonholes the rest of mankind. 'There was a frankness which would not have been tolerated in normal society and possibly this preserved our sanity,' Phyllis Liddelow said. 'We respected each other's idiosyncracies.'

The Liddelows were accommodated in a hut they privately called 'the melting pot' because there were blood lines extending so far across the globe: Spain, Portugal, Sweden, Australia, Siam, the British Isles. All of the inhabitants, including about twelve children, were Eurasian or Chinese, but with the breadth of mind that they had developed in their 'education' during the past years the sisters could enjoy the more vivid and textured existence led by this group.

Phyllis was hilarious about what she and Doris thought of as 'the dawn chorus' – the fractious beginning of each demanding day when the grumbling and complaining and airing of ancient arguments filled the air with noisy dissonance. 'But by twilight there was peace: amiable conversation, a few songs, ending with a nursery rhyme for the very young.' Some degree of discord in the daylight hours was evidently a cultural necessity, understood by all, but at root there was tremendous loyalty and generosity.

The Liddelows were deeply intrigued by two ladies in the hut who were constantly at loggerheads because they brought out the worst in each other. Much later on when they came to England the sisters instantly recognized the characteristics of one of these women in the style of the comedian Harry Worth: an infallible knack of unintentionally rubbing people up the wrong way. The other protagonist produced the same effect but apparently with full intention. Phyllis described her as 'a "dainty" little lady, a purist. In spite of being clothed in rags she would sit on a tree stump and sip her drink from a coconut shell with her little finger poised as if she were drinking from bone china. The clash with the gaucheness of "Harry Worth" was quite inevitable. But when Harry Worth fell very sick it was "Dainty" who nursed her. Whilst feeding Harry tenderly, "Dainty" remarked one day, "When you're well I shall revert to the wall of silence, you know . . ." '

Convent bred, the Liddelows were often wide-eyed at the less genteel manifestations of internal tumult. Both the diet and the lack of it meant that raucous indigestion was among the most prevalent of the minor scourges of the camps, and its audible expression was given full rein. 'One particular person had *great* pleasure in "resounding", whether in broad daylight or at bedtime. Life in the raw!' Phyllis commented, with a rueful grin.

One useful advantage of living in the melting pot was the notably more adventurous attitude of the Eurasians towards possible sources of protein. While the Europeans gagged at the dead monkey which was one day flung unceremoniously into the kitchens by the Japanese, there no living creature was entirely safe. One morning at *tenko* there was a reek sufficiently pungent for the guard to pinch his nose as he counted. The women were despatched to find its source and a Thai lady called Mrs Ling discovered an injured skunk. She promptly killed and skinned the animal and it provided a positive feast for supper that night in the hut. 'Very powerful odour,' was Phyllis's judgement. 'An experience not to be repeated or recommended.'

Another day, as she lay ill with malaria on the *bali-bali* in the afternoon when only the sick and the young children were present, a snake flopped down so close to Phyllis that she was too terrified to move. A mother's scream from the sleeping place opposite attracted Mrs Ling who acted promptly again and that night the snake provided the evening meal. It tasted like salt fish. Emboldened by these two experiences, Phyllis trapped the grasshoppers which fed on the leaves of plants on the banks of the stream and dropped them into the heated palm oil which was intended as fuel for the lamps in the huts but was constantly finding its way into a diet bereft of fats. 'We so enjoyed our "prawns". The imagination played extraordinary tricks on the taste buds!' On another occasion, after a night of violent thunderstorms, the baleful stream produced a miracle, banks littered with such quantities of tiny fish that the women were cautioned not to overload their shrunken stomachs. This was an event that was subsequently discussed at great length since it seemed so extraordinarly providential.

Extreme hunger proved to breed hallucinations and Belalau could offer a positively unnatural beauty to prisoners wandering about the recesses of the clearing, light-headed with starvation or the aftermath of sickness:

I have never seen such beautiful butterflies or so many varieties. (Phyllis Briggs recorded.) Some were very large, others tiny. Some looked like autumn leaves falling, others were blue-black with orange velvet bodies. The most common were deep blue and purple, although there was one variety pale green and black which was particularly pretty. There were also large numbers of dragonflies down by the river, coloured scarlet, dark red, yellow and blue.

Ferns grew all along the river banks and at the foot of many trees. Some were pink tipped, almost a coral colour. Others were blue and green like shot silk. At first I used to like arranging them in half coconuts shells but latterly I only picked them for funerals. I shall always connect ferns with dear friends who have gone. The coffins were very rough boxes made of boards that didn't even join together properly and we used to cover the coffin tops with ferns to fill in the gaps and make them more decent. . . .

This was the stark reality behind the beauty. The tops of the ferns were eaten to improve the awful taste of boiled grass. The lovely, pale mauve, wild sweet peas which grew abundantly even in the twilight beneath the trees were fried in the fuel that was meant for the lamps, the pretence being that they gave a flavour of mushrooms. The same attempt at self-delusion that turned grasshoppers into prawns transformed fern-tops into 'asparagus'.

The truth was that nothing could stop the want which bred illness, illness which brought weakness and weakness which could not withstand the hardship of living so much like prehistoric beings in a jungle clearing cut off from the rest of the earth. Every small task required a major effort from women who were now so emaciated that the once sturdy Aussie, Betty Jeffrey, discovered that by bending her elbow she could span both her wrist and her upper arm with her finger and thumb.

In order to bathe in the quite gently flowing stream, Phyllis Briggs used to wade into the flow and simply cling to a rock, allowing the water to sluice her, so reducing the effort of washing herself; but there was no let-up from the heavy manual tasks. There was still the appalling burden of finding and collecting firewood. The geography of the camp, which set the communal kitchens at the lower level and across the bridge, meant that those in the outlying huts had to embark upon a mighty trek to collect their food. The steep bank on the other side was a daily Everest and it was constantly necessary to cut new steps into it with the infernal *chungkals*, but it remained treacherous. Shelagh Brown, who had now become Captain of her hut via a formal rotation of the office that was constantly being disrupted by sickness and death, one day slipped on this ascent and spilled the whole container of mushy rice, representing breakfast for her particular tribe, into the clinging mud. The upset produced one of those tremulous moments of chagrin and horror that are normally left behind with similar disasters in childhood, except that here it was of truly grim importance. Others, to her immense relief, rallied round and made up the loss.

Norah Chambers had a grim confrontation with the growing frailty: 'One day the Japs called together those who could both stand and walk, which was a diminishing band. We went down to the guardhouse and there eighty sacks of rice were stacked. We had to shoulder these sacks and carry them up the hill and put them in a shed. My goodness, that was tough – up and down, up and down we went carrying these sacks until we lost all our breath and our backs felt as if they were broken.' On the last trip even Norah's strength failed. She stopped, utterly drained and struggling to breathe, and was only rescued by a Dutch-Indonesian woman, called 'Tante' Peuk, who shoved a spoonful of sugar into her mouth. This minimal succour proved sufficient to allow Norah to regain her hut.

There was a history to this kindness which perfectly expresses the degree of humanity that the camps bred. 'Tante' Peuk had formerly been one of the 'free women', effectively the prostitutes of the Japanese in the more expansive years of their dominance of the East. In return for favours given in the past, these women were still a little better off than the rest through their easier access to the black market.

With this knowledge Norah, when Ena was afflicted by a severe attack of jaundice in addition to the beriberi which had caused her such a crisis on the pier at Muntok, took 'Tante' Peuk her own wedding ring for sale so that she could buy her sister some food. The transaction went through and when 'Tante' Peuk in her turn fell ill and was lying alone in a hut at the top of the hill, Norah carried water to her from the stream, twice a day up the crippling slope. One day, returning to her hut after one of these trips, Norah put her hand into her pocket and found that her ring had been restored to her.

These were the small dramas of a minuscule world that might have existed on another planet for all its connection with the rest of the earth. In the early months of 1945 the European war boiled to its Wagnerian conclusion quite unremarked by the women in Belalau. VE Day – Victory in Europe – was proclaimed on 8 May 1945, but Betty Jeffrey's diary entry for that date shows a total unawareness of its significance. '*8 May*. We have been here for nearly a month but no sign of the Red Cross parcels promised to us. They are here, up at the guardhouse, but the Japs won't give them to us because the Americans sank the ship that was carrying the receipt for them! What will they think up next?'

The momentous events of the succeeding months went by without penetrating the almost languorous haze of hunger and sickness in which the prisoners moved, or ceased to move as they gave up the fight. By July there were only five survivors of the fifteen especially vigorous British women who had lived in Garage 9 at Irenelaan. The sola topi which invariably crowned the tall, thin missionary, Miss Livingstone, had passed on to another, that fine and scrupulous lady having no further requirement for it. The discovery that this area of Sumatra was known throughout the Indies for the virulence of its malaria had moved all the more punctilious people to write their wills.

Even the last, inadequate haven of the camps, the hospital, was finally buckling under the weight of the demands upon it and the fact that the nurses, for all their devotion, were by this time no more impervious to the rigours of the existence than were their charges. The hospital staff were reduced to working for spells of an hour at a time followed by a rest, then another hour if they could manage it.

A call went out for volunteers to nurse and Shelagh Brown was among the auxiliaries who came in to patch up the gaps in the duty roster. She quickly became involved in another nightmare: '"Shorty", an Australian nurse, was going off to rest and I was left in charge. I was simply told by Shorty who was in need of the most attention – she said cryptically of one, "Be careful she doesn't bite you" – and then I was left to it. The worst problem came from a Dutch lady who began to make awful noises and seemed to be choking and could not speak the little English she knew. Luckily Sister Rhynelda, a super Dutch nun, was on call all the time. I got her and she took one look down the Dutch lady's throat and jumped right up in the air. She rushed off for some forceps, delved and produced an endless worm from the patient.'

The medicines to hand in the hospital were nothing less than pitiful. Quinine tree bark was virtually all that was available to fight malaria, and the beriberi raged unchecked. The appalling tropical ulcers and the infected insect bites that plagued so many were treated only with palm oil, which was kept in a beer bottle, then covered with bits of rag. The nun who for years had made her daily vocation the boiling of these remnants in an old oil-drum kept up this service to the end.

As the tide turned inexorably against survival another daily duty was initiated in the hospital. Each morning an estimate was made of how many would die that day so that graves could be prepared. There was just sufficient energy to dig in the mornings. By the afternoon it had evaporated. That was the degree of desperation in Belalau as 1945 unfolded.

The most memorable Japanese contribution to these months of steady decline had a quality that was in keeping with the slightly surreal nature of this strange, hermetic place. As the Japanese fleets were being annihilated across the breadth of the Pacific and their armies were pushed back relentlessly towards the sacred homeland, they produced, in this forgotten corner of this remote island conquest, a full-blown military band. Not food or medicine or hope or news of loved ones, but a military band!

The concert was announced to the astounded inmates on the previous day, but its venue was at the top of the hill and, in addition to the prevailing incredulity, the sheer effort of making the climb persuaded most of the prisoners to stay at home. The Japanese were furious. In the early afternoon guards arrived at the Liddelows' hut with lowered bayonets and drove the inhabitants out, convincing many that the massacre of the captives, which had lurked in the women's minds for months as a possible ending to their long ordeal, was now at hand.

All over the clearing there was the same rumpus. Betty Jeffrey recorded the event:

At 2.30pm along came "Gold Teeth", the new interpreter, and he screamed at us to "lekas" (hurry) up the hill. He was swinging a great stick wildly over our heads so we did not waste any time and all scrambled up that steep bank to the top of the camp.

We were amazed at what we saw. There were about thirty Japs *all dressed alike and all shaved*, a sight we had never seen before and their expressions were entirely different. There was no sign of hatred on their faces at all. They were simply men who loved good music and played it well. They played all German music: Mozart, Strauss, mostly overtures and waltzes we all knew well.

One fellow sang a Japanese marching song. It was obvious that he was Western-trained. He had a delightful voice, even the Japanese words sounding soft and clear, not a bit like the 'clack, clack' we are used to hearing. Both band and audience were in beautiful surroundings in the shade of the rubber trees. We sat on the ground or on the trunks of fallen trees; the band had proper chairs they had brought with them. For two hours we were all to forget we were prisoners and most of us wanted to howl when the music started. I know I had a terrible struggle for the first ten minutes . . .

The group of Eurasians around Phyllis and Doris offered no such resistance, weeping unashamedly at the first gentleness and generosity the captors had offered since the women had struggled from the sea.

Chapter 15

Elsewhere in the world, in the middle months of 1945, as the women sank into their final apathy in that remote jungle, men were planning the single most momentous act of war in the whole of history. As the Japanese gave ground grudgingly, fighting island by island back across the Pacific, the decision was made to attempt to end the long battle at a single stroke by the unleashing of a weapon of unparalleled ferocity: the atomic bomb.

The justification for the use of such a devastating implement was the saving of the lives of untold Allied Servicemen who would otherwise have been obliged to fight a fanatical enemy to the death. At the same time the Allied High Command were aware that they were placing the vast array of prisoners taken by the Japanese in their years of conquest in considerable jeopardy. Just as the full lethal potential of the atomic bomb was not entirely known, the reaction of the Japanese to its descent upon them could not be predicted. But their capability for savagery was well proven and it seemed highly likely that they would wreak a terrible revenge on those in their power. It was also of some concern that, in a war that was spread over such an immense area, thousands of miles separated the main Allied armies from the outlying Japanese possessions, so that even if the atomic device produced an instantaneous surrender from Tokyo it would not be possible to impose control over all their lands simultaneously. In the hiatus there would be infinite opportunity for a vengeful blood-letting.

There was a further entailment to facing this particular foe. Given the Japanese indifference to the conventions relating to prisoners of war, it was not even known with any certainty where large numbers of the prisoner of war camps were located, and Sumatra was an area of particular mystery.

In these circumstances, the discovery and retrieval of the captives would clearly rest on diplomacy and stratagems, rather than direct action; in effect, a dangerous game would have to be played with the lives of thousands of helpless prisoners as the prize.

So it was that in July 1945, a young Major in the Royal Marines, a South African called Gideon Jacobs, was briefed for a mission so lonely but so crucial that if it had been conjured up as a fictional adventure it would have appeared far-fetched: a vehicle for some such single-handed invincible as Errol Flynn. Jacobs was told that a decisive blow was about to be struck at the Japanese and briefed about the special peril of their prisoners.

His task was to parachute into Sumatra with a handful of men, and to remain in hiding until the Japanese surrendered, when he was to begin at once the process of locating the camps and the setting up of a rescue operation. The logic behind this plan was that a larger force, quite apart from the difficulties of conveying them to the heavily defended island, might stampede the Japanese into immediate reprisals. A tiny group, too small to be dangerous, would establish an immediate Allied presence, open a line of communication to the Japanese Command, and have the opportunity to convey, by implication, the weight of the great armies over the horizon.

The corollary to all this, of course, although unstated, was that the method, if it were a total failure, would not materially worsen the prisoners' plight in relation to the Japanese and would involve the loss of no more than a handful of men. Thus, to the bitter end the imprisonment of the women remained a curious affair, a miniscule side issue to the larger purposes of the great nations which were bludgeoning each other, an embarrassment to the Allies now just as it had been, in its turn, to the Japanese.

This is by no means to diminish the high seriousness of Major Jacob's mission and certainly not the gallantry required to undertake it. Jacobs was twenty-three years old and attached to the Intelligence Headquarters of South-East Asia Command in Colombo, from where he set out with two Australian wireless operators, a Dutchman and a Chinese who had lived in Java before the invasion. Jacobs could speak Afrikaans, with which he would be able to make himself intelligible to the Hollanders he might encounter, but his knowledge of Sumatra was confined to Intelligence reports he had prepared at SEAC Headquarters. He had already operated behind the Japanese lines, however, and was to prove immensely resourceful in the chaos that he entered. He was to find a skein of difficulties and complications in Sumatra greater even than his masters had envisaged.

The women, in spite of their isolation in Belalau, were aware by small signs and portents that some great upheaval was taking place beyond the wire, but, ironically, when events of central importance to their future were actually in train, the riotous growth of rumour was much abated. Their separation into small enclaves was a factor, but principally it was the torpor of the last months that made them almost indifferent to any news. Rumour was equated with hope and hope was at its lowest ebb.

They were fully aware, having had such ample opportunity to observe the temperament of their captors, that a massacre was possible if the Japanese were defeated, but their reaction to this prospect was not panic, rather an infinite sadness that the goal of freedom might elude them when they had endured so much. Death of the kind that had become routine loomed larger than any future risk from machine guns, bayonets, or whatever apparatus the guards would employ to eradicate their prisoners.

On 10 August Phyllis Briggs acknowledged that Mary Jenkin, her quiet, charming friend of all these years, could not live much longer – 'in fact her emaciated body was in such a state we hoped it would not be long. Helen Mackenzie was very good and helped me every morning to bathe her and make her as comfortable as possible and at night I used to go over to the hospital and tuck her up and arrange the mosquito net around her. At this stage we were all so weak that we couldn't do as much as we wanted to for one another.

'On 16 August Mary was much worse. She dozed most of the day and at 7pm the last thing she said was, "I can't do any more – I'm going to join Charlie" [this was her husband]. I spoke to her and said I would see Robert [Mary's son] when I got home, to give her love and to say how brave she had been. She gave a little smile then soon after became unconscious and died within an hour.'

She died quite unaware that on 14 August 1945 the Japanese had agreed to an unconditional surrender. It was on the 6th of that month that the first atomic bomb had been dropped on Hiroshima, killing seventy-one thousand people in its initial blast, and the second fell on Nagasaki three days later, with an instant death toll of eighty thousand. No hint of these colossal events reached the camp for another two weeks, the problems there remaining precisely as before, although in retrospect there were tragedies both great and small which were made especially poignant by their timing. There were deaths, inevitably, but among the minutiae Netta Smith remembered counselling Jennie MacAlister, who was very ill, to sell her engagement ring to buy food, the ring being the very last relic of those wedding preparations interrupted by the Japanese advance through Malaya so long ago. Molly Ismail, in similar distress, sold the ring which her mother had bequeathed her.

Within this vacuum the strangest occurrence was the revelation that the men, too, had made the journey from Banka Island and, for all these months, had been imprisoned on the very same estate barely a mile away. In less depleted times the discovery would have been a major sensation, but the women's capacity for astonishment was also withering. It came about through a strange announcement by the Japanese: all children with fathers or brothers in the men's camp could go to visit them. This news, at least, stirred an almost forgotten instinct. Betty Jeffrey: 'Flo [Trotter, another of the Australian sisters] and I were flat out cutting children's hair so that they would look presentable. The little girls were sweet, dressed in frocks made at the last moment from cast-offs and each one wore a hair-ribbon.

'The excitement was at fever pitch when the bell rang for them to assemble at the guardhouse. When they got there their names were listed and then their excitement died suddenly. The Japs called the names of those who could not go and that is how many wives and children learnt that their husbands and daddies had died, some of them more than a year ago.' For all the callousness of its beginning the visit was a success, the four-year-olds encountering their fathers for the first time that they could remember: 'All were surprised to find such tall men after seeing squat little Nipponese for so long. Some were frightened of the big men and cried until they came home.'

This concession to humanity, however flawed, aroused considerable speculation that peace was in sight, but there was an equally pervasive rumour that a vast pit had been dug in the neighbouring jungle which could well be intended to serve as a mass grave. This was precisely the delicate balance between the acceptance of defeat and unfettered vengeance that had been foreseen in Colombo, and the fate of those at Belalau, it was to prove, was to remain on the knife's edge until the very last.

At the surrender, Major Jacobs had emerged from the jungle to confront the Japanese High Command at Medan in Northern Sumatra and had found the initial stages of contact as precarious and taxing as was to be expected on a heavily defended island with the nearest physical threat being the British Army in Burma, far to the north. Sumatra was garrisoned by some eighty thousand Japanese; the air force there was largely intact and, since the bulk of the soldiers belonged to the same formations which had conquered Malaya and the Dutch East Indies with such contemptuous ease, their warlike spirit was not greatly impaired.

Jacobs performed prodigies of tact and bluff and established himself in the role that had been assigned to him by Colombo. A Japanese Army colonel and an interpreter were seconded to his little group of parachutists and, travelling in Japanese military aircraft, he visited camp after camp on the island: British and Indian Servicemen's camps, male civilians' camps, and the women's camps of the north and centre. Belalau, however, was to escape his net until the very last.

Jacobs' message, to those who assumed that their freedom began with his appearance among them, was difficult to convey. Until the Allies could land in force in Sumatra they would have to remain in their camps and under Japanese supervision. There was no other way to avoid a greater chaos and, in addition, a fresh hazard now threatened the prisoners and made the Major's task even more fraught.

The Japanese rallying cry of the early stages of the conquest – 'Asia for the Asians' – had borne fruit. Although an Asia dominated by Japan had scarcely proved paradisiacal, the concept survived and in Indonesia, as elsewhere, a powerful and aggressive nationalist movement emerged as the grip of Nippon wavered. These early freedom-fighters, founders in the long term of the modern Indonesian republic, were strongly opposed to the restoration of a European dominance. The weakness and fallibility that had forced the Europeans to concede Malaya and the Indies so briskly had not gone unremarked. The spectacle of thousands of Europeans in the total thrall of Asiatics in the camps, and with a status below that of coolies, had played its part in ending a myth. In the great upheaval which the Japanese had set in motion, the assumption that the Allies would now return as liberators was no longer clear cut by any means.

Chillingly, in terms of those concerned with the retrieval of the prisoners, the nationalists, shortly after the surrender, fell upon a Swiss community at Brastagi, just to the south of Medan, killing twenty-six of these innocent neutrals, men, women and children. But Major Jacobs could convey none of this to those in the camps as a reason for their remaining under Japanese guard, and among the multifarious problems he had to contend with was the pent-up anger of the prisoners towards their captors.

To offer an outlet for this resentment he asked prisoners to begin assembling evidence of brutalities to hasten the process of justice when the Allies arrived, and it was via this remarkable skein of circumstances that the Major and the women of Belalau eventually conjoined. For reasons that remained a mystery to him, the Japanese withheld the existence of both the men's and the women's camp on the estate in the south-west, and it required a shrewd piece of detective work to pierce the profound isolation of those imprisoned there among the blanketing jungle and the rubber trees.

By an extraordinary quirk of fate it was the massacre on the beach at Banka Island which provided the first clue to their existence. Sister Vivien Bullwinkel of the AANS was not the only survivor of that holocaust. When the men were separated from the women and led away round the headland to be executed, two of their number, although wounded and left for dead, in fact remained alive. One of these was Eric Germann, the American who had suffered such curious indignities from the women in the course of his brave actions at the time of the sinking of the *Vyner Brooke*. He was still in the men's camp at Belalau, and so still to be discovered.

The other was a Royal Navy stoker called Ernest Lloyd, who was in a Servicemen's camp with which Jacobs was in contact. Lloyd was to play a crucial part in the finding of the women, but it was by a further chance that his experiences came to light. Major Jacobs was glancing quickly through a pile of the reports he had asked for from the prisoners when one of these caught his eye because it was submitted by a fellow Royal Marine. The Marine had come ashore on Banka Island after the massacre and had seen the bodies of the nurses before he was captured further inland.

The account was sufficiently gruesome for Jacobs to continue through the reports in search of further evidence and so came across the story of Stoker Lloyd. Lloyd, of course, from his encounter with the doomed Australian nurses on the beaches of Banka before the massacre, was aware that a much larger number of them had been involved in the sinking of the *Vyner Brooke*.

No trace of Australian Army sisters had emerged in Jacobs' enquiries at this stage but, when he sought more information in the camps, a number of prisoners corroborated the landing of many women, including Australian nurses, on Banka Island as survivors of sunken ships. There were rumours that these women had been taken to a camp in the interior of Sumatra where they had all died of malaria. A Eurasian was found who knew of the camp at Benkulen but he believed, too, that most of the inmates there had died. There was enough of an enigma, however, for Jacobs to persist in spite of considerable Japanese evasiveness and eventually to extract from them for the first time the name of Loebok Linggau. He flew there immediately, filled with foreboding as to what he might find.

In the event, the long awaited deliverance came to Belalau in such a muted fashion that the announcement of peace more closely resembled the cancellation of a social event than the ending of a war. On 26 August, twelve days after his Emperor had conceded to the world that the Japanese adventure was no more, Captain Siki mounted a wooden table at the top of the hill and made a short speech. The gist of it was as follows: 'The war is ended. There is peace and we will all soon be leaving Sumatra. Now we will be friends.'

The Japanese circumlocutions teased out this address and the Captain's words were translated so haltingly into Malay by an interpreter that when the key phrase was uttered a Dutchwoman pushed him aside and continued the interpretation into both Malay and English. The effect was less than electric. 'There were no loud outbursts of celebration or hilarity,' wrote Elizabeth Simons, 'although in their excitement some of the women ran around kissing everybody. One or two fainted. For half an hour I just sat where I was under a rubber tree and "howled". The sense of relief was overwhelming and I just let go.'

Elizabeth and her friend Mavis Hannah were only at the gathering by chance. The announcement earlier that day that the Commandant would address the prisoners at 3pm was greeted with the apathy of women too often bidden to endless harangues in the hot sun, and little inclined now to tackle the climb up the hill. In full expectation that they would eventually be hounded there by the guards, many of them let the hour come and go. It was a change of mind at the last listless moment that took Elizabeth and Mavis to the gathering, but there were scores of others who were physically incapable of making their way to the climactic moment of all those years. Even Margot Turner, after such a prodigious expenditure of effort to help herself and others reach this goal, was laid low with fever and had to wait for the news to be brought to the hospital.

'I think most of us were so stunned we would not let ourselves believe it at first,' said Phyllis Briggs. In her diary Shelagh Brown awarded the event an exclamation mark: 'Peace! We were all ordered to assemble under the trees up the hill. Captain Siki appeared all polished up in his uniform. Much "umphing" to his minions who returned to the guard-house and brought back a table and a chair. Ugh, we thought, a long meeting . . . To our surprise he mounted the chair and stood on the table and announced "The war is over." '

It took most of the rest of the day for the magnitude of what had been said to sink in. Shelagh's sang-froid evaporated as she returned to the business of lighting the evening cooking fire and found that the only usable cooking pot left was leaking. It dawned upon her slowly that this no longer mattered enormously. She almost filled the pot with tears.

By nightfall the jubilation had come, overpowering the weakness and the listlessness. All over the camp there were repeated croaky renderings of 'God Save the King' and the national songs of Holland. Services of thanksgiving were held and for one Australian sister there was an immediate response which seemed to her to have been divinely guided. The previous day, with infinite reluctance, starvation had persuaded her to sell her four back teeth on their gold bridge to buy food. She had given them to a *Hei Hoe* for conveyance to the black market and had believed them gone for ever, but in the effulgence of peace he returned them to her that night.

The circumstances lying behind the long delay in the revelation that the war had ended can probably never now be precisely ascertained. On 20 August there had been a visit from a high-ranking Japanese officer that was mysteriously free of the elaborate preparations that usually accompanied an official arrival. The women were obliged to remove a heap of tapioca roots that were rotting in the camp approach in the usual fashion and distribute them among the huts, but otherwise the visit bore the signs of haste that might accompany an emergency.

When the officer arrived the women were made to stand to attention and bow beside their bed-spaces in the huts rather than parading outside, and the inspection was conducted with a glum and abstracted air as if it were to be the foundation for a brisk and weighty decision. Or so, on later reflection, the women decided. At the time they noticed that, for all the plethora of gold braid on the officer's uniform jacket, there was a huge patch on the seat of his trousers.

Had this Chaplinesque figure been holding the women's lives in his hands? Were the prisoners in this most remote of the camps being held back as a bargaining weapon in some last-ditch negotiation that might arise when the Allies came? Was Banka Island exerting its last malignant influence over the women – the site of a massacre, was it the intention to destroy the evidence by obliterating all who were known to have landed on its shores?

Whatever the explanation the Japanese visitor may well have been there to make some final evaluation and certainly these captives had in some way been singled out as a special case. Major Jacobs, when he arrived with his team, described the conditions at Loebok Linggau as the worst that he had encountered, and he had been consistently appalled by the state of the prisoners he had met, especially the women and the huge-eyed stick figures that the children had become. He radioed Colombo to call up an air-drop of food and medical supplies by the vast, four-engined Liberator bombers which, like much else in the world that was to open up to them again, were to astound the women by their size and power.

The impact of the men, when they walked over from their camp and brushed contemptuously past the guards, was not markedly less awe-inspiring. They took over all the chores of the camp at once, chopping down trees for fuel, and plunging into the jungle to return with wild pigs and deer and the fruits which they found rotting on the trees almost within sight of those who were dying for the lack of them. They also cooked the food and set about amending the squalor of the place while the women contemplated them with a wonderment born of such long deprivation. 'I had never thought much about the hair on men's legs before,' Betty Jeffrey confided to her diary as she lay in the hospital recovering from yet another attack of malaria. 'But at the moment a large Dutchman is working just outside the hospital doorway, making a decent path, and his hairy legs are a delight to gaze upon after seeing shiny, hairless, bandy yellow legs for so long.'

The Japanese, providing the last evidence of their singular mentality, went into reckless reverse once the decision had been made that the prisoners were to rejoin the human race. They opened their storerooms and poured forth all they had been holding back down the years: precious medical supplies from the hundreds of Red Cross parcels they had kept, blankets, towels, mosquito nets, tinned butter and meats, Klim, coffee, sugar, and rice in greater profusion than the contracted stomachs of the prisoners could readily ingest.

In an absurd over-elaboration of generosity, somehow macabre since it was being extended to beings they had practically killed, they produced lipstick, silk stockings, underwear and Chinese hair oil, the lipstick, in this frenzy of donation, even being offered to the men! The Japanese military clothing stores were made available, and strange, hybrid figures began to be seen around the camp wearing Japanese Army boots and shorts and shirts with lavish lipstick, and giving off wafts of Chinese hair oil, used as perfume.

The natives now entered the camp at will, looking for barter, and Elizabeth Simons, a consistently business-like prisoner, described the state of trading:

The Japs had no food supplies which made any appeal to us so our new clothing and footwear were soon being used on what had been the Black Market, now thoroughly open and respectable. The natives had few clothes but plenty of food; we now had clothes but no food; soon the stocks had been rearranged to our mutual satisfaction.

Tired of working for others and for our living we made a deal with a Siamese woman to make our drinks in return for a supply of coffee for her own use. Sitting back sipping coffee *with sugar* first thing each morning, we felt like the upper ten. Even in our new found luxury nothing was wasted. We strained into service all our knowledge of vitamins and diet together with the tricks that years of camp life had taught us. I remember clasping a chicken by the legs with one hand, wings and head in a sort of all-in wrestler's hold, before I cut its throat carefully and caught the blood for later frying. From this beginning until we reached the beak we wasted nothing of that chicken, for which I had exchanged a pair of boots. . . .

On a return visit to the men's camp Shelagh Brown was entertained by two of the former captives, the men rising politely when she arrived, their good manners returning with a shock after all the years of hectoring and bawling and face-slapping. There was a slight difference, however, to the normal course of social exchange, not least the presence nearby of a small, scrawny hen tied up by one leg. 'Whilst leisurely sipping coffee the wee hen dropped dead before our eyes. Nothing was said but both men immediately got up and while one lit a fire the other prepared the creature for the pot. It was cooking away in no time . . .'

For all the miraculous improvements and the burgeoning of hope and enterprise, the awful years still loomed. Norah Chambers was immobilized with a leg ailment at the time when the men first appeared and she had to watch her husband, John, walking slowly towards her, giving her time to study his emaciated appearance: 'It was still a miracle that he was there before me because he had gone into captivity already a very sick man. His strength must have been remarkable.'

Marguerite Carruthers was not as fortunate as far as her husband, Andrew, was concerned. In the men's camp William McDougall observed their reunion in the hut reserved for beriberi cases in the men's compound:

Carruthers' wife came from the women's camp to find her husband. When I first saw Carruthers, standing in line on my first roll-call in Palembang Jail he had been a slender, gracefully formed chap. Now the last roll-call had sounded and except for his eyes and voice and shining hope he was nearly unrecognizable. She shuddered, halted and closed her eyes when she entered our thatch-roofed hospital. Quickly, however, she recovered herself and walked down the aisle towards her husband's bed at the other end of the ward. She passed the patients who had both dysentery and beriberi, each one of them a sodden, living stench. Their eyes were slits in swollen, putty-coloured faces. Serum oozed through rag bandages, soaked blankets of rice sacking, and dripped through bamboo slats to the earthen floor. It was as though their bodies were inexhaustible reservoirs whose contents were being forced by hydraulic pressure through distended skins.

Since April 1942, Mrs Carruthers had waited for this moment. And her husband too. Now it had come and she was walking to meet him, the last man in a row of beriberi cases. Attendants had managed to prop him up a little bit, so he was not lying flat. She reached his bed and smiled and kissed him. 'Don't worry now,' he told her. 'I'm going to be all right. Vitamin injections are all I need and the Allies will have those when they come.' But one day followed another and no Allies came. We were too far from anywhere.

Andrew Carruthers, aged twenty-seven, died on 9 September 1945, still full of hope and with Marguerite beside him, just one week before the final rescue was made. When the terrible arithmetic of the camps was done the men proved to have had a considerably higher mortality rate than the women. Among the British men originally imprisoned in Palembang Jail there was a death rate of nearly fifty-five per cent. In the women's camps it was thirty per cent among the British and twenty per cent for the Dutch. The British of both sexes patently suffered from the disturbance of the vital money-food equation by having lost so much through shipwreck, although the matter of morale was clearly of crucial importance.

Major Jacobs, who was in a unique position to judge, expressed 'a great admiration for these women and the heroic role they had played in the camps'. He found the level of their morale, even at the nadir in which he made his first contacts, noticeably higher than that of the men. 'Perhaps the women were more adaptable or had greater inner resources than the men, but they seemed to withstand the rigours of imprisonment more stoically.'

Both men and women curiously lacked any vengeful feelings towards their captors in the immediate aftermath of the relinquishing of their life and death powers. The greatest gratification was in being able largely to ignore them and they receded quickly into a faceless unimportance, a part of the broad mass of Asiatics, perceived much as they had been before they stormed the Eastern world. If the Japanese temperament cried out for self-importance and endless sway over the arrogant white intruders, as plainly it did, they did well to exploit their opportunity so forcefully.

Captain Siki, who was to receive fifteen years' imprisonment for his role in administering death and degradation, was seen standing alone and silent by the wire as the Australian nurses, the first group to leave, climbed into the familiar Japanese lorries but with British or Dutch drivers at their wheels. Nobody bothered even to catcall.

An Australian Air Force plane was due to land, at considerable risk, at the airfield at Lahat, a hundred miles away, to fly out the twenty-four sisters remaining from the sixty-five who had set out from Singapore in February 1942, together with the worst of the sick from the hospital. This last journey was not uneventful. The railway station at Loebok Linggau was reached at 7am on the morning of 15 September, but the Indonesian train driver refused to move the train in spite of the blandishments of the women's escort, the Australians in Major Jacobs' party and some Dutch paratroopers who had now joined them. The driver had been making the run to Lahat for years, invariably starting at 8am, and he was not prepared to make an exception. Japanese soldiers gathered ominously around during this delay and at Lahat, where the aircraft had not yet arrived, there was a threatening appearance by a large group of nationalists.

On the aeroplane, when it landed, was the Matron-in-Chief of the AANS and another Army nurse, both in immaculate uniforms but, to the astonishment of those who had missed every development in the outside world for three and a half years, wearing slacks instead of skirts! The ex-prisoners wore their uniforms, too, as they had promised themselves they would when freedom came, but when they reached Singapore they felt acutely conscious of their dirtiness and raggedness and their appalling physical state. All of them were struck by the bountiful bosoms and bottoms of the women of this other world until they realized that it was their own loss of such upholstery which was infinitely more extraordinary. There was an excited welcome in the city, then a billowing of unlimited shower water and blissful soap-suds, clean, cool white sheets and pillow-cases and the dim knowledge that it was at last truly over.

The success of the Australian foray paved the way for a shuttle of aircraft to Lahat on succeeding days. Phyllis Briggs left the Belalau estate on 16 September wearing a Japanese private's uniform, complete down to the yellow leather boots with the curious separate compartments for the big toes. She took with her a little pack containing the linen dress which Mary Anderson had left to her when she died and a pair of tennis shoes with the toes cut out which had belonged to Mary Jenkin. She weighed less than six stones and her hands were covered with scabies although she was thankful that she was free of the swollen legs and distended rice-belly of so many of her companions. When she reached the haven of a clean, fresh bed in a Singapore hospital the ward sister came to talk to her and during their conversation Phyllis noticed that the nurse had gone silent and was staring in horror: 'A bed bug had crept out of my little bag and was walking across the snow white sheet. We had tried so hard to keep ourselves free from vermin.' From shame and the weakness she had held at bay for so long, Phyllis wept.

Shelagh Brown left on 19 September, cautiously stocked up with enough hard-boiled eggs to last for a far longer journey. She travelled in a Dakota, remembering this because people were at that time speaking so frequently of Dakotas and Jeeps as indispensable aids to mobility. They were part of a whole new language which seemed to have sprung up while the women had been away. Nurse Kong sat beside her on the journey, when, that is, there was time to sit: there were many sick on the plane and they helped to nurse them, laughingly agreeing that freedom had not brought a decrease in the handling of bed-pans. There were children on the aircraft, too, and a young nurse in crisp uniform who was dispensing milk to them. As she moved about and the plane rocked in the turbulent air of those parts a little of the milk spilled and the children sitting on the floor held up their matchstick arms so that they could catch the drips.

Over Singapore a brilliant sunset echoed the lurid skyscape of fire reflected on smoke pall that was the last memory as the city receded behind the evacuation fleet of 1942 but now, in panorama, a vast Allied armada could be seen, enveloping those same waters and bespeaking an infinite strength and security.

Norah Chambers was in the last group to leave the camp and, as she boarded the lorry and it began to draw away, she heard the rhythms of the 'Bolero', that demanding piece which had so taxed the abilities of the 'orchestra' in its heyday. She turned to see the Dutch nuns lined up in a row offering her this most subtle and delicate tribute to the gift of music which she had been able to bestow. 'I'm afraid,' said Norah, 'I unashamedly wept.'

The nuns, as exemplars of a calling that makes deprivation and sacrifice the starting point of a dedicated existence, were not accorded the catharsis of flying away from Sumatra and all its associations with these demanding years. Their task, precisely, was to remain where there was want and need and this they did, travelling no further than to Palembang where they began the work of tending children orphaned by the war.

In Singapore all of the women, however vigorous they may have seemed to their peers in imprisonment, were hospital cases in the eyes of the outside world. Many came afterwards to be accommodated in Raffles Hotel while they waited for ships or trains or planes to their ultimate destinations. This would make it appear that the wheel had come full circle and they were restored intact to the life that they had known. This was not so, nor could it be, because, in the cataclysm that had befallen them, that world had come to an end.

Epilogue

Compared with the women's dreams of what freedom would mean, the reality was, at first, very hard to assimilate. One of them found a graphic image to convey the immediate aftermath of the imprisonment. She likened the transition to the world outside to passing through a decompression chamber, that staging post in the return to the surface of a deep-sea diver who has spent a long time in the ocean's depths. The chamber allows for the unusual pressures to which the diver has been subjected to equalize with those of normal existence. The analogy only falters in that the women were offered no such assistance in making very much the same adjustment.

Raffles Hotel, almost a war-victim in its own right, was much subdued. It would take time to retrieve its glamour and could work no immediate magic. At this time it was virtually a hostel for ex-prisoners awaiting onward movement and was now luxurious only to those accustomed to two feet of bed-space each and nothing to eat. The hotel and the hospitals were haunted by men seeking news of their womenfolk and, for those who had endured a three-and-a-half-year vacuum in their joint lives, there were encounters which were especially poignant.

Denis Russell-Roberts described his quest for news of Ruth: 'A message reached me telling me to go to Alexandra Hospital where the women prisoners from Sumatra and Java were due to arrive. . . . I was standing in the hall of the hospital when those poor women walked up the steps. How ill and weary they looked, how unkempt, how thin. I felt a lump come into my throat and for the very first time a little stab of pain, of dread of what might be. Then I saw Christine [Bundy] and she saw me. She was overcome and found it difficult to say anything. She squeezed my hand and whispered in my ear, "I'm so sorry, Denis." It was just like that.'

The Red Cross functioned as an agency for dealing with missing persons. It was through the Red Cross that Phyllis Briggs discovered that her fiancé, Tony Cochrane, was missing presumed dead. Time

263

proved the presumption to be correct and Phyllis believed that he must have perished at sea during the evacuation in February 1942. For those to whom Malaya was home there were immediate reunions, but many were marred by the news that had to be conveyed. Molly Ismail had a joyful welcome from her father, who had been sheltered by a Chinese friend in Singapore in the intervening years, but had to tell him of Mrs Ismail's death. Shelagh Brown faced the same ordeal when she met her father, newly-released from Changi Jail. The Browns and the Ismails were among the many, restored to their homeland and their families, who found themselves temporarily pauperized, without jobs, homes, possessions or money. This was, in some ways, the sharpest indication of the havoc which the Japanese incursion had wrought.

Norah Chambers learned that her father had died in Changi and now there were fresh partings that were immensely painful. Of the close-knit group of friends that Norah had formed in the camps the first to leave Malaya was Audrey Owen – 'We all went along to see her off and it was an awful feeling.' Audrey was reunited with her husband in Malaya and for all the joy of finding him alive she was prey, as they started back to England, to the particular malaise of all those who had based their existence on the eternal continuance of the colonial life: 'It was a restless time. You had to wonder where you were going to from there. Would we come back to Malaya? What was the right direction to take?'

Ena Murray had a memorable reunion with her husband, Ken, also released from Changi, to whom she had so wistfully written those anniversary letters which were never sent, but there was a heartrending severance from the little girl that she had mothered for so long. June Bourhill's father was located in Australia and she flew to join him there while the Murrays returned to England. She had been precisely like a daughter to Ena who was never to have a child of her own.

The life of the little Russian boy, Mischa Warmen, continued in its bewildering pattern. In Singapore he remained in the care of Mamie Colley and the missionary, Miss Cullen. He had no recollection of life outside the camps and, taken on a drive through the city, he kept enquiring anxiously, 'When are we going to reach the wire?' Miss Cullen wanted to adopt him but an enquiry via a Jewish society dealing with displaced persons traced a family connection in Shanghai and Mischa was eventually sent there to live with relatives he had never previously seen (see page 272).

The orphaned children who had remained in Sumatra in the care of the Dutch nuns made a slow adjustment to normality, continuing for many weeks in the grave listlessness that made them seem prematurely aged, before their childish spirits began gradually to return. It was a complicated process to trace remaining members of their families or otherwise resettle them. The last of these children left Palembang in March 1946 and it was then that Sister Catherinia faced a significant moment in her life. She was one of only eleven survivors of the twenty-four teaching nuns who had followed their Mother Superior on that long trek from the school at Lahat which had led to captivity, and it was time for her to return to her convent.

'I didn't want to go,' said this strong and dedicated woman. 'I wanted to jump out of the car that was taking me there. I was thirty-eight by that time and I wanted to be free – just free. The need had been within me for some time – "Now you should be yourself again and pursue a normal woman's vocation outside the convent." But I struggled with myself and I came through. I did return to the convent and it was the right thing to do.' Thirty-two years later, in 1978, she was still doing important work in neighbouring Java, and from time to time would meet the five surviving nuns of the Charitas hospital in Palembang, also still in harness. One of the highlights of the return of Margot Turner and Betty Jeffrey to Sumatra was the reunion with these sisters – a moment of high emotion.

Phyllis Briggs faced an even more profound crisis. Her brother, Tom, invited her to stay with him and his wife in New Zealand and she flew there on 30 September 1945. At first there was the pleasure of being with family again, but then: 'I was so accustomed to being surrounded by hordes of other people that it was frightening to be alone – even to be in a bedroom alone. I had *longed* to be by myself but when it came to it I was afraid even to cross a road alone, to go into a shop or on a bus. It required a lot of courage to do any of those things.'

Phyllis fought her way back towards normality. She had a perm, a facial massage once a week – 'anything that made me feel like a human being again'. She recovered enough to decide to go back to Malaya to resume her nursing career. First she had to return to England and on the night before she sailed, staying with friends of her brother, she went to bed and was suddenly overwhelmed by panic. 'All at once I thought, "I really am alone; I've left my brother, my fiancé is lost, I have to start a job again." I couldn't face it. I walked up and down that bedroom three or four times, and when I got near to the window I felt that I wanted to jump. It was a terrible struggle to resist the feeling. Eventually I got back into bed. I hung on to the pillow very tightly to stop myself from getting out again and somehow the night passed.' The next morning Phyllis felt able to face the world again.

The Liddelow sisters returned to the world with a burden of naïvety that left them as vulnerable as young maidens from an earlier century. Phyllis was now an attractive nineteen-year-old who had had no way of judging her appeal to the opposite sex until she encountered the British and American servicemen who once again thronged Singapore, this time in the high spirits of having won a war. Phyllis loved dancing and was hungry for fun and pleasant company. 'In camp we had talked about kissing a lot and felt starved of romance. Now I was physically mature but mentally still in early adolescence. I was terribly upset when what I thought was to be a simple walk with a young man turned out to be a "grab-affair". Men who thought me good fun at first would later think I was a tease. They would become indignant and often leave me high and dry on a date and I just didn't understand their attitude.'

The sisters combed the missing persons organizations of Singapore but could find no trace of either their father or their brother, Colin. Their mother was still living in Phuket in much reduced circumstances and shattered by the loss of her husband. 'She had an awful, haunted look on her face,' Phyllis said of the reunion with her. 'The look of those whose relatives have gone missing in war. We've since seen the expression on our travels in Israel. My mother died of cancer in 1950 but her spirit had ebbed long before.'

Doris Liddelow, sixteen when freedom came, went back to school but very half-heartedly. In the camps she had been tutored by the missionary, Miss Prouse, specifically for the School Certificate examination, and she found herself bored at having to cover the same ground. 'The real trouble was that I had grown out of school life. I had learnt more of the world outside than my schoolmates and school became like another prison.'

Jane Reid, sister of the bellicose brothers of the early camps, James and Dirk, was also sixteen and encountered difficulties with her schooling too. When the family went to live in Scotland she had to begin in a class for eleven-year-olds and work her way up. A teacher who knew nothing of her experiences called her a dunce and made her life miserable. She couldn't bear to remain in school and left with no qualifications. She married and had three children. 'The camps were an education in one way. I'd work at anything now, no matter how lowly. I'm not too proud to say I won't do it.'

Harry Dyne, second in command to the Reid brothers in the war games of Irenelaan, was thirteen when he resumed his studies and found it tough going, but he rose to become Vice-Captain of the school, as well as captain of the rugger team, a remarkable transformation from the shy little boy who entered captivity. He was to father a family of five. His solicitor's office in Singapore is quite close to the patents agency of his fellow captive, Zaida Short, and they often meet in the business quarter of the city.

The surviving Australian Army nurses were rapidly repatriated and arrived home to a rapturous welcome. Mavis Hannah: 'There were presents, flowers – it was overwhelming, too much for us if anything. Everyone tried to do things for you, bring you things, be extremely kind. But they couldn't understand what it had been like and how you'd changed and that you missed the people with whom you'd had so much in common.'

Another of the Australian sisters, Jenny Greer: 'Despite the wonderful welcome it seemed a very lonely time. So much so that we used to try to meet the others from camp for lunch or for drinks after duty every day until we got used to being among civilians and living a different life altogether.'

Betty Jeffrey required hospital treatment for two years after her release, suffering from a combination of tuberculosis, malaria and beriberi, but she found the strength to travel all over her home state of Victoria with Vivien Bullwinkel raising funds for a memorial building dedicated to the nurses of the camps. Their efforts accumulated £123,000 and led to the founding of a residential educational establishment, the Nurses' Memorial Centre in St Kilda's Road, Melbourne. Betty was subsequently to become an administrator there. Vivien Bullwinkel's further contribution was to testify at the War Crimes Trials in Tokyo, describing the massacre on the beach at Banka Island. Sister Nesta James, another of the Australians, told the tribunal of the terrible journey from Muntok to Loebok Linggau. Both these events were no more than small contributions to the full, grisly catalogue of the treatment of prisoners by the Japanese.

The nurses found less difficulty than others in picking up the threads of their existences because of the continuity which their profession gave them. The British civilian women had to adjust to a world that no longer offered the particular niche that they had occupied. The colonial life was never resumed in quite the form that they had known it. Most of the British took advantage of the free passage back to Britain which was offered to them. They travelled in the same troopships that were returning the Servicemen to the homeland and these were memorably lively voyages with parties and dancing and all the other gaieties of people celebrating, eventually, the fact that among the millions of dead of the war, world-wide, they were still alive.

The women's reception in Britain was distinctly muted. So far from offering a gala welcome of the kind that the Australians received, the Home Office asked relatives and friends not to meet the ships when they docked. There was no formal Press coverage of the return of this group of war-victims. The somewhat shamefaced public attitude of the authorities towards the whole ordeal continued until the end. The official recognition that they had upheld the dignity of their country in

The Queen and I bid you a very warm welcome home.

Through all the great trials and sufferings which
you have undergone at the hands of the Japanese, you
and your comrades have been constantly in our thoughts.
We know from the accounts we have already received how
heavy those sufferings have been.   We know also that
these have been endured by you with the highest courage.

We mourn with you the deaths of so many of your
gallant comrades.

With all our hearts, we hope that your return from
captivity will bring you and your families a full measure
of happiness, which you may long enjoy together.

George R.I.

September 1945.

captivity was contained in a stock letter to each survivor signed by King
George VI.

There was no central government fund to help those in financial need.
Clothes rationing was still in force in Britain and extra clothing
coupons were sometimes made available. When Norah Chambers
presented hers in a shop a woman assistant enquired severely as to why
she should have the additional vouchers. When Japanese reparations
began in 1946 the admissibility of claims from ex-prisoners was
announced via a newspaper advertisement. Application had to be
made in writing to the Colonial Office. Molly Ismail only saw this
advertisement by chance and wrote off. She received £35, the standard
amount, a year later.

It was not in the temperament of these women to make a fuss in such
a matter. The prevailing code of behaviour suggested a decent reticence
about the war years and as brisk as possible a return to normal life.
Mamie Colley remembered a vow made by her and her friends in

Sumatra that they would not become 'camp bores' if they were ever released. In this decision was the beginning of the long silence that surrounded the story of these women prisoners.

Present-day prisoners, hostages certainly, are examined exhaustively for psychological after-effects and are offered help in readjustment. These women were never studied from that point of view and were offered no such assistance. The long separation from men and the women's success at fending for themselves was a common source of turbulence when relationships were resumed. Norah Chambers: 'I think it was difficult for both sides. Before the war I wouldn't have said boo to a goose but I came out of the camps much more confident and wilful. If one was married it meant that one had to start all over again.'

The relationship between Norah and her daughter Sally had also to be resumed afresh. Sally had spent the war in England and then Ireland in the care of relatives. 'When we first saw each other again,' Norah said, 'I wanted to rush up and give her a big hug but somehow I felt it wouldn't work. It was very strange – I looked at her and she looked at me and we didn't know what to do. We gradually got to know each other again but it took time.' There was an important turning-point. 'I used to sing a great deal before the war and when Sally was a toddler I sat her on my lap and sang Cyril Scott's "Lullaby" to her, which she loved. After camp I lost my voice and could never sing again but one day Sally presented me with the music to that song and I was so touched that she had remembered.' Norah's passion for music continued to be expressed through her conductorship of the choir of St Mark's, a large church in the principal town of St Helier in Jersey, where she and John settled after a short spell back in Malaya in the early 1950s. Ena and Ken Murray live a few miles away on the same island, Ena's flair as a producer, so valuable in the camps, being put at the disposal of local musical and dramatic productions. Her new interest in domestic matters, discovered in the same inimical circumstances, was not diminished by returning to running a home and she believes that her relationship with her husband improved through their enforced separation: 'I found that marriage was better than before. I had improved – was more tolerant, less quick-tempered. Perhaps the experience made one much more sensitive to others.'

A number of marriages failed to survive. At least one of the women returned to find that her husband had left her. Phyllis and Doris Liddelow both married Englishmen after the war but both marriages ended in divorce, the sisters attributing the breakdowns to an ingrained habit of independence on their parts which made for difficulties in their married lives. Both became health visitors and are neighbours in the same street in the new town of Milton

Keynes. Molly Ismail, when she came to England, was reunited with her fiancé, Frank, but the feelings which had existed between them when they defied an air-raid to buy an engagement ring in Singapore had not endured. Molly met and married a delightful, died-in-the-wool Londoner called Jimmy Smith in the 1950s. His job as a Civil Servant eventually took them both to the Far East, to Hong Kong, but they made their final home in London.

Several marriages followed quickly on the release from the camps. Mavis Hannah became Mrs Allgrove, marrying, in 1946, an English survivor of the labour force on the Japanese 'Railway of Death' which Allied POWs were forced to build through Siam. She and her husband eventually settled in Essex where Mavis has long been involved in charitable activities and is a member of numerous committees. Every year on ANZAC Day, 25 April, she places her own wreath on the Cenotaph in memory of those of her comrades among the Australian nurses who never came back. One other of the Aussies, Jenny Pemberton, née Greer, settled in England and she and Mavis often meet.

Christine Bundy married Norman Cleveley, who, as a Lieutenant in the Royal Signals, tried vainly to pass a message from the *Mata Hari* to the Japanese warships which brought them both to imprisonment. Jennie MacAlister, who was preparing her trousseau as the Japanese advanced down Malaya, at last completed her wedding arrangements and married her planter, Bob Taylor. Their marital home was far from the scene of their engagement – the Mull of Kintyre.

When Phyllis Briggs went back to Malaya to nurse she met and married Robbie Thom, who had also been a prisoner, captured by the Germans at Dunkirk. They never discussed the war years, but their experiences of captivity clearly formed a powerful unspoken bond. 'In the early years,' said Phyllis, 'I would often wake up screaming and he would comfort me. He would pat me and say, "I'm here, I'm here." '

Shelagh Brown married the Reverend Arthur Lea, whom she had known in Malaya before the war, and for a spell his parish was in a Canadian village so remote that water had to be fetched in buckets. Shelagh bore this discomfort with a stoicism she might not have displayed before receiving such an education in hardship. Universally the women found their attitude to material possessions drastically altered. Ever afterwards there was a freedom from that form of enslavement which is imposed by goods and chattels. None of them regretted that.

Shelagh spent the compensation she received on a second-hand piano, which led to another unforeseen by-product of the lost years. From their early lessons on that instrument her son went on to become a professional musician and her daughter a teacher of music.

Since 1949 Shelagh has campaigned persistently, via the Commonwealth War Graves Commission and the Foreign Office, for proper maintenance of the known graves of civilian women in Sumatra. Soon after the war a number of the dead were moved to the Muntok civil cemetery by the Dutch authorities and new wooden crosses were erected. These were never replaced with permanent memorials and when the Dutch withdrew from the Indies the graves reverted to the care of Indonesians, who had no special regard for these foreign plots. As late as 1966 the work of transferring the relatives of military personnel to the War Cemetery at Djakarta in Java was continuing by the War Graves Commission, but there was no organization specifically charged with the management of the graves of civilians with no such connection, and they were left to the ravages of the jungle in Muntok and Loebok Linggau. Shelagh has a letter from the Commission, dated September 1966, which concludes: 'I regret that we have no complete record of the civilian graves at Muntok as the Commission have no responsibility for civilian graves and were merely acting as agents for the UK government.'

The long correspondence has therefore produced no important results but there was recently installed in the Lady Chapel of St Mark's in St Helier, Norah Chambers' church, a simple cross made from a piece of oak a century old by the husband of Audrey Owen. Around its base is inscribed the words: 'In the memory of those women who died in prison camps in Sumatra whose graves will never be found.'

It is small and far from where the women died, but the memories of those who lived are indelible, and so too is the comradeship, the humour, the tolerance, even the bickering: all the ingredients of that immense bond between the prisoners that the passage of the years has never broken. For all the legacy of ill health that remained with many, there was a continuing wonderment at having survived at all. 'Ever since, I've felt that I've been living on borrowed time,' said Mamie Colley. Perhaps this feeling explains the total absence of self-pity among the women, and their unshakeable equanimity.

When Betty Jeffrey was at Palembang railway station during her return to Sumatra in 1979 and standing on the selfsame spot where the women, sick and dying alike, were packed into the fetid and filthy wagons in the course of that terrible journey in 1945, she was asked what sensations the return had brought to her. 'I feel,' she said, with unforgettable emphasis, 'as if I'd never left the blasted place!'

Postscript

Mischa Warmen, the little Russian orphan – who had been looked after by several of the women in camp before being sent to relatives in Shanghai after the war – had lost touch with all of the women. None of them knew where he was until, following the first publication of this book in 1982, the authors received a phone call from Mischa's cousin, Marilyn Branston, who had read the book in London. She told us that Mischa was married and a successful accountant in America. Mischa himself then came to England for very moving reunions with all his former 'aunts' from camp, including Gladys Band (née Cullen), who had wanted to adopt him.

The fate of the three young RAF men, who saved Norah Chambers and her sister Ena from the sea after their shipwreck (see page 69), had never been known to Norah until one of them, James Brindle, read this book and immediately contacted her. It turned out that he and one of his companions had also been captured and imprisoned for three and a half years, while the third man had been shot by the Japanese. At last Norah was able to thank her rescuer, who was delighted to know that she had survived.

Paul Hilton last saw his mother Maudie in 1936 when he went off to boarding school in England. After the war, all he received were a piece of needlework from the camps and a few other tiny possessions, plus the knowledge that she was dead (see page 197). Reading this book told him, for the first time, of his mother's life in camp, and through it he was also able to get in touch with some of her surviving friends, who could tell him more about the circumstances of her death.

Appendix I: The Course of the Second World War in the Far East

1941 7/8 Dec – Japanese attacks on Pearl Harbor, Hong Kong, Malaya, Singapore

10 Dec – sinking of the *Prince of Wales* and *Repulse*

Christmas Day – Hong Kong capitulates. The Japanese enter Burma

1942 January – Japanese begin invasion of Dutch East Indies

1 Feb – British forces in Malaya retreat to Singapore

14 Feb – Japanese invade Sumatra

15 Feb – British surrender in Singapore

8 March – Dutch capitulate in Dutch East Indies. Rangoon taken by Japanese in March, and India threatened after Mandalay falls

April – US surrender in Bataan. Multiple Japanese advances in Pacific Islands

May – Corregidor taken, and Japanese overrun Philippines, but Allies win the Battle of the Coral Sea (8 May) and stop the Japanese advance to the South

7 June – Japanese lose in Battle of Midway

August – Americans land in Guadalcanal – signifies beginning of Allied counter-offensive

December – British and Indian troops begin Burma advance

1943 Allies begin 'island-hopping' offensive in SW Pacific – landings in New Georgia, New Guinea, New Britain

August – Americans recapture Aleutian Islands

American air-raids on Japan begin

1944 Advance of American forces in the Central Pacific

March – reoccupation of Gilbert and Marshall Islands

June/July – recapture of the Marianas, Saipan and Guam. Battle of the Philippine Sea.

October – US victory in the naval Battle of Leyte Gulf. Americans bomb Tokyo.

1945 British, American and Chinese troops retake Burma
  4 Feb – Manila occupied and Philippines regained by end of Feb
  19 Feb – Americans land in Iwo Jima, Japan
  6 Aug – dropping of first Atomic bomb on Hiroshima
  9 Aug – second Atomic bomb on Nagasaki
  2 Sept – formal ceremony of surrender

Appendix II: *Alice in Internment Land* (abridged) by Margaret Dryburgh

'Is this a barracks?' said Alice, looking around a dusty square, enclosed by wooden sheds with thatched roofs. 'I see no soldiers but – surely those are the women and children I have seen before, on "The Hill". Can they still be interned?'

'Yes, alas,' said a voice at her feet. Alice noticed a black cat.

'Midnight, at your service,' said he, looking important. 'I can give you any information you want.'

'Why are these people not free yet?' asked Alice.

Midnight looked a little crestfallen. 'That I cannot tell you,' he said, 'for we get no outside news here.'

'How distressing,' said Alice. 'Please tell me how they fare here. What are these buildings?'

'This is the Main Entrance, where we are standing,' said Midnight. 'On your right is the Hospital, on your left a dormitory for the Hospital sisters and Roman Catholic nuns. Right opposite, at the other end, are the kitchens. The two blocks on the right of the square are occupied by the British, the two on the left by the Dutch. The shed in the centre is meant for the children and acts as school, playground and church.'

'It certainly isn't a palace-de-luxe,' said Alice. 'I expect they all feel distinctly aggrieved.'

'No more than I am,' broke in a fretful voice.

Alice saw a long thin figure in red and yellow, with a pipe dangling round his neck. 'The Pied Piper, surely!' she said in great surprise. 'What are you doing here?' 'It's what I am *not* doing here that annoys me,' he said glaring at Midnight. 'Word was brought that this camp was over-run with rats of an outside variety. The tale went that one was so busy eating the stuffing of a mattress being repaired, that he was sewn inside, and only discovered by his squeaks when sat upon, and yet I was not invited to deal with the scourge,' and the Piper cast a baleful glance at Midnight, who nonchalantly licked his lips. 'A curse upon you,' shouted the Piper, 'may you meet with a bad end,' and he vanished.

'Rats are not the only trouble here,' said a new voice.

Alice saw a worried looking little man, carrying a very large notebook.

'I am the Compiler of Camp Complaints,' said he.

'Let me hear some of them,' said Alice.

'With pleasure,' said the Compiler. 'Sit down -- that is if you can find anything to sit on. Our few odd chairs are falling to bits.'

The Compiler opened his book.

'A is for Ants that we find on our shelves.

'B is for Bathroom and bugs in our beds.

'I can understand a complaint about bugs, but why a bathroom?' said Alice.

'Come and see for yourself,' said the Compiler.

He led Alice to the central section.

'This is the Bathroom for two hundred people,' he said.

Alice looked round incredulously. She noticed some roughly constructed compartments.

'These are latrines, I suppose,' she said. 'Only seven!'

'Only seven,' repeated the Compiler. 'Look inside.'

Alice saw a deep drain with a slightly raised cement foothold on each side of it – nothing more.

'No wonder they complain,' said Alice. 'How are these cleaned?'

'Each day a bathroom squad flushes them with pails of water, sending the contents to the Septic Tank just outside. That has to be emptied each day by a noble band of hygiene specialists, affectionately known as the B.A.D. Brigade.'

'I should think it was a very good brigade,' said Alice.

'Oh yes, the B.A.D. Brigade consists of British, Australians and Dutch who go round together hunting for germs. The bathers bring their own water to the bathroom and bathe in public. They complain that they are dirty before they leave the bathroom, for the floor is full of holes, filled with water, muddied by the feet of those coming in.'

'My list goes right through the alphabet,' said the Compiler, turning over his pages, 'in fact, there is no end to complaints. The Dutch complain about the British and vice versa; there are complaints about the shop, the rations, the bed spaces, work and slacking – but some people find a kind of enjoyment in complaining, and would be wretched without a cause to grumble.'

'I think I will have a look at the dining-room,' said Alice.

She wiped away a tear, as she gazed at the pathetic assortment of enamel mugs, broken plates, coconut shells, old tins, and glass bottles that formed the equipment of the diners. Changing the subject she asked Midnight what the internees did to amuse themselves.

'They read all the books they can get. A librarian changes books in the woodshed twice a week. The centre shed acts as a rendez-vous, gossip corner, school, and church, and a public hall, where *announcements* are made by the *authorities*; on occasions, it is a concert hall.'

'Oh, what kind of concerts do they have?' asked Alice.

'They have songs by a choir that practises in the kitchen, solos, and a special choir which calls itself a vocal orchestra. It aspires to classical music and hums it in four parts, the result gives quite the effect of an orchestra. Once a Variety Show, with songs and dances in costume, was produced. The Japanese visitors were so pleased that they gave the performers bits of soap and tins of British army rations. However, concerts have been impossible of late, because of the blackout. Still there are mild forms of amusement – cards, auction sales of clothes, gossip about the guards who have nicknames. Oh! I forgot to mention, the writing of recipes is very popular.

'That reminds me, you had better see Mrs Feed-Em. There she is, outside the kitchen,' said Midnight. 'Go and talk to her.'

'How are you, Mrs Feed-Em?'

'Oh, not so well as I was when I came,' she said.

'How is that?' asked Alice.

'Come into the kitchen and I will tell you some of my troubles,' said Mrs Feed-Em.

Alice looked at a ramshackle shed, with a long brick fireplace along one side where four large fires were burning. Roman Catholic sisters, in their long robes, were stirring huge cauldrons of rice. 'This is the Dutch Communal Kitchen,' said Mrs Feed-Em. 'The British did individual cooking at first; the kitchen was a regular inferno in those days, because of the smoke from so many fireplaces and full of noise. When the military authorities took over, they made the British cook communally. Come and see the kitchen.'

They passed into a shed, more decrepit than the first, where there were four cauldrons supported by precarious-looking piles of bricks and stones, with an iron ring or home-made grid of bars, to support the big pots.

'Are those safe?' asked Alice apprehensively.

'Not very,' said Mrs Feed-Em. 'That is one reason for my worries. The women have to make them with anything they can find. No wonder there is a collapse sometimes. Once, the wall fell out as the cook tried to steady herself while lifting the cauldron.

'Have a look at the rest of the establishment. This is the woodshed, where a squad deals with the problem of carrying, sawing and chopping the logs sent in – hard work, as you may imagine. Axes are scarce, one for at least 137 people, so ours often "Loses its head", as it seems to fly off on the slightest provocation. Here is the British vegetable shed.' They approached an open shed, with rough tables and benches. 'The vegetable cutters have their set days too; my department is quite well organized,' said Mrs Feed-Em, and the glimmer of a smile lit up her worn features. 'From 3.30am when the fire-lighters start the day's work, until 6pm when the fires are all put out, everything goes by clockwork.'

'Now that I have seen the cooking arrangements, I would like to know more about the food,' said Alice. 'Have you thought out any exciting recipes?'

A look of gloom descended on Mrs Feed-em's face.

'I am more than satisfied if I can give them the barest necessities nowadays,' she said. 'Here is the British storehouse. Look inside.'

Alice obeyed, and saw another tumble-down shed where some empty kerosene tins rested on a bench and some rice sacks lay on the ground.

'Where are the stores?' asked Alice in surprise.

'This is a low time, but something will come in,' said Mrs Feed-Em. 'We have three sources of supply; come and see them.'

She pointed to three automatic machines between the storehouses and a little door in the corner of the camp. The first was labelled 'RATIONS', the second 'SHOP', and the third 'BM'.

'We press the button each day,' said Mrs Feed-Em, 'not knowing what will come out. Rice, of course, is a dead cert, usually a supply, unpolished or white, for five days arrives. Often the bags are not full, though we are credited with the whole amount. Vegetables come daily but they are often faded, and never are there sufficient for all.'

'Does meat come every day?' enquired Alice.

Mrs Feed-Em had to sit down from shock.

'Meat!' she exclaimed, 'I should think not; pork once a month is our average.'

'Well, the rations sound very meagre,' said Alice. 'I don't wonder underfeeding is among the complaints. Does the SHOP not help matters?'

'Considerably,' said Mrs Feed-em. 'Once it came on Sundays and the contents of the bullock cart were checked and shared out in the shed. Now the goods come by the back entrance; we never know when they will arrive. There is great excitement when the gate creaks and many eyes watch expectantly for it to open. Sometimes the shop brings fruit, eggs, curry biscuits, coffee, beans and even sweets. These are sold at very high prices, but are bought eagerly by all who can afford them.'

'What about the BM machine?' asked Alice.

Mrs Feed-em looked round blankly. 'What are you talking about?' she said.

'Well, I saw a third machine, labelled BM,' said Alice.

'Are you sure?' said Mrs Feed-Em.

'Absolutely,' said Alice, looking at the spot where the machine had been. 'Why,' she faltered, 'where is it now? Has it disappeared?'

Mrs Feed-Em smiled. 'Move back a step,' she said.

As Alice obeyed, the machine came into view again.

'We have to camouflage it,' explained Mrs Feed-Em, 'as it is not suppoed to be here at all. Press the button and see what happens.'

Alice somewhat fearfully obeyed. To her surprise a black figure appeared, grinning, carrying a parcel.

'You are too early,' he said. 'This button should be pressed only by night, when I can't be seen, for I am not supposed to exist. Black Market, you know,' he whispered. 'I had better vanish, I think,' and with these words, he suddenly disappeared.

'There are various ways of sending messages to the BM,' explained Mrs Feed-Em. 'Sometimes the guards oblige; it has even been said that orders for sugar and others things have been sung to a hymn tune, about the time for devotions. In the darkness, baskets are deposited at agreed spots, then at dawn, the selling begins, at sky-high prices of course.'

'But what about the poorer people?' asked Alice.

'Oh, many of them have sold their jewellery and clothes. Some, of course, have only been able to sniff and covet. They have the very slight satisfaction of feeling virtuous when *authority* burst in occasionally and threatens dire punishment to all concerned in such nefarious traffic.'

'I'm sure you must be tired of hearing about food,' said a new voice.

Alice turned, and saw a scholastic figure at her side.

'Are you a professor?' she asked respectfully.

'Correct,' replied the gentleman. 'I am Professor Toromento, LMT.'

'That degree is quite unknown to me,' said Alice.

'I daresay,' said the professor. 'It means Licentiate of Mental Torture. I specialise in experimenting on the emotions,' swaggered the professor.

'In what way?' asked Alice.

'Various ways of course,' he replied. 'I have tried the effect of a Mental Vacuum on the internees. Formerly, news used to leak through from the hospital but I have put a stop to that, and now rigidly exclude all news of the outside world.'

'How cruel,' sighed Alice.

'Maybe,' said Professor Toromento with a sardonic grin, 'come and see my apparatus.'

Wonderingly, Alice followed him to where a kind of seesaw was erected, only one plank being visible. It was joined to a barrel-shaped machine labelled 'Mental Vacuum' on one side and 'Secrecy' on the other.

'What a strange machine, how does it work?' asked Alice.

'Well,' said the professor patronizingly, 'as we are pastmasters in the Secret Service, we easily create the Mental Vacuum that is our goal. But nature abhors a vacuum, so this one is soon filled by Rumours. We know when the barrel is full, for other people gather in groups, talking and smiling and the spirits of the campers rise mysteriously.'

As he spoke, he turned a handle, and the plank rose.

'Oh, I am beginning to understand now,' said Alice.

'When there is such a wave of optimism it is time for me to act. Watch.'

He inserted something into the barrel through a slit, and the plank began to descend.

'What happened?' enquired Alice.

'I sent an old newspaper into the camp, with news of our initial successes – quite enough to change the balance, as you see. Watch again.'

The plank began to rise again; when it was quite high, the Professor passed a torpedo-like object through the slit. Down came the plank with a terrific bang. 'A bolt from the blue,' said the professor blandly. 'A sudden order to get ready to change camp, or an insinuation that things may worsen in a few months. Ha, ha! I do enjoy seeing the change from gaiety to gloom. Now they are afraid to believe anything they hear. As "Be prepared" is our motto, we arrange Alerts at all hours of the day or night, so that no one knows if they are real or faked. Now I shall explain another of my experiments, known as Delayed Action. I announce that something will happen shortly, and then postpone the event at will. I love to see the people hastily packing their goods, ready to move at a moment's notice. After a fortnight, they relapse into uncertainty!'

'But how wearing to the nerves!' said Alice.

'Why should they have nerves?' asked the professor. 'When they are listless, I use the opposite method of Precipitation. Without warning, I give orders for sudden action. It is funny to see the commotion, like an anthill being disturbed,' and the professor laughed heartily. 'Oh yes, and by the way, there is another little form of torture I use. I have allowed no communication with friends and relatives overseas except one postcard.'

'In two years!' gasped Alice.

'Of course,' chuckled the professor. 'These insignificant women can mean nothing to their kinsfolk. We made a concession to those with husbands in neighbouring camps. We always let them know if their husbands have died.'

'Oh you stupid ignorant monster of cruelty,' burst out Alice indignantly.

A look of apprehension, almost of fear, came into the professor's eyes. Astonished, Alice looked round, and saw the shadowy figure of a Red Cross nurse approaching. She raised an accusing finger.

'What have you done with the hundreds of letters and parcels sent so lovingly and trustingly to those pining under your guardianship?'

The professor hastily broke in. 'There is a parcel on its way now. It will be distributed almost immediately.'

'When was it sent?' demanded the nurse.

'Only 18 months ago, but what is that to complain about in a war of several years' duration?'

The professor hastily departed, and the nurse faded out leaving Alice alone, to ponder on what she had heard. She was acclaimed by a cheerful voice, asking 'Would you care to see my Conjuring Show?'

'I certainly need brightening up, after what I have heard and seen,' said Alice.

Suddenly a stout figure in a tight uniform appeared from nowhere.

'I am the WIZARD of WIC and can effect most marvellous transformations with a wave of my hand,' he said.

'What is WIC?' asked Alice.

'Women's Internment Camp, of course,' replied the Wizard. 'Shall I repeat some of my performances for you? Shut your eyes. Now open them.'

Alice saw the compound covered with yellow dust, with a few clumps of grass here and there. The wizard waved his hand. Down came a shower of rain and Alice saw a quagmire of squelchy mud. It gradually took the form of regular rows of sweet potatoes and tapioca plants, divided into plots by narrow yellow paths.

'What an improvement,' said Alice, 'how and why was it made?'

'We though the women were not working hard enough, so we threatened that as food would be short, they must plant their own vegetables. We used our own famous methods, of course. We encouraged them to dig plots for themselves, and supplied them with a great variety of seeds. Just when the first shoots were appearing and people showed enthusiasm, we scrapped that scheme. Pressed labour was used to dig up the whole compound. The women had to dig and manure (from the Septic Tank) and water the plants each day.'

'With water carried in from the hydrant, while they had to use dirty well water for personal use,' said Alice severely.

The Wizard looked annoyed.

'Who has been telling tales?' he demanded. 'It was unfortunate that our scheme synchronised with the worst drought known for years. But we succeeded,' he remarked brightly. 'Look at those luxuriant plants – quite a credit.'

'Yes, but look at these miserable little yellow ones,' said Alice, but the Wizard was gazing elsewhere.

'Now for another change,' he said. He waved his arm and the compound became yellow and dirty as before.

'Why this change?' asked Alice.

'Orders came suddenly to move camp and so we ordered the plants to be pulled up,' exclaimed the Wizard.

'Were there any roots?' asked Alice.

'Oh, a few small ones,' replied the Wizard, 'but there were plenty of leaves to eat. They provided food for two whole days, or was it three?'

'Three days, after weeks of strenuous toil!' exclaimed Alice.

'Oh, discipline is good for the character,' said the Wizard. 'What right have these women to complain about using their hands? Our women take it as a matter of course.'

'Well, I don't think much of that transformation,' said Alice. 'It's as bad as the other ones by which you have changed buxom women into walking skeletons, and well-dressed ladies into Cinderellas –' but Alice found herself talking into space, the Wizard had gone.

'Now I wonder if there is anything else to see here?' mused Alice.

'Yes,' said a sad voice.

Alice, looking round, saw a worn woman by her side, carrying an empty disinfectant bottle in one hand and a grey bandage in the other.

'I am Hygeia,' said the figure, 'in a sad condition, as you can see. Come and sit outside the Hospital, for I feel too weak to stand, and I shall tell you my sad tale.'

'From what I have heard and seen,' said Alice, 'I should think you have a desperate task, trying to combat unhygienic conditions.'

Hygeia held up her empty bottle. 'With unlimited supplies it would have been difficult enough, but I have had nothing to help me – only a few drops of disinfectant, a small number of pills, and bandages washed over and over again. Look at this one,' and she showed Alice her discoloured bandage. 'Even old rags have been difficult to get. Would you like a peep inside our clinic, though there isn't much to see?'

Alice saw a tiny room, with a table holding a meagre assortment of ointments and powders.

'This is all we have,' said Hygeia, 'in spite of frequent appeals.'

'How lucky that you have doctors and nurses among your internees,' said Alice encouragingly.

'Yes, but workmen, however accomplished, cannot do much without tools or instruments,' moaned Hygeia. 'Look in the hospital next door. Can you see any bedpans, bedrests or air pillows? Are there any invalid requirements, as hot bottles, thermometers? No, even towels are scarce. Occasionally a small consignment of lint and sticking plaster is brought in, but it is used immediately. Oh dear,' and Hygeia put her head on her hands and sobbed. 'How I long for buckets of Keatings Powder, and Chloride of Lime, for soap, and hot water. I can tell you it is utter misery to take ill in the middle of the night, for there is neither light nor water nor anything available!'

'I suppose the diet, or lack of it, is responsible for many ills,' said Alice.

'Yes,' sighed Hygeia, 'it is the main cause. The whole camp is badly debilitated and unable to resist germs. Nerves are strained by uncertainty and ignorance of the world happenings outside of the camp. Our foes are numerous. See what menaces us continually.'

Alice saw a miserable-looking figure holding a cigarette tin passing by.

'Diarrhoea,' said Hygeia.

'Why has it a tin?' asked Alice.

'No toilet paper or rags available,' explained Hygeia, 'so water is used. There go Dysentery and Typhoid whom I cannot fight without medicine and nourishing food.'

'Who is this yellow-faced creature?' asked Alice.

'Malaria, of course,' said Hygeia. 'The swamp round the camp breeds mosquitoes, so we cannot escape their unwelcome attentions. Here comes Beri-Beri, suffering from our unbalanced diet.'

Alice saw a figure with puffy eyes and feet, limping slowly along.

'A pitiable sight indeed,' she murmured.

Toothache and Eyestrain followed, while Heartstrain, due to the lifting of heavy weights, could hardly drag herself along. Last in the grim procession came a cloaked figure, whose name Alice did not need to ask.

'So Death has visited the camp,' she whispered.

'Nine times already,' sighed Hygeia, 'and even the dead are deprived of their due. The only mortuary is an open shed, coffins are often very late in arriving, the hearse is an unswept lorry and no respect is shown by the guards.'

'A tale of woe indeed,' said Alice. 'What will the world say when all these tragedies are brought to light? All that makes life lovely and worthy seems to have been snatched ruthlessly from these women.'

'Not all,' piped a clear voice. Alice raised her head. Sad Hygeia had gone and in her place stood a tiny figure in iridescent raiment.

'I am Hope,' she said. 'In spite of rumours and disappointments, delays and hardships, I live on, and never quite die away. One day, the internees will surely regain freedom and reunion with their loved ones; then my work will not have been in vain.' Hope vanished, but a beautiful rainbow stretched its brilliant arc over the drab buildings, cheering Alice as she left the camp.

Bibliography

Attiwill, K., *The Singapore Story* (Frederick Muller, 1959)

Barber, Noel, *Sinister Twilight* (Collins, 1968)

Braddon, Russell, *The Naked Island* (The Bodley Head, 1952)

Caffrey, Kate, *Out in the Midday Sun* (Deutsch, 1974)

Gibson, Michael, *The Rise of Japan* (Wayland Ltd, 1972)

Jackson, Daphne, *Java Nightmare* (Tabb House, 1979)

Jacobs, G. F., *Prelude to the Monsoon* (Purnell, 1965)

Jeffrey, Betty, *White Coolies* (Angus & Robertson, 1954)

Keith, Agnes Newton, *Three Came Home* (Michael Joseph, 1948)

Low, N. I., *When Singapore was Syonan-To* (E. Universities Press, 1973)

Lucas, Celia, *Prisoners of Santo Thomas* (Leo Cooper, 1975)

McDougall, William H., *By Eastern Windows* (Arthur Barker, 1951)

Russell, Lord, of Liverpool, *The Knights of Bushido* (Cassell, 1958)

Russell-Roberts, Denis, *Spotlight on Singapore* (Times Press & Anthony Gibbs and Phillips, 1965)

Shinozaki, Mamoru, *Syonan – My Story* (Asia Pacific Press, 1975)

Simons, Elizabeth, *While History Passed* (Heinemann, 1954)

Smyth, Sir John, VC, *The Will to Live* (Cassell, 1970)

The Last Japanese Soldier: Corporal Yokoi's 28 Incredible Years in the Guam Jungle (Tom Stacey Ltd, 1972)

Storry, Richard, *A History of Modern Japan* (Penguin Books, 1960)

Taylor, A. J. P., *The Second World War* (Hamish Hamilton, 1975)

The authors and publishers would like to thank the following for permission to reproduce extracts from the publications mentioned: Purnell, *Prelude to the Monsoon*, by G. F. Jacobs; Angus & Robertson, *White Coolies*, by Betty Jeffrey; E. Universities Press, *When Singapore was Syonan-To*, by N. I. Low; Arthur Barker, *By Eastern Windows*, by William H. McDougall; Cassell's, *The Knights of Bushido*, by Lord Russell of Liverpool; and Heinemann, *While History Passed*, by Elizabeth Simons.

Index